Business Accounting for Solicitors

Business Accounting for Solicitors

Louise M Watson BA, CA
Chartered Accountant

Robert A B Watson BA, LLM
Deputy Director of the Centre for Professional Legal Studies at the University of Strathclyde

Edinburgh
Butterworths
2000

United Kingdom	Butterworths, a Division of Reed Elsevier (UK) Ltd, 4 Hill Street, EDINBURGH EH2 3JZ and Halsbury House, 35 Chancery Lane, LONDON WC2A 1EL
Australia	Butterworths, a Division of Reed International Books Australia Pty Ltd, CHATSWOOD, New South Wales
Canada	Butterworths Canada Ltd, MARKHAM, Ontario
Hong Kong	Butterworths Asia (Hong Kong), HONG KONG
India	Butterworths India, NEW DELHI
Ireland	Butterworth (Ireland) Ltd, DUBLIN
Malaysia	Malayan Law Journal Sdn Bhd, KUALA LUMPUR
New Zealand	Butterworths of New Zealand Ltd, WELLINGTON
Singapore	Butterworths Asia, SINGAPORE
South Africa	Butterworths Publishers (Pty) Ltd, DURBAN
USA	Lexis Law Publishing, CHARLOTTESVILLE, Virginia

A CIP Catalogue record for this book is available from the British Library.

ISBN 0 406 04655 7

Typeset by Phoenix Photosetting, Chatham, Kent
Printed by Thomson Litho Ltd, East Kilbride

Visit us at our website: http://www.butterworthsscotland.com

Foreword

This book constitutes a major step in the right direction. For decades solicitors in Scotland have been conceding ground to accountants largely as a result of their failure to grasp numeracy and technology issues. Part of the problem has been the lack of dedicated materials in the Scottish market place.

I still have vaguely disconcerting memories of the accountancy element of my Law Degree in the late 1970s. It seemed to consist largely of pontificating about a 'true and fair view' which I have to say did not exactly equip me for the rigours of professional practice in a post-scale fee era.

We live in an age where there is considerable blurring between the professions. It is now even more important for Scottish solicitors to embrace accounting. The Law Society of Scotland in its review of legal education acknowledged that greater emphasis requires to be placed on business skills.

This book more than fills the gap. I require to declare an interest and it is that I know Robert Watson as a respected former colleague at Strathclyde University. His professionalism and involvement with the Diploma in Legal Practice over a number of years make him uniquely qualified to undertake such a project. The authors have delivered. This book is essential reading and not just for law students as there are few in private practice who would not benefit from its messages.

Douglas R. Mill LLB, BA, MBA, WS, SSC, NP
Secretary and Chief Executive
The Law Society of Scotland

To Robert and Euan

Preface

In days since long departed, a competent solicitor could make a decent living without necessarily being an astute business person. The level of fee income relative to its associated costs could, in the main, accommodate a fairly lax approach to the running of a law firm. However, the departure of scale fees coupled to marked changes in the framework within which law must be practised, including the seemingly relentless increase in competitive pressures facing practitioners, all contrive to make the possession of business acumen and a sound sense of commercial awareness a virtual necessity for the average lawyer of today.

The study of accountancy related issues to law is considered to be a fundamental step in the development of such skills.

The Solicitors (Scotland) Accounts Rules, designed primarily to offer protection to clients, but simultaneously helping to preserve the reputation of the legal profession as a whole, also demand a level of accountancy knowledge if their provisions are to be applied correctly and consistently over time by legal practitioners. Breaching the Accounts Rules, whether by design or incompetence, is an event that must be avoided by all conscientious solicitors. The old adage that 'you can delegate work, but not responsibility' is readily applicable within a legal practice generally, but especially so with respect to the processes necessary to accord with the terms of the Accounts Rules and other related provisions.

Again an understanding of accountancy is a pre-requisite to the successful application of the above Rules.

This book has been written in an attempt to give existing as well as future members of the legal profession a simple foundation in accountancy upon which they may build through experience and further study the portfolio of knowledge and skills necessary to cope in the present day legal environment.

It is, by design, a basic text for non-accountants who have little or seemingly no mathematical abilities. Nor does the book assume any level of prior knowledge of the subject area.

Some topics are addressed in a reasonable level of detail owing to the fact that they underpin virtually all forms of accounting systems, irrespective of the nature of commercial activity, and without which the proper understanding of the Solicitors Accounts Rules, etc is unlikely ever to be achieved. The principles of double-entry accounting fall into this category.

Other topics are dealt with on a relatively more superficial basis, owing principally to limitations on space. The reader should still receive a reasonable insight into these subject areas, however, even although the depth of study afforded to them amounts to no more than a quick cantor around their boundaries. Corporate accounting reports are studied on this basis for example.

Within the book the use of 'T' accounts has been adopted on a reasonably widespread basis during the sections dealing with double-entry accounting. In the writers' opinion, using this style of presentation more readily assists those new to basic bookkeeping come to terms with the principles of double-entry accounting. It should however be noted that the format of individual accounts in practice may differ, although they will of course still be governed by the same underlying principles.

Once a basic level of competency in this method of accounting has been achieved, examining the effects of various business transactions in terms of the way they are recorded in a double-entry accounting system also serves as a convenient means by which the reader may come to appreciate the relationships existing between different aspects of a business.

The book has been written to be as far as possible a self-contained, self-teach accountancy manual requiring minimum reference to further source material. Where the book is adopted as a core text for the Diploma in Legal Practice, the role of the lecturer will be more focused on promoting learning efficiency on the part of readers in order that they may acquire maximum knowledge in the shortest time (with minimum stress).

Louise Watson and Robert Watson
August 2000

Acknowledgements

Writing a book is much like building your own home. They both seem to take about ten years to complete.

To all our family, friends and colleagues who have watched, supported and tolerated the 'bricks' being laid, our sincere thanks. A special thanks to those who have rolled up their sleeves and assisted with no thought of reward other than the comfort derived from helping a fellow human being.

Material for the project has come from a variety of sources. Again our heartfelt thanks to all those who contributed, some albeit unwittingly. Without their input the finished article would have been much the poorer.

The writing of any textbook invariably means that a disproportionate workload is placed on people beyond purely the authors. This book is no different. Consequently it would be remiss of us not to take the opportunity to express our sincere gratitude to a few key individuals by name, as follows: to Liz McCallum for her patience and word-processing skills, to Cinzia Biondi and Lorna E. Gillies for research assistance given, to the staff of Butterworths Publishing for their professional support and tolerance, to Alison Attack of Kidstons, Solicitors and especially Tony Sinclair of French Duncan, Chartered Accountants for contributions with respect to the chapters dealing with solicitors accounts, to the Law Society of Scotland for permissions granted to reproduce written material, and finally to all former and future students for providing the motivation and inspiration necessary for the writers to bring this book to a conclusion.

Mistakes, of which there are bound to be some if not many, are all ours.

Louise M Watson
Robert A B Watson
August 2000

Contents

Bibliography

Davies, M, Paterson, R, and Wilson, A, *Generally Accepted Accounting Practice in the United Kingdom* (6th edn, 1999) Butterworths Tolley/Ernst & Young, Croydon

Department of Trade and Industry *Limited Liability Partnerships – A Consultation Document*, Department of Trade and Industry (September 1998)

Institute of Chartered Accountants in Scotland *Making Corporate Reports Work*, (1988) Kogan Page

Johnson, H and Whittan, A, *A Practical Foundation in Accounting* (3rd edn, 1987) Allen and Unwin Ltd

Wood, F, *Business Accounting Volume 1* (6th edn, 1993) Pitman Publishing

Chapter One: Introduction to accountancy

The main activities of professional accountants can be considered as being twofold; the first relates to the recording of financial data, the other is concerned with the communication of accounting information. Such activities are evident throughout the business world, including within legal firms.

Solicitors are frequently required to accept responsibility for the accuracy of their financial records (for example, having regard to the provisions of the Solicitors (Scotland) Accounts Rules 1997). Solicitors are also called upon in a whole variety of situations to be able to read, interpret and understand the contents of various forms of financial statements, be it in relation to their clients' affairs or with respect to the running of the firm itself. Failure to be properly equipped to perform such duties to a level commensurate with their professional standing can carry severe consequences.

It follows that solicitors should be aware of accounting issues if only in so far as they impinge on the practice of law.

In order that at least a basic appreciation of the discipline of accountancy can be attained, it would be useful to review its basic foundations and then give very brief consideration to the heavily regulated environment in which professional accountants operate.

THE BASIC ASSUMPTIONS UNDERPINNING ACCOUNTANCY

The practice of every-day accounting is carried out having regard to several basic assumptions which are known as *accounting conventions* (or *concepts*). Accounting conventions are universal and applicable throughout the world. The main conventions can be summarised as follows:

(1) Business entity
(2) Accounting period (or Periodicity)
(3) Money measurement
(4) Historic cost
(5) Realisation
(6) Matching (or Accruals)
(7) Consistency
(8) Prudence (or Conservatism)
(9) Materiality
(10) Going concern (or Continuity)
(11) Objectivity
(12) Dual aspect

(1) Business entity

Under this concept it is assumed that the business is a separate entity, quite distinct from the affairs of its owner and, as a consequence, only the transactions and dealings of the business have their effects noted in its financial records.

This concept sits comfortably with company law for example, where companies have a distinct legal persona and it is relatively simple to understand it within that context.

However, in contrast, the concept appears to be in conflict with the law relating to sole traders and partnerships where the line between the entity and the owner is more blurred. Nevertheless, in order that meaningful records can be maintained, the convention must be applied. This means that a separately identifiable business entity still has to be recognised in such circumstances with accounting records maintained accordingly.

(2) Accounting period (or periodicity)

Under this convention accounting statements are prepared for a specific period which in most cases is one year. Reporting on an annual basis is now the norm for most organisations and indeed, is compulsory for UK companies.

Organisations are largely bound by the practicalities of their business in deciding when their accounting period should begin. Common sense should prevail when initially determining the commencement date for an organisation's accounting period which, once decided, will probably exist well into the future. For example, where the trading activity of a business is heavily cyclical throughout the course of a year, it makes sense to avoid having a financial year-end which falls within busy trading periods. The additional work associated with the end of an accounting period should, ideally, fall within a quiet trading period for the organisation concerned.

Where businesses have no marked cyclical variations in trading activity, which will generally be the case for solicitors, the most practical financial period will probably be chosen to coincide with the tax year.

(3) Money measurement

Applying the concept of money measurement means that only transactions, facts, events, etc, that can be quantified in monetary terms are noted in the accounting records of the business.

An unfortunate consequence of this convention is that important facts of direct relevance to the organisation may be totally ignored. Financial reports may not, therefore, tell anything like the whole story regarding the quality of a firm's products or services, of its management or workforce, of potential threats or opportunities likely to be faced in the future.

(4) Historic cost

This concept dictates that the historic or original cost of an item should be used for accounting purposes. The fact that it is such an objective practice, providing accountants with a readily identifiable figure with which to work, is an obvious advantage.

The concept is not without problems though, especially when applied over inflationary periods. In a situation where inflation exists, using the original purchase price of an asset in preference to its current market value may well mean that financial statements provide a misleading picture of the business. For this reason, many organisations periodically re-value major assets (such as property) and use the revaluation figure for accounting purposes in preference to relying on their historic cost.

(5) Realisation

This concept is concerned with identifying the correct point in time when revenue can be recognised for accounting purposes. Under the convention, revenue is normally recognised at the moment an item is sold. This, of course, may or may not coincide with the transfer of any related cash.

(6) Matching (or accruals)

Under the matching convention, revenues earned by an organisation should be matched with the expenses incurred in earning those revenues.

For the purposes of applying this particular convention, the fact that determines the accounting period into which a revenue or expense is deemed to fall is not so much the point in time when money actually changes hands. Rather, it is the moment that revenue is earned or expense incurred that is the relevant factor.

As an example, take the situation where a legal firm purchased a new office car exactly two-thirds of the way through its financial year. If the firm paid £150 as a full 12 months' road tax on the same day as it bought the car, then in four months time (ie at the end of its financial year) an accounting adjustment will have to be made to reflect the fact that the firm has effectively paid part of the next financial year's expenses in advance. This adjustment will involve setting only £50 of the road tax against the revenues of the current financial year, with the balance of £100 being attributed to the following financial year. If no adjustment was made, expenses will not have been properly matched to the revenues generated by the use of the vehicle.

(7) Consistency

There is frequently more than one way to account for a particular transaction. If an organisation adopts a certain accounting approach with respect to some matter, then the concept of consistency states that the same approach should be followed in the future.

Assuming an organisation adopts consistent accounting practices from one period to the next, then more meaningful comparisons between the results of the business over successive financial periods will be possible. This will assist those using the accounts to gain a better insight into how well or badly the business is performing.

(8) Prudence (or conservatism)

Accountants often have to make judgements about the future when performing their role. There is an underlying assumption in accountancy that a prudent or conservative approach should always be adopted in determining the profits of a business. Accordingly, accountants generally do not anticipate possible profits but always anticipate possible losses.

The application of the prudence concept is perhaps most easily illustrated in the context of stock valuations of trading companies. For example, at the end of an accounting period, a retailer of fashion clothing will reflect the value of stocks remaining by reference to the lower of their cost price or the amount that they would probably realise if sold. So if the trader has only one item of designer clothing in stock at the financial year-end, which cost £1,000 but because it is now out of fashion will probably only be sold for £150, then the trader will include the latter figure in the accounting statements. By valuing the stock at the lower figure, the trader will have acted in accordance with the prudence concept.

(9) Materiality

The materiality convention allows accountants to use a measure of discretion when carrying out their role. It basically means that time and effort should not be spent on the elaborate recording of some trivial item. In a sense, therefore, the convention reflects the practicalities of business.

(10) Going concern (or continuity)

Unless there is clear evidence to the contrary, there is an underlying assumption in accountancy that organisations will continue in operational existence for the foreseeable future. This is the going concern concept.

The importance of such an assumption can be seen, for example, with respect to the value placed upon business assets shown in its accounting statements. Where a business has assets that will be used over several years, a widely adopted accounting technique is to apportion the value of such assets over those accounting periods benefitting from its use (again, this is another example of the matching concept in action). This approach assumes that the business will continue to trade into the future for at least for the working life of the assets. However, if the concept of going concern was not applied in this way, a totally different basis would have to be used for valuing such assets. If continuity was not assumed, assets would probably have to be valued in the accounts on the basis of what they would raise if sold off at that time. This could have a rather dramatic effect on financial statements, especially for businesses using specialist machinery with a strictly limited resale value.

(11) Objectivity

Accountancy functions should be performed with the minimum of bias. The concept of objectivity means that accountants should retain an independence of mind and view the business through the eyes of an unbiased outsider.

(12) Dual aspect

As will be seen in the next chapter of this book, the main system used to record financial information relating to a business is known as *double-entry bookkeeping*. The concept of dual aspect can be regarded as the seed from which double-entry bookkeeping grew. Under the dual aspect concept it is assumed that every transaction affects business resources in two ways. More will be seen of the operation of the dual aspect concept in due course.

The review of accounting conventions above outlines the main assumptions which are made when carrying out the accounting function. An awareness of them is important if financial statements are to be understood and the information contained within them interpreted fully by their users.

OVERVIEW OF THE ACCOUNTANCY PROFESSION

It would also be appropriate to be aware generally of the fairly heavily regulated environment that exists and within which the practice of accountancy is conducted.

Accountants, like lawyers, have several different branches in which to specialise. For example, accountants may work within professional firms and handle work relating to audit, tax, general accounts preparation services, etc for a broad range of clients. They may also work in industry for companies and produce financial information for management decision-making purposes. Individuals involved in the latter style of work are termed 'management accountants'. Other accountants may also be employed by companies but spend their time collecting financial data that will be refined down into statements eventually to be released by the company to the outside world. These people can be called 'financial accountants'. Accountants also operate within the public sector, in local government for example, and in other civil service agencies. Large organisations in the public or private sector will usually have their own internal audit department, which is again a further example of the specialised work performed by accountants. Finally, there is even a branch of accountancy that works almost exclusively with the legal profession. 'Law accountants' can provide a range of specialised services to law firms.

There are many different professional bodies of which accountants could be a member. For example, Chartered Accountants (CAs) may belong to one of the separate Institutes of Chartered Accountants to be found in Scotland or Ireland, or to the joint Institute of England and Wales. Alternatively, and dependent upon main vocation, an individual may be a member of the Chartered Institute of Management Accountants (CIMA) or of the Chartered Institute of Public Finance and Accountancy (CIPFA). The Chartered Association of Certified Accountants (CACA) is another example of a professional organisation for accountants.

Although distinctly separate, the above accountancy bodies very often work collectively to promote and resolve accountancy issues both at national and international levels. Accountants are proud of the extent of self-regulation they enjoy and are keen to retain such powers. Consequently they are almost continuously active in relation to accountancy issues through collaborative bodies such as the International Accounting Standards Committee, the Financial Reporting Council, and the Urgent Issues Task Force.

The production of *Statements of Standard Accounting Practice* (SSAPs) is another example of the fruits of collaboration. SSAPs provide guidance to accountants on appropriate accounting practices. Professionally qualified accountants are expected to do their best to follow the substance of the various SSAPs that exist. SSAPs are slowly being updated and superceded by *Financial Reporting Standards* (FRSs).

Although SSAPs and FRSs do not result in identical accounting practices, they do serve a very important role in helping to standardise them as much as possible. The contents of SSAPs and FRSs are consistent with the laws of the UK and the Republic of Ireland. Similarly they are compatible with the contents of European Community Directives [1].

In conclusion, it should be evident by now that accountancy is far from being an undisciplined business activity. It is based on firm foundations and is subject to reasonably definite parameters.

---

1   For comprehensive guidance on the application of SSAPs, FRSs and other regulatory pronouncements relevant to current accounting practice, reference should be made to M Davies, R Paterson and A Wilson *Generally Accepted Accounting Practice in the United Kingdom* (6th edn, Butterworths/Tolley/Ernst & Young, Croydon, 1999). GAAP is regarded by many to constitute the accountant's bible.

Chapter Two: Recording financial information

WHY KEEP BUSINESS RECORDS?

Solicitors, like any other business persons, need to know how well their organisation is doing from a commercial point of view. It is considered sound business practice for the solicitor to know how profitable the firm is, how much it owns and how much it owes. In other words, is the firm solvent and capable of meeting its financial obligations as they fall due?

Furthermore, besides meeting the personal demands of the solicitor, records must be maintained which are also capable of satisfying any legal requirements imposed by, for example, the Inland Revenue, Customs and Excise, the Department of Social Security and certainly not forgetting The Law Society of Scotland[1]. Failure to comply with the requirements of such organisations can have serious consequences.

The above bodies, besides creating the need for proper business records in the first place, also largely determine just how detailed such records will be. In practical terms, once the records are at a stage where they are capable of satisfying the demands of external agencies, it is really up to the owners to dictate the final level of sophistication of the accounting system having due regard to their needs.

It is one thing to have comprehensive accounting records, but it is something else to have these records organised in such a way that they are efficient both when it comes to recording details affecting the business in the first instance, and when producing information which can be used beneficially by the owners and/or managers of the business.

HOW SHOULD BUSINESS TRANSACTIONS BE RECORDED?

At its simplest, the proprietor of a business might list all relevant events in a diary, reviewing the entries in this book on any occasion when information was required. For all but the simplest of businesses, it is not difficult to envisage that such a system would be time-consuming to operate and, almost certainly, would be totally impractical when it came to both recording the affairs of larger organisations and subsequently extracting information therefrom. Given such shortfalls and the susceptibility to errors in general, it follows that some other more suitable method should be used to record the activities of businesses.

It was noticed as long ago as the fifteenth century that business transactions could be grouped into clearly definable categories, depending on whether they related to

---

1 For example, the Solicitors (Scotland) Accounts Rules 1997; see appendix 1.

Assets, Liabilities, Capital, Income or *Expenditure* and further, that if simple basic rules were followed, it was possible to have a self-checking system for recording business transactions.

Fixed and current assets

Assets can really be regarded as the resources owned by the business for use within that business. It is possible to divide them into *fixed assets* or *current assets*, depending on their nature and the activities of the business in general. The principal characteristics of fixed assets are (i) that they are not bought primarily for the purpose of immediate resale for profit, and (ii) that they are essentially of a long term nature where their use extends over many accounting periods. Examples of fixed assets commonly used in a solicitor's firm could include *office property, motor vehicles, computer equipment*, and *office fixtures and fittings*.

In contrast, assets such as *cash* and *debts owed to the firm* are examples of current assets. If the business is involved in trading (that is buying goods for the purpose of reselling them at a profit) as opposed to providing say, legal services, the *stock* in which it trades can also be considered as a current asset. Also, it is reasonably common practice for trading organisations to supply goods on credit—that is, although the goods are received by the customer, there will be an agreed period of delay before the customer is due to pay for the goods previously received. Very often professional services are provided on such a basis; for example a solicitor may handle the sale of property for a client, invoicing the client upon completion of the work. Where goods or services are sold on this basis, the customer or client will be termed a *debtor* of the supplying firm until the point in time where the debt is extinguished by the debtor settling the outstanding invoice. Debtors can be regarded as another example of a current asset.

On the whole, current assets are more short-term in nature and are more capable of being quickly turned into cash, assuming that they are not cash already. They are sometimes also referred to as *circulating assets*. If reference is made to the activities of a basic trading firm, it is relatively easy to see where this term arose: beginning with *cash*, the trader may use this to pay for *trading stock* which can then be sold on to a customer. If this customer does not pay for the goods immediately, a *debtor* is created. When the debtor eventually pays, *cash* is received and so the whole cycle continues.

Regard must be shown to the main activities of the business when deciding whether an item should be classified as a current or as a fixed asset, since it is quite possible that the item could fall into either camp depending on the nature of the business. In the above explanation of the type of items which could be regarded as fixed assets in the context of a legal firm, motor vehicles were quoted as an example. However, if a business trades in motor vehicles, as a car dealer does, then cars, vans etc should properly be regarded as the trading stock of that business and as such should be classified as current assets. Another example can be seen with respect to office equipment—to a solicitor's firm this will almost certainly be shown as a separate heading under fixed assets, since such equipment is for use within the business to help generate profit on an ongoing basis and is not bought in the hope that it could be immediately resold at a profit. Nevertheless, to another business, such as an office supplies company, the office equipment is trading stock and should be shown in the records as a current asset.

Short- and long-term liabilities

Liabilities are basically amounts owed by the business to some other party. They can be split into either *current liabilities* (that is, short-term liabilities) or *long-term liabilities*, depending on the length of time remaining before settlement is due. Normally, debts due for repayment in less than one year from a given point in time are classified as current liabilities, with amounts which have more than a year to run being termed long-term liabilities of the business.

Examples of items which fall into the latter classification could include a long-term loan negotiated by a solicitor for the purchase of a new car for the firm or a mortgage being used to finance the purchase of the firm's offices.

A bank overdraft, on the other hand, being technically due for repayment upon demand by the firm's bank, will properly be regarded as a current liability. In addition, if a trading business is considered again, and that business buys goods for resale on credit from a supplier, then the supplier will be considered a *creditor* to the business and as such a current liability. Once the business pays for the goods previously received, then the creditor (that is, the current liability) will be extinguished.

Capital

The *capital* of a business represents the residual claim on the business by the owner(s) of that business. For example, when solicitors start a legal practice, capital introduced at the inception of the business will be the total value which the partners have committed to the firm. This may take the form of cash or it could be some other asset such as when one of the partners introduces a car or office premises, the latter being examples of fixed assets as seen previously. The contribution from each partner must be quantified in monetary terms in order to establish the capital input by each of the partners on the one hand and to establish the total capital of the firm on the other.

By the same token, if a partner subsequently withdraws cash from the firm or permanently removes another business asset for private use (eg a word processor), then the partner's capital in question will be reduced by the relevant amount. Such transactions have a special accounting term, namely *drawings*, and as mentioned will have the effect of reducing a partner's claim on the business.

The effect of profits or losses on capital

Perhaps the main reason for someone being in business is to make a profit, which in turn will increase their wealth. It is possible to calculate the size of profits generated by the business over a specific period of time by subtracting the *expenses* incurred in that period from the *revenues* generated. Where a gain is the end result, this will increase the owners' capital stake in the firm (assuming that it is not taken out of the business as drawings) and conversely, where there is a loss situation, the owners will see a reduction in their capital by the amount of loss.

As far as a solicitor in private practice is concerned, it is possible to list the more common forms of business expenses and revenues as follows:

Business Expenses	*Business Revenues*
Wages and salaries*	Fee income
Heating and lighting	Commissions received
Postage and telephone	Investment income
Insurances	
Professional subscriptions	
Stationery	
Marketing and advertising	
Sundry expenses	
Rent and rates	
Motor vehicles expenses	
Printing and photocopying	
Travelling expenses	
Bank interest and charges	

[* It is worth noting that the business expenses of 'wages and salaries' shown above relate to payments to employees. Partners' emoluments are treated differently and so are not regarded as business expenses, but rather *appropriations of profit*[1].]

These lists are not intended to be comprehensive. Various other forms of legitimate business expenses and revenues will be introduced at appropriate stages later on.

The formal accounting process of matching business expenses incurred to revenues generated over a given period of time in a legal practice results in the production of a financial report called the *Profit and Loss Account*, more about which follows in subsequent chapters[2].

THE ACCOUNTING EQUATION

In the 15th century, besides identifying the above general headings under which the effects of transactions could be grouped, it was also noticed that a definite relationship existed between them and that it was possible for this relationship to be used as a basis for recording the effects of business transactions. It was further observed that if a set of simple rules were followed when recording transactions in the books and records of a business, then the fundamental relationship is never disturbed. The relationship between Assets, Capital and Liabilities can be expressed by the following statement:

'The resources owned by the business should always equate to the claims against such resources'.

In other words,

$$ASSETS = CAPITAL + LIABILITIES$$

This is known in the accountancy world as the *Accounting Equation* and in essence is the foundation for another form of financial report called *The Balance Sheet*[3]. It is

---

1   See Chapters 7 and 8.
2   This report would be known as the *Trading, Profit and Loss Account* for trading businesses, ie those buying and selling goods as their main line of business. A solicitor does not 'trade' in this sense, hence the truncated title used for legal practices and indeed for other professional firms.
3   The Balance Sheet is examined in greater depth in Chapter 3.

possible to expand the accounting equation to include income and expenditure as follows:

$$\text{ASSETS} = \text{CAPITAL} + \text{LIABILITIES} + (\text{INCOME} - \text{EXPENDITURE})$$

Business transactions **always** affect the Accounting Equation in such a way that *either*: (i) its alternate sides are increased or decreased by the same amount, *or*, (ii) items in only one side are altered in such a self-cancelling way that the net effect on the equation is to leave it unchanged. In either case, the equation should always balance.

For example, to illustrate point (i), on the earlier occasion where a partner of a legal firm introduced a car into the business, the effect of the transaction is, on the one hand, to increase the assets owned by the business (that is, the motor vehicles) and, on the other, to increase the partner's capital by the same amount, being the value of the car. Here both sides of the accounting equation are being increased by the same amount. Alternatively, where a partner withdraws £1,000 cash from the firm's bank account, the effect of this transaction is to reduce the assets of the business (ie the money held at the bank) and to reduce the partner's capital (as seen earlier, drawings have this effect on capital) in each case by £1,000. Here each side of the equation is being reduced by the same amount.

To give an example of point (ii), where a transaction results in compensating changes to one side of the equation so that a net effect is zero, consider the situation where someone who owes the solicitor £500 in respect of work done previously now decides to pay in cash. In this instance one category of asset (the debtor, whoever that may be) is being reduced by £500 whilst simultaneously another category of asset (cash) is being increased by £500. Thinking in terms of the accounting equation, it can be seen that the equation remains unaffected by this transaction.

In all of the above examples, none of the transactions have the effect of throwing the accounting equation out of balance. Furthermore, it is possible to see from looking at such examples that any individual transaction always seems to have a double effect. This *duality of effect*[1] gave rise to a system of recording business transactions known as *double-entry bookkeeping*.

THE PRINCIPLES OF DOUBLE-ENTRY

Double-entry bookkeeping is an ancient system first described in detail by a Franciscan monk Luca Pacioli in 1494 which, with very little modification, still underpins virtually all modern accounting systems. In essence, like so many good ideas, it is relatively simple.

Under this system, an *account* is created for each separately identifiable item (or group of items as the case may be) in the business, whether it is related to assets, liabilities, capital, income or expenditure. **The owner/manager of the business decides on the number of accounts to operate, depending on the degree of detail required of the business records.** The more detailed the recording process, then the greater the number of accounts which would have to be set up. Each account is used to record changes in the monetary value of the item concerned. If there is an increase

---

1   'Dual aspect' is another example of an accounting concept, as outlined in Chapter 1.

or a decrease in the value of a particular item, then a record of this change must be shown in the relevant account.

Generally, every account used in the business is set out in exactly the same way, whether it is being used to record a change to an asset, a liability, capital or some form of income or expenditure. A simplified format for any account can be shown as follows:

[Name of the Account]

'Debit' side	'Credit' side

It can be seen that each account should be clearly named and that the left-hand side of an account is always known as the *Debit* side with the *Credit* side being on the right. Very often 'debit' and 'credit' will be shortened to *Dr* and *Cr* respectively. For fairly obvious reasons, accounts set out in this way are referred to as '*T*' accounts. When information is recorded on the left-hand side of an account, this is known as making a *debit entry*. Alternatively, when details of a transaction are entered on the right-hand side, this is known, logically enough, as a *credit entry*.

Developing this basic structure a little results in the following:

Dr   [Name of the A/C]   Cr

Date (i)	Details (ii)	Folio (iii)	£ (iv)	Date (i)	Details (ii)	Folio (iii)	£ (iv)

The account still retains a debit and a credit side, with the information contained on either side being organised in exactly the same way. That is, in column (i) the *date* of the transaction which affected this account would be shown. Column (ii), the *details* column, would contain the name of the other account affected by the transaction (remembering that each transaction has a double effect on business items). In this respect, the *details* column acts as a cross reference to that other account. The *folio* column, (iii) also assists in keeping track of the other account affected and is a more specific reference to it—for example, it could give a specific page reference where the other account is located. Finally, column (iv) would contain the monetary value of the transaction.

Traditionally, the accounts of a business were kept in a large bound book called a *ledger*, with each account having a separate page within this ledger; hence the term *ledger account*. Although things have now moved on somewhat from this type of set-up, the basic concept of accounts being grouped together into ledgers still remains.

The next matter to be considered is the process of recording business transactions into the accounts using the double-entry system of bookkeeping.

The ground rules

The following rules must be adhered to at all times if the double-entry system is to work successfully:

Rule One: This rule determines the type of entry which should be made in a particular account to record the effects of a business transaction.

General Category	To Record	Action Required
(1) Asset	An increase in an asset account	Debit the account in question [that is, enter the date and other details of the transaction on the left-hand side of the relevant account]
	A decrease in an asset account	Credit the account [that is, enter the date and other details of the transaction on the right-hand side of the relevant account]
(2) Capital	An increase	Credit the account
	A decrease	Debit the account
(3) Liability	An increase	Credit the account
	A decrease	Debit the account
(4) Income	An increase	Credit the account
	A decrease	Debit the account
(5) Expense	An increase	Debit the account
	A decrease	Credit the account

Note the similarity in treatment of accounts falling into the general categories of **Assets** and **Expenses**. Here any *increase* in an account would result in a *debit* entry being made to that account, with a *decrease* being recorded as a *credit* entry. In direct contrast, **Capital**, **Liability** and **Income** accounts are treated in exactly the opposite way—that is, *increases* in the accounts are recorded as *credit* entries, with *decreases* shown as *debit* entries.

To assist in remembering the contents of this rule, it is useful to think of a slightly re-arranged equation which is itself based on the Accounting Equation. That is,

Assets = Capital + Liabilities

or   Assets = Capital + Liabilities + (Income – Expenses)

or   **Assets + Expenses = Capital + Liabilities + Income**

Rule Two: Recalling the double effect of business transactions noticed earlier, then:

'*Every debit entry must have a corresponding credit entry and vice versa*'.

In other words, a business transaction *never* results in only a single entry. There must always be *two* entries made in the accounts to record a business transaction. After all, it is called the 'double-entry' bookkeeping system.

Rule Three: '*The Accounting Equation should always balance*'

If Rules One and Two are followed correctly then this will always be the case. Again, it cannot be over-emphasised that the above Rules must be observed at all times if the double-entry system is to work correctly.

Before looking at an illustration of a double-entry bookkeeping system in operation, it may be worthwhile to examine the various practical steps involved when applying the Rules:

First step: Identify the business transaction which has occurred.

Second step: Looking more closely at the transaction, decide:
(a) the names of the accounts which have been affected;
and (b) under which general category each of the accounts fall (that is, do they relate to Assets, Capital, Liabilities, Income or Expenses?)

Third and final step: Apply the appropriate double-entry rules to record either an increase or a decrease in the accounts affected.

Applying the practical steps

ILLUSTRATION 2.1

Kevin Hall, a solicitor of some years standing with one of the major legal practices in Glasgow, decided to start his own practice specialising in criminal law. He began on 1 April 1999 and had the following business transactions which are to be recorded using the principles of double-entry bookkeeping:

1 April — Kevin Hall opened a business account with his local branch of the Bank of Scotia and immediately lodged £2,500. On the same date, he transferred his car into the name of his firm at a value of £3,000. The car is to be used purely for business purposes.

4 April — He moved into a small office near the Sheriff Court. The rent for the office is £400 per calendar month, payable in advance. He paid April's rental charge today by cheque.

5 April — Kevin bought a secondhand desk and a couple of filing cabinets for £300, paying by cheque.

6 April — He bought a small computer system from 'Computer Supplies Ltd.' for £1,500. The company offered two months interest-free credit. Kevin decided to take advantage of the offer, which effectively meant that he could delay payment until early June.

7 April — He withdrew £200 cash from the firm's bank account and deposited this money into an old cash box which a friend had given him. He keeps the cash box in the bottom drawer of his filing cabinet at the office. The cash will be used for minor forms of business expenditure.

8 April — He bought some pens, pencils and other office stationery for £25 using cash from the cash box.

11 April — He bought £20 worth of petrol for the car, paying by cheque.

12 April — He paid for a holiday weekend using his business cheque book. The holiday cost £225.

13 April — He carried out some agency work for another legal firm, Gee and Co at the Sheriff Court. The agreed fee was £80. Hall sent his invoice off to Gee and Co with payment due on or before Friday, 22 April 1999.

14 April — He performed more work for Gee and Co on the same terms as before. The fee on this occasion was £150.

15 April — He paid a telephone bill of £35 by cheque.

18 April — He bought tea, coffee, sugar and some milk for use at the office for £5, paying by cash from the cash box.

19 April — He paid an electricity bill by cheque. The office is electrically heated and the bill amounted to £50.

20 April — He received a cheque for £80 from Gee and Co in respect of work done earlier in the month. The cheque was immediately lodged in the firm's bank account.

21 April — He received interest on his firm's bank account amounting to £15. The sum was automatically transferred by the bank to Hall's business account.

22 April — The Bank of Scotia charged Hall's business account £20 in respect of service charges. This amount was automatically deducted from Hall's account.

25 April — Hall carried out more agency work, this time for Wright & Co. He was paid by cheque the same day. The cheque for £55 was immediately lodged with the bank.

Later on that day, Hall spoke at a Law Society of Scotland seminar. His fee for the afternoon seminar was £180, which he expects to receive before the end of next month. He delivered his invoice on the day of the lecture.

26 April — He received a £150 cheque from Gee and Co in payment of his invoice dated 14 April.

Hall also filled the car up with petrol and bought a gallon of oil to keep in its boot. He paid the £30 charge by cheque.

27 April — He bought some milk and some toilet paper for the office. The total cost was £10 and was paid from the cash box.

28 April — He paid a cleaning company £45 by cheque for cleaning his office throughout April.

29 April — Hall represented a client of Smithys (Solicitors) on an agency basis. He sent off an invoice for £40 to Smithys the same day, with payment due within two weeks of the invoice date.

Applying the various steps which should be taken when recording such information, it would be possible to re-organise the above summary of Hall's transactions in the following manner. Note that the first step—that is, the identification of the actual business transaction—has largely already been done given the way in which Hall's transactions for April have been shown thus far in the illustration. The transactions are listed in date order of occurrence:

(a) Date of the transaction	(b) Name of the accounts affected by the transaction and the general category into which each falls (shown in brackets)		(c) Effect of the transaction on each account	(d) Action required to record those of K. Hall
APRIL				
1 (Two transactions happened on this date)	(i) Cash at Bank	(Asset)	Increase	Debit the 'Cash at bank' account, £2,500
	K. Hall—Capital	(Capital)	Increase	Credit the 'K. Hall — Capital' account, £2,500
"	(ii) Motor Vehicles	(Asset)	Increase	Debit the 'Motor Vehicles' account, £3,000
	K. Hall—Capital	(Capital)	Increase	Credit the 'K. Hall — Capital' account, £3,000
4	Rent	(Expense)	Increase	Debit 'Rent' account, £400
	Cash at Bank	(Asset)	Decrease	Credit 'Cash at Bank' account, £400
5	Office Furniture	(Asset)	Increase	Debit 'Office Furniture' account, £300
	Cash at Bank	(Asset)	Decrease	Credit 'Cash at Bank' account, £300
6	Office Equipment	(Asset)	Increase	Debit 'Office Equipment' account, £1,500
	Computer Supplies Ltd.	(being a Creditor this account is a Liability)	Increase	Credit 'Computer Supplies Ltd.' account, £1,500
7	Cash at Bank	(Asset)	Decrease	Credit 'Cash at Bank' account, £200
	Cash in Hand	(Asset)	Increase	Debit 'Cash in Hand' account, £200
8	Stationery	(Expense)	Increase	Debit 'Stationery' account, £25
	Cash in Hand	(Asset)	Decrease	Credit 'Cash in Hand' account, £25
11	Motor Vehicle Running Costs	(Expense)	Increase	Debit 'Motor Vehicle Running Costs' account, £20
	Cash at Bank	(Asset)	Decrease	Credit 'Cash at Bank' account, £20

(a) Date of the transaction	(b) Name of the accounts affected by the transaction and the general category into which each falls (shown in brackets)		(c) Effect of the transaction on each account	(d) Action required to record those of K. Hall
APRIL				
12	Cash at Bank	(Asset)	Decrease	Credit 'Cash at Bank' account, £225
	K. Hall—Drawings	(Capital)	Although the transaction involves an increase in Drawings, its actual effect is to *reduce* the owner's claim on the business (that is, Capital). Accordingly, use the double-entry rule to record a decrease in Capital but in the Drawings account.	Debit 'K. Hall — Drawings' account, £225
13	Fees Rendered	(Income)	Increase	Credit 'Fees Rendered' account, £80
	Gee & Co	(being a Debtor this account is an Asset)	Increase	Debit 'Gee & Co' account, £80
14	Fees Rendered	(Income)	Increase	Credit 'Fees Rendered' account, £150
	Gee & Co	(Asset)	Increase	Debit 'Gee & Co' account, £150
15	Telephone	(Expense)	Increase	Debit 'Telephone' account, £35
	Cash at Bank	(Asset)	Decrease	Credit 'Cash at Bank' account, £35
18	Sundry Expenses	(Expense)	Increase	Debit 'Sundry Expenses' account, £5
	Cash in Hand	(Asset)	Decrease	Credit 'Cash in Hand' account, £5
19	Heating and Lighting	(Expense)	Increase	Debit ' Heating and Lighting' account, £50
	Cash at Bank	(Asset)	Decrease	Credit 'Cash at Bank' account, £50
20	Gee & Co	(Asset)	Decrease (since there is a reduction in the indebtedness of Gee & Co to K. Hall)	Credit 'Gee & Co' account, £80
	Cash at Bank	(Asset)	Increase	Debit 'Cash at Bank' account, £80
21	Bank Interest Received	(Income)	Increase	Credit 'Bank Interest Received' account, £15
	Cash at Bank	(Asset)	Increase	Debit 'Cash at Bank' account, £15
22	Bank Charges	(Expense)	Increase	Debit 'Bank Charges' account, £20
	Cash at Bank	(Asset)	Decrease	Credit 'Cash at Bank' account, £20
25	(i) Fees Rendered	(Income)	Increase	Credit 'Fees Rendered' account, £55
	Cash at Bank	(Asset)	Increase	Debit 'Cash at Bank' account, £55
"	(ii) Fees Rendered	(Income)	Increase	Credit 'Fees Rendered' account, £180
	Law Society of Scotland	(being a Debtor, this account is an Asset)	Increase	Debit 'Law Society of Scotland' account, £180
26	(i) Gee & Co	(Asset)	Decrease	Credit 'Gee & Co' account, £150
	Cash at Bank	(Asset)	Increase	Debit 'Cash at Bank' account, £150
"	(ii) Motor Vehicle Running Costs	(Expense)	Increase	Debit 'Motor Vehicle Running Costs' account, £30
	Cash at Bank	(Asset)	Decrease	Credit 'Cash at Bank' account, £30

(a) Date of the transaction	(b) Name of the accounts affected by the transaction and the general category into which each falls (shown in brackets)		(c) Effect of the transaction on each account	(d) Action required to record those of K. Hall
APRIL				
27	Sundry Expenses	(Expense)	Increase	Debit 'Sundry Expenses' account, £10
	Cash in Hand	(Asset)	Decrease	Credit 'Cash in Hand' account, £10
28	Office Cleaning	(Expense)	Increase	Debit 'Office Cleaning' account, £45
	Cash at Bank	(Asset)	Decrease	Credit 'Cash at Bank' account, £45
29	Fees Rendered	(Income)	Increase	Credit 'Fees Rendered' account, £40
	Smithys (Solicitors)	(being a Debtor, this account is an Asset)	Increase	Debit 'Smithys (Solicitors)' account, £40

Illustration 2.1 has been set out purely as a learning aid on how to use double-entry principles to record business transactions. Essentially, columns (b) and (c) represent no more than the background thought-process a bookkeeper would go through for each separately identifiable transaction. Column (d) on the other hand reflects the 'doing' part, whereby actual entries are made in the various T accounts of K. Hall on the date on which they occurred. From a practical viewpoint, it is not necessary to create such a table when recording business transactions. Anyone who is familiar with double-entry bookkeeping should be capable of looking at a transaction and then making the appropriate entries directly in the accounting records.

If all of the above transactions had been recorded in K. Hall's accounts, the position as follows would have been the result:

CASH AT BANK

APRIL	£	APRIL	£
1 K. Hall—Capital	2,500	4 Rent	400
20 Gee & Co	80	5 Office furniture	300
21 Bank interest		7 Cash in hand	200
received	15	11 Motor vehicle	
25 Fees rendered	55	running costs	20
26 Gee & Co	150	12 K. Hall—Drawings	225
		15 Telephone	35
		19 Heating & Lighting	50
		22 Bank charges	20
		26 Motor vehicle	
		running costs	30
		28 Office cleaning	45

K. HALL—CAPITAL

APRIL	£	APRIL	£
		1 Cash at Bank	2,500
		1 Motor vehicles	3,000

MOTOR VEHICLES

APRIL	£	APRIL	£
1 K. Hall—Capital	3,000		

RENT

APRIL	£	APRIL	£
4 Cash at Bank	400		

OFFICE FURNITURE

APRIL	£	APRIL	£
5 Cash at Bank	300		

OFFICE EQUIPMENT

APRIL	£	APRIL	£
6 Computer Supplies Ltd.	1,500		

COMPUTER SUPPLIES LTD.

APRIL	£	APRIL	£
		6 Office equipment	1,500

CASH IN HAND

APRIL	£	APRIL	£
7 Cash at Bank	200	8 Office stationery	25
		18 Sundry expenses	5
		27 Sundry expenses	10

OFFICE STATIONERY

APRIL	£	APRIL	£
8 Cash in Hand	25		

MOTOR VEHICLE RUNNING COSTS

APRIL	£	APRIL	£
11 Cash at Bank	20		
26 Cash at Bank	30		

K. HALL—DRAWINGS

APRIL	£	APRIL	£
12 Cash at Bank	225		

GEE & CO

APRIL	£	APRIL	£
13 Fees Rendered	80	20 Cash at Bank	80
14 Fees Rendered	150	26 Cash at Bank	150

FEES RENDERED

APRIL	£	APRIL	£
		13 Gee & Co	80
		14 Gee & Co	150
		25 Cash at Bank	55
		25 Law Society of Scotland	180
		29 Smithys (Solicitors)	40

TELEPHONE

APRIL	£	APRIL	£
15 Cash at Bank	35		

SUNDRY EXPENSES

APRIL	£	APRIL	£
18 Cash in Hand	5		
27 Cash in Hand	10		

HEATING AND LIGHTING

APRIL	£	APRIL	£
19 Cash at Bank	50		

BANK INTEREST RECEIVED

APRIL	£	APRIL	£
		21 Cash at Bank	15

BANK CHARGES

APRIL	£	APRIL	£
22 Cash at Bank	20		

LAW SOCIETY OF SCOTLAND

APRIL	£	APRIL	£
25 Fees Rendered	180		

OFFICE CLEANING

APRIL	£	APRIL	£
28 Cash at Bank	45		

SMITHYS (SOLICITORS)

APRIL	£	APRIL	£
29 Fees Rendered	40		

Upon first sight of the above it would be no surprise if the reader succumbed to the effects of information overload, whatever form that may take. However, there is absolutely no need for this to be the case, assuming the accounts are analysed in a logical manner. If reference is made again first to the original details of K. Hall's business transactions and, secondly, to column (d) in the table shown earlier, it will therefore be possible to trace each of the entries appearing in each of the above T accounts. The reader is in fact advised to carry out this review as it will undoubtedly assist in understanding the workings of a double-entry bookkeeping system.

BALANCING OFF THE ACCOUNTS AND EXTRACTING A TRIAL BALANCE

From time to time it is good business practice to check the accuracy of the accounting records. The most effective way of performing such a task is to *balance off* each account and thereafter extract a *trial balance*. In a solicitor's practice it would be reasonable to do this at the end of each month. It is possible to do it more frequently, but it will obviously involve more work on the part of the firm's cash room staff (and/or partner) which may be spent more beneficially elsewhere[1]. On the other hand, the accounts could be balanced off and a trial balance extracted at more than one-month intervals, but this would mean that errors would go undetected for longer periods and because of such may be more difficult to find and rectify.

Looking at the Cash in Hand account of the K. Hall illustration, the following procedure is adopted to balance the account off at the end of April:

ILLUSTRATION 2.2

					Explanatory Notes
		CASH IN HAND			
APRIL	£	APRIL		£	
7 Cash at Bank	200	8	Office stationery	25	
		18	Sundry expenses	5	
		27	Sundry expenses	10	
		30	Balance c/f	160	(1)
	200			200	(2)
MAY					
1 Balance b/f	160				(3)

Explanatory Notes

(1)   Enter an amount on one side of the account so that it balances on a figure equal to that of the other, higher, side of the account. In this case, the debit side totals £200 and the credit entries for April amount to £40 (that is, £25 + £5 + £10). Another credit entry of £160 (that is, £200 − £40) is required to bring both sides of the account up to the same figure of £200. The date to be entered will be that on which the procedure is being carried out, being the last day in April in this illustration. The narrative entered in the account is in accordance with standard practice. The term 'c/f' simply means 'carried forward'.

(2)   The total figure for the account (that is, £200) is entered on each side of the account as shown.

(3)   Remembering that: 'every debit has a corresponding credit and vice versa', then the corresponding entry to that already made under explanatory note (1) will be a debit entry of £160 on the first day of the new month in the Cash in Hand account. Again custom dictates the narrative used. The term 'b/f' means 'brought forward'[2].

The Cash in Hand account of K. Hall above can be said to have a *debit balance of £160*. In other words, at the end of April, the total of all the debit entries exceeded the total of the credit entries by £160. In contrast, the Fees Rendered account has a *credit balance of £505* at the end of April, as shown thus:

---

1   If a firm's system is computerised, the amount of work involved in the task will be relatively insignificant. Press a button and the process should be performed automatically.

2   As alternatives, instead of c/f and b/f, it is possible to use 'c/d' and 'b/d' respectively, meaning 'carried down' and 'brought down'.

FEES RENDERED

APRIL		£	APRIL		£
30	Balance c/f	505*	13	Gee & Co	80
			14	Gee & Co	150
			25	Cash at Bank	55
			25	Law Society of Scotland	180
			29	Smithys (Solicitors)	40
		505			505*
			MAY		
			1	Balance b/f	505

*   It so happens in this account that the balancing figure is the same as the total figure of £505, given that there have been no other debit entries in the account throughout April.

Another example of an account being balanced off at the end of April for K. Hall can be seen with respect to the Telephone account:

ILLUSTRATION 2.3

TELEPHONE

APRIL		£	APRIL		£
15	Cash at Bank	35	30	Balance c/f	35
MAY					
1	Balance b/f	35			

In this instance, given that there was only one entry in the account before it was balanced off, it is perfectly acceptable to simply rule the account off as shown since the total figure is self-evident. The telephone account has a *debit balance of £35*.

Similar procedures would be carried out for each and every one of K. Hall's accounts. Once this process has been completed, it is possible to list the accounts' balances in a *trial balance* as shown in **Illustration 2.4**.

ILLUSTRATION 2.4

Kevin Hall (Solicitor)
Trial Balance as at 30 April 1999

	DR £	CR £
Cash at Bank	1,475	
K. Hall—Capital		5,500
Motor Vehicles	3,000	
Rent	400	
Office furniture	300	
Office equipment	1,500	
Computer Supplies Ltd.		1,500
Cash in Hand	160	
Office stationery	25	
Motor vehicle running costs	50	
K. Hall—Drawings	225	
Fees Rendered		505
Telephone	35	
Sundry expenses	15	
Heating and lighting	50	
Bank interest received		15
Bank charges	20	
Law Society of Scotland	180	
Office cleaning	45	
Smithys (Solicitors)	40	
	7,520	7,520

It is appropriate at this stage to comment on the general nature and content of a trial balance.

First of all, as familiarity with its content is developed, it will be noticed that certain accounts contained within the trial balance will normally have debit balances, whilst others will have credit balances. In the normal course of events it is expected that there will be debit balances remaining at the end of a given time period in the various asset accounts of a business, as well as in the different expense accounts. In contrast, capital accounts, liability accounts and income accounts will generally contain credit balances.

Next, when listing account balances in a trial balance, it is perfectly acceptable to omit any account that has a zero balance. For example, this is the case with respect to the Gee & Co account in K. Hall's records—both sides of this account total £230, so there is no closing balance at the end of April to be carried down into May.

It is also acceptable practice to group the balances in all of the individual debtors accounts together and express this as a total figure under 'Debtors' in the trial balance. Accordingly, although the debit balance on the Law Society of Scotland account (£180) and on Smithys (Solicitors) account (£40) have been shown separately in this illustration, it would be acceptable to show one total figure of £220 annotated as 'Debtors' in the trial balance. By adopting this approach it means that the relevant information is being shown in a summarised form in the trial balance, so leaving it free of cluttering detail. The benefits of such a practice would be especially noticeable in cases where a firm has many hundreds, or even thousands, of debtors. Exactly the same approach can be adopted with respect to the individual creditors' accounts, with a total 'Creditors' figure being shown in the trial balance.

The trial balance also serves as a useful collection point for information which will later be used in the preparation of a firm's accounting statements, such as the Profit and Loss Account, and the Balance Sheet, which are collectively known as the *final accounts* of a business. The final accounts are designed to convey summarised accounting information to the people using them. Hence the grouping of the individual debtors' and creditors' accounts into only two total figures in the trial balance is consistent with the refining or summarising process which ends with the drafting of the final accounts.

Finally, it is important to note that the trial balance is simply a list of balances remaining in the accounts on a certain date and serves as an arithmetical check on the accuracy of such accounting records—it is *not* part of the double-entry system. The balancing figure for each side of the trial balance should be the same, as it is in the above example, being £7,520. This figure in itself is unimportant—what is important is that the total debit balances at a given date should equal the total credit balances of the firm's accounts. The fact that they are in agreement provides a significant measure of assurance that the accounting records are correct.

Trial balance errors

If the two totals shown in a trial balance do not agree then it is clear that there must have been some sort of error. The main types of errors which cause the trial balance totals to be out of balance, can be summarised as follows:

(1)   **Single entry**. If only one aspect of a particular transaction has been entered in an account with no corresponding entry in another account then the trial balance totals will not agree. For example, the correct action to record the payment of a telephone bill by cheque would be to: (a) debit the Telephone account for the appropriate amount, say £25, and (b) to credit the Cash at Bank account by £25. If the person recording the transaction only made one of these entries without the other, then an error results.

(2)   **Errors of addition**. Simple arithmetical errors will also affect the trial balance totals.

(3)   **Transposition errors**. Looking at the example above in (1) where a telephone bill for £25 was paid by cheque, if one of the two entries necessary to record this transaction had its figures transposed—that is, £52 was entered as the charge in the Telephone account instead of £25—then an error occurs.

Although the occurrence of any of the above will affect the trial balance totals, other mistakes can happen which, unfortunately, fail to be highlighted by the trial balance since they will not upset the agreement of its totals. Examples of the latter type of errors include the following:

(1)   **Compensating errors**. Here one type of error will have its effects cancelled by another (quite separate) error in the opposite direction. That is, if the Cash in Hand account of K. Hall had been added up incorrectly resulting in its debit balance being £20 too much and if the Fees Rendered account also had its credit balance overstated by £20, then the errors will cancel each other. The Trial Balance totals will still agree, but on a figure £20 higher than it should be.

(2)   **Error of Original Entry**. If a transaction is properly recorded having regard to the principles of double entry, but the wrong figure is used, this can be termed as an error of original entry. As long as the rules of double entry are observed then it would be difficult to detect this error at the trial balance stage, since the trial balance totals will not be thrown out of balance.

(3) **Complete reversal of entries**. In the earlier instance where K. Hall paid his office rent of £400 by cheque, the correct way to record this transaction was seen to be to debit the Rent account £400 and credit the Cash at Bank account £400. If instead the Rent account was credited and the Cash at Bank account debited by £400, then there would have been a complete reversal of entries which, although not affecting the trial balance totals, is incorrect.

(4) **Error of Omission**. If a transaction is overlooked with no entries being made in the accounts, then the records are incomplete owing to this omission.

(5) **Error of Commission**. In this case, the correct figure is used with the rules of double-entry also being correctly followed, but the wrong account is used. For example, in the K. Hall illustration when he lectured at a Law Society seminar and invoiced the Society in respect of his fees of £180, the correct method of recording this particular transaction was to debit The Law Society of Scotland account £180 and credit the Fees Rendered account for the same amount. If instead Hall had debited, say, Gee & Co's account in error, then although the correct general class of account had been used (that is, another debtor's account), there has still been a mistake given that the debit entries of £180 should have been made to the Law Society of Scotland's account.

(6) **Error of Principle**. An error of principle is made when the wrong account completely is used to record a transaction. For example, if a firm buys a motor vehicle for £1,000 paying by cheque, and records the transaction by, say, debiting an expense account (eg Motor Vehicle Running Costs account) instead of an asset account (that is, Motor Vehicles account) then the wrong general category of account has been used. If this happened, then the error will not necessarily be picked up at the trial balance stage, assuming of course that the other aspect of the transaction has been completed correctly (being a credit entry of £1,000 in the Cash at Bank account).

In all of the above instances, the errors involved will not in themselves cause the trial balance total figures for the debit and credit columns to disagree. Thus, although the extraction of a trial balance will help in the detection of errors, it should not be regarded as a fail-safe procedure.

Once an error of whatever nature has been detected, it should be corrected. Generally, the best approach to error correction is to first of all work out what the correct position should be with respect to the account(s) involved. Then, after comparing the correct closing position with the erroneous position which presently exists, make any necessary adjusting entries to bring the accounting records back into line[1].

SPECIAL MEANING OF 'SALES' AND 'PURCHASES' IN TRADING BUSINESSES

The K. Hall illustrations were of a solicitor who was in business to provide a service. Other professionals, such as accountants, architects, surveyors and dentists for example, are similarly in business providing services rather than selling more tangible products. In contrast, a great many commercial concerns are trading organisations—they purchase a tradable commodity at a certain price and then sell

---

1   Very often an explanation of the processes used to correct errors will be recorded in a book called *The Journal*. Basically The Journal is like a diary given that it will allow people to look back at some later date to see why certain (probably unusual) entries were made in the accounting records.

on the same goods at a higher price, so making a profit. The commodity bought and sold in this way can generally be referred to as *trading stock* or simply *stock* and can be regarded as a current asset of the business, as mentioned earlier in this chapter.

In order for the double-entry system to work, as well as to provide the people running trading businesses with relevant and worthwhile information, it is necessary to establish several different accounts to record specific types of stock movement. Accounts are opened to record purchases of the stock, sales of the stock, any returns of stock to the firm by its customers, and, any returns by the firm to its own suppliers. Generally, these accounts will be known, respectively, as the *Purchases* account, the *Sales* account, the *Returns Inwards* account (also known as the *Sales Returns* account) and the *Returns Outwards* account (also known as the *Purchases Returns* account). Finally, the *Stock* account itself will be used to record the opening/closing values of stock held by the firm at the end of an accounting period[1].

All of the accounts will conform to the general principles of double-entry bookkeeping. Furthermore, they can all be regarded in essence as falling under the general heading of 'Assets'. It follows that the double-entry rules applied to record increases or decreases in such accounts should be consistent with the general treatment of assets (a debit entry will therefore record an increase, with a credit entry being used to record a decrease).

ILLUSTRATION 2.5

Consider the following transactions of David and Sheila Alexander who have a stall selling fashionware at the local street market. The transactions all happen in May 1999. Further assume that on 1 May, the Alexanders have £1,000 cash in hand with a further £2,500 in the business bank account:

(i)   **David and Sheila buy £150 worth of T-shirts from a wholesaler, paying cash on 2 May.**

Transaction involved:	The purchase of trading stock for cash.
Accounts affected and their general nature:	The *Purchases* account (asset), the *Cash in Hand* account (asset).
Action required to record the transaction:	Since the firm's stock level will be increasing, the Purchases account should be *debited* with £150; the Cash in Hand account should be *credited* with £150, to record a decrease in the asset of Cash in Hand.
	That is:

PURCHASES					CASH IN HAND				
MAY	£	MAY		£	MAY	£	MAY		£
2 Cash in Hand	150				1 Balance b/f	1,000	2 Purchases		150

(ii)   **On 3 May, they sell some T-shirts to a customer for £50 who pays cash.**

Transaction involved:	The sale of trading stock for cash.
Accounts affected and their general nature:	The *Sales* account (asset), the *Cash in Hand* account (asset).
Action required to record the transaction:	The firm's asset of stock is decreasing, so the Sales account should be *credited* with £50; the Cash in Hand account is increasing and accordingly this account should be *debited* with £50.
	That is:

---

1   The correct valuation of a firm's stock is important owing to the effect which the resulting figure has on that firm's reported profit for the period, as well as on its apparent financial position. The stock valuation process can be quite involved. See Chapters 3 and 4.

CASH IN HAND

	£	MAY		£	MAY		£
in Hand	50	1	Balance b/f	1,000	2	Purchases	150
		3	Sales	50			

...jeans on credit from another wholesaler, Flashers

Transaction involved:	The purchase of stock on credit.
Accounts affected and their general nature:	The *Purchases* account (asset), a creditor's account in the name of *Flashers Ltd.* (liability).
Action required to record the transaction:	The Purchases account should be *debited* with £200 to record an increase in the asset of ...; Flashers Ltd.'s account should be ...ed with £200 given that a liability has ... established.

PURCHASES

MAY		£	MAY
2	Cash in Hand	150	
4	Flashers Ltd.	200	

FLASHERS LTD.

	£	MAY		£
		4	Purchases	200

(iv) On 10 May, David and Sheila ... Flashers Ltd. the £... owed, by cheque.

Transaction involved:	The payment of a creditor by cheque.
Accounts affected and their general nature:	The *Cash at Bank* account (asset), the *Flashers Ltd.* account (liability).
Action required to record the transaction:	The Cash at Bank account should be *credited* with £200, since this particular asset is being reduced; the Flashers Ltd. account should be *debited* with £200 so recording a decrease in a liability. That is:

CASH AT BANK

MAY		£	MAY		£
1	Balance b/f	2,500	10	Flashers Ltd.	200

FLASHERS LTD.

MAY		£	MAY		£
10	Cash at Bank	200	4	Purchases	200

(v) On 11 May, they sell goods to the value of £300 to Alf Young, a fellow retailer. Alf has been given one week to pay for the goods, being the credit terms offered to him by David.

Transaction involved:	The sale of stock on credit.
Accounts affected and their general nature:	The *Sales* account (asset), a debtor's account in the name of *Alf Young* (asset).
Action required to record the transaction:	The Sales account will be *credited* with £300, since the asset of trading stock is being reduced; the Alf Young account will be *debited* with £300 in order that the establishing of a debtor's account is recorded (the debit entry will record an increase in this particular form of asset). That is:

SALES

MAY		£	MAY		£
			3	Cash in Hand	50
			11	Alf Young	300

ALF YOUNG

MAY		£	MAY		£
11	Sales	300			

(vi)   On 18 May, A. Young pays £300 in cash to Sheila and David in respect of the goods bought previously.

Transaction involved:	The receipt of cash from a debtor.
Accounts affected and their general nature:	The *Cash in Hand* account (asset), the *Alf Young* account (asset).
Action required to record the transaction:	The Cash in Hand account should be *debited* with £300 to record an increase in this asset; the Alf Young account will be *credited* with £300 since it is recording a decrease in an asset (remembering that before this latest transaction Alf Young was a debtor of David and Sheila Alexander's business). That is:

	CASH IN HAND						ALF YOUNG				
MAY		£	MAY		£	MAY		£	MAY		£
1	Balance b/f	1,000	2	Purchases	150	11	Sales	300	18	Cash in Hand	300
3	Sales	50									
18	Alf Young	300									

(vii)   On 19 May, another customer returns two pairs of jeans which have faulty zips. David agrees that the goods were not of satisfactory quality and gives the customer a full cash refund of £50.

Transaction involved:	Cash refund in respect of goods returned inwards.
Accounts affected and their general nature:	The *Cash in Hand* account (asset), the *Returns Inwards* account (asset, since it relates to the movement of stock).
Action required to record the transaction:	The Cash in Hand account should be *credited* with £50 to record a decrease in this asset; the Returns Inwards account should be *debited* with £50. That is:

	CASH IN HAND						RETURNS INWARDS				
MAY		£	MAY		£	MAY		£	MAY		£
1	Balance b/f	1,000	2	Purchases	150	19	Cash in Hand	50			
3	Sales	50	19	Returns							
18	Alf Young	300		Inwards	50						

(viii)   On 20 May, David sends the jeans with the broken zips back to his own supplier, who immediately issues a £25 cheque being the cost price of the goods. David lodged the cheque with his bank.

Transaction involved:	Refund by a supplier in respect of goods returned outwards.
Accounts affected and their general nature:	The *Cash at Bank* account (asset), the *Returns Outwards* account (again since this particular account is used to record a certain type of stock movement it can be categorised as an asset account).
Action required to record the transaction:	The Cash at Bank account should be *debited* with £25 so recording an increase in this asset; the Returns Outwards account should correspondingly be *credited* with £25. That is:

	CASH AT BANK						RETURNS OUTWARDS				
MAY		£	MAY		£	MAY		£	MAY		£
1	Balance b/f	2,500	10	Flashers Ltd.	200				20	Cash at Bank	25
20	Returns										
	Outwards	25									

In conclusion of **Illustration 2.5**, it can be imagined that after the last transaction of David and Sheila on 20 May, they will still have some jeans and T-shirts left to sell. If they decided to extract a trial balance for their business at this date then, as far as the remaining stock was concerned, they would have to place a value on it and record this value through the *Stock* account[1].

Furthermore, bearing in mind the earlier observation on how it would normally be expected for certain accounts to have either a debit or credit balance in the trial balance, the above accounts which were used to record specific movements in a firm's trading stock also have such characteristics. For example, it would normally be the case for the Purchases account and the Returns Inwards account to have debit balances, with the Sales account and Returns Outwards account having credit balances.

Finally it should be stressed that the various accounts used to record different kinds of stock movements should *only* be used to record transactions involving the trading commodity. They must *not* be used to record, say, the purchase or sale of a fixed asset (like a motor vehicle, or a computer for the office) which should be recorded through its own separate account.

ALTERNATIVE ACCOUNT LAYOUT

Throughout this chapter and indeed for the remainder of the text, a two sided layout has been used when looking at the accounts of a business. The principal reason for this is that it should aid the understanding of the double-entry process given that there is a clear distinction between a debit entry to an account (an entry made in the left-hand side) and a credit entry (one made on the right-hand side). However, very often in practice the format is slightly different. That is, although the various principles of double-entry still apply, the individual accounts are laid out slightly differently:

Account Name: ....

Date	Details	Folio	Dr £	Cr £	Balance £

1 The actual accounting treatment of opening and closing stocks of a trading business will be left until later. See Chapters 3 and 4.

It can be seen that this alternative format contains much the same information as a traditional T account, as can be expected, but furthermore the T account style has been abandoned and a *Balance* column has been added to show the balance remaining in the account immediately after the last transaction. The figure appearing in the *Balance* column will generally be followed by a Dr or Cr notation to emphasise its nature.

For example, if the Cash at Bank account of David and Sheila Alexander at 20 May 1999 was to be set out in this revised format, it would appear as follows:

Account Name: Cash at Bank

Date	Details	Folio	Dr £	Cr £	Balance £
MAY					
1	Balance b/f	—	2,500		2,500 Dr
10	Flashers Ltd.	—		200	2,300 Dr
20	Returns	—	25		2,325 Dr

QUESTIONS[1]

1. Identify from the following list the items which are ASSETS and those which are LIABILITIES.
   - (a) Motor vehicles
   - (b) Office equipment
   - (c) Office premises
   - (d) Owing money to the bank
   - (e) Debtors
   - (f) Creditors for goods
   - (g) Bank balance
   - (h) Fixtures and fittings

2. Categorise the following items into Assets, Liabilities, Capital, Income or Expenditure:
   - (a) Building
   - (b) Motor car
   - (c) Rent
   - (d) Loan from bank
   - (e) Fees received
   - (f) Bank overdraft
   - (g) Cash in hand
   - (h) Debtors
   - (i) Item input by owner
   - (j) Electricity
   - (k) Postage
   - (l) Stock
   - (m) Interest received
   - (n) Petrol
   - (o) Creditor
   - (p) Office equipment
   - (q) Telephone bill

1 For suggested solutions see p 269.

3. Complete the gaps in the following table:

	Assets (£)	Liabilities (£)	Capital (£)
(a)	7,500	3,000	*
(b)	*	5,000	7,000
(c)	10,000	8,000	*
(d)	17,600	*	5,600
(e)	*	3,900	11,100
(f)	70,000	*	15,600

4. State which of the following are assets and which are liabilities:
    (a) Office furniture (f) Loan from B Ltd
    (b) Bank overdraft (g) Premises
    (c) Cash in hand (h) Stock of goods
    (d) Creditors for goods (i) We owe for goods
    (e) Debtors (j) Motor vehicles

5. Mr Basset sets up a new business, but has not yet started trading. He has bought a motor vehicle £3,500; premises £10,000; stock of goods £2,500, (although he has not paid in full for the stock—amount still owing £600). He borrowed £7,500 from his mother and £2,000 from his sister. After all of these transactions he has £250 cash in hand and has a bank overdraft of £750. Calculate the amount of his capital.

6. (i) Which two accounts are affected by each of the following transactions?
        (a) Car purchased for cash
        (b) Electricity paid by cheque
        (c) Amount owed to us received in cash
        (d) Building purchased through bank loan
        (e) Stock purchased on credit
        (f) Office equipment purchased on credit
        (g) Loan from Bloggs repaid by cash
        (h) Fee note raised in the name of G & Co
        (i) G & Co pay fee note by cheque
        (j) Cash paid into bank

    (ii) For each of the above accounts state its general nature (that is Asset/Liability/Expense etc) and then note whether the account has been increased or decreased.

7. In each of the following examples show which accounts are to be debited and which are to be credited:
    (a) A pays cash into his business
    (b) F & Co pay amount due to us by cheque
    (c) Car purchased by cheque
    (d) Electricity paid by cash
    (e) Fee note sent to ABC Ltd
    (f) ABC Ltd send cheque re above
    (g) Receive loan from bank directly into A's business bank account
    (h) Pay DC Ltd by cheque amount owing

(i) Petrol paid by cash

(j) Building purchased by bank loan

8. Prepare T accounts for the following transactions of Acme & Co:

1 July   Mr Acme pays £3,000 into the company bank a/c from his own funds.

2 July   Mr A transfers his car (valued at £3,500) to the business.

3 July   Mr A withdraws £100 from the bank to put in his cash box. Mr A buys £20 of petrol in cash.

4 July   Mr A pays for office equipment by cheque, £570.

8 July   Mr A carries out work for BC Ltd and raises an invoice for £1,000 to be paid within 30 days.

9 July   Mr A pays British Telecom £340 by cheque for the installation of his phone system.

10 July   Mr A pays £200 towards his public liability insurance.

15 July   Mr A buys a computer from Compo Ltd on credit for £1,500.

16 July   Mr A works for CM Ltd and invoices £500—to be paid within 30 days.

20 July   BC Ltd pays the £1,000 previously invoiced.

21 July   Mr A buys coffee, tea and biscuits and other sundries for the office for £12 from the cash box.

28 July   The car breaks down and has to be repaired—cost £190 paid by cheque.

30 July   Mr A pays £250 as a first instalment to Compo Ltd by cheque.

9. Charlie D has decided to start up his own business. (i) Record the following transactions in T accounts and then (ii) prepare a trial balance as at 31 May 1997 after balancing off each of the accounts.

1997

1 May   Charlie introduced capital by paying £27,000 into the bank.

2 May   Paid by cheque £15,000 for a small office on the High Street.

7 May   Paid by cheque £1,500 for furniture for the office.

10 May   Received cheque from his father for £5,000 as a loan.

15 May   Bought a secondhand car for £7,500 by cheque.

20 May   Withdrew £150 cash from the bank and paid it into his cash box.

27 May   Bought a fax machine for £450 by cheque.

30 May   Bought two filing cabinets for £150 on credit from A. Supplier.

10. J Jones decides to start up on his own as a solicitor. He places £3,000 of his own money in a bank account opened specifically for the business. He manages to find an office to rent, but has to pay £500 rent in advance. He writes a cheque from his bank account to cover it. To furnish the office, he buys a desk, three chairs, a telephone, a fax machine and a kettle at a total cost of £1,200, for which he again pays by cheque.

He decides that rather than buy a new car he will manage with his current car valued at £4,500—he introduces this to the business. The insurance on the car expires soon, so he visits his insurers Noinsure Ltd to advise them that the car will now be used for business use. His premium is to be £350; the insurers agree to credit facilities and the amount is to be paid in ten instalments of £35. The first instalment is due at the end of the month.

Next he visits the local printers and gets his business cards and headed stationery. The printer, Blueprint, gives him an invoice for £85, which is payable within 30 days. His first client, A Dollar, requires some conveyancing work carried out. He duly does this and sends out a fee note for £280—payable within 30 days.

The University of Strathclyde has also asked that he present a course to solicitors. He does this and at the same time issues his invoice for £300 plus £30 expenses. Since he was able to catch the sometimes elusive cashier, he receives a cheque for the £330 immediately—he banks the cheque that day, and draws £120 cash to put in the petty cash box in the office.

Using cash, he fills the car with petrol for £25 and buys some office sundries (paper clips, pencils, pens) for £10 and some tea, coffee and biscuits, for £7. Finally the office cleaner pops round the door looking for payment. He pays £50 for the month's cleaning from the cash box. He remembers to write a cheque for £35 to Noinsure and goes to the post office and buys stamps for £10 from petty cash. He posts the letter and goes back to the office. He knows that he really should record the month's transactions now before he forgets what has happened and whilst he still knows where his receipts and other documentation are, but he does not know where to start.

Required: You are required to advise him which T accounts to open and note whether these are Assets, Liabilities, Capital, Income or Expenditure and then post the amounts to the correct accounts.

Note: In attempting this question it will probably be easier to number each transaction as it occurs for ease of posting the entries to the T accounts.

Chapter Three: Simple accounting statements

It was seen in an earlier chapter that an owner of a business is primarily concerned with two things. That is, on the one hand, the owner will need to know how well the business is doing and, on the other, whether the firm will be able to meet its commitments as they fall due.

The main source of this information is the *final accounts*. The term 'final accounts' in common usage is taken to mean both the Trading and Profit and Loss Account together with the Balance Sheet of the business.

THE TRADING AND PROFIT AND LOSS ACCOUNT

The principal objective of this account is to quantify how profitable a business has been over a specific period of time.

Looking a little more closely at the Trading and Profit and Loss Account, it can be considered as having two distinct but related parts. First of all, the *Trading account* is used to calculate the *gross profit* of the business for a period of time. The gross profit represents the excess of the value of the sales for a period over the cost of the goods sold. This figure is significant in trading organisations since it is regarded as a key indicator of the basic profitability of the business and, because of this fact, it is often incorporated into ratios and used for the purpose of financial analysis. It is possible that a firm could make a gross loss, but this is a relatively rare occurrence.

The second part of the statement is the *Profit and Loss account*, which will show the *net profit* (or *net loss*) made over the same period of time. The starting point of the Profit and Loss account is the gross profit brought forward from the Trading account. Other forms of income which are subordinate to the firm's main trading business will be added to the gross profit at this stage. For example, if the firm receives rental income in respect of part of its offices let to a third party, this amount will be added to the gross profit.

Once this has been done, any selling or administrative expenses arising in the accounting period will be set off against the new figure, allowing the calculation of the net profit or loss.

Assuming a net profit is made then, logically enough, this will belong to the owner of the business. A net profit will have the effect of increasing the proprietor's capital. In contrast, a net loss reduces the owner's capital stake in the business.

It should be noted that both the Trading account and the Profit and Loss account are still part of the double-entry book-keeping system. Consequently, any debit or credit entry made to either account must have a corresponding entry in some other account. It is also normal practice to show the Profit and Loss account immediately following the Trading account and, for the majority of purposes, to display them as a single entity.

In order to show the relationships between the Trading and Profit and Loss account and the other accounts in a business's records, it will be worthwhile to work through a simple example.

ILLUSTRATION 3.1

The following trial balance has been extracted from K. Anderson's accounting records on 31 May 1999:

K. Anderson
Trial Balance as at 31 May 1999

	Dr. £	Cr. £
Capital at 1.6.98		22,000
Bank	13,000	
Cash	3,000	
Drawings	17,000	
Sales		100,000
Purchases	60,000	
Motor vehicle (cost)	12,000	
Motor vehicle running costs	4,000	
Heating and lighting	2,000	
Rent	3,000	
General office expenses	1,000	
Trade creditors		8,000
Trade debtors	15,000	
	130,000	130,000

Note: Assume that K. Anderson sold all of the goods bought during the year to 31 May 1999 and that there was no initial stock of goods on the first day of the trading year. That is, assume no opening or closing stock balances.

Required: Prepare a Trading and Profit and Loss Account for K. Anderson for the year to 31 May 1999.

Bearing in mind that the Trading and Profit and Loss Account is part of the double-entry system, in order to appreciate fully what is happening at this stage it will be helpful to look at the entries which would be made on the 31 May 1999 in the accounts.

The Trading and Profit and Loss account, as mentioned earlier, is concerned with the calculation of the profitability of a business. Consequently, as a general rule, only those accounts which affect profitability should be considered at this stage. Such accounts and the entries which would be made to them at the year end are as shown. It should be noted that the entries shown in italics in the T accounts represent the entries which are necessary to close the accounts off at the end of the financial period (in this case 31 May 1999) by transferring the balances over to either the Trading account or the Profit and Loss account.

	SALES						PURCHASES		
MAY		£	MAY		£	MAY		£	MAY	£
31	*Trading*	100,000	31		100,000	31		60,000	31 *Trading*	60,000

As can be seen, the corresponding entries to those made in the Sales and Purchases accounts will appear in the period's Trading account. The gross profit can then be calculated and carried forward into the Profit and Loss account. Next, the various expense accounts will be closed off by transferring their balances to the Profit and Loss account, thus:

MOTOR VEHICLE RUNNING COSTS					HEATING AND LIGHTING				
MAY		£	MAY	£	MAY		£	MAY	£
31		4,000	31 Profit and Loss	4,000	31		2,000	31 Profit and Loss	2,000

RENT					GENERAL OFFICE EXPENSES				
MAY		£	MAY	£	MAY		£	MAY	£
31		3,000	31 Profit and Loss	3,000	31		1,000	31 Profit and Loss	1,000

K. Anderson
Trading and Profit and Loss Account for the year ended 31 May 1999

	£		£
Purchases	60,000	Sales	100,000
Gross Profit c/f	40,000		
	100,000		100,000
Motor vehicle running costs	4,000	Gross Profit b/f	40,000
Heating and lighting	2,000		
Rent	3,000		
General office expenses	1,000		
Net profit	30,000		
	40,000		40,000

Explanatory Notes

(1) Only those accounts affecting the calculation of K. Anderson's profitability are considered at this stage. The other accounts so far omitted will be dealt with later when the Balance Sheet is being drafted.

(2) With respect to the Trading and Profit and Loss Account, note that it covers a **period of time**. That is, this account summarises the sales and purchases together with the various forms of expenditure which have occurred during the year to 31 May 1999.

(3) It can be seen that the Trading account (the upper section of the Trading and Profit and Loss account) highlights a gross profit for the period of £40,000 which is immediately carried forward into the Profit and Loss account. Thereafter the various expenses associated with running the business are off-set against the gross profit figure. The resulting net profit is £30,000. Bearing in mind the rule 'every debit has a corresponding credit', the entry corresponding to that of the net profit figure will appear as a credit entry of £30,000 in Anderson's Capital account.

(4) As seen earlier in Chapter two, the balance on the Drawings account represents the value which the owner has taken out of the business, either in cash or in kind (eg stock for personal use), throughout the year to 31 May 1999. It is *not* a business expense but rather it is an appropriation of profit. Hence, it is not incorporated in the calculation of the firm's net profit.

THE BALANCE SHEET

The Trading and Profit and Loss account is one part of the final accounts of K. Anderson's business. The other part is a statement called the *Balance Sheet.*

In a way it is a little unfortunate that the term 'final accounts' is taken to include the balance sheet of a business since the balance sheet is *not* actually an account. Rather, it is a list of balances remaining in the accounting records at the end of the financial period after all the details necessary to formulate the Trading and Profit and Loss account have been drawn off. Therefore, it is not part of the double-entry system as it does not conform to the debit and credit rules of double-entry. The main function of the balance sheet is to show what the business owns and what it owes at a given point in time.

A glance back at K. Anderson's trial balance at 31 May 1999 and to the contents of the Trading and Profit and Loss account will reveal that so far certain accounts have not been considered. The omission of the Drawings account has already been highlighted and this, like the others ignored up until now, will be dealt with in the preparation of a balance sheet.

However, taking a step back from the actual preparation of the balance sheet for the moment, the accounts which were not used in the formulation of the Trading and Profit and Loss account will be as follows:

	CAPITAL					BANK		
MAY		£	MAY	£	MAY		£	MAY	£
			31	22,000	31		13,000		

	CASH					DRAWINGS		
MAY		£	MAY	£	MAY		£	MAY	£
31		3,000			31		17,000		

	MOTOR VEHICLES (COST)					TRADE CREDITORS		
MAY		£	MAY	£	MAY		£	MAY	£
31		12,000						31	8,000

	TRADE DEBTORS		
MAY		£	MAY	£
31		15,000		

The book-keeping procedures which are carried out at this stage generally involve simply balancing each of the accounts off at the end of one financial year (that is, in K. Anderson's case, on 31 May 1999) and carrying the balancing figure forward, in the same account, to the first day of the new financial period (in this illustration, this date will be 1 June 1999 being the day after the previous year end). That is, looking at K. Anderson's Bank account:

	BANK		
MAY	£	MAY	£
31	13,000	31 Bal c/f	13,000
JUNE			
1 Bal b/f			
	13,000		

Similar procedures would be used for K. Anderson's Cash account, the Motor Vehicle (cost) account, the Trade Creditors account and the Trade Debtors account [1].

---

1   The Trade Creditors account in this example has only been shown as a single account in order to simplify the illustration as far as possible. In reality, this figure would be a total of all the credit balances existing on the individual trade creditors' accounts. Financial year end procedures would simply mean that each of the individual creditors' accounts would be debited with a balancing figure on 31 May, the corresponding credit being on the same account on 1 June 1999. Similarly, Trade Debtors have been treated as the one composite figure in the K. Anderson example. Individual debtors' accounts would be credited on 31 May with an appropriate balancing figure, with the related debit entry appearing on 1 June 1999 in the same account.

However, the accounting treatment of the Capital account and the Drawings account is a little different. That is, first of all the balance on the Drawings account would be transferred to the Capital account. The former account would now be cleared, free to start recording any drawings by the proprietor in the new financial year. Next, the balance which was left in the Profit and Loss account (in this case the net profit of £30,000) will be transferred to the Capital account as well. Finally, the Capital account will be squared off with the balancing figure being carried forward into the new financial period, again in the same account. That is:

DRAWINGS				CAPITAL					
MAY	£	MAY	£	MAY	£	MAY	£
31	17,000	31 Capital	17,000	31 Drawings	17,000	31 Bal b/f	22,000
						Profit and	
				31 Bal c/f	35,000	31 Loss	30,000
					52,000		52,000
						JUNE	
						1 Bal b/f	35,000

In drafting a balance sheet, all that is required is simply to list the closing balances on each of the above accounts although, that said, slightly more detail than this would be provided with respect to the owner's Capital.

It may have been noticed that each of those accounts relate either to assets, liabilities or capital. It follows, therefore, that the balance sheet is simply a more elaborate version of the accounting equation introduced in Chapter two, where it was shown that:

ASSETS = CAPITAL plus LIABILITIES

ILLUSTRATION 3.1, K. ANDERSON (continued)

Required: Prepare a balance sheet as at 31 May, 1999 for K. Anderson.

Suggested solution:

K. Anderson
Balance Sheet as at 31 May 1999

Fixed Assets	£	£	Capital	£	£
Motor vehicles (cost)		12,000	Opening Balance		22,000
			Add: Net profit for		
			the year	30,000	
Current Assets			*Less:* Drawings	(17,000)	
Trade debtors	15,000				13,000
Bank	13,000				
Cash	3,000				35,000
		31,000	**Current Liabilities**		
			Trade creditors		8,000
		43,000			43,000

Explanatory Notes

(1) The balance sheet is a financial statement showing the assets, liabilities and capital of the business on a particular date which in this case is 31 May 1999. Its aim is to communicate financial information to people who will be using it.

(2) In the format adopted here, the assets of the business have been shown on the left-hand side of the balance sheet, with the Capital and the liabilities (both of which can be regarded as claims against the assets) being shown on the right-hand side. This layout is known as the *horizontal* format.

(3)   Concentrating on the left-hand side of the balance sheet, it can be seen that it has been divided into two main sections, being *fixed assets* and *current assets*. The fixed assets category includes all of those business assets that are intended for long-term use within the organisation. In contrast, the current assets category shows assets which are essentially short-term in nature, being assets which are cash or which are shortly to be converted into cash (eg trade debtors). If K. Anderson had any closing stock of goods on 31 May 1999, then the value of stocks held at this date would also be shown here in the current assets section.

(4)   Generally, assets are shown in a certain order, depending on their degree of permanence. Fixed assets therefore appear before current assets. Items appearing within each of these sections are similarly structured. For example, if Anderson had owned property, then a figure in respect of the value of that property would have been shown in the fixed assets section before the £12,000 relating to Motor Vehicles. Similarly, the current assets section will begin with those assets which will be the most difficult to turn into cash and end with the cash figure itself. If there had been any closing stock, the figure in respect of this would have appeared above Trade Debtors.

(5)   The total of the fixed assets plus current assets can be seen to be £43,000 in this example. This figure represents the *total assets* of the business.

(6)   The right-hand side of the balance sheet shows details of the owner's *Capital* and of *current liabilities* which when combined, represent the claims on the assets of the business. Again bearing in mind the accounting equation of Assets = Capital + Liabilities, it should not come as a surprise to see that the total figure on the right-hand side of the balance sheet is also £43,000.

(7)   It is customary for the balance sheet to show the change in the proprietor's Capital from its level at the beginning of the financial year to its position as at the balance sheet date. K. Anderson began the year with £22,000 and experienced a net increase of £13,000 [being net profit received during the year of £30,000 less drawings of £17,000] to leave his Capital at £35,000 at 31 May 1999. The figure of £35,000 can be termed the owner's *net worth*[1]. Broadly speaking, it is the amount of money K. Anderson could expect to receive if the entity was dissolved at this moment in time.

(8)   Liabilities falling within the current liabilities section are also listed in a certain manner, with the timing of when they are due to be paid determining the order in which they appear. The longer a liability has before it is due to be paid, then the higher up the list of current liabilities it would be displayed. So, for example, if K. Anderson had a bank overdraft, details of this liability would normally be shown below Trade Creditors. The reasoning here is that a bank overdraft is normally repayable on demand, whereas by definition Trade Creditors offer a period of credit before settlement is due.

COLUMNAR PRESENTATION OF ACCOUNTING STATEMENTS

It will be appreciated that business people frequently have to use final accounts for decision making purposes as well as for reasons of financial control. Solicitors will regularly come into contact with final accounts when acting as professional advisers on behalf of clients as well as when fulfilling their duties as business managers within their own practice or of the organisation in which they are employed. In all probability, the accounting statements being used by the solicitor in such situations will be presented in a different manner to that examined within the context of the foregoing K. Anderson illustration. The Trading and Profit and Loss account relating to K. Anderson, for example, was introduced within the context of how such an account would appear in the records of Anderson's business and how it was connected to many other different ledger accounts by virtue of the double-entry system. In essence therefore, Anderson's Trading and Profit and Loss Account was considered as a working document. The final accounts with which solicitors and others come into contact, will be a more formalised version which, in all probability, will be *columnar* or *vertical* in layout.

---

1   Another term for the owner's net worth is 'owner's equity'.

Looking again at the details relating to the previous illustration of K. Anderson, but this time re-arranging the way in which it is displayed to that of a columnar format, the following statement results:

ILLUSTRATION 3.2

K. Anderson
Trading and Profit and Loss Account for the year ended 31 May 1999

	£	£
Sales		100,000
Less: Cost of Goods Sold		
Purchases		(60,000)
Gross Profit		40,000
Less: Expenses		
Motor vehicle running costs	4,000	
Heating and lighting	2,000	
Rent	3,000	
General office expenses	1,000	
		(10,000)
Net Profit		30,000

It is also possible to re-arrange the balance sheet into a similar format. That is,

K. Anderson
Balance Sheet as at 31 May 1999

	£	£
Fixed Assets		
Motor vehicles, at cost		12,000
Current Assets		
Trade debtors	15,000	
Bank	13,000	
Cash	3,000	
	31,000	
Less: Current Liabilities		
Trade creditors	(8,000)	
Net Current Assets		23,000
		35,000
Represented by:		
Capital:		
Balance at 1 June 1999		22,000
Add: Net Profit for year	30,000	
Less: Drawings	(17,000)	
		13,000
		35,000

One of the advantages claimed on behalf of this format is that it is more informative to lay users of accounting statements than the horizontal format seen earlier. Although the Trading and Profit and Loss account still accords with the principles of double-entry, it is generally believed that the columnar version makes it easier to see the relationship between key measures of profitability and, furthermore, is prima facie more user friendly than the traditional horizontal version.

Similar general comments on ease of use can also be made regarding the columnar balance sheet. In addition, by re-arranging the balance sheet in this way, another key figure is highlighted, namely *Net Current Assets*. These are the excess of current assets over current liabilities. In K. Anderson's case, net current assets amount to £23,000. This figure can be regarded as the *working capital* of the entity in that it represents the money and other assets available for conducting the day-to-day operations of the business[1].

It was mentioned earlier that the vertical method of presentation is the more commonly used version. Accordingly, it will be this format for final accounting reports which will be adopted for the remainder of this text.

COST OF GOODS SOLD

Looking back to the Trading account of K. Anderson in **Illustration 3.2**, it can be seen that the only item to be considered under the heading of 'Cost of Goods Sold' was in fact Purchases of £60,000. This illustration was deliberately simplified by omitting other items which would normally be considered at this point. In particular, any *opening* and/or *closing stocks* of trading organisations fall into this category.

If K. Anderson did have some stock on the first day of his trading period, then the value of such opening stock should be taken as the starting point for calculating the period's Cost of Goods Sold. Next, the figure representing the total value of trading stock purchases made during the financial period should be added. Finally, the value of any stock remaining unsold on the last day of the trading period (that is, the closing stock) should be deducted, thereby arriving at the Cost of Goods Sold figure. The latter figure will then be set-off against the value of Sales during the same period of time to produce the amount of gross profit.

ILLUSTRATION 3.3

General trader I. Peters began a new financial year on 1 January 1999. On that date Peters had stock valued at £500 in the store room. During the year to 31 December 1999, Peters purchased a further £4,000 worth of stock. At the end of that particular year the trading stock was valued at £750. Receipts from Sales over the year amounted to £8,750.

Required: Prepare I. Peters' Trading Account for the year to 31 December 1999.
Solution:

I. Peters
Trading Account for the Year Ended 31 December 1999

	£	£
Sales		8,750
Less: Cost of Goods Sold		
Opening stock at 1.1.99	500	
Add: Purchases	4,000	
	4,500	
Less: Closing stock at 31.12.99	(750)	
		(3,750)
Gross Profit		5,000

1   The term 'net working capital' can be used to describe the excess of current assets over current liabilities. The term 'gross working capital' is used for the total value of current assets.

It is worth noting that the closing stock valuation of £750, besides being used to help calculate the Cost of Goods Sold figure in the Trading account, will also appear in I. Peters' balance sheet on 31 December 1999. Closing stock is quite properly regarded as an asset of the business, given that it will be available for sale in the subsequent accounting period. In order that a true reflection is achieved of what I. Peters owns on 31 December 1999 it will therefore be necessary to show the closing stock figure in the current assets section of the balance sheet. Looking ahead to Peters' next trading period, the closing stock figure of £750 in the year to 31 December 1999 will become the opening stock figure for the year to 31 December 2000.

WORKING FROM THE TRIAL BALANCE

In order that the accounting process which results in the production of a set of final accounts could be understood, it was necessary to look earlier in this chapter at individual accounts and to examine the entries which would be made in them at the end of an accounting period. In so far as the non-accountant is concerned, it is sufficient that a reasonable appreciation of such procedures is achieved.

Solicitors must feel comfortable when using a set of final accounts, both for reasons of looking after their own business interests and those of their clients. One of the best ways for attaining a working knowledge of a set of final accounts is, quite simply, practice in drafting. With this in mind, but to avoid the cluttering detail of having to make all the entries in the individual accounts, the intention now is to use the information contained within, chiefly, the trial balance to produce a set of final accounts. Where appropriate, additional source information will be provided by way of notes accompanying the trial balance. Detailed 'behind-the-scene' double-entries will, in effect, be taken as assumed knowledge.

ILLUSTRATION 3.4

Required: Prepare a Trading and Profit and Loss account for the year to 30 June 1999 together with a Balance Sheet as at the same date from the following information provided to you by a client, T. Canyon:

T. Canyon
Trial Balance as at 30 June 1999

	£	£
Motor vehicles, at cost	10,000	
Opening stock, 1.7.98	1,000	
Debtors	1,200	
Creditors		1,600
Purchases	9,000	
Sales		25,000
Cash at bank	11,350	
Telephone expenses	350	
Motor vehicle expenses	450	
Rent and rates	900	
Heating and lighting	250	
Cleaning	100	
Drawings	7,000	
Capital, 1.7.98		15,000
	41,600	41,600

Notes:
(1)   Closing stock at 30 June 1999 was valued at £1,500.

Suggested solution:

T. Canyon
Trading and Profit and Loss Account for the year ended 30 June 1999

	£	£
Sales		25,000
Less: Cost of goods sold		
Opening stock, 1.7.98	1,000	
Add: Purchases	9,000	
	10,000	
Less: Closing stock, 30.6.99	(1,500)	
		(8,500)
Gross profit		16,500
Less: Expenses		
Telephone	350	
Motor vehicle expenses	450	
Rent and rates	900	
Heating and lighting	250	
Cleaning	100	
		(2,050)
Net profit		14,450

T. Canyon
Balance Sheet as at 30 June 1999

	£	£
Fixed Assets		
Motor vehicles, at cost		10,000
Current Assets		
Stock	1,500	
Debtors	1,200	
Cash at bank	11,350	
	14,050	
Less: Current Liabilities		
Creditors	(1,600)	
Net Current Assets		12,450
		22,450
Represented by:		
Capital, 1.7.98		15,000
Add: Net Profit for the year	14,450	
Less: Drawings	(7,000)	
		7,450
		22,450

BASIC ANALYSIS OF FINAL ACCOUNTS

After drafting T. Canyon's final accounts the next logical step is to use them for a given purpose, for example to assess profitability and/or the financial position of the business. Although the process of interpreting financial statements will be considered in more depth in later chapters, it is still useful at this stage to highlight a few key points from the final accounts of T. Canyon.

For example, with respect to profitability, examining the Trading and Profit and Loss account reveals:

—T. Canyon had a net profit for the year of £14,450

This looks good for a couple of reasons. First of all, it is not a net loss. It is always better to make a profit rather than a loss. Secondly, the level of net profit relative to turnover (that is, Sales of £25,000) also appears adequate.

—Total expenses of £2,050

Bearing in mind that the gross profit figure is £16,500, total expenses of £2,050 look modest.

On the basis of the available information, T. Canyon's business is producing an acceptable level of profit. However, in order to assess profitability for the year to 30 June 1999 more fully, it would be useful to have other figures to use as a benchmark rather than using only this year's Trading and Profit and Loss account. For example if T. Canyon had been in business for a number of years, comparing the results of the year to 30 June 1999 with those of previous years may prove enlightening—that is, how have the net profit/gross profit/turnover/total expenses figures changed over the years?

Alternatively, another useful benchmark can be achieved through the use of *budgets*. That is, before the present financial year began, T. Canyon may have predicted how the financial year was going to unfold. By comparing the actual results at the end of the year with the forecast results for the same period, it would be possible to form an opinion of how well (or badly for that matter) the business has done over the year. It is also sound management practice for significant variances between actual and budgeted figures to be examined and reasonable explanations obtained.

The balance sheet of T. Canyon can be used to assess the financial position of the firm. For example, points worth noting here include:

—Net current assets amount to £12,450

As has been seen in an earlier illustration, the net current assets figure represents the excess of current assets over current liabilities. In this example it provides assurance that T. Canyon is able to meet short-term commitments as they fall due by having sufficient assets which can be turned into cash at short notice, assuming that they are not cash already[1]. The total value of current assets of T. Canyon amounts to £14,050 which more than covers the creditors figure of £1,600, being the only current liability.

—The owner's net worth is £22,450

In other words, if the business was wound up at 30 June 1999, T. Canyon could expect to receive that amount once all the assets have been turned into cash and any liabilities met.

Even from this very restricted review of T. Canyon's financial position as portrayed by the balance sheet, it would be fair to say that the financial position of the business was sound.

---

1 In the present context, 'short-term' refers to a period extending to approximately one year.

Although the above illustration involved a trading company, the principles of reading a set of final accounts outlined in the T. Canyon example apply equally to other types of businesses, including solicitors.

CAPITAL v REVENUE EXPENDITURE

It is important in a solicitor's practice, and indeed in any business, to maintain a clear distinction between *capital* and *revenue expenditure*.

Capital expenditure is incurred when a firm either buys a fixed asset or makes improvements to existing fixed assets in an attempt to enhance their value. For example, if a solicitor bought an office, the cost of it would be classified as capital expenditure. If an extension was added to it in the future, such costs would again be regarded as capital expenditure. When capital expenditure is incurred, this will result in additions to the balance sheet of the organisation involved.

The 'cost' of a fixed asset will include expenditure on items which are necessary to get the fixed asset fully operational. For example, consider the situation where a firm of solicitors wished to open a new branch office on a brown-field site in an urban area of a Scottish city. The cost of this fixed asset to the firm could include all of the following types of expenditure: the price of the land; the costs of demolishing any existing buildings and clearing the site; fees of the building professionals involved in the project (architects, surveyors, engineers, etc); construction costs; associated legal fees. All of the above costs would be combined and shown under the heading of 'Office property' in the fixed assets section of the solicitors' balance sheet.

It is important to note that capital expenditure is not charged to a single accounting period's Profit and Loss account. It will be seen in the following chapter that the cost of a fixed asset is normally spread over those accounting periods which benefit from its use. The value of a fixed asset used up in an accounting period and consequently charged to that period's Profit and Loss account, is known as a *depreciation charge*.

Revenue expenditure on the other hand, will be charged directly to the Profit and Loss account of the period in which it was incurred. Revenue expenditure is expenditure on items necessary to run the business on a day-to-day basis. For example, the cost of a new car for use within a solicitor's office will be regarded as capital expenditure, but the costs of operating the vehicle fall into the category of revenue expenditure. Therefore, motor vehicle running costs such as petrol, road tax and servicing charges, are all forms of revenue expenditure which will appear in the solicitor's Profit and Loss account covering the period in which they were incurred.

The following illustration will also help demonstrate the difference between the two principal types of expenditure.

ILLUSTRATION 3.5

Elliot and Co (Solicitors)

NATURE OF EXPENDITURE	TYPE OF EXPENDITURE
(a) The firm buys a new office	Capital
(b) The cost of painting the outside of the office during the construction phase	Capital
(c) The cost of repainting the outside of the office four years after it was completed	Revenue
(d) Office heating and lighting costs	Revenue
(e) Office cleaning costs	Revenue
(f) The firm purchases a new microcomputer and printer	Capital
(g) The costs of buying software to use in the microcomputer	Capital
(h) The firm buys a box of printer ribbons	Revenue

The correct definition of expenditure is important if the final accounts of a business are to accurately reflect reality. If an item of capital expenditure was erroneously treated as revenue expenditure in the accounting records, this would result in expenses appearing in that period's Profit and Loss account being overstated, with an artificially low net profit figure being reported. Furthermore, the fixed assets figure shown in the firm's balance sheet at the end of the accounting period would also be too low given that the value of the asset acquired has been omitted. In this case the balance sheet simply would not give a true picture of the fixed assets owned by the business.

Alternatively, if the reverse was to happen, with revenue expenditure being improperly treated as capital expenditure, then the net profit for the period would be overstated as would the figure supposedly reflecting the value of fixed assets in the balance sheet of the practice.

QUESTIONS[1]

1. P Marwick began trading on 1 June 1998. Marwick sells videos from a stall in the local market. The following trial balance was extracted from the accounting records at 31 May 1999:

P Marwick
Trial balance as at 31 May 1999

	Dr £	Cr £
Capital, 1.6.98		6,500
Bank	7,000	
Cash	550	
Sales		16,000
Purchases	7,000	
General expenses	1,400	
Trade creditors		1,300

1 For suggested solutions see p 273.

	Dr £	Cr £
Trade debtors	200	
Stall site rental	1,200	
Insurances	450	
Stall, at cost	1,500	
Drawings	4,500	
	23,800	23,800

Note:

(1)   Marwick had no opening or closing stocks.

Prepare a Trading and Profit and Loss Account for the year ended 31 May 1999 together with a balance sheet as at that date.

2.   N Goldberger owns a small jewellery shop. Details of the accounting year to 31 December 1999 are as follows:

N Goldberger (Jeweller)
Trial Balance as at 31 December 1999

	Dr £	Cr £
Motor vehicle, at cost	10,000	
Fixtures and fittings, at cost	10,000	
Office equipment, at cost	2,000	
Cash at bank	19,750	
Creditors		4,000
Rent and rates	7,500	
Electricity costs	1,250	
Staff wages	9,000	
Sales		75,000
Purchases	25,000	
Insurances	2,500	
Motor vehicle expenses	1,500	
Stationery	500	
Drawings—N Goldberger	25,000	
Capital, 1.1.99		40,500
Telephone	500	
Stock at 1.1.99	5,000	
	119,500	119,500

Note:

(1)   The stock which Goldberger held at 31.12.99 was valued at £5,000.
(2)   Ignore depreciation.

Goldberger has asked you to prepare a set of final accounts in respect of the above trading year.

3. Gilberts is a successful legal practice operating in the East of Scotland. The firm specialises in employment law. The practice has supplied the following information and asked that a Profit and Loss account for the 6-month period to 30 September 1999 be prepared together with a balance sheet as at that date.

Gilberts (Solicitors)
Trial balance as at 30 September 1999

	Dr £	Cr £
Office property, at cost	125,000	
Office equipment, at cost	15,000	
Office furniture and fittings, at cost	10,000	
Motor vehicles, at cost	30,000	
Cash at bank	29,750	
Debtors	2,500	
Creditors		1,000
Capital, 1.4.99—K. Gilbert		206,500
Fees rendered		150,000
Office wages	80,000	
Telephone	2,000	
Heating and lighting	3,000	
Insurances	1,500	
Subscriptions to professional journals	250	
Motor vehicle running costs	4,000	
Stationery	1,000	
Property maintenance	2,500	
Office equipment maintenance	250	
Travel expenses	750	
Drawings—K Gilbert	50,000	
	357,500	357,500

Note:

(1) Ignore depreciation.

4. Casper has been in business as a merchant importing Italian porcelain for a number of years. The latest available trial balance is shown below together with some additional information. On the basis of the details supplied, prepare Casper's final accounts for the year to 30 November 1999, commenting briefly on the results.

Casper
Trial Balance as at 30 November 1999

	Dr £	Cr £
Capital, at 1.12.98		41,750
Motor vehicle, at cost	7,500	
Premises, at cost	32,500	
Fixtures and fittings, at cost	15,000	
Bank (overdraft)		7,800

	Dr £	Cr £
Debtors	4,500	
Creditors		10,000
Loan: N E Breaker		12,000
Stock, 1.12.98	3,250	
Sales		43,000
Purchases	18,250	
Rates	2,350	
Gas	900	
Heating and lighting	1,250	
Wages	18,000	
Telephone	1,600	
Postages and stationery	750	
Motor vehicle running costs	1,900	
Drawings	5,500	
Loan interest paid	1,300	
	114,550	114,550

Notes:

(1)   Closing stock at 30.11.99 was valued at £4,250.
(2)   The loan for N E Breaker is due to be paid by 1 February 2000.
(3)   Ignore depreciation on fixed assets.

5.   F and J Quinn Ltd is a company which supplies the veterinary profession. Classify the following list of transactions into capital and revenue expenditure:

   (a)   purchase of a new pick-up truck;
   (b)   insurance, road tax, petrol and servicing costs relating to the new truck;
   (c)   plastic containers for various drugs;
   (d)   receptionist's salary;
   (e)   costs of installing a new telephone system;
   (f)   costs of carriage on sales and purchases borne by F and J Quinn Ltd;
   (g)   buildings insurance;
   (h)   stationery;
   (i)   rent and rates on warehouse;
   (j)   directors' salaries;
   (k)   fitting out costs of a new laboratory.

6.   The legal firm of Harpie and Henderson has been in practice for a number of years. In an attempt to make the firm more cost-effective the partners have decided to buy a new microcomputer together with a laser printer. The recommended retail price of the new equipment was £5,499 but the firm managed to secure a £499 discount. Delivery was separate and cost an additional £50.

The computer supply company also quoted for the provision of various ancillary services as follows:

— computer installation and testing costs, £250;
— supply and installation of specialist wiring, £150;
— staff training in order that they could operate the computer, £500;
— custom designed computer software, £750;
— insurance for fire, theft and accidental damage, £100 per annum;
— maintenance of computer system, £200 per annum;
— initial supply and delivery of computer paper, £25;
— two spare toner cartridges for the laser printer, £90 each.

Harpie and Henderson decided to accept all of the additional items and services at the prices quoted.

Required:
(a) Calculate the acquisition cost of the microcomputer system to Harpie and Henderson as it would appear in the firm's balance sheet and
(b) Identify the costs which would appear in the Profit and Loss account relating to the financial period in which the above events occurred.
Ignore VAT.

Chapter Four: Accounting adjustments—Part one

It will be appreciated by this stage that the recording of business transactions by the use of double-entry principles in a solicitors' practice, and indeed in any business, is a somewhat mechanical process. Every time a transaction occurs, the rules of double-entry are followed to record the events into the firm's books. At the end of the accounting period, balances are extracted from the accounts to form a trial balance with the period's financial statements being drafted thereafter.

However, in the normal course of events a certain amount of fine-tuning is necessary at the end of the period to ensure that the final accounts adequately reflect reality. *Accounting adjustments* are needed so that the expenses of an accounting period are properly matched to associated revenue in accordance with the Matching convention[1].

In deciding whether or not an accounting adjustment is to be made, regard should be shown to another accounting convention, namely that of Materiality. Under this latter convention, only significant accounting adjustments need occur. Solicitors' practices will generally require adjustments to reflect some or indeed all of the following:

(1)   depreciation of fixed assets;
(2)   bad debts and provisions for doubtful debts;
(3)   accrued and prepaid expenses;
(4)   work in progress.

A final type of accounting adjustment which is of little direct relevance to legal practice but which is still nevertheless very important in the context of trading organisations is in relation to:

(5)   stock

It is intended to consider the first of the above accounting adjustments in this chapter, namely depreciation of fixed assets, with the remainder being examined in the following chapter.

DEPRECIATION OF FIXED ASSETS

ILLUSTRATION 4.1

Frederickson started as a sole practitioner specialising in criminal law. A few weeks after the inception of the business, Frederickson bought a car for £16,000 to be used exclusively for business purposes. Ignoring the purchase price of the car, Frederickson's practice generated a net profit of £20,000 over the year. However, Frederickson is unsure as to the charge to be levied against the profits of the year for the use of the vehicle. Remembering that the overriding

---

1 See Chapter 1.

objective in such situations should be to try and match the costs incurred by the business against the revenues generated over a given period, it follows that some method should be applied which results in the cost of the vehicle being fairly charged against those accounting periods benefiting from its use.

In the light of this approach, therefore, it would be inappropriate for Frederickson to write-off the full cost of the car in the first year, since the resulting net profit in Year One would be heavily understated at only £4,000 (that is, £20,000 less £16,000). Also, if the full cost of the vehicle was, in fact, charged against the first year, this would mean that profit levels in subsequent trading periods would be overstated, given that the vehicle would still be getting used for the benefit of the firm but at no cost (other than running costs such as fuel, insurance, etc which are considered quite separately). Users of the final accounting statements would be misled as to the true profit levels over such periods.

The cost of the vehicle should preferably be *depreciated* over its estimated working life, with an appropriate *depreciation charge* being made in each accounting period in which the asset has been in use. The charge should reflect the value of the fixed asset consumed in each period. The depreciation charge relating to each year would be shown as an expense in the relevant Profit and Loss account.

The balance sheet would be used to summarise the total amount of depreciation so far provided against the fixed assets of the business. In the latter financial statement, it is normal to detail the nature of each category of fixed asset belonging to the business and to show the cost of such assets and the *accumulated depreciation* (that is, total depreciation) so far written off. By so doing, it would be possible for the users of a balance sheet to see the *net book value* (NBV) of each category of fixed assets held by the business at a given point in time. The net book value of an asset can be regarded as an estimate of how much the asset is worth to the firm in the future.

FACTORS WHICH CAUSE DEPRECIATION OF FIXED ASSETS

In the case of a motor vehicle, as in the Frederickson illustration, the main factor which results in the diminution of value is simply wear and tear through normal everyday use. *Physical deterioration* is only one cause of depreciation, but others exist. For example, *obsolescence* or *inadequacy* are other factors. Many legal firms a few years ago used electronic typewriters. With the advent of word-processors and laser printers, a firm using old technology is almost automatically operating at a disadvantage. The electronic typewriter in itself may be in perfect working order, but compared to the efficiency gains possible through the use of a word-processing system, the former has become inadequate. Old manual typewriters besides being inadequate must also surely be on the verge of obsolescence.

   Although largely irrelevant to the work of a solicitor, *depletion* is another example of why a depreciation charge should appear in the Profit and Loss account of, say, a quarrying business. As minerals are extracted from the quarry, the value of this particular fixed asset is being reduced. It would be appropriate to reflect the fact by including a depreciation charge in the Profit and Loss account of the company concerned.

ESTIMATING THE VALUE OF FIXED ASSETS CONSUMED DURING AN ACCOUNTING PERIOD

Once the fact that virtually all fixed assets gradually reduce in value over the years is recognised, the next consideration is how to estimate the actual depreciation charge to be written off as an expense in any given accounting period. One way would be to value the asset on the first and last days of the financial period, taking the difference in value as the depreciation charge. When one considers the number of fixed assets which larger businesses use, coupled with the fee costs of professional valuers, this may be neither the most practical nor the most economical way to calculate depreciation charges.

There are several techniques for estimating depreciation charges on fixed assets. The actual approach adopted will depend on the circumstances, having regard to the nature of the fixed asset in question, what the generally accepted accounting approach is for such an asset and, of course, the preference of the owners and/or managers of the business.

The straight-line method

One of the most common techniques used to calculate a depreciation charge is the *straight-line* method. Here the annual depreciation charge is found by dividing the cost of the asset *less* an estimate of any residual value by an estimate of the length of its working life.

ILLUSTRATION 4.1 (continued)

If the Frederickson illustration above is continued by assuming that the car lasts for three years, at the end of which time it is worth £1,000, the annual depreciation charge can be calculated as follows:

$$\text{Annual depreciation charge} = \frac{\text{Original cost } \textit{less} \text{ estimated residual value}}{\text{length of working life in years}}$$

$$= \frac{£16,000 - £1,000}{3}$$

$$= £5,000$$

Frederickson will show a depreciation charge of £5,000 as an expense in the Profit and Loss account for *each* of the three years in which the asset was used. In Year One, therefore, the firm's final net profit will be £20,000 − £5,000 = £15,000.

If consideration is given to the appearance of Frederickson's balance sheet at the end of each of the three trading years over which the vehicle was used, the position after the relevant accounting entries have been made can be summarised as follows:

(1) [Extract] *Balance Sheet as at the end of Year One*

Fixed Assets	Cost	Accumulated Depreciation	Net book value
	£	£	£
Motor vehicles	16,000	5,000	11,000

(2) [Extract] *Balance Sheet as at the end of Year Two*

Fixed Assets	Cost	Accumulated Depreciation	Net book value
	£	£	£
Motor vehicles	16,000	10,000	6,000

(3) [Extract] *Balance Sheet as at the end of Year Three*

Fixed Assets	Cost	Accumulated Depreciation	Net book value
	£	£	£
Motor vehicles	16,000	15,000	1,000

It can be seen that the balance sheet highlights the gradual increase in accumulated depreciation over the three-year period and, consequently, the gradual reduction in the net book value (NBV) of the car over the same period until, at the end of the third year, the asset is shown in the books as being worth £1,000.

One advantage of the straight-line method is the ease with which it can be applied. Once the annual flat-rate charge has been worked out, the same figure can be written into the accounting records at the end of each trading year thereafter. The main disadvantage is that the charge will not take into consideration how heavily the asset has been used in any one accounting period. Taking it to extremes, Frederickson would allow a depreciation charge of £5,000 per annum irrespective of whether the car travelled one mile in the year or one hundred thousand miles.

It is worthwhile noting that where a depreciation policy is expressed in terms such as, for example, '. . . the annual depreciation charge on plant and equipment is to be allowed at 15% *on cost'*, the inference is that the straight line method is in use.

The reducing-balance method

Another popular way of calculating the annual depreciation charge on fixed assets is to apply the *reducing-balance* method. Unlike the straight-line method which gives a flat-rate charge each year an asset is in use, the reducing-balance technique produces a relatively higher depreciation charge in the early years of an asset's life with a gradually decreasing charge the older the asset grows. Under the latter system a fixed percentage is applied annually to the net book value of the asset at the beginning of each accounting period.

ILLUSTRATION 4.1 (continued)

Consider the following example. At the start of Frederickson's second year, a new computer system was bought for the firm at a cost of £4,000. It is expected that it will last for four years, at the end of which time it will be worth approximately £250. The computer system is to be depreciated at a rate of 50% per annum using the reducing-balance method.

The depreciation charges being written-off to Frederickson's Profit and Loss accounts in the Years 2–5 would be as follows:

	Computer Equipment	£	
Year Two:	Cost	4,000	
	Less: depreciation charge for the year (being 50% of £4,000)	2,000	charged as an expense to the period's Profit & Loss account
	Closing NBV at the end of Year Two	2,000	
Year Three:	Opening NBV	2,000	
	Less: depreciation charge for the year (being 50% of £2,000)	1,000	charged as an expense to the period's Profit & Loss account
	Closing NBV at the end of Year Three	1,000	

Year Four:	Opening NBV	1,000	
	Less: depreciation charge for the year (being 50% of £1,000)	500	charged as an expense to the period's Profit & Loss account
	Closing NBV at the end of Year Four	500	
Year Five:	Opening NBV	500	
	Less: depreciation charge for the year (being 50% of £500)	250	charged as an expense to the period's Profit & Loss account
	Closing NBV at the end of Year Five	250	

It can be seen that by using this particular method the majority of the cost of the asset is written off early in its lifespan and by the time Year Five is reached, the annual depreciation charge is quite modest.

In so far as Frederickson's balance sheets over Years 2–5 inclusive are concerned, the information which would ultimately be shown with respect to the computer equipment would be:

(1) [Extract]   *Balance Sheet as at the end of Year Two*

Fixed Assets	Cost £	Accumulated Depreciation £	Net book value £
Computer equipment	4,000	2,000	2,000

(2) [Extract]   *Balance Sheet as at the end of Year Three*

Fixed Assets	Cost £	Accumulated Depreciation £	Net book value £
Computer equipment	4,000	3,000	1,000

(3) [Extract]   *Balance Sheet as at the end of Year Four*

Fixed Assets	Cost £	Accumulated Depreciation £	Net book value £
Computer equipment	4,000	3,500	500

(4) [Extract]   *Balance Sheet as at the end of Year Five*

Fixed Assets	Cost £	Accumulated Depreciation £	Net book value £
Computer equipment	4,000	3,750	250

The above illustration was simplified to the extent that the reducing-balance depreciation rate of 50% was actually given. By applying this rate, the illustration ended rather neatly on the estimated residual value of £250 for the computer equipment. Even if the rate had not been stated, it would still nevertheless have been possible to calculate it from the other background information available. The appropriate rate could have been found by applying the following formula:

$$r = 1 - \sqrt[n]{\frac{s}{c}} \times 100 \quad \text{where,}$$

r = depreciation rate (%'age)
n = estimated working life of the asset in years
s = the asset's residual value at the end of its life span
c = the cost of the asset

So, in the case of Frederickson's computer equipment:

$$\text{The depreciation rate (expressed as a percentage)} = 1 - \sqrt[4]{\frac{250}{4,000}} \times 1000$$

$$= 1 - 0.50 \times 100$$

$$= \underline{\underline{50\%}}$$

It may come as a relief to know that solicitors do not normally have to make such calculations during a typical working day.

Other techniques for depreciating fixed assets

Although the straight-line and reducing-balance methods described above are the ones most frequently used in the context of a solicitor's practice, there are other ways of apportioning the cost of fixed assets over their economic working lives. It was mentioned earlier that one of the main disadvantages of the straight-line method is that it takes little account of asset use. The reducing-balance method similarly suffers from such a drawback. However, the *production units* method is based on the assumption that the more an asset is used, then the greater the depreciation charge should be in any given period.

A simple example shows how the annual depreciation charge can be calculated using this technique:

ILLUSTRATION 4.2

Assumptions:

— A manufacturing machine has an expected total output of 100,000 steel washers
— The machine cost £5,500 and it has an estimated scrap value of £500
— During the financial year in question, the machine produced 25,000 washers

Required:

Using the production units method, calculate an appropriate depreciation charge for the machine.

Solution:

$$\text{Depreciation charge per unit produced} = \frac{\text{Cost of the machine} - \text{its estimated scrap value}}{\text{Total number of washers the machine will produce}}$$

$$= \frac{£5,500 - £500}{100,000}$$

$$= £0.05$$

Therefore, given that the machine produced 25,000 washers during the financial year in question, the depreciation charge to be written-off to the period's Profit and Loss account will be 25,000 × 5 pence = £1,250.

Another depreciation method very similar to that of the production units method, is one based on the number of hours the asset was used over a financial period relative to the total number of hours for which it is expected to operate. The *machine hours* method can be illustrated as follows.

ILLUSTRATION 4.3

Assumptions:

— An item of machinery cost £1,100 and is expected to work for approximately 1,000 hours
— Its scrap value at the end of this time will be £100
— During the financial year just finished, the machine was used for 300 hours

Required:

Using the machine hours method, calculate the year's depreciation charge.

Solution:

$$\text{Hourly depreciation charge} = \frac{\text{Cost of the machine} - \text{scrap value}}{\text{Total working life, in hours}}$$

$$= \frac{£1,100 - £100}{1,000 \text{ hours}}$$

$$= \underline{\underline{£1}}$$

Therefore, the depreciation charge for the year would be 300 hours @ £1 per hour = £300

Straight-line, reducing-balance, production units and machine hours are examples of methods which could be used to calculate the annual depreciation charge on a business's fixed assets[1]. A business would have to select a method appropriate in the circumstances.

Further decisions would also be necessary with respect to the overall depreciation policy of a firm. Besides choosing the method of depreciation for different categories of fixed assets, consideration would have to be given to the action to be followed when fixed assets are bought or disposed of during a financial year. In such circumstances, the two main alternative schools of thought are:

(1) that a full year's depreciation charge is allowed in the year of acquisition with no charge in the year of disposal, irrespective of when the asset is acquired or disposed of; or alternatively,
(2) that the depreciation charge is directly related to the length of time that the asset was used within the business. If an asset was bought three months into a financial year, only nine-twelfths of the full annual depreciation charge would be written-off to the period's Profit and Loss account. Similarly, if the asset was sold at the end of the eighth month of a financial year, the depreciation charge in respect of that asset for the financial year in which the disposal took place would be restricted to eight-twelfths of the full year's charge.

Once the solicitor's practice has formulated a rational depreciation policy with respect to the treatment of its fixed assets, this policy should then be applied *consistently* over successive accounting periods. It is possible for a business to change its depreciation policy if deemed appropriate in the circumstances, but such a decision should not be taken without good reason given the effects which the change will have on its financial statements[2].

---

1 Other techniques for calculating depreciation on fixed assets exist but are considered to be outwith the scope of this text.
2 If a limited company, for example, decides to alter its depreciation policy and if the change has a material effect on its reported results, then a full explanation of the effects of such a change must be included in the final accounts for that financial period.

ACCOUNTING FOR DEPRECIATION CHARGES

All accounting adjustments basically involve two main stages. The first is to quantify the adjustment arithmetically; the second involves writing the relevant figure(s) into the books and records of the business. As far as depreciation charges are concerned, the first stage has already been addressed and it only remains to look at the actual accounting entries to be made.

The three main accounts which are involved in the recording of depreciation charges are:

(1)   the depreciation expense account;
(2)   the asset account; and
(3)   the accumulated depreciation account for the asset concerned.

The interaction between these different accounts on the one hand and the details which are eventually shown in the Profit and Loss account and the balance sheet on the other, can be seen in a simple example.

ILLUSTRATION 4.4

Assumptions:

— The background information is taken from the Frederickson illustration used earlier. To recap and to introduce further assumptions:
— Frederickson started the legal practice on 1 January 1994, the date on which the motor vehicle was bought for £16,000. The car has an estimated life span of three years at which time it is expected to be worth £1,000. The computer equipment costing £4,000, was purchased on the first day of the business' second trading year. The equipment is to be depreciated over four years and it has an estimated scrap value of £250.
— It is Frederickson's depreciation policy to allow a full year's charge in the year of acquisition, irrespective of when the asset was bought during the accounting period, with no allowance for depreciation in the year of disposal. Motor vehicles are depreciated using the straight-line method whilst the reducing-balance method, at 50% per annum, is applied to the computer equipment.
— The financial year end is 31 December each year.

Required:

Show the entries in the asset accounts, the Depreciation expense account and the Accumulated depreciation accounts which would be necessary to process the depreciation charges for the car and the computer equipment in each of the first three years of Frederickson's practice. Also, provide extracts from the Profit and Loss accounts and balance sheets covering the same periods.

Solution:

(i)   *Year to 31 December 1994 (Year One)*

MOTOR VEHICLES		
	£	£
(1) 1.1.94 Bank	16,000	

DEPRECIATION EXPENSE		
	£	£
(2) 31.12.94 Accum. depreciation (Motor Vehicles) 5,000		31.12.94 Profit and Loss a/c 5,000 (3)

ACCUMULATED DEPRECIATION (MOTOR VEHICLES)	
£	£
	31.12.94 Depreciation Expense 5,000 (2)

Explanatory Notes

(1)   The corresponding entry to the debit entry for £16,000 appearing in the Motor vehicles account is a credit for the same amount in the firm's Bank account in the cash book. The Bank account entries are ignored in this example.

(2)   The car's depreciation charge of £5,000 is initially recorded in the records as follows:

DR Depreciation Expense   £5,000
          CR Accumulated depreciation (Motor vehicle)   £5,000

(3)   The corresponding entry to the £5,000 credited to the Depreciation expense account will be a debit of £5,000 to the period's Profit and Loss account. The effect of this double entry is to clear the Depreciation expense account ready to begin a new period.

(4)   The balances remaining in the Motor vehicle account and the Accumulated depreciation account will be reflected in the balance sheet drawn up on the 31 December 1994 and will be carried forward into the next financial year.

(ii)   *Year to 31 December 1995 (Year Two)*

MOTOR VEHICLES			COMPUTER EQUIPMENT		
	£	£		£	£
(1) 1.1.95 Bal b/f 16,000			(2) 1.1.95 Bank 4,000		

DEPRECIATION EXPENSE			ACCUMULATED DEPRECIATION (MOTOR VEHICLES)		
	£	£		£	£
(3) 31.12.95 Accumulated depreciation (Motor vehicle) 5,000	31.12.95 Profit and Loss a/c 7,000 (5)			1.1.95 Bal b/f 5,000 (1) 31.12.95 Depreciation expense 5,000 (3)	
(4) 31.12.95 Accumulated depreciation (Computer equip-ment) 2,000					
7,000	7,000				

ACCUMULATED DEPRECIATION (COMPUTER EQUIPMENT)		
£	£	
	31.12.95 Depreciation expense 2,000 (4)	

Explanatory Notes

(1)   As mentioned above, the cost price of the car of £16,000 has been brought forward from the previous financial year, as has the £5,000 opening credit balance in the vehicle's Accumulated depreciation account.

(2)   The computer equipment was purchased on 1 January 1995 for £4,000. The accounting entries for this transaction would be:

DR Computer Equipment   £4,000
          CR Bank   £4,000

Again for the purpose of this illustration the entries to the latter account are ignored.

(3), (4)   The year's depreciation charge relating to each asset is brought into the accounts as follows:

for the car   *DR* Depreciation expense   £5,000
                    CR Accumulated depreciation (Motor vehicle)   £5,000

for the computer equipment

DR Depreciation expense   £2,000
          CR Accumulated depreciation
                    (Computer equipment)   £2,000

(5)   The next step is to transfer the year's depreciation charges on the fixed assets to the Profit and Loss account for that period. To accomplish this, all that is necessary is:

DR Profit and Loss	£7,000
CR Depreciation expense	£7,000

Once again, this entry will have the effect of clearing the Depreciation expense account ready to begin the next financial year's transactions.

(6)   Finally, the balances remaining in the records at 31 December 1995, in the two asset accounts (Motor vehicle and Computer equipment) and in their respective Accumulated depreciation accounts, will be carried forward to 1 January 1996, being the first day of the new trading period. Such balances existing at 31 December 1995 will appear in the balance sheet of the same date.

(iii)   *Year to 31 December 1996 (Year Three)*

MOTOR VEHICLE

	£		£
(1) 1.1.96 Bal b/f	16,000		

DEPRECIATION EXPENSE

	£			£
(2) 31.12.96 Accumulated depreciation (Motor vehicle)	5,000	31.12.96 Profit and Loss a/c	6,000 (4)	
(3) 31.12.96 Accumulated depreciation (Computer equipment)	1,000			
	6,000		6,000	

ACCUMULATED DEPRECIATION (COMPUTER EQUIPMENT)

	£		£
		1.1.96 Bal b/f	2,000 (1)
		31.12.96 Depreciation expense	1,000 (3)

COMPUTER EQUIPMENT

	£		£
(1) 1.1.96 Bal b/f	4,000		

ACCUMULATED DEPRECIATION (MOTOR VEHICLE)

	£		£
		1.1.96 Bal b/f	10,000 (1)
		31.12.96 Depreciation expense	5,000 (2)

Explanatory Notes

(1)   The opening balances in each asset account as well as in its respective Accumulated depreciation account are brought forward from the previous accounting period.

(2), (3)   The depreciation charges for the year to 31 December 1996 with respect to the car and the computer equipment are incorporated into the accounting records.

(4)   The end of year balance on the Depreciation expense account (£6,000) is transferred to the period's Profit and Loss account.

(5)   The balances in the two asset accounts and in the two Accumulated depreciation accounts are again carried forward into the next accounting period. Once more such balances appear in Frederickson's balance sheet as at 31 December 1996.

The second part of the solution to the example, that is, where extracts from the Profit and Loss account and the balance sheet for each year are to be displayed, is relatively straightforward since it is simply a combination of the extracts shown earlier in this chapter[1].

---

1   See the earlier consideration of the straight-line and reducing-balance methods of depreciating assets for the motor vehicle and computer equipment respectively.

ILLUSTRATION 4.5

(i)   Profit and Loss Account Extracts for the
**   Years to 31 December 1994, 1995 and 1996**

Frederickson & Co., Solicitors
Profit and Loss account (Extract) for the year ended:

	31 December 1994		31 December 1995		31 December 1996	
	£	£	£	£	£	£
Gross profit b/f		x		x		x
Less: Expenses						
Depreciation:						
Motor vehicles	5,000		5,000		5,000	
Computer equipment	–	5,000	2,000	7,000	1,000	6,000

(ii)   Balance Sheet Extracts as at
**   31 December 1994, 1995 and 1996**

Frederickson & Co., Solicitors

(a)   *Balance Sheet (Extract) as at 31 December 1994*

Fixed Assets	Cost	Accumulated Depreciation	N.B.V.
	£	£	£
Motor vehicle	16,000	5,000	11,000

(b)   *Balance Sheet (Extract) as at 31 December 1995*

Fixed Assets	Cost	Accumulated Depreciation	N.B.V.
	£	£	£
Motor vehicle	16,000	10,000	6,000
Computer equipment	4,000	2,000	2,000
	20,000	12,000	8,000

(c)   *Balance Sheet (Extract) as at 31 December 1996*

Fixed Assets	Cost	Accumulated Depreciation	N.B.V.
	£	£	£
Motor vehicle	16,000	15,000	1,000
Computer equipment	4,000	3,000	1,000
	20,000	18,000	2,000

It can be seen in this illustration that the process of making the annual allowance in the accounting records to reflect the value of fixed assets used up in the accounting period follows the same pattern each year. It should also be noted, however, that the accounting adjustments to provide for depreciation on assets is very much a test of one's skill at estimating since in most cases the actual value of the fixed asset consumed during a period will not be known with certainty.

It is only upon the disposal of an asset that all the relevant information comes to hand and it becomes possible to assess the full extent of the depreciation which has occurred over its working life within the organisation concerned. At this stage it will probably be necessary to make a further accounting adjustment, the nature of which depends on the relationship between the cost of the fixed asset, the total depreciation written-off from the date of acquisition to the date of disposal and the value of any proceeds generated by the disposal of the asset.

DISPOSAL OF FIXED ASSETS

When an asset is scrapped or sold off by the firm, the accuracy of the depreciation policy which had been used for the asset can be assessed. In cases where, on the one hand, the cost of the asset plus the value of any further capital expenditure incurred thereon, is matched exactly on the other by the total of the accumulated depreciation plus the disposal proceeds, no further accounting adjustment is necessary. But where the two total figures do not equate, there will have been a *gain* or *loss on disposal* of the fixed asset and an appropriate adjustment will be necessary.

Gain on disposal

Assume that Frederickson sold the car on 1 April 1997 (Year Four) for £1,750. The gain on the disposal can be calculated arithmetically as follows:

		£
Accumulated depreciation 1.1.94 to 1.4.97	=	15,000*
Add: Proceeds from sale of car	=	1,750
		16,750
Less: Cost price of car		(16,000)
Gain on disposal		750

[*Note:* Remember that Frederickson's depreciation policy means that no allowance for depreciation is provided in the year of an asset's disposal].

The gain of £750 on disposal of the motor vehicle would be detailed as such in the Profit and Loss account for the year to 31 December 1997, appearing there as a credit entry. This can be seen if the background accounting entries necessary to record the disposal are examined:

ILLUSTRATION 4.6

MOTOR VEHICLE

	£		£
(1) 1.1.97 Bal b/f	16,000	1.4.97 Disposal of Motor Vehicle	16,000 (2)

ACCUMULATED DEPRECIATION (MOTOR VEHICLE)

	£		£
(3) 1.4.97 Disposal of Motor Vehicle	15,000	1.1.97 Bal b/f	15,000 (1)

DISPOSAL OF MOTOR VEHICLE

	£		£
(2) 1.4.97 Motor Vehicle	16,000	(3) 1.4.97 Accumulated depreciation (Motor Vehicle)	15,000
(5) 1.4.97 Profit & Loss	750	(4) 1.4.97 Bank	1,750
	16,750		16,750

BANK

	£		£
(1) 1.1.97 Bal b/f	xxx		
(4) 1.4.97 Disposal of Motor Vehicle	1,750		

Explanatory Notes

(1)   The opening balances on the relevant accounts have been brought forward from the previous financial year.

(2), (3)   On 1 April 1997 when the car is sold, the balances on the Motor vehicle account and on the Accumulated depreciation (Motor vehicle) account are transferred over to the Disposal of Motor Vehicle account. It follows that no mention of this fixed asset will appear in the balance sheet from this date on.

(4)   The proceeds from the sale of the car will be recorded thus:

> *DR*   Bank   £1,750
> *CR*   Disposal of Motor Vehicle   £1,750

(5)   To close off the Disposal of Motor Vehicle account, this account should be debited with £750 whilst the corresponding credit will be made in the period's Profit and Loss account.

Loss on disposal

Assuming instead that Frederickson sold the car on 1 April 1997 for £600, this will give rise to a loss of £400 on disposal which would be charged to the period's Profit and Loss account in the same way as any other business expense:

	£
Accumulated depreciation 1.1.94 to 1.4.97 =	15,000
Add: Proceeds from sale of car	600
	15,600
Less: Cost price of car	(16,000)
Loss on disposal	(400)

The £400 loss on disposal of the motor vehicle will be debited to the Profit and Loss account. In this instance, the background accounting entries will be as follows:

The Motor Vehicle and the Accumulated depreciation (Motor Vehicle) account will appear the same as under the previous example where the effects of a gain on disposal of a fixed asset was considered. Furthermore, the only difference to the Bank account from the earlier example will be a debit entry of £600 on 1 April 1997 instead of the £1,750. The main difference will be in the Disposal of Motor Vehicle account. Thus:

ILLUSTRATION 4.7

DISPOSAL OF MOTOR VEHICLE

	£			£
1.4.97 Motor vehicle	16,000	1.4.97	Accumulated depreciation (Motor vehicle)	15,000
		1.4.97	Bank	600
		1.4.97	Profit & Loss a/c	400
	16,000			16,000

In either case, where a gain or loss on disposal of a fixed asset is realised, it is normal accounting treatment to show the relevant adjustment in the Profit and Loss account of the period in which the disposal occurs.

Before leaving this section, it is worth mentioning again that the net book value of fixed assets shown in the balance sheet represents the perceived future value of those assets to the business. The net book value does not necessarily reflect the open market value of an asset at a given point in time. For example, consider the case where an entity buys a piece of specialised machinery which has been custom-built and is expected to last for ten years. The firm could normally expect to write this particular asset off over the full ten-year period of its use. In this way, each successive accounting period is being fairly charged for the value of the fixed asset consumed in that period.

It is quite possible that the asset is worth only its scrap value to any organisation other than the one using it. It could be argued therefore that its cost should be immediately written-off in the period in which it was bought. The effect of this action would, it could be counter-argued, seriously distort the true profitability of the firm involved—that is, the profit level in the year of acquisition would be heavily under-estimated given the full cost of the asset is being charged as depreciation to the Profit and Loss account—leaving profit to be over-estimated in every remaining financial year of its working life (given the absence of depreciation charges for the asset in such periods).

On balance in such circumstances, the profitability of the enterprise and its financial position at any given point in time will be more accurately represented by assuming that the organisation will be capable of using the asset for the duration of its normal working life in the ten-year period.

QUESTIONS[1]

1. A solicitor purchased a boardroom table and chairs for use within the practice for £2,350 on the first day of the new financial year. It is intended to replace them in five years time, at which point it is estimated that their resale value will be £350. Calculate the annual depreciation charge which would be shown in the firm's Profit and Loss account for each of the five years, assuming that the straight-line method is used to depreciate this particular type of fixed asset.

2. Assuming the same details apply as in question one above, show the information which would be included in the balance sheets of the firm at the end of each of the five years in which the furniture was used.

3. Alderston and Williamson (Solicitors) bought a new car for £16,000 on the opening day of a new financial year. It is the firm's policy to depreciate motor vehicles using the reducing-balance method at a rate of 25% per annum. The firm replaces cars every three years. It is expected that the car will be worth £6,750 at the end of the three-year period. Calculate the depreciation charge which would be written off to the firm's Profit and Loss account for each of the three years in which the car was owned.

4. Assuming the same details apply as in question three above, show the information which would be included in the balance sheets of Alderston and Williamson at the end of each of the three years over which the vehicle was owned.

5. Donaldsons is a legal practice specialising in matrimonial work. The firm was established on 1 January 1996 and owns the following fixed assets:

1   For suggested solutions see p 279.

	Cost (£)	Date of Purchase	Depreciation Policy
Office property	100,000	1.1.96	2% per annum on cost, straight-line
Office furniture and Fittings	5,000	1.3.96	10% per annum on cost, straight-line
Computer equipment	25,000	1.3.96	20% per annum, reducing balance
Motor vehicles	30,000	1.4.96	25% per annum, reducing balance

A full year's depreciation charge is to be provided in the year of an asset's acquisition, irrespective of when the asset is acquired. No depreciation charge is allowed in the year of an asset's disposal.

Donaldsons financial year runs from 1 January to 31 December each year.

Required:

    (i)   Calculate the total depreciation charge which will be written off against the firm's Profit and Loss account for the year to 31 December 1996. Furthermore,

   (ii)   show an extract of Donaldsons balance sheet as at that date.

6.   Assuming the same information as in question five, with the exception that the financial year in question is now the year to 31 December 1997, calculate:

    (i)   the depreciation charge written off to the Profit and Loss account for that year, and,

   (ii)   show an extract of the balance sheet as at 31 December 1997.

7.   (a)   McNamarras is a practice dealing almost exclusively with criminal court work. McNamarras' financial year runs from 1 January to 31 December each year. The firm's main asset is a motor vehicle which was bought on 1 January 1995 for £18,000. The firm's motor vehicle depreciation policy is to charge 20% of the car's cost to the Profit and Loss account for each year, based on complete months of ownership.

   Calculate the depreciation charge on the vehicle for the financial year to 31 December 1995 which would be charged to Profit and Loss account in respect of that period, and, show an extract of the balance sheet as at that date.

(b)   McNamarras sold the car on 1 June 1996. Calculate the gain or loss realised on the sale of the vehicle assuming that it was sold for:

   (i)   £13,000

  (ii)   £12,000

   Also, in each of the above instances, state the information which would be shown in McNamarras' Profit and Loss account for the year to 31 December 1996 with respect to the car.

8.   Donald and MacGregor (Solicitors) are in the second year of business. The partners commenced in practice on 1 January 1996 and have a financial year ending on 31 December. Besides other fixed assets, the firm owns three motor vehicles, details of which are as follows:

	Cost (£)	Date of Purchase
Car A	20,000	1.1.96
Car B	20,000	1.4.96
Car C	10,000	1.7.96

The cars are depreciated using the reducing balance method, at a rate of 25% per annum, based on each complete month of ownership in any accounting year.

On 1 October 1997, the partners decided to sell car C for £8,000.

Required:

(a)   (i)   Calculate the total depreciation charge which would be written off in the firm's Profit and Loss account for the year to 31 December 1996, and
      (ii) show the balance sheet extract as at that date;

(b)   (i)   Calculate the gain or loss realised on the sale of car C which would be detailed in the Profit and Loss account for the year to 31 December 1997. Also,
      (ii) state the total depreciation charge on the cars in that year which will appear in the Profit and Loss account. Finally,
      (iii) provide a balance sheet extract based on the available information at 31 December 1997.

[All calculations should be rounded up to the nearest £]

9.   Assuming the same details as in question eight above, show the necessary accounting entries to record the following:

1996
   (i)   the purchase of the three cars (ignore entries to the firm's Bank account)
   (ii) the year's depreciation charge
   (iii) the transfer of the balance in the Depreciation expense account to the period's Profit and Loss account at the end of the financial year

1997
   (i)   the disposal of car C on 1.10.97
   (ii) the year's depreciation charge
   (iii) the transfer of the balance in the Depreciation expense account to the period's Profit and Loss account at the end of the financial year

and finally,

   (iv) show the various entries which have been made over 1997 to the Motor vehicles account, and the Accumulated depreciation (Motor vehicles) account and highlight the balances carried forward to the subsequent financial year on these accounts.

Chapter Five: Accounting adjustments—Part two

The previous chapter looked at the way in which a legal business can make an allowance for depreciation on its fixed assets. Other accounting adjustments yet to be considered are:

1   bad debts and provisions for doubtful debts;
2   accrued and prepaid expenses;
3   work in progress; and
4   stock.

BAD DEBTS AND PROVISIONS FOR DOUBTFUL DEBTS

Another example of a year-end accounting adjustment which a solicitor's practice would normally expect to carry out can be seen with respect to the treatment of potential bad debts. It is a common occurrence for work to be done on behalf of a client with no fee changing hands until the work of the solicitor is finished. That said, where the legal work involved is of a protracted nature, it would be normal for the solicitor to raise interim invoices. Even in the latter case, invoices are still being raised on clients retrospectively, after work has been done on their behalf[1]. In other words, solicitors are providing credit facilities for clients.

This means that the 'Fee Income' figure which appears at the top of a solicitors' Profit and Loss account will probably be a combination of money actually received from clients, and, amounts still outstanding where clients have yet to pay their dues[2]. Unfortunately, some clients for whatever reason do not pay. If this fact is ignored, the Prudence concept is also being ignored and the profit levels of the practice will probably be overstated. In an attempt to avoid this happening, a business could establish a *provision for doubtful debts*. In this way the legal practice is anticipating potential non-payment of invoices by clients. As a direct consequence of maintaining this provision, the final accounts of the practice will accord more closely with reality.

Before looking at provisions for doubtful debts, it would be beneficial at this stage to review the accounting treatment of known *bad debts*.

---

1   This is not to say that solicitors cannot, or should not, obtain professional fees in advance if carrying out work for a client. Indeed, with some clients this would be a preferable course of action to one where the work is done, even partially, in advance of the fee note being raised.
2   For a further discussion on the definition of Fee Income, see Chapter 7 on Partnership Accounts.

Bad debts

If it becomes clear at any stage during the financial year that a client is not going to pay what is owed, and after all practical steps have been taken by the solicitor to recover the outstanding amount, it will be necessary to write off the sum as a bad debt.

ILLUSTRATION 5.1

Kippen and Co. (Solicitors) specialise in civil litigation. The firm's financial year runs from 1 January to 31 December. The following transactions involving its clients occurred during the year to 31 December 1996:

(1)   10 June   —   Armstrong and Co goes into liquidation. There is no prospect of the firm recovering the £500 owed by this particular client. The partners decide that the sum should be written off as a bad debt.

Action required: *DR* Bad debts   £500
                      CR Armstrong and Co   £500

(2)   30 September—   Dundas is declared bankrupt, owing £250 to the practice which the partners feel is now irrecoverable and should be treated as a bad debt.

Action required: *DR* Bad debts   £250
                      CR Dundas   £250

(3)   11 December —   Young, a client, is refusing to pay an outstanding firm's invoice for £50. The partner who dealt with the work has intimated that Young has been a particularly troublesome client and, given that the sum doesn't justify court action, is quite prepared to write the £50 off as a bad debt and refuse to act on Young's behalf in the future.

Action required: *DR* Bad debts   £50
                      CR Young   £50

The firm's Bad debts account would now appear:

BAD DEBTS

1996		£	1996	£
10.6	Armstrong and Co	500		
30.9	Dundas	250		
11.12	Young	50		

At the end of the firm's financial year, the balance on the Bad debts account will be cleared off like any other form of business expense to the Profit and Loss account as follows:

BAD DEBTS

1996		£	1996		£
10.6	Armstrong and Co	500	31.12	Profit and Loss a/c	800
30.9	Dundas	250			
11.12	Young	50			
		800			800

The accounts of the individual clients involved here will all be squared off, with no balances remaining[1].

Thus, on the 31 December 1996, being the end of Kippen and Co.'s financial year, £800 will be charged to the firm's Profit and Loss account. As far as the balance sheet is concerned, all the

---

1   The individual ledger accounts of Armstrong and Co, Dundas and Young will be found in the firm's Client Ledger. See Chapters Nine and Ten for a discussion on the need for separation of clients' affairs from those of the firm for the purpose of record keeping. All of the entries envisaged in this illustration will be made in the 'office column' of the clients' records.

debit balances remaining in the firm's other individual clients' accounts will be added together with the total figure being displayed as 'Client Debtors' in the balance sheet under the heading of Current Assets. It is important to stress again that the latter figure which appears in the balance sheet, will be net of all known bad debts written off during the year.

Provision for doubtful debts

Dealing with known bad debts is not, therefore, something which is only carried out at the end of a financial period. Rather it is a continuous process which occurs throughout the financial year. Unfortunately, the end of year debtors figure as defined above, although shown net of all known bad debts, may well still contain amounts which are in doubt and which will never be collected by the solicitor. As mentioned earlier, if the firm's profit is not to be overstated, an adjustment should be made via the Provision for Doubtful Debts account at the end of the accounting period to reflect this fact and to provide against future non-payment of debts owed to the firm.

Once more the process of making a year-end adjustment to provide for doubtful debts can be broken down into stages. The first stage is to calculate the size of the provision; the second stage is to make the necessary accounting entries.

Methods of estimating potential bad debts

There are various techniques solicitors have at their disposal to estimate doubtful debts:

(1) *Specific provision*. This method would involve the solicitor reviewing the contents of the firm's Clients Ledger, for example, and selecting debts which may be difficult to collect. The size of the provision for doubtful debts at the end of the period will be the total figure derived from this process.

(2) *General provision*. It may be possible to estimate potential future bad debts on the basis of past experience. By examining the percentage of the debtors figures which at the end of previous years subsequently turned into bad debts, it could be possible to express the provision for doubtful debts for the present financial year as a percentage of the year-end debtors figure. For example, if a solicitor's client debtors totalled £5,000, and it has been found that around 10% of clients invoices are never paid, the provision for doubtful debts could be calculated thus: £5,000 × 10% = £500. The percentage figure being applied (in this case 10%) can itself be adjusted each year to take into account factors such as the general economic climate prevailing at the time, the level of local economic activity, etc.

(3) The third method involves the solicitor reviewing all debtors and categorising them on the basis of the length of time for which they have been outstanding. After that an appropriate percentage figure would be applied to each category to highlight the level of potential bad debts. The overall provision for doubtful debts for the firm is found by totalling the likely bad debts in each category.

Accounting for a provision for doubtful debts

Once the solicitor has quantified the extent of the year-end debtors figure which is in doubt, it will be necessary to incorporate the level of the provision into the firm's records. This can be done as follows:

(1) In the financial year in which the provision for doubtful debts is first established:

	£
DR The Profit and Loss	with the full amount of the
CR The Provision for Doubtful Debts	provision

For example, Wolfson & Co (Solicitors) decided to set up a provision for doubtful debts at the end of its first year of business. An adequate provision was estimated at £1,500. The accounting entries to record this figure would be to *debit* the Profit and Loss account, £1,500, and to *credit* the Provision for Doubtful Debts account, £1,500.

When a provision for doubtful debts has been in existence for at least one prior accounting period, and:

(2) the provision is to be increased to reflect the fact that a greater amount of the outstanding debt is in doubt, the accounting entries will be:

	£
DR The Profit and Loss	with only the amount needed to bring the provision up to
CR The Provision for Doubtful Debts	its new higher level from its previous level

For example, at the end of Wolfson's second year, it was decided to increase the provision for doubtful debts to £2,500. The accounting entries required would be to *debit* the Profit and Loss account, £1,000, and to *credit* the Provision for Doubtful Debts account £1,000.

(3) if the provision is to be decreased at the end of the accounting period, the entries will be:

	£
DR The Provision for Doubtful Debts	with only the amount needed to bring the provision down
CR The Profit and Loss	from its previous level to the new lower level

For example, at the end of Wolfson's third year, in light of the firm's increased success rate in recovering debts, the provision for doubtful debts is to be reduced to £2,000. To achieve this, *debit* the Provision for Doubtful Debts account, £500 and *credit* the Profit and Loss account, £500.

In each of the above examples, at the end of each of Wolfson's financial years, the balance on the Provision for Doubtful Debts account should be stated in the relevant balance sheet.

ILLUSTRATION 5.2

	Notes	*Wolfson and Co, Solicitors* Balance Sheet (Extract) as at the:					
		(end of Year One)		*(end of Year Two)*		*(end of Year Three)*	
	Notes	£	£	£	£	£	£
Current Assets							
Client debtors	(1)	12,000		11,000		11,500	
less: Provision for Doubtful Debts	(2)	(*1,500*)	10,500	(*2,500*)	8,500	(*2,000*)	9,500

Explanatory Notes

(1) The client debtors balances at the end of the three years in question are simply assumed figures. Notwithstanding such assumptions, the figures will still be net of all known bad debts written off during the year to the Profit and Loss account.

(2) The figure shown under the heading of Provision for Doubtful Debts here will be the total balance standing at the credit of the Provision for Doubtful Debts account on the date the balance sheet is drawn up.

In summary, the Profit and Loss account of an entity will show the full extent of known bad debts written off during the period and it will also show any adjustment which has been made to the Provision for Doubtful Debts account (assuming one exists). The balance sheet, on the other hand, simply states the balances on the relevant accounts on a given date and shows the relationship between them.

It should be remembered that the control of the level of debtors is vitally important in a solicitor's business. Sound financial management of a practice demands tight control over debtors and this can only be achieved through regular checks on outstanding debts with appropriate follow-up action with respect to slow payers. All other things being equal, debtors tend to pay those creditors who pester them most[1]!

ACCRUED AND PREPAID EXPENSES

Other examples of accounting adjustments which are often necessary at the close of an accounting period in order to ensure the expenses incurred for that period are properly matched to revenue, are in relation to *prepaid* and *accrued expenses*. It is perhaps easiest to explain the nature and accounting treatment of prepaid and accrued expenses by way of short examples.

---

1 See Chapter 13 dealing with aspects of the financial control of a legal practice.

Prepaid expenses

ILLUSTRATION 5.3

J and A Boyce (Solicitors) prepare accounts to 31 December each year. The office is rented at a cost of £3,600 per annum. The rent is payable quarterly, in advance. The following payments were made in 1996:

Expense: Office Rent

Date of Payment	Amount £	To cover rental period
5.1.96	900	1.1.96–31.3.96
1.4.96	900	1.4.96–30.6.96
1.7.96	900	1.7.96–30.9.96
1.10.96	900	1.10.96–31.12.96
23.12.96	900	1.1.97–31.3.97

The Office Rent account would therefore appear as follows:

OFFICE RENT

1996		£	*1996*		£
5.1	Bank	900			
1.4	Bank	900			
1.7	Bank	900			
1.10	Bank	900			
23.12	Bank	900			

It is clear that the total rent due for the 1996 financial year (£3,600) has been paid by 1 October 1996 and it is this amount which should be transferred to the period's Profit and Loss account. The additional payment of £900 on 23 December 1996 relates to the following financial year and is, therefore, a prepaid expense (or payment in advance). An accounting adjustment should be made so that the reported profit level for the period to 31 December 1996 is not artificially depressed, as it would be if the balance at 31 December 1996 on the Office Rent account (that is, £4,500) was transferred to the period's Profit and Loss account.

One way to process the required adjustment is simply to *credit* the Office Rent account, £900 on 31 December 1996, and *debit* the same account on 1 January 1997 after the transfer of the correct figure to the Profit and Loss account. That is:

OFFICE RENT

1996		£	*1996*		£
5.1		900	31.12	Profit and Loss	3,600
1.4		900	31.12	Prepaid bal c/f	900
1.7		900			
1.10		900			
23.12		900			
		4,500			4,500
1997		£	*1997*		£
1.1	Prepaid bal b/f	900			

The prepaid office rent can properly be regarded as an asset. The balance sheet of J & A Boyce (Solicitors) would contain details of the prepaid expense within the Current Assets section of its balance sheet. It is usual for prepaid expenses to be included with, or shown immediately after, the debtors figure.

Accrued expenses

In direct contrast to prepaid expenses, accrued expenses are amounts which relate to a certain financial period but at the end of that period remain unpaid.

ILLUSTRATION 5.4

During 1996, J & A Boyce also leased a photocopier at an annual cost of £2,000. The actual cash paid for the photocopier during the year was £1,500, leaving a balance of £500 due but unpaid at 31 December 1996. The correct figure to be transferred as an expense to the period's Profit and Loss account is £2,000. The adjustment necessary to take the accrued expense of £500 into account is to *debit* the Photocopier Expense account, £500 on 31 December 1996, and to *credit* the same account on the first day of the new trading year, 1 January 1997:

Office Rent

1996		£	*1996*		£
5.5	Bank	500	31.12	Profit and Loss	2,000
8.9	Bank	750			
1.12	Bank	250			
31.12	Accrued bal c/f	500			
		2,000			2,000
1997			*1997*		
			1.1	Accrued bal b/f	500

The accrued photocopier expenses of £500 would appear in the Current Liabilities section of the firm's balance sheet as at 31 December 1996. It would be normal for the accrued expenses to be included with, or shown immediately after, the firm's creditors figure.

WORK IN PROGRESS

It is not difficult to imagine that the work of a solicitor does not naturally segment itself on the basis of the firm's accounting years. Legal cases and other transactions will inevitably straddle the date marking the end of the financial period. Work will have been done on behalf of clients, but because the solicitor has not been in a position to see the various matters through to completion, not all the invoices will have been dispatched to the clients involved. This can be termed *work in progress* (WIP).

It is a very subjective task to place a value on a firm's work in progress at any given point in time, however it is now required, for taxation purposes, that some attempt is made where such costs are material. The cost of a partner's time will not be included in the calculation since that is akin to an appropriation of profit[1]. If the firm has chargeable staff, that is fee earning employees, then some attempt must be made to allocate the *cost* of work done. Such costs (assuming they are in fact recoverable) would include a proportion of gross salaries, employer's national insurance, any pension contributions etc and direct expenses relating to the job, for example, search dues. It may be that some office costs (for example, secretary's time) could also be considered. These costs are effectively carried forward as work in progress to be matched against income in some future accounting period when the work is finally invoiced.

Basically, when a firm does include work in progress as part of its income computation, any increase in work in progress experienced over the financial period will be added to the value of the invoices actually rendered, whilst any reduction in work in progress will be deducted.

---

1 See chapter 7.

ILLUSTRATION 5.5

Clarke and Millar commenced business as a legal firm on 1 January 1996. Their partnership agreement states that work in progress (WIP) should be valued at the end of each accounting period. At the end of their first year, WIP was valued at £25,000. At the end of their second year, the valuation in respect of WIP stood at £20,000. Fees rendered to 31 December 1996 and to 31 December 1997 amounted to £100,000 in each case. The firm's total income for each year can be found thus:

Clarke and Millar, Solicitors
Profit and Loss Account (Extracts) for the year ending ....

31 December 1996

(i)		£	£
Fees Rendered			100,000
Add: Increase in Work in Progress			
Work in progress, 31.12.96		25,000	
less, work in progress, 1.1.96		NIL	25,000
			125,000

31 December 1997

(ii)		£	£
Fees Rendered			100,000
Less: Decrease in Work in Progress			
Work in progress, 31.12.97		20,000	
less: work in progress, 1.1.97		(25,000)	(5,000)
			95,000

It can be seen in each of the above years that the change in the level of WIP is found by deducting the opening WIP figure from the closing WIP figure.

It is possible to account for a firm's work in progress at the end of the financial period by *crediting* the Fees Rendered account with the value of the closing WIP thereby increasing the earnings of the period. The value of the closing WIP will also appear under Current Assets in the firm's Balance Sheet. The corresponding *debit* entry will be to the same account on the first day of the next trading period.

STOCK

The final accounting adjustment to be examined is in relation to *stock*. Solicitors' annual financial statements will make no mention of trading stock since lawyers simply do not buy goods for the purposes of resale. Nevertheless, the importance of this particular adjustment should never be underestimated, given its potential effect on the reported profitability and financial position of other businesses which do in fact trade in physical commodities.

For example, it was seen in the previous chapter that the opening and closing stock figures of a trading entity are important elements of the calculation of a period's gross profit[1]. That is, gross profit is found by deducting the cost of goods sold from the period's Sales figure, with the cost of goods sold being calculated, thus:

---

1   For example, see the I Peters and T Canyon illustrations contained in Chapter Three.

Cost of Goods Sold	£
Opening stock	x
Add: Purchases	x
	xx
Less: Closing stock	(x)
	x

It is not difficult to see how an over-valuation of a company's closing stock could improve its reported profit level for the period. By increasing the closing stock valuation, the cost of goods sold is reduced which in turn means that the reported gross profit is increased[1]. Furthermore, given that closing stock features as a Current Asset in the balance sheet, the same over-valuation could also affect the company's apparent financial position.

The closing stock figure is, therefore, a significant factor when determining how successful a trading enterprise has been over a period. Internal management are certainly aware of this fact as are external auditors, evidenced by their attendance at stock-counts, an event in the corporate calendar very seldom missed by them.

Nature of stock

In a trading organisation the term 'stock' can cover the tradable commodity in a variety of forms. For example, stock can comprise the following categories:

1 goods for resale held in a finished condition;
2 goods for resale held in a partially complete condition;
3 raw materials and components purchased for incorporation into products for resale.

In order for a company to ascertain the closing stock figure, a stock-count is necessary. Once the existence of stock, in whatever form, has been physically verified, the next step is to place a value on it.

Stock valuation methods

The generally accepted accounting practice with respect to the valuation of stock, is that it should be shown at the *lower of cost or net realisable value*[2].

(1) *Cost*

At its simplest, *cost* is what is paid for the goods to be resold. Statement of Standard Accounting Practice 9 (SSAP 9) goes further and defines cost as '... that expenditure which has been incurred in the normal course of business in bringing the product or service to its present location and condition'[3]. Ascertaining the cost price of stock can be a fairly difficult process at the best of times, but more so in periods where prices have been fluctuating or where the nature of the business involves carrying a large

---

1 In contrast an under-valuation of closing stock would have the effect of reducing the reported gross profit from its 'true' level.
2 See *UK GAAP* (6th edn, 1999, Butterworths Tolley, Croydon), p 981.
3 Statement of Standard Accounting Practice 9, para 17.

quantity of stock items. The determination of the cost of stock in many situations becomes, therefore, reliant on methods of approximation.

There are several methods frequently used by trading organisations to calculate an approximate cost for stock:

Weighted Average—In this case, the cost of items held in stock is determined by reference to their average purchase price, with due allowance also being made with respect to the quantity of items purchased at each different buying price.

Fifo —'First in, first out'. The assumption here is that those goods purchased first are sold first. Thus, the stock remaining at the end of a period is assumed to consist of those items purchased most recently.

Lifo —'Last in, first out'. In contrast to the Fifo method above, the assumption here is that those goods bought last are the first to be sold. Closing stock is therefore regarded as consisting of items bought earliest.

ILLUSTRATION 5.6

A A Phillips was a trader who bought and sold a single product line. Over the course of the first trading week the following identical units of stock were bought and sold:

DAY	PURCHASES	SALES
One	100 units at £12.50 per unit	—
Three	400 units at £10 per unit	—
Four	—	100 units at £20 per unit

Required:

On the basis of the above information, calculate the value of Phillips' closing stock at the end of Day Five using the (a) Weighted Average (b) Fifo, and, (c) Lifo methods of stock valuation.

Solution:

(a)   *Weighted Average*

No. of Units Bought	Unit Price £	Total Price £
100	12.50	1,250
400	10.00	4,000
500		5,250

Average cost per unit £5,250 divided by 500 = £10.50

Value of closing stock at end of Day Five = 400 units @ £10.50 = £4,200

(b)   *Fifo*
Under this stock valuation method, the 100 units sold on Day Four are assumed to be the 100 units bought on Day One.

Value of closing stock at end of Day Five = 400 units @ £10   = £4,000

(c)   *Lifo*
Applying the Lifo method implies that the 100 units sold came from those bought on Day Three.

Value of closing stock at end of Day Five = 100 units @ £12.50 =   1,250
plus 300 units @ £10.00 =   3,000
£4,250

It is clear from the above example that the cost price of closing stock is affected by the valuation method used. Once the most appropriate method for determining the cost of stock has been selected by the company, it should be applied consistently within the business from one year to the next.

(ii) *Net realisable value*

After an estimate has been obtained for the cost of the closing stock, the next step under SSAP 9 is to compare this figure with the *net realisable value* of the stock concerned. 'Net realisable value' can be defined as '... actual or estimated selling price *less* any further costs necessary to complete the product together with all costs to be incurred in marketing, selling and distribution'[1].

Examples of situations where the net realisable value might be less than cost would include the following:

(1) where stocks held in store have physically deteriorated or become obsolete;
(2) where the selling price of the product has fallen significantly;
(3) where the organisation has taken the decision to deliberately sell products at a loss for a period of time as part of some overall marketing strategy;
(4) where there have been costly mistakes in either purchasing or in the manufacturing of the product.

By selecting the lower of cost or net realisable value for the stock figure, the business is actively applying the concept of Prudence.

Accounting for stock

Once the stock valuation figure has been determined, the next step is to incorporate it into the accounting records. Again this is perhaps best explained by way of an example.

ILLUSTRATION 5.7

Kelvin Kling started a small trading business on 1 January 1996. His financial year end is 31 December. The following details of the business have been made available:

		£
(a)	*Year to 31 December 1996*	
	Purchases	25,000
	Sales	40,000
	Opening stock	—

Closing stock has been valued on 31 December 1996 at £2,500.

		£
(b)	*Year to 31 December 1997*	
	Purchases	30,000
	Sales	50,000
	Opening stock (being the previous year's closing stock)	2,500

The closing stock figure at 31 December 1997 was estimated at £3,500.

---

1 SSAP 9, para 21.

Required:

Explain the accounting entries necessary at the end of the 1996 and 1997 years in relation to the items mentioned above.

Suggested Solution:

1996

(1)   The balances on the Purchases account and the Sales account would be transferred over to the period's Trading account so clearing off both of the former accounts, ready to begin the next financial year. That is:

    (a)   *DR*   Sales   £40,000

               CR   Trading   £40,000

    (b)   *DR*   Trading   £25,000

               CR   Purchases   £25,000

(2)   The value of the closing stock has been stated at £2,500. To bring this figure into the accounts:

        DR   Stock   £2,500

            CR   Trading   £2,500

(3)   The Stock account should thereafter be balanced off, with the closing balance of £2,500 in 1996 being brought down into 1997 as the opening stock figure for that year. The Stock account would appear thus:

STOCK ACCOUNT

1996		£	1996		£
31.12	Trading a/c	2,500	31.12	Bal c/f	2,500
1997					
1.1	Bal b/f	2,500			

(4)   The Trading account on 31 December 1996 would appear, therefore:

TRADING ACCOUNT

1996		£	1996		£
31.12	Purchases	5,000	31.12	Sales	40,000
			31.12	Stock (closing)	2,500

1997

(1)   The value of the stock brought forward in the Stock account from 1996 (ie the opening stock on 1 January 1997) was £2,500. This amount should be transferred to the period's Trading account:

        DR   Trading   £2,500

            CR   Stock   £2,500

(2)   The treatment of the Purchases and Sales accounts should follow the same pattern as at the end of the previous financial year. That is,

    (a)   *DR*   Sales   £50,000

                CR   Trading   £50,000

    (b)   *DR*   Trading   £30,000

                CR   Purchases   £30,000

(3)   The closing stock is valued at £3,500 on 31 December 1997. Once more, to bring this figure into the records:

        DR   Stock   £3,500

            CR   Trading   £3,500

(4)   The Stock account at the end of 1997 would now appear:

STOCK ACCOUNT

1997		£	1997		£
1.1	Bal b/f	2,500	31.12	Trading a/c	2,500
31.12	Trading a/c	3,500	31.12	Bal c/f	3,500
		6,000			6,000

1998		
1.1	Bal b/f	3,500

(5)   The Trading account, once more in its 'raw' form, would appear:

TRADING ACCOUNT

1997		£	1997		£
31.12	Stock (opening)	2,500	31.12	Sales	50,000
31.12	Purchases	30,000	31.12	Stock (closing)	3,500

The balance on this account at the end of 1997 represents the gross profit for the year (in this case £21,000) which would be transferred over to the period's Profit and Loss account.

It is possible to re-organise the Trading account as it appears above into the format more familiar to users of accounting statements as follows:

Kelvin Kling
Trading account for the period to 31 December 1997

	£	£
Sales		50,000
Less: Cost of Goods Sold		
Opening stock, 1.1.97	2,500	
Add: Purchases	30,000	
	32,500	
Less: Closing stock, 31.12.97	(3,500)	
		(29,000)
Gross Profit		21,000

The Trading account for 1996 could also have been shown in a similar format, although it would obviously not have contained an Opening Stock figure.

Accounting adjustments of the nature examined here are carried out at the end of a financial period in order that the expenses of that period are properly matched with the revenues which have been generated. Some time was spent looking at the entries associated with each type of adjustment primarily to give the reader an adequate background of the various items which will eventually appear in the final accounting statements of a business.

In the normal course of events, it would be usual for the trial balance to be extracted from the books and records of an organisation and, thereafter, for the necessary accounting adjustments to be carried out. The adjustments must be completed before the Trading and Profit and Loss account and the Balance Sheet can be properly prepared.

THE EXTENDED TRIAL BALANCE

It is common practice for those involved in drafting final accounting statements to use an *extended trial balance* or *worksheet*. This approach involves having a single working document which, ultimately, provides the figures to be used in the period's

Trading and Profit and Loss account and Balance Sheet. The basic layout of an extended trial balance is as follows:

EXTENDED TRIAL BALANCE

Account Name	Trial Balance DR CR £ £	Adjustments DR CR £ £	Trading A/C DR CR £ £	Profit and Loss A/C DR CR £ £	Balance Sheet DR CR £ £

The simplest way to explain the workings of an extended trial balance is by illustration.

ILLUSTRATION 5.8

The trial balance of Nick Casio, general trader, on 30 June 1996 appears as follows:

Trial Balance as at 30 June 1996

	DR £	CR £
Shop fixtures & fittings, at cost	70,000	
Truck, at cost	52,500	
Accumulated depreciation: shop fixtures & fittings		14,000
: truck		26,250
Capital		271,500
Bank	5,250	
Trade debtors	17,150	
Trade creditors		12,250
Stock, at 1.7.95	175,000	
Sales		691,250
Purchases	601,650	
Wages and salaries	52,500	
Telephone	1,750	
Rates	10,500	
Bad debts	350	
Provision for doubtful debts		1,400
Proprietor's drawings	30,000	
	1,016,650	1,016,650

Notes:

(a)   It is Casio's policy to depreciate shop fixtures and fittings at 10% per annum, and the truck at 25% per annum. The straight-line method of depreciation is used in both cases.
(b)   Casio has decided to increase the provision for doubtful debts to £1,715.
(c)   Salaries due but unpaid at the financial year end of 30 June 1996 were £8,750. Furthermore, a charge of £385 in respect of telephone calls was also outstanding at this date.
(d)   Casio has paid £875 for rates in advance in respect of the next financial year.
(e)   The closing stock at 30 June 1996 was £210,000.

Required:

Prepare the final accounts of Nick Casio for the year to 30 June 1996 after having first drafted an appropriate accounting worksheet.

Suggested solution:

Nick Casio, General Trader Worksheet	Trial Balance DR £	Trial Balance CR £	Adjustments DR £	Adjustments CR £	Trading Account DR £	Trading Account CR £	P + L Account DR £	P + L Account CR £	Balance Sheet DR £	Balance Sheet CR £
Shop fixtures & fittings, at cost	70,000								70,000	
Truck, at cost	52,500								52,500	
Accumulated depreciation										
: shop fixtures & fittings		14,000		7,000(i)						21,000
: truck		26,250		13,125(ii)						39,375
Capital		271,500								271,500
Bank	5,250								5,250	
Trade debtors	17,150								17,150	
Trade creditors		12,250								12,250
Stock, at 1.7.95	175,000				175,000					
Sales		691,250				691,250				
Purchases	601,650				601,650					
Wages and Salaries	52,500		8,750(iv)				61,250			
Telephone	1,750		385(v)				2,135			
Rates	10,500			875(vi)			9,625			
Bad debts	350						350			
Provision for doubtful debts		1,400		315(iii)						1,715
Proprietor's drawings	30,000								30,000	
	1,016,650	1,016,650								
Depreciation expense, shop fixtures & fittings			7,000(i)				7,000			
Depreciation expense, truck			13,125(ii)				13,125			
Provision for doubtful debts			315(iii)				315			
Accrued expenses										
: salaries				8,750(iv)						8,750
: telephone				385(v)						385
Prepaid expenses : rates			875(vi)						875	
Stock 30.6.96 c/f			210,000(vii)						210,000	
Stock 30.6.96				210,000(vii)		210,000				
			240,450	240,450						
Gross Profit (balancing figure)					124,600(viii)			124,600(viii)		
					901,250	901,250				
Net Profit (balancing figure)							30,800(ix)			30,800(ix)
							124,600	124,600	385,775	385,775

The finished accounting statements of Nick Casio can now be more formerly drafted by using the information contained within the appropriate columns of the worksheet, as follows:

Nick Casio, General Trader
Trading, Profit and Loss Account for the year to 30 June 1996

	£	£	£
Sales			691,250
Less: Cost of Goods Sold			
Opening stock, 1.7.95		175,000	
Add: Purchases		601,650	
		776,650	
Less: Closing stock, 30.6.95		(210,000)	566,650
Gross profit			124,600
Less: Expenses			
Wages and salaries		61,250	
Telephone		2,135	
Rates		9,625	
Bad debts		350	
Increase in Provision for doubtful debts		315	
Depreciation: Shop fixtures and fittings	7,000		
Truck	13,125	20,125	
			93,800
Net profit for year			30,800

Nick Casio
Balance Sheet as at 30 June 1996

	Cost	Accumulated Depreciation	N.B.V.
	£	£	£
Fixed Assets			
Shop fixtures and fittings	70,000	21,000	49,000
Truck	52,500	39,375	13,125
	122,500	60,375	62,125
Current Assets			
Stock		210,000	
Trade debtors	17,150		
less: Provision for doubtful debts	(1,715)	15,435	
Prepaid expenses		875	
Bank		5,250	
		231,560	
Less: Current Liabilities			
Trade creditors		12,250	
Accrued expenses		9,135	
		(21,385)	
Net Current Assets			210,175
			272,300
Represented by			
Proprietor's Capital			271,500
Add: Profit for the year			30,800
			302,300
Less: Drawings			(30,000)
			272,300

Looking back at Casio's worksheet, the following comments can be made. First of all, the worksheet starts with the trial balance on 30 June 1996. Next, the notes relating to all the various year end accounting adjustments are considered. The entries necessary to effect the adjustments are posted to the various accounts (see the 'Adjustments' columns in the extended trial balance. Note that 'every debit has a corresponding credit'). Thereafter, the details contained in the 'Trial Balance' and 'Adjustments' columns are drawn off and placed in one of the remaining columns as appropriate. That is, to either the Dr or Cr columns in the Trading Account, Profit and Loss Account or Balance Sheet. The gross profit and net profit figures are the missing figures which serve to balance the relevant sets of columns.

Ultimately, final accounts consisting of a Trading and Profit and Loss Account together with a Balance Sheet, can be prepared in conventional format from the information contained in the latter columns of the worksheet. It would not normally be the case for the worksheet to be made available to the end users of accounting statements.

QUESTIONS[1]

1.   Wilson and Wilson is a legal practice which has been in existence for many years. The partners plan to retire in the near future and, as a result, the business is

1   For suggested solutions see p 287.

gradually being wound down. Upon a recent review of the firm's Client Ledger, the following client debtors were evident:

CLIENT NAME	BALANCE £
Chalmers Frozen Foods Ltd	2,650 (DR)
Mrs R Patton	360 (DR)
K & C Development Ltd	8,750 (DR)
F Staedtler	400 (DR)
TOTAL DEBTORS BALANCES	12,160

The senior partner has decided that the monies owed by F Staedtler (£400) and Mrs R Patton (£360) are irrecoverable and consequently that both should now be written off as bad debts.

Required:

   (i)   Describe the accounting entries necessary in the books of Wilson and Wilson to record the debts being written off.

  (ii)   State the figure which would be shown in the relevant period's Profit and Loss account in respect of bad debts written off during the year.

 (iii)   State the Client debtors figure which would appear in the Current Assets section of the firm's balance sheet drawn up on the last day of the financial year.

2.   Leggatt and Company are a firm of solicitors that began in business on 1 July 1996. The firm's financial year end is 30 June. The following information has been extracted from the firm's trial balance drawn up on the 30 June 1997:

Leggatt and Co
Trial balance extract as at 30 June 1997

	DR £	CR £
Bad debts written off	2,250	
Client debtors	24,650	

It has since been discovered that owing to an oversight by the cashier, no adjustment had been made in the accounts to write off a debt for £350 which was recognised as being irrecoverable earlier in the year. Furthermore, the partners have decided to establish a provision for doubtful debts. The provision is to be set at 5% of the closing balance on the Client debtors account at the end of each financial year.

Required:

State:

   (i)   the correct amount of bad debts written off to the firm's Profit and Loss account for the year to 30 June 1997;

  (ii)   the information that would appear in the same Profit and Loss account with respect to the provision for doubtful debts;

Finally:

 (iii)   provide a balance sheet extract as at 30 June 1997 showing the relevant details concerning the firm's Client debtors.

3. Assuming the same background information as in the preceding question, state:
    (i)   the appropriate details which would appear in Leggatt and Co's Profit and Loss account for the year to 30 June 1998 in each of the following alternative situations:

Year to 30 June 1998   £

    (a) Bad debts written off during the period   =   2,000
         Client debtors at period end   =   27,000
         Provision for doubtful debts (5% of £27,000)   =   1,350
    (b) Bad debts written off during the period   =   2,000
         Client debtors at period end   =   20,000
         Provision for doubtful debts (5% of £20,000)   =   1,000
    (c) Bad debts written off during the period   =   2,000
         Client debtors at period end   =   24,300
         Provision for doubtful debts (5% of £24,300)   =   1,215

    (ii) in each of the cases (a) to (c) above, provide a balance sheet extract showing all the relevant information.

4. An extract from the trial balance of Campbell N Kippoch (Solicitors) on the last day of their 1996 financial year appeared as follows:

Campbell N Kippoch (Solicitors)
Trial Balance as at 30 June 1996

	£	£
Office equipment, cost	17,500	
Office furniture and fittings, cost	12,000	
Motor vehicle, cost	11,000	
Accumulated depreciation—office equipment		2,650
—office furniture and fittings		1,800
—motor vehicle		3,000
Office rent	2,950	
Office rates	4,000	
Heating and lighting	1,750	
Office wages	38,200	
Vehicle running expenses	3,450	
etc, etc	....	....
	150,000	150,000

    Upon further examination it transpires that:
    (i)   Rent payable on the firm's office accommodation is paid quarterly in advance on 1 June, 1 September, 1 December and 1 March each year. The last payment of £750 made by Campbell N Kippoch on 1 June 1996 and included in the above trial balance, contains £500 which relates to the first two months of the next financial year.
    (ii) An invoice amounting to £800 in respect of office rates had been received prior to 30 June 1996, although its details had not been included in the records of the firm at the time when the trial balance was extracted. Office rates for the year to 30 June 1996 should be £4,800.

(iii) The last electricity bill paid by the firm was received at the beginning of May 1996. The partners have estimated that the value of electricity used by the firm, but for which no payment has yet been made, amounts to £125.

Required:

For each of the business expenses detailed in (i)–(iii) above, state the figure which should be shown in the firm's Profit and Loss account for the year to 30 June 1996. Furthermore, indicate the details which should also appear in the firm's balance sheet as of that date in relation to the above items.

5. The Office rent and rates account of P Squires (Solicitor) per the trial balance extracted on the final day of the firm's first financial year showed a debit balance of £3,600. However, no allowance had been made at that point in respect of the following:
    (i)   Rent paid in advance in respect of a subsequent financial year amounted to £425; and
    (ii) rates due but unpaid at the period end amounted to £300.

Required:

State the figure for Office rent and rates which would appear in P Squire's Profit and Loss account in respect of the first financial year. Furthermore, state what information would be shown in the firm's first balance sheet in relation to Office rent and rates.

6. Evans and Bevans set up their legal practice on 1 August 1996. It was agreed at the outset that the firm should consider the value of work in progress when drafting the final accounts at the end of each financial year. On 31 July 1997, the end of the first financial year, WIP was valued at £30,000. Fees actually invoiced to clients over the duration of the first year totalled £120,000.

    At the close of their second financial year, WIP was agreed at £32,500, with fees rendered for the year amounting to £125,000. The third financial year saw the figures standing at £28,000 and £130,000 respectively.

Required:

    (i)   Provide extracts from the firm's Profit and Loss accounts for its opening three years of business;
    (ii) State what information you would expect to see in Evans and Bevans' balance sheets at the end of each financial period in relation to fees rendered and/or WIP.

7. Assuming that a legal firm considers work in progress as part of its income calculations, explain the effect which an over-valuation of closing work in progress would have on the reported profitability and financial position of that business.

8. Condor (Plastics) Ltd began trading on 1 September 1996. The company's financial year end is 31 August. The following details of the business have been made available

    (a) *Year to 31 August 1997*   £
         Sales   100,000
         Purchases   75,000
         Trading stock, 1.9.96   NIL
         Trading stock (valuation), 31.8.97   15,000

    (b) *Year to 31 August 1998*   £
         Sales   125,000
         Purchases   85,000
         Trading stock, 1.9.97   15,000
         Trading stock (valuation), 31.8.98   20,000

Required:

Provide extracts from the company's Profit and Loss account and balance sheet so far as the information permits with respect to (a) and (b) above.

9. Describe the effects on the reported profitability and/or financial position of a company if the value of its closing stock at the end of a financial period is over/under estimated.

10. O B Knobe has been in practice as a solicitor for a number of years. Although the only qualified solicitor in the firm, O B Knobe employs a number of paralegal staff. The following information has been provided:

O B Knobe,
Trial Balance as at 30 June 1996

	Dr	Cr
	£	£
Office premises, at cost	144,000	
Office fixtures and fittings, at cost	35,140	
Motor vehicles, at cost	50,000	
Accumulated depreciation: Office premises		13,025
Office fixtures & fittings		17,116
Motor vehicles		13,550
Capital		128,274
Debtors	6,037	
Cash in hand	100	
Bank overdraft		29,123
Fees rendered		305,000
Work in progress, 1.7.95	33,970	
Postages	3,450	
Rates	12,000	
Insurance	4,625	

Office wages and salaries	107,084	
Staff travel expenses	12,100	
General expenses	15,000	
Telephone	8,000	
Heating and lighting	14,600	
Stationery	11,732	
Bank interest and charges	2,750	
Bad debts	5,000	
Drawings—O B Knobe	40,500	
	506,088	506,088

Notes:

(1) The firm depreciates its fixed assets on the following basis:

Office premises	— 5% charge per annum, reducing balance method
Office fixtures and fittings	— 15% charge per annum, straight line method
Motor vehicles	— 20% charge per annum, reducing balance method

(2) Knobe has estimated that the value of Work in Progress at 30 June 1996 is £29,500.

(3) In order that the final accounts of the business more accurately reflect the fortunes of the firm over the year to 30 June 1996, the following accounting adjustments are to be incorporated:

(a) A member of staff delayed lodging an expense claim in respect of travel over the months of May and June 1996. This expense, which remained unpaid at 30 June 1996, amounted to £150.

(b) A telephone bill for £450 arrived in the office on 7 July 1996. The invoice amounted to £450 and related to telephone charges for the month of June 1996.

(c) A rates bill was received at the end of May 1996 for the quarter ending 31 August 1996. The bill totalled £3,000 and was paid on 1 June 1996.

(d) £850 was paid by the firm during the year to 30 June 1996 relating to building insurance for the month of July 1996.

(4) Knobe has decided to establish a Provision for doubtful debts at a level equivalent to 5% of the year end debtors figure.

Required:

After first preparing an accounting worksheet, draft a Profit and Loss Account for the year to 30 June 1996 together with a balance sheet as at the same date.

[All calculations to the nearest £].

11. T Dimple, a solicitor in private practice specialising in employment law, has provided you with the firm's trial balance at 31 December 1996 together with a few notes. On the basis of this information, prepare a set of final accounts for T Dimple's practice for the year ended 31 December 1996. [All calculations to the nearest £. In this question there is no requirement to draft an accounting worksheet].

T Dimple, Solicitor
Trial Balance as at 31 December 1996

	Dr £	Cr £
Freehold office premises, at cost	99,650	
Office furniture and fittings, at cost	30,724	
Motor vehicles, at cost	28,500	
Provision for depreciation: Furniture and fittings		16,300
Motor vehicles		11,000
Client debtors	4,610	
Bank	23,645	
Cash in hand	186	
Capital—T Dimple		98,465
Drawings	24,000	
Creditors		5,250
Fees rendered		162,625
Commissions received		836
Work in progress, 1.1.96	21,300	
Office wages and salaries	50,531	
Heating and lighting	2,477	
Provision for bad debts		530
Rates	956	
Sundry office expenses	324	
Postage and telephone	1,488	
Stationery	1,300	
Insurance	860	
Bad debts written off	500	
Staff travel expenses	1,655	
Vehicle running costs	2,300	
	295,006	295,006

Notes:

(1) It is the firm's policy to depreciate its fixed assets, thus:

Office furniture and fittings:	10% per annum, reducing balance method
Motor vehicles:	25% per annum, reducing balance method
Freehold office premises:	no depreciation charge to be provided

(2) At the year end, rates on the office premises paid in advance in respect of the subsequent financial year amounted to £200.

(3) Insurance paid in advance, £160.

(4) Dimple checked the office electricity meters on 31 December 1996 and calculated that £300 worth of electricity had been used but remains unpaid.

(5) Upon a review of the debtors ledger, Dimple identifies a further bad debt of £150 which had not been considered prior to the date when the trial balance was prepared. Furthermore, Dimple believes that the Provision for bad debts should be set at a level equivalent to 5% of the year end Client debtors figure.

(6) An invoice in respect of repairs carried out on one of the firm's cars in November 1996, arrived in the office in mid-January 1997. The invoice was for £450.

(7) Dimple has valued closing Work in progress at £22,500 on 31 December 1996.

Chapter Six: Bank reconciliations

A solicitor's firm will use its cash book on a daily basis to record receipts and payments of money. It is standard practice to regularly compare the balance per the firm's cash book with the balance shown in the bank statement which has been received from its bank. Almost inevitably there will be two different figures involved, necessitating further work to ascertain the reasons for the apparent discrepancy existing between the two sets of records (that is, the firm's and the bank's). This process usually concludes in the preparation of a document called a *bank reconciliation statement*. The primary purpose of the statement is to provide a full explanation of any variance which exists.

Formal requirements exist which compel solicitors to perform bank reconciliations for not only their own firm but also in respect of the clients' funds that are under their control. When the number of transactions handled by a solicitor's firm over, say, a month is considered, it is not difficult to appreciate that it will be beneficial to adopt an efficient approach in the performance of this routine task.

PREPARING A BANK RECONCILIATION STATEMENT

In order to carry out a bank reconciliation, it is useful to regard the process as comprising four basic steps.

(1) The two records must be directly compared to reveal any differences. The contents of the firm's cash book will, therefore, be compared to the bank statement received from its bank.

(2) Any items appearing within the bank statement, which have so far been omitted by the firm from its own records for whatever reason, can be used to help update its cash book.

(3) Remaining differences should then be grouped together by reference to their general nature.

(4) A bank reconciliation statement should be prepared to prove that any difference between the balance on the bank statement on a given date and the balance per the firm's cash book on the same date can be fully explained.

The above process can be considered in more detail as follows.

(1) *Upon receipt of the bank statement from the bank, this document's contents should be compared with the information contained within the firm's cash book.*

On a practical level whilst carrying out this comparison, the opportunity should be taken to begin reducing the volume of data under consideration. So if an entry in the cash book is accurately reflected in the bank statement, the two figures can safely be ignored from that point on in the reconciliation process. Corresponding items in the cash book and bank statement should simply be physically ticked off as they are in need of no further scrutiny. As the comparison continues with an increasing number of corresponding items being matched, so the remaining data will be gradually reduced until only non-matching items remain.

(2)   *Any items appearing within the bank statement which have so far been omitted by the firm from its own records can be used to update its cash book.*

It is a relatively common occurrence for items to appear in a bank statement for which there appears to be no matching entry in the firm's own cash book. For example, this could be the effect of payment by *standing order* or *direct debit* being processed by the bank as the result of some prior instruction given by the firm. A standing order is where the bank has been given authority by a customer to make a regular payment on some stated future date(s) to a third party. A direct debit is much the same in effect, since money is withdrawn from the account in payment of a third party. In the case of payment by direct debit, however, the authority to make deductions from the bank account will have been granted directly to the third party concerned. Furthermore with respect to direct debits, in the event that the amount payable to the third party has to be changed, it will be the third party that has to take the necessary steps to have this done. In contrast where a creditor of the firm is paid via standing order, then it will be the firm that has to make any changes.

Other examples of deductions being made directly by the bank that may only become apparent when the bank statement is received by the firm, are bank interest and other charges which are levied from time to time by the bank.

It is not uncommon for income to be received and paid directly into the firm's bank account without its knowledge. For example, if clients settled an invoice by instructing their bank to pay the firm directly through the banking system rather than sending a cheque to the firm, then it may well be that the latter will only become aware of the *credit transfer* once its bank balance is checked. This may also be the case where investment income (interest, dividends received, etc) has been paid directly into the firm's account. It is also possible that the Legal Aid Board has made a direct payment to the firm's bank account.

In all of the cases above, it is quite feasible that the person responsible for writing up the firm's accounting records omitted the transactions at the time when they happened. Setting up a diary system to record regular payments or receipts as per any agreement with suppliers or customers will cut down this aspect of the reconciliation task. It also improves control of the firm's cash resources when cash flow is tight.

Another event that may be highlighted by comparison of the contents of the bank statement with the entries in the cash book can be the effect of a *dishonoured cheque*. If the firm had previously received a cheque in payment of an invoice from a client and the cheque failed to clear the banking system, the cheque will be dishonoured. The net effect of this means that the firm will not have the value of the cheque credited to its account at the bank.

A cheque could be dishonoured for several reasons. Sometimes a payment might have been countermanded (ie stopped by the person who sent the cheque), or it may simply be the result of an error on the face of the cheque (that is, if it was unsigned, or if the payment narrative did not match with the figures, etc). Alternatively, it may have been caused by insufficient funds being available to the person that sent the cheque to the firm, or it might even have been caused by the cheque becoming out of date (if a cheque is not lodged within six months of its date, then it can be considered stale by the banks in which case non-payment will be the result).

In the case of a dishonoured cheque, the firm will have to take appropriate remedial action which will probably involve first of all adjusting its records to reflect the true situation, then contacting its client to arrange for the outstanding debt to be settled by some other means. However, a point worth noting is that the bank statement may have once again been used as an aid to help ensure that the contents of the firm's records, and its cash book in particular, are fully up-to-date.

It is also possible that the comparison process will reveal an error either on the part of the bank or on that of the firm. In either case, the error should be corrected.

Once the cash book has been fully updated, this will produce one of the key figures that will be used later within the actual bank reconciliation statement itself (that is, the *adjusted* cash book balance).

Finally in this stage, it should be noted that all of the information used for the purpose of updating the cash book can again safely be ticked off and ignored for the remainder of the overall bank reconciliation process.

(3) *The remaining differences existing between the bank statement and the cash book should now be reviewed, with like items being grouped.*

In the normal course of events it is likely that the only discrepancies remaining between the cash book and the bank statement are the result of *timing differences*. Timing differences can occur in relation to payments as well as receipts and should be grouped accordingly when they are displayed in the bank reconciliation statement.

It is quite common for a cheque to take several days to complete its full life cycle, from the time it was originally drafted until the moment the relevant sum clears the banking system. If the firm sends a cheque in payment to a supplier after first making the relevant entries to its accounting records, there is likely to be at least a few days delay before the cheque completes its journey as confirmed by the value of the cheque being deducted from the firm's account at its bank. However, if the firm had received a bank statement in the intervening period (being after the transaction had been entered into its cash book but before the cheque has had sufficient time to clear the banking system) then this will of course give rise to a legitimate variance between the balances in the bank statement and in the cash book. This is an example of a timing difference on the payments side which has been caused by an *unpresented cheque*.

On the other hand, if the firm had received a cheque, made the relevant entry into its cash book and thereafter banked the cheque but only shortly after the bank had first extracted a statement detailing the firm's account, then this again will be an example of a timing difference but this time on the receipts side. The difference on this occasion is termed an *outstanding lodgement*. Outstanding lodgements can also be known as *late credits*. Another example of an outstanding lodgement could be seen where the bank's night safe had been used by the firm to lodge its cash receipts for the day. If the firm completed its cash book that day, including making an entry to show the cash being transferred to its bank, and if the bank had again run off a statement at the close of business that same day (being before the bank staff had been given the opportunity to count the cash and make the necessary credit to the firm's account), then once more a difference will be evident between the balance per the bank statement and the balance per the firm's cash book.

As mentioned earlier in this section, timing differences should be grouped together depending on whether they are unpresented cheques or outstanding lodgements. Once all items at variance between the bank statement and the cash book have been considered, all that remains will be to draft the actual bank reconciliation statement itself.

(4)   *Preparing the bank reconciliation statement*

The bank reconciliation statement is simply a document to show that the firm's balance per its bank statement equates to its balance per the cash book. It is not a part of the double entry system. A typical bank reconciliation statement can be drafted as follows.

ILLUSTRATION 6.1

Bank Reconciliation Statement as on 30 June 2000		
	£	£
1. Balance in hand as per bank statement		100
2. *Add:* Outstanding lodgements:		
Lodgement on 29/6/00	40	
Lodgement on 30/6/00	20	60
		160
3. *Less:* Unpresented cheques:		
Cheque No:		
136	35	
144	10	
145	50	(95)
4. Balance in hand per the cash book		65

The figures used above are purely for illustrative purposes.

Explanatory notes

(1)   The balance per the bank statement will normally be the final balance displayed in it. The starting point for the reconciliation statement will be the balance in hand on 30 June as per the bank statement, which in the above case is a favourable balance of £100.

(2)   All outstanding lodgements which have been omitted from the bank statement owing to timing will be listed, totalled and shown in the bank reconciliation statement. It can be seen that the effect of the outstanding lodgements will be to increase the balance in hand as per the bank statement.

(3)   As with outstanding lodgements, all unpresented cheques are listed, totalled and shown in the bank reconciliation statement. The effect of unpresented cheques, once considered, will be to reduce the balance in hand at the bank.

(4)   The final line is the end result of the arithmetical computation carried out within the bank reconciliation statement. This should also match the balance in the cash book once it has been bought up-to-date in light of all the information contained within the bank statement. In the event that the bank reconciliation statement fails to produce a figure identical to the (adjusted) cash book balance, then a review of work already done is the only option until such times as the desired result is achieved.

A SIMPLE WORKED EXAMPLE OF THE BANK RECONCILIATION PROCESS

The following worked example shows an extract of a cash book (bank columns) for the month of May, a bank statement received from the bank covering the same period and the bank reconciliation statement that has been prepared confirming all to be in order.

ILLUSTRATION 6.2

Bryden Graham & Co
Cash book extract, May 2000

DR			CR			
Date	*Narrative*	*(£)*	*Date*	*Narrative*	*Cheq.*	*(£)*
1 May	Bal b/f	1,000	4 May	D. Norman	0021	50
5 May	P. Lambert	25	8 May	Petty cash		10
9 May	J. Venglos	300	21 May	I. Greaves	0022	20
19 May	B. Scott	150	25 May	S. Byrne	0023	500
20 May	S. Lavery	175	" "	G. Gibson	0024	20
22 May	B. Simpson	250	29 May	T. Baird	0025	200
30 May	F. Ewing	400	30 May	BEQ Ltd.	0026	100
" "	D. Goodyear	200	31 May	R. MacDuff	0027	300
31 May	R. Smith	700	" "	Bal c/f		2,000
		3,200				3,200
1 June	Bal b/f	2,000				

Scottish National Bank
Bank statement: Bryden Graham & Co, 141 St James' Road, GLASGOW
Firms A/C No: 1

May		Dr (£)	Cr (£)	Balance (£)
1	Bal b/f			1,000 Cr
5			25	1,025 Cr
8	Cheque 0021	50		975 Cr
"		10		965 Cr
9			300	1,265 Cr
19			150	1,415 Cr
"	Direct debit	225		1,190 Cr
20			175	1,365 Cr
22			250	1,615 Cr
26	Cheque 0022	20		1,595 Cr
"	Cheque 0024	20		1,575 Cr
"	Standing order	75		1,500 Cr
30			300	1,800 Cr
"			200	2,000 Cr
31	Cheque 0025	200		1,800 Cr
June				
1	Bal b/f			1,800 Cr

Applying the four main steps to carrying out a bank reconciliation, (1) compare the two documents and mark off corresponding entries; (2) fully up-date the cash book; (3) group together remaining differences; and, (4) prepare the bank reconciliation statement, results in the following:

[**Note:** assume ticks and other symbols have been added by the person carrying out the reconciliation process.]

Bryden Graham & Co
Cash book extract, May 2000

DR			CR			
Date	Narrative	(£)	Date	Narrative	Cheq.	(£)
1 May	Bal b/f	1000✓	4 May	D. Norman	0021	50✓
5 May	P. Lambert	25✓	8 May	Petty cash		10✓
9 May	J. Venglos	300✓	21 May	I. Greaves	0022	20✓
19 May	B. Scott	150✓	25 May	S. Byrne	0023	500#
20 May	S. Lavery	175✓	" "	G. Gibson	0024	20✓
22 May	B. Simpson	250✓	29 May	T. Baird	0025	200✓
30 May	F. Ewing	400?✓	30 May	BEQ Ltd.	0026	100#
" "	D. Goodyear	200✓	31 May	R. MacDuff	0027	300#
31 May	R. Smith	700#	" "	Bal c/f		2,000
		3,200				3,200
1 June	Bal b/f	2,000	1 June	Insurances		225✓
			" "	Profession. Subs.		75✓
			" "	Error correction		100✓
			" "	Bal c/f		1,600
		2,000				2,000
1 June	Bal b/f	1,600				

Scottish National Bank
Bank statement: Bryden Graham & Co, 141 St James' Road, GLASGOW
Firm's A/C No: 1

		Dr (£)	Cr (£)	Balance (£)
May				
1	Bal b/f			✓1,000 Cr
5			25✓	1,025 Cr
8	Cheque 0021	50✓		975 Cr
"		10✓		965 Cr
9			300✓	1,265 Cr
19			150✓	1,415 Cr
"	Direct debit	225?✓		1,190 Cr
20			175✓	1,365 Cr
22			250✓	1,615 Cr
26	Cheque 0022	20✓		1,595 Cr
"	Cheque 0024	20✓		1,575 Cr
"	Standing order	75?✓		1,500 Cr
30			300?✓	1,800 Cr
"			200✓	2,000 Cr
31	Cheque 0025	200✓		1,800 Cr
June				
1	Bal b/f			1,800 Cr

It can be seen above that although most entries at the bank immediately corresponded with those in the cash book, a few items only matched once additional work was carried out in their respect.

For example, the receipt from F. Ewing on 30 May was originally entered in the cash book as £400 but upon checking the bank statement (and, it is assumed, the relevant back-up documentation) this was found to be a mistake, with the correct sum received being £300. An adjusting entry of £100 to the cash book (credit side) rectifies the situation[1].

---

1   Illustration 6.2 deliberately ignores corrective entries to the firm's records other than those made to the cash book. In a practical situation, all records that were incorrect must be amended. However, it is assumed in the case of the £300 received from F. Ewing that the sum was simply originally overstated in the cash book. The credit entry of £100 will be sufficient to correct that error.

For all such items, the procedure followed as part of the reconciliation process was first to highlight them with a question mark and then tick them off once any corrective action occurred. This practice can also be seen for the direct debit and standing order entries in the bank statement (dated 19 and 26 May respectively). Very often the bank statement will provide an abbreviation of the name of the organisation to which the payment has been made. This will assist the firm in writing up its own records by minimising the amount of background detective-work necessary to clarify the nature of any particular transaction. The direct debit of £225 and standing order of £75 in the example are assumed to be payments for insurance and professional subscriptions respectively and have been entered into the cash book accordingly.

The items labelled with a '#' in the cash book are timing differences which will be shown in the bank reconciliation statement along with the balance in hand on 1 June per the bank statement (ie £1,800) and as per the cash book (ie £1,600), thus:

ILLUSTRATION 6.2 (continued)

Bryden Graham & Co
Bank Reconciliation Statement as on 1 June 2000

	£	£
Balance in hand as per bank statement		1,800
Add: Outstanding lodgements		700
		2,500
Less: Unpresented cheques:		
Cheque No:		
0023	500	
0026	100	
0027	300	(900)
Balance in hand as per the cash book		1,600

The above statement clearly shows that the balance in hand figure per the bank statement can be fully reconciled with firm's (adjusted) cash book balance on a given date.

BANK RECONCILIATIONS: AN EXAMPLE OF GOOD BUSINESS PRACTICE

Firm's funds

Mistakes can happen anywhere, be it at the bank or in the firm's records. Carrying out routine checks like a bank reconciliation helps ensure that records are accurate and reliable. Performing a bank reconciliation on a regular basis is an essential task rather than just good practice[1].

Clients' funds

It is important to note that the Solicitors Accounts Rules specifically require solicitors to prepare, at no less than monthly intervals, a separate bank reconciliation

---

1   See Solicitors (Scotland) Accounts Rules 1977, secton 12(4).

statement in relation to clients funds. This document is then compared to another statement drawn up by the solicitor which contains a list of all balances due by the firm to its clients. A third statement is then prepared by the firm to show that the total figures as contained within the other two documents are fully reconcilable with one another. The Accounts Rules go on to specify that all of the aforementioned statements must be drafted on the same date and kept for a period of three years from that date[1].

In addition, if a legal firm handles investment funds on behalf of its clients, then the Accounts Rules set out similar procedures which must be followed with respect to such funds[2].

ADDITIONAL CONSIDERATIONS

For anyone inexperienced in the comparison of the contents of cash books and bank statements there are a few potential sources of confusion which may cause some difficulty until they are fully understood.

(1)   *Cash book debit balance = bank statement credit balance*

The fact that a positive cash in hand figure is displayed as a debit balance in the cash book but appears as a credit balance in the bank statement occasionally causes some angst. It should be borne in mind though that if a firm has physically deposited one of its assets (being money) at the bank for safekeeping, then logically the bank will have to show the full extent of its liability to that firm by means of a credit entry in its (the bank's) records. As far as the firm's records are concerned though, they will show the existence of an asset by carrying a debit balance in the relevant account which in this case will be in its cash book.

The opposite holds true as well. If a firm is in overdraft at the bank, the bank statement will display a debit balance to reflect the fact that it is the firm that owes it money. Consistent with this, the firm's cash book will have a credit balance given its liability to the bank.

(2)   *The arithmetical effects in the bank reconciliation statement of a closing debit balance in the bank statement*

In the Bryden Graham & Co bank reconciliation statement exhibited earlier (see **Illustration 6.2**), it can be seen that the value of the outstanding lodgement of £700 was added to the balance in hand per the bank statement. However, if the balance in hand per the bank statement had been an overdraft (ie a debit balance) of say, £1,900, then the effect of including the outstanding lodgments would have been to *reduce* the overdraft to £1,200. Care has to be taken when dealing with what is essentially a negative starting figure.

1   See Solicitors (Scotland) Accounts Rules 1997, section 13.
2   See Solicitors (Scotland) Accounts Rules 1997, section 14.

Similarly, caution should also be shown when considering the effects of unpresented cheques in the bank reconciliation statement. It should be noted that unpresented cheques will either reduce a positive bank balance, or increase an overdraft.

A short example may be useful at this point to illustrate the above points.

ILLUSTRATION 6.3

Keple and Hempie, Solicitors
Cash book (Extract), July 2000

DR			CR			
Date	*Narrative*	*(£)*	*Date*	*Narrative*	*Cheq.*	*(£)*
1 July	Bal b/f	200✓	15 July	J. Golding	017	400#
31 July	Cash	350#	20 July	F. Burns	018	75✓
" "	Bal c/f	150	23 July	A. Trusk	019	225✓
		700				700
			1 Aug	Bal b/f		150

National Bank of UK
Bank Statement: Keple and Hempie, 222 Union Street, Aberdeen
Firm's A/C: No 1

		Dr (£)	Cr (£)	Balance (£)
July				
1	Bal b/f			✓200 Cr
24	Cheque 018	75✓		✓125 Cr
29	Cheque 019	225✓		✓100 Dr
August				
1	Bal b/f			100 Dr

Keple and Hempie, Solicitors
Bank Reconciliation Statement as on 1 August 2000

	£
Overdraft per bank statement (Note: being a debit balance)	(100)
Add: Outstanding lodgement	350
	250
Less: Unpresented cheque no: 017	(400)
Deficit per cash book (Note: shown as a credit balance)	(150)

(3) *Other potential sources of confusion*

Another potential difficulty which may be encountered with respect to bank reconciliations is when the person preparing the actual bank reconciliation statement chooses to begin the statement with the balance in hand per the cash book (as adjusted) and ends with the balance in hand per the bank statement. Adopting this alternative approach to drafting a bank reconciliation statement is, of course, perfectly acceptable. Whichever of the two main alternative methods is chosen, consistency in its application would be one sure way of minimising unnecessary confusion both on the part of the person drafting the document and for those having to use it later.

Finally, on a different point, it is possible for some items used in the bank reconciliation process to appear in subsequent statements. For example, a particular unpresented cheque may have been listed in a bank reconciliation statement and if it has still not been presented by the time of the next bank reconciliation, it will have to be shown again and in successive statements until such times as the recipient of the cheque decides to bank it. Items of this nature can sometimes cause difficulty if overlooked as the bank reconciliation statement will not be able to reconcile the balances shown in the bank statement and firm's cash book.

PRACTICAL BANKING

If a business is to operate at its most efficient in terms of its banking practices, then it follows that it must be familiar with all the facilities that its bank offers and be able to use them as and when required. This is particularly true of a legal firm where, besides caring for its own funds, it often has stewardship over funds belonging to its clients. Inefficiencies within this aspect of the business can be expensive both in terms of wasted time on the part of the solicitor and in terms of failing to maximise the return on all sums banked.

On the latter point, the fact that many legal firms commonly handle reasonably significant sums of clients' money on a daily basis makes the firm attractive to banks as a customer. Solicitors should be aware of this, as it may well be an influential factor in negotiations with the bank when determining matters such as (a) the interest rates payable on the balance on the general clients account, or on the balance on the firm's own account if in surplus (or on its bank overdraft if not), or (b) the level of bank charges that will be applied. That stated, the solicitor would be advised to retain a wide perspective during negotiations and, in particular, bear in mind that a quality service from the bank could well be worth more to the firm over time than, say, an extra fraction of one per cent on the interest rate offered.

Present day information technology capabilities offer many advantages to the legal firm with respect to its banking practices. Using such technology it is now simple for a solicitor to check the extent of funds available on a daily basis. This is particularly important when one considers that a solicitor acting on behalf of a client must first ensure that cleared funds are available from that client before any transaction can be progressed on his or her behalf. If a solicitor issues a client account cheque where there are insufficient funds available to meet the commitment, then the solicitor will be in clear breach of the Solicitors Accounts Rules.

It is absolutely essential therefore for solicitors acting on behalf of clients to allow sufficient time for transfers from clients to clear the banking system before issuing a client account cheque to progress a particular transaction.

It is important to bear in mind that cheques may take anything from three to nine days to clear, depending on the nature of the issuing institution. A cheque may have been drawn by a client on the same branch as actually used by the legal firm, in which case it would be normal to expect clearance safely within three working days of lodgement. Alternatively the cheque may have originated abroad or be drawn upon a Building Society which in either case would mean a longer wait for cleared funds.

It is possible to request the firm's bank to specially present a cheque to the issuing branch. This speeds up the process involved, allowing earlier confirmation of cleared funds. Special presentation of a cheque means that it effectively by-passes the normal (and somewhat cumbersome) bank clearing house system since the firm's bank will post a cheque directly to the issuing branch on which it has been drawn before following this up with a telephone call to ensure the transfer of funds can be honoured.

Another way to reduce the time that it takes to obtain cleared funds is to make bank transfers electronically. Transfers via either Clearing House Automated Payment System (CHAPS) or Bankers Automated Clearance Service (BACS) are processed much quicker through the banking system. Electronic CHAPS transfers between banks are guaranteed to be completed during the same day as the instructions were issued (assuming that instructions were given to the bank prior to 2.30 pm that day). CHAPS transfers should not be regarded as instantaneous, however. BACS transfers allow immediate access to cleared funds.

Irrespective of the method adopted to transfer funds, be it by traditional cheque or via an electronic medium, it is again stressed that solicitors must ensure that they are in possession of cleared funds before placing reliance on the funds to progress a client transaction. Where the solicitor does not have a computer banking link then a telephone enquiry to the bank, in order to confirm whether funds have been cleared, will avoid error.

Finally, although it is advisable for the legal firm to be aware of the complete array of banking facilities available and to make full practical use of them as situations dictate, the fact should not be overlooked that these facilities will almost certainly be subject to bank charges. A solicitor should try to balance the economic cost of adopting particular banking practices against their benefits (either to the firm or to the clients, depending on whichever is the more appropriate in the circumstances) before selecting the most cost-effective solution. Where it is possible to legitimately pass on banking charges to clients then from the business perspective of the firm this should of course be done.

QUESTIONS[1]

1. Draft a bank reconciliation statement as on 1 August 2000 on behalf of Maguire Swanson & Co., Solicitors, from the following available information:
    Balance in hand per bank column of firm's cash book = £3,500
    Cheques issued to suppliers but still not appearing in the firm's bank statement:

Cheque No. 9801	£250
Cheque No. 9807	£1,150
Cheque No. 9809	£100

    Lodgements made by the firm which have not yet appeared in its bank statement:
    £950 cash
    cheques for £50 and £450
    Credit balance per the statement received from the firm's bank = £3,550.

2. The following information has been extracted from the firm's records by the cashier of F. Muldroch & Co. (Solicitors):
    (a) A cash lodgement of £850 was made by the firm at its bank's nightsafe. This sum, although entered correctly in the firm's cash book, does not yet appear in the latest bank statement.
    (b) Several cheques sent by the firm to suppliers have so far not been presented for payment by the recipients. Details of the cheques involved are:

---

1 For suggested solutions see p 297.

Cheque No.	Amount (£)
90445	750
90449	150
90452	650
90458	450

(c) The undernoted items appeared in the firm's bank statement but have not yet been recorded in its cash book:

   (i) A payment by standing order to Edinburgh City Council, £345.

   (ii) A direct debit to the firm's account for £455 in favour of Northern Insurances Ltd.

   (iii) A direct debit charge by Elite Cleaning Co. Ltd for £200.

   (iv) A further payment by standing order to G. Penman, Insurance Services Ltd, £250.

   (v) Credit transfers received directly by the firm's bank from the Scottish Legal Aid Board amounting to £4,250.

(d) The balance in hand per the firm's cash book (that is, the debit balance) prior to updating in light of the above information was £2,250. On the same date, the balance in hand (that is, the credit balance) per the bank statement was £6,400.

Required:

(a) Find the firm's revised cash book balance once all the relevant information above has been used to update it; and

(b) prepare a bank reconciliation statement to show that the balance in hand per the bank statement can be reconciled to the firm's adjusted cash book balance.

3. The following information has been extracted from the records of S & R Robertson, Solicitors, Dundee:

Cash Book Extract (bank columns only)
April 2000

Debit			Credit			
Date	*Description*	*£*	*Date*	*Description*	*Ch.No.*	*£*
1	Bal b/f	2,500	3	To cash		75
3	P. Mullins	5,450	"	I. Shaw	714	320
5	P. Neville	500	"	W. Prentice	715	415
6	R. Anderson	175	6	R. Watson	716	125
7	G. Mackay	855	7	D. McMillan	717	60
12	J. Robertson	1,450	9	A. Potts	718	15
15	R. Douglas	2,000	"	To cash		65
19	R. Keane	50	"	A. Watson	719	800
25	R. Russell	550	18	A. Swinburne	720	515
27	B. Whyte	190	"	Quik Clean Ltd	721	150
30	S. Dicks	350	25	M. Murdie	722	90
"	Cash	25	30	Bal c/f		11,465
		14,095				14,095

A copy of the firm's April bank statement follows:

Scotia Bank PLC
Inverurie Branch
S&R Robertson (solicitors), Dundass House, Leven Street, DUNDEE

April, 2000		Withdrawals Dr £	Pay-ins Cr £	Balance £
1	Bal b/f			2,500 CR
3		75		2,425 CR
"			5,450	7,875 CR
6			675	8,550 CR
7			855	9,405 CR
"	Cheq. 714	320		9,085 CR
"	Cheq. 716	125		8,960 CR
9		65		8,895 CR
11	Cheq. 718	15		8,880 CR
"	Cheq. 717	60		8,820 CR
"	Cheq. 719	800		8,020 CR
"	Giro credit: SLAB		2,500	10,520 CR
12			1,450	11,970 CR
"	DD: CGU Assur.	550		11,420 CR
"	DD: Keyplan Ltd	650		10,770 CR
15			2,000	12,770 CR
16	Bank interest		2	12,772 CR
"	Bank charges	200		12,572 CR
"	Giro credit: Divis receiv'd		325	12,897 CR
19			50	12,947 CR
23	Cheq. 720	515		12,432 CR
"	Cheq. 721	150		12,282 CR
25			550	12,832 CR
27			190	13,022 CR
May				
1	Bal b/f			13,022 CR

Required:

On the basis of the above information,
(a) determine the true cash book balance as carried forward into May, and
(b) draft a statement reconciling the balance in hand per the April bank statement to the revised cash book figure.

4. Prepare a bank reconciliation statement for Simpsons (Solicitors) as on 1 February 2000 after first adjusting the firm's cash book in light of the information contained within the January bank statement.

Cash Book (Extract)

January.

DR

Date	Narrative	(£)	Date	Narrative	Cheq.	(£)
1	Bal b/f	4,200	1	To cash		250
12	Dunbrooks Ltd	500	6	Browns	088	10,000
18	K. Charlton	750	"	Postages	089	55
22	A. Maguire	250	"	Travel	090	545
29	P. Cohen	400	19	To cash		300
31	G. Johns	2,000	24	Insurances	091	125
"	Bal c/f	3,625	31	N. Fleming	092	450
		11,725				11,725

February						
1			1	Bal b/f		3,625

Northern Bank Plc
Union Street Branch
S. Simpson, Solicitors, 111 Union Street, Aberdeen

		Dr £	Cr £	Balance £
January				
1	Opening bal b/f			4,200 Cr
"		250		3,950 Cr
12			500	4,450 Cr
"	Cheq. 0088	10,000		5,550 Dr
15	Cheq. 0089	55		5,605 Dr
19		300		5,905 Dr
22	Cheq. 0090	545		6,450 Dr
"			1,000	5,450 Dr
29			400	5,050 Dr
"	DD: Govans Security	500		5,550 Dr
"	Giro credit: Divis rec'd		850	4,700 Dr
31	Cheq. 0091	125		4,825 Dr
February				
1	Opening bal b/f			4,825 Dr

5. Further to the information given in Question 4, Simpsons had various transactions throughout the month of February resulting in its cash book and bank statement appearing thus:

Cash Book (Extract)

February

DR				CR			
Date	Narrative	(£)		Date	Narrative	Cheq.	(£)
1	J. Mulholland	4,800		1	Bal b/f		3,275
19	Tolbooths Ltd	800		4	To cash		200
"	A. Maguire	250		12	Travel		225
"	S. Simpson: Loan	1,500		14	To cash		240
"	B. Cummings	700		24	Insurance	093	125
28	G. Sylvestre	900		25	Postages	094	15
"	E. Walsh	45		28	Spot Clean	095	85
"	Cash	50		"	Bal c/f		4,880
		9,045					9,045

March
1   Bal b/f   4,880

Northern Bank Plc
Union Street Branch
S. Simpson, Solicitors, 111 Union Street, Aberdeen

		Dr £	Cr £	Balance £
February				
1	Opening bal b/f			4,825 Dr
"			2,000	2,825 Dr
"			4,800	1,975 Cr
4		200		1,775 Cr
14		225		1,550 Cr
"		240		1,310 Cr
19			800	2,110 Cr
"			250	2,360 Cr
"			1,500	3,860 Cr
"			700	4,560 Cr
26	Cheq. 093	125		4,435 Cr
28	Cheq. 094	15		4,420 Cr
"			50	4,470 Cr
"	DD: Govans Security	500		3,970 Cr
March				
1	Opening bal b/f			3,970 Cr

Required:

Complete the bank reconciliation process for Simpsons, Solicitors, as on 1 March by first making any necessary adjustments to the firm's cash book and thereafter by drafting a bank reconciliation statement.

Chapter Seven: Introduction to partnership accounting

PARTNERSHIPS AS BUSINESS ORGANISATIONS

A widely accepted definition of a partnership is the relationship '... which subsists between persons carrying on a business in common with a view to profit'[1]. Partnerships are commonly used forms of business organisation, especially among the professions like those of the solicitor, the architect, the surveyor, the dentist, the accountant, etc. They are also used as vehicles for trading organisations in the strict sense, although the fact that each partner generally has unlimited liability[2] for all partnership debts serves to restrict the number of trading concerns that adopt this business 'persona'.

Unlimited liability is an obvious drawback and the risk of loss should be carefully weighed against the benefits that operating as a partnership can bring before a decision in favour of a partnership structure is made. There are advantages in having such a status, including the fact that partnerships enjoy a higher degree of business privacy than limited companies since the latter have to accord with legislative disclosure requirements[3]. The costs of maintaining the business entity may also be considerably lower for a partnership than for a comparably sized limited company, given the need for companies to have their affairs regularly audited by professional accountants and to have fairly routine administrative matters formally documented and lodged with the Registrar of Companies[4]. Nevertheless, business losses falling on partners beyond the level of their capital contributions, possibly to the extent of personal bankruptcy, could far outweigh such advantages. Inherent business risk must always be carefully assessed to enable a rational conclusion to be drawn on the most appropriate organisational medium in the circumstances.

It should be stressed that the brief comparison above between the relative merits of corporate or partnership status is based on the traditional view of the latter type of business organisation. It is likely that in the near future a new form of limited liability partnership will be recognisable in law. If this happens and professional firms of accountants and solicitors, for example, choose to organise their business affairs in this way, there will almost certainly need to be sacrifice by practitioners in terms of some of the advantages they could normally expect when trading as a

---

1 See Partnership Act 1890, s 1(1).
2 In some situations however a partner may have limited liability. See Limited Partnerships Act 1907 and the later comments on the new form of limited liability partnerships.
3 See the various provisions contained within the Companies Acts.
4 This advantage may be lost to an extent in the case of legal partnerships. In certain respects, given that they are dealing with funds belonging to their clients, solicitors' practices are subjected to more onerous regulatory provisions than partnerships of other disciplines, resulting in greater costs being incurred by the former. See the 'Solicitors (Scotland) Accounts Rules 1997' and the 'Solicitors (Scotland) Accounts Certificate Rules 1997'. For example the advantage could be further eroded if a limited liability partnership was involved. See later.

partnership form, as outlined above. It follows that the distinction between the corporate and partnership form will not be as marked as at present.

An in-depth discussion of limited liability partnerships is considered outwith the scope of this book. Unless the contrary is stated, therefore, it should be assumed that any subsequent reference to partnership relates to the traditional partnership form[1].

The accounting requirements of a partnership basically stem from the need to produce information for use by the Inland Revenue and other regulatory authorities (such as HM Customs and Excise or professional bodies, like the Law Society of Scotland for solicitors) and the fact that periodic accounting statements are beneficial to the partners when attempting to ascertain how well, or how badly, their business is performing. The accepted format for accounting statements used by partnerships in this respect is the Profit and Loss account and Balance Sheet as indeed it is for sole traders/practitioners. However, the content of these statements is slightly different for partnerships and largely reflects the terms of the Partnership Agreement or, in the absence of such, the relevant sections of the Partnership Act 1890.

PARTNERSHIP AGREEMENTS

It is understandable that when people start a business together one of the prime concerns is to minimise costs. In the context of a partnership, especially where there is no legal requirement imposed on the partners to have their business affairs regulated by means of a formal partnership agreement, it could prove to be a false economy to neglect this aspect given the extent of private as well as business assets which will be placed at risk. The partnership agreement will act as the partnership rule book and will be a ready source of reference in the event of any dispute which may subsequently arise between partners. It can also help minimise the number of disputes, or even prevent them arising in the first place, with commensurate savings in partners' time and effort.

It is possible to consider the contents of partnership agreements by splitting items into those which have direct or indirect influences on partnership accounting and other more general matters which, although still important, are of slightly less significance in the present context. Focusing on the first of these categories, a factor of undoubted significance in any partnership agreement is the extent of each partner's capital contribution to the business.

Partner's capital contributions

The agreement should state the level of capital contribution expected from each partner at the inception of the business as well as addressing the matter at key points in the life of the partnership (for example when a new partner is admitted). Capital contributions could be in cash or in kind (for example where a partner introduces a motor vehicle to the business or even property as their share of capital).

---

1   For a useful review of the background to limited liability partnerships, reference should be made to the DTI publication, September 1998, 'Limited Liability Partnership Draft Bill, A Consultative Document'. Also see Charlotte Waelde and James Burrell, 'A New Era in Partnership Law' (1999) JLSS 27.

Consideration should also be given to the desired level of gearing of the business where external borrowing is compared with the partners' capital input. In professional partnerships, it would normally be expected that the base funding requirement including the working capital of the business should be met from the capital contributions of the partners involved, with a borrowing arrangement in place (for example, a bank overdraft) to smooth fluctuations in day-to-day income and expenditure. In youthful partnerships in particular, it may not be possible to achieve this objective from day one, although it should still be considered a target for the prudent firm.

If the desired gearing ratio is stated in the agreement, it follows that there should be guidance on the source of capital from each of the partners. A contribution from the partner's private funds is the favoured option, but given the costs of establishing a business in the early years, it is not difficult to imagine the situation where partners have to borrow to meet their share of the capital. In such circumstances, it is advisable that all partners are fully aware of the extent of such borrowing given that it would be in no-one's interest for one partner to get into personal financial difficulties given the potential knock-on effects to the firm. Hidden debt within the capital of a partnership is simply not good business practice. If borrowing above the desired level is inevitable, as it may well be in the case of a business start-up, then consideration should be given to whether the partnership as an entity does the borrowing or whether it should be left to individual partners, or even a combination of the two.

Partner's capital, current and drawings accounts

The level of capital contribution is recorded through the partner's Capital account. It is often the case that each partner has a fixed *Capital account* containing a static credit balance, together with a *Current account* which is used to record day-to-day transactions affecting the partner's claim on the business[1].

It is also commonly accepted practice for a *Drawings account* to be maintained for each partner. This account gathers together all of the withdrawals (either in cash or in kind) that a partner makes from the business during the year. The magnitude of partners' drawings permitted during any one financial year should be addressed by the partnership agreement. The limit will probably be calculated on the basis of the previous year's profit less an amount to provide a reasonable safety margin for any potential down-turn in business activity during the current year. A further sum may also be deducted to reflect a provision for income tax. Levels of partners' drawings are normally set at the beginning of each year with a revision after six months or so, once the true profits picture starts to form. At the accounting year end the balance on each partner's Drawings account should be transferred to the appropriate Current account to leave the former account clear to start another period.

The partnership agreement should also state whether or not *interest on partners' drawings* is to be levied by the partnership and, if so, the applicable rate, as well as what happens if partners exceed the level of permitted drawings and/or allow their capital contributions to fall below the required amount. On the matter of interest

---

1   See later section dealing with the division of Partnership Profits/Losses for examples of items which would be recorded through partners' Current accounts.

being charged on partners' drawings, it may be considered fair to discourage partners from taking their draw from partnership funds early in the financial year since it could adversely affect the firm's cash flows later on. Charging interest on drawings, from the date they occurred to the end of the financial period, is one way of regulating this activity. Any interest charges applied must be reasonable since the objective here is not to prevent drawings altogether, but rather to ensure partners draw funds at a sensible rate having due regard to the firm's cash flow position and the profitability of the business in general.

Finally in this area as an alternative to the combined use of a fixed Capital account, a Current account and a Drawings account, it is open to partners to maintain a single, *fluctuating Capital account* with this being used to record matters which would otherwise have been dealt with in one of the former accounts. The choice of which system to adopt belongs to the partners, but it should be borne in mind that if the latter option is chosen (that is, the fluctuating Capital account) then by restricting the number of accounts used to record a partner's relationship with the firm, there may well be a loss of clarity in the records.

Preparation of partnership accounts

Another matter which should be considered in partnership agreements concerns the actual preparation of the partnership accounts. The agreement should clearly state the accounting year end date; who is to prepare the accounting statements; the procedures to be adopted in certain specified situations (for example, when a new partner is admitted, or an old partner dies/retires, or if there is a change in the profit/loss sharing ratios among existing partners[1]) and it should clearly define key elements in the partnership accounts. In particular under the latter heading, income and the appropriation of partnership profits and losses need careful consideration.

Income and the appropriation of partnership profits and losses

Income

It is important that the existence of different sources of income is recognised in the partnership agreement and a fair basis established for the apportionment among partners of profits or losses from these sources. In defining the income of the firm, any gains/losses accruing upon changes in the value of partnership assets or liabilities (that is, capital profits or losses) and partners' private earnings (for example, from non-executive directorships, private commissions, etc) must be considered, as well as revenues which have been generated purely from the normal course of business. It is possible that what the partners regard as a fair basis for the share-out of profits from normal trading activities would be inappropriate for the distribution of a gain on, for example, the sale of office property. Similarly, if an individual partner generates income from work falling outside the umbrella of a normal partnership business, the agreement should regulate this in order that a partner knows when responsibility for declaring income to fellow partners ends and

---

1 The necessary accounting procedures are considered in detail later on. See Chapter 8.

when he or she can start to retain income free from partnership obligations. Perhaps the safest solution here would be for partners to regard all earnings as belonging to the partnership in the first instance. Exceptions would still have to be catered for in the agreement and common sense rules applied. For example, consider dividend income accruing to individual partners from the investment of their own money in quoted stocks and shares. In terms of fairness, and indeed practicality, this income should properly be regarded outwith the definition of income belonging to the firm.

Consideration must also be given to the basis for determining the fee income of the firm since a number of alternative accounting techniques exist. Fee income could be defined as the invoices rendered to clients in an accounting period including or excluding, as the case may be, a valuation in respect of work-in-progress (WIP). Alternatively, fee income might be restricted to include only the fees actually collected from clients. The basis most suitable in the circumstances should be selected and applied.

In terms of the business expenses which are to be off-set against income, the partnership agreement should again state the accounting basis to be used which, in turn, must be consistent with the one chosen to determine the firm's fee income. That is, should it be all expenses incurred (even if some/all have not been paid in the financial period in question) or, should it be only those expenses actually paid which are recognised as the relevant business expenditure to be matched to the income of the period?

The partnership agreement must address such issues at the outset and ensure their consistent application throughout the duration of the partnership. It is always possible to change the accounting bases adopted by a partnership so long as it would be fair and reasonable to do so. This, however, would be an infrequent occurrence and many partnerships will never have to make such alterations.

Appropriation of partnership profits and losses

As mentioned above, it is important for the partnership agreement to address the issue of the manner in which any resultant profit or loss of the firm is appropriated among its partners. The guiding light here must be that the system adopted should be fair and reasonable to all partners with individuals receiving just reward for their endeavours in the business. There are many factors which should be considered and if dissatisfaction among partners is to be avoided, it is important that a suitable blend of these be found and agreed upon by all concerned.

It was mentioned earlier in this chapter that a set of partnership accounts is slightly different in appearance from those of a sole trader or sole practitioner. One such difference can be seen in the Profit and Loss account. Once the net profit is calculated in a partnership, the amount is transferred into the *Appropriation account*. It is in this account that it is possible to see the allocation of the partnership profits, or losses for that matter, among the various partners.

Assuming that drawings are allowed by the partnership agreement, with partners being charged interest thereon, the sum of the interest charged levied against each partner will be shown in the Appropriation account.

Another issue which should be addressed is whether or not there should be an allowance for *interest on the capital contributions of the partners*. It follows that a decision may then be necessary on the rate of interest to be applied to capital balances. Assuming interest is to be permitted, it is suggested that a suitable rate would equate to that offered on a ninety-day building society account. Once the monetary value of the interest due to each partner has been calculated, the sum will be accounted for in the Appropriation account.

The next question which can arise is whether *salaries* should be paid to certain partners in return for their specialist knowledge, or their role in the management of the firm, etc. If a salary is payable, the agreement should either stipulate the amount involved or provide a mechanism for its proper calculation. A salary would be a preferential apportionment of partnership profits. Other examples of pay-outs of this nature could be commissions payable to certain key partners which are based on partnership profit levels or, alternatively, a guaranteed profit share which would be credited to a specified partner. The common factor in all such apportionments is that they would occur, in the normal course of events, before a general profits distribution to the partners.

Once provision for specific rewards has been made, the partnership agreement should stipulate *the basis on which the remaining profits or losses are to be shared out*. For illustration, in a three partner firm of A, B and C it could be agreed that any resultant profits are split in the proportions 1:2:3 respectively. In other words, A would get ⅙th, B ⅔ths and C ½ths of any profit. When such profit shares exist, consideration should be given to the relative rewards of the most senior to junior partner. In this example C (being the assumed senior partner) receives three times the profit share of A (the assumed junior partner) which could be regarded as an acceptable norm in the context of professional firms. The greater the gap between the earnings of the senior and junior partner, then the stronger the case for the introduction of some minimum profit share (expressed in monetary terms) for the 'poorer' partner. Indeed, it is possible that the partnership agreement could provide that junior partners will not be responsible for any losses in the first couple of years of their appointment, vis-à-vis other partners. Alternatively, the firm could have two sets of profit sharing ratios. That is, continuing with the above example, A, B and C might agree that profits up to £60,000 should be distributed on the basis of 1:2:3 respectively, and for the balance beyond this sum to be split equally.

Arguably it is in times of partnership losses when the minds of the individual partners are most focused on the basis of apportionment. In preparation for lean times, it would be wise for the agreement to provide guidance on the ranking of any preferential apportionments of profit. Decisions would have to be taken in advance, therefore, on matters such as whether or not there should be preferential apportionments to certain partners if there are insufficient profits to go round all of the partners in the firm and, if so, whether such apportionments should be allowed to create or exacerbate a loss situation. Again, the way in which apportionments are made among the partners must be fair to all concerned and stipulated in the partnership agreement.

It can be seen that this is a complex area, especially if one considers the changing real value of money. One way of simplifying the entire process is by using a *points based system*. Here, partnership profits/losses are shared among partners on the basis of the number of points each partner has in relation to the total points in issue. Partners acquire points as appropriate in the circumstances. They could be awarded additional points for such activities mentioned earlier which benefit the firm as a whole (that is, to reflect the input of specialist knowledge, management functions, etc). Partners might also gradually gain points for each year of partnership service, up to a certain limit.

The points based system can also be applied in what could be regarded as a negative sense. For example, once partners near retirement age, they could start to gradually lose points. The justification is to discourage old partners from staying with the firm beyond the stage where they actively contribute to the overall well-being of the firm.

The classic shape of an individual partner's points profile appears, therefore, as follows:

INDIVIDUAL PARTNER'S POINTS PROFILE

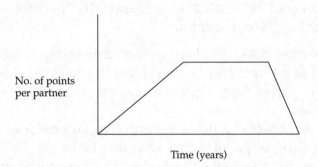

If the points system is to be used, adequate provisions to this effect must be incorporated into the partnership agreement at the outset.

OTHER MATTERS WITHIN A PARTNERSHIP AGREEMENT

Although each of the items so far considered will, in one way or another, affect the content of the partnership accounts there are of course other issues which should also be dealt with in the partnership agreement if this is to be a credible, working document. Matters such as the names of partners and that of the partnership itself, its place of business, the date of commencement (and dissolution, if the business has been established for a clearly definable period of time), details of expected standards of behaviour (both in a personal and business sense), procedures to be followed upon the onset of illness or disability of any of the partners, details of any binding agreements between partners which would persist after a partner leaves the firm (for example, restrictive covenants), details of non-profit making/charitable/public service activities in which a partner may become involved, the procedures to be followed in the event of internal disputes and so on, should all be directly addressed in the partnership agreement or at least have reference made to them and to how any problems evolving from them should be handled within the firm.

THE PARTNERSHIP ACT 1890

It will be self-evident by now that the use of a formal partnership agreement is strongly recommended to govern the affairs of this type of business entity. The principal legislation which regulates partnerships is the Partnership Act 1890 and it is the provisions of this Act which will be applied in the absence of any agreement to the contrary, be it formal or informal. The section of the 1890 Act of most relevance to partnership accounts is section 24. This section provides, inter alia, that when no agreement to the contrary exists among partners the following will apply:

(1)   all profits or losses will be shared equally;
(2)   no salaries will be payable to any partners;
(3)   no interest will be charged on partners' drawings;
(4)   no interest will be given on partners' capital contributions;
(5)   if a partner subscribes finance in addition to his agreed capital contribution, this additional sum will be treated as a loan to the partnership and will attract interest at a rate of 5% per annum.

In the event of a partner making a loan to the partnership firm, the interest will be charged to the period's Profit and Loss account in the same way as a loan from an independent third party. Such interest payments would *not* appear in the Appropriation account.

The Partnership Act itself should be regarded as compulsory reading for anyone involved in the drafting of partnership agreements, be they solicitors acting in an advisory capacity on behalf of clients (the contrary would be unthinkable) or even the contracting parties themselves, who will in all probability be laymen to the discipline of law, if for no other reason than to serve as a useful checklist for items that should be considered before individuals bind themselves together in a partnership.

PARTNERSHIP ACCOUNTING STATEMENTS

The accounting statements of any partnership must highlight its financial performance over an accounting period and show its financial position at the end of any such period. The statements should also reflect the business relationships existing among partners. As mentioned earlier, the actual layout of a set of partnership accounting statements is similar to that of the sole trader and is as follows:

ILLUSTRATION 7.1

Simple Partnership Accounting Statements of a Trading Firm

A. B. C. Partnership, General Traders
Trading and Profit and Loss Account for the year ended
31 December 1999

	£	£
Sales		X
Less: Cost of Goods Sold		
Opening Stock at 1.1.99	X	
Add: Purchases	X	
	X	
Less: Stock at 31.12.99	(X)	
		(X)
GROSS PROFIT		X

Less: Expenses				
Rent and Rates		X		
Heating and Lighting		X		
Wages and Salaries		X		
Interest and Bank Charges		X		
Motor Vehicle Expenses		X		
Printing and Stationery		X		
Salesmen's Commission		X		
Telephone Charges		X		
Depreciation Charges—on Motor Vehicles	X			
—on Fixtures and Fittings	X	X		(X)
NET PROFIT				*X

	A	B	C	
Appropriated Thus				
Partners' salary—	X	–	–	X
Interest on Partners' Capital—	X	X	X	X
Less: Interest Charged on Drawings	(X)	(X)	(X)	(X)
Share of Profits:	X	X	X	X
Appropriated profits for the period	X	X	X	*X

Note: Figures denoted * will be the same.

A. B. C. Partnership, General Traders
Balance Sheet as at 31 December 1999

	Notes	Cost £	Accumulated Depreciation £	NBV £
Fixed Assets				
Motor Vehicles		X	X	X
Fixtures and Fittings		X	X	X
		X	X	X
Current Assets				
Stock			X	
Trade Debtors			X	
Prepaid Expenses			X	
Bank			X	
Cash in hand			X	
			X	
Current Liabilities				
Trade Creditors			X	
Accrued expenses			X	
			(X)	
Net Current Assets				X
				*X
Represented by:		A	B	C
Partners' Capital Accounts:		X	X	X	X
Partners' Current Accounts:		X	X	X	X
		X	X	X	*X

Note:

(1) It would be usual to supplement the information given in the Balance Sheet by showing the movements which have occurred in the partners' current accounts over the accounting period. This can be done as follows:

Movements in Partners' Current Accounts

	A £	B £	C £
Balance at 1.1.99	X	X	X
Add: Appropriations of Profit for the Period	X	X	X
	X	X	X
Less: Drawings	(X)	(X)	(X)
Balance at 31.12.99	X	X	X

(2) Figures denoted * in the balance sheet will be the same.

In terms of professional partnerships (architects, surveyors, etc) the main difference in their accounting statements, in contrast to the above example of a trading firm's statements would be the absence of a Trading Account. Fee income would be shown instead, with the rest of the Profit and Loss and Appropriation Account flowing from there. In cases where the partnership is a firm of solicitors, the Balance Sheet of such a business would clearly show, separately, details of any funds held on behalf of its clients.

ILLUSTRATION 7.2

Illustration of the Accounting Statements of a Solicitors' Firm

Mrs. A. Jefferson and Mr. P. McEnroy are in partnership as solicitors. The firm of Jefferson McEnroy & Co. has its financial year from 1 January to 31 December each year. The partners of the firm have asked you, as their adviser on financial matters, to prepare a Profit and Loss Account and an Appropriation Account for the period ended 31 December 1999 together with a Balance Sheet as at that date. The following information has been provided:

Jefferson, McEnroy & Co., Solicitors
Trial Balance as at 31 December 1999

	£	£
Partners' Capital Accounts, 1.1.99— A. Jefferson		90,000
P. McEnroy		44,000
Partners' Current Accounts, 1.1.99—A. Jefferson	6,540	
P. McEnroy	3,686	
Partners' Drawings—A. Jefferson	20,000	
P. McEnroy	20,000	
Firm's Bank (Overdraft)		36,296
Cash in Hand	100	
Clients Bank—On current account	46,854	
On deposit receipt	329,000	
Client's ledger		362,414
Fees rendered		334,420
Work in progress (incl. fees not yet rendered) at 1.1.99	34,320	
Offices premises—Cost	172,000	
—Accumulated depreciation to 1.1.99		19,732
Office furniture & fittings—Cost	57,140	
—Accumulated depreciation to 1.1.99		22,856
Office wages & salaries	161,572	
Rates & insurance	16,250	
Stationery	11,432	
Sundry expenses	9,256	
Telephone & postages	15,068	
Bank Interest and charges	6,500	
	909,718	909,718

Notes

(1) Depreciation is to be provided on fixed assets as follows:
Office Premises = 3% per annum reducing balance method.
Office Furniture & Fittings = 20% per annum straight line method.

(2) Work-in-progress (WIP) (incl fees not yet rendered) at 31 December 1999 was valued by the partners at £30,800. The partners have agreed that a valuation in respect of WIP should be included in the firm's financial statements.

(3) From a review of the firm's partnership agreement you find the following details which should be taken into account:
(a) Profits/losses to be shared equally between A. Jefferson and P. McEnroy.
(b) Partners' Capital Account balances at the beginning of the year to attract interest at a rate of 5% per annum;
(c) Mrs. Jefferson to receive a salary of £20,000 per annum.
(d) The drawings made by the partners over the course of the year (£20,000 each) are not subject to interest charges.

(4) Upon examination of the Clients' Ledger it was evident that total credit balances amounted to £372,846 and total debit balances £10,432. Included in the list of debit balances was an amount for £420, being outlays on behalf of a client. Both partners have agreed to write this amount off given that the debt is considered irrecoverable.

(5) Accounting adjustments should also be made to reflect the following:
(a) Insurance premiums amounting to £3,000 have been paid in advance.
The premiums are for insurance cover on the office premises until 30 May 2000.
(b) A telephone bill was received after the year end amounting to £4,926. It related to the three months to the end of February 2000, and included charges for calls and faxes to Europe where the firm was hoping to establish a branch network.

Jefferson McEnroy & Co.
Solicitors
Profit and Loss Account for the Year to 31 December 1999

	£	£
Fees rendered	334,420	
Add: Work in Progress at 31.12.99	30,800	
	365,220	
Less: Work in Progress at 1.1.99	(34,320)	
		330,900
Less: Expenses		
Office wages & salaries	161,572	
Rates and insurance	13,250	
Stationery	11,432	
Sundry expenses	9,256	
Telephone & postages	16,710	
Bank Interest and charges	6,500	
Bad debts w/o	420	
Depreciation—office premises	4,568	
—office furniture & fittings	11,428	15,996
		(235,136)
Net Profit		95,764

Appropriated thus:

	A. Jefferson £	P. McEnroy £	Total £
Salary	20,000	–	20,000
Interest on Capital	4,500	2,200	6,700
Share of Profit	34,532	34,532	69,064
	59,032	36,732	95,764

Jefferson McEnroy & Co.
Solicitors
Balance Sheet as at 31st December 1999

	Cost £	Acc. Depn. £	NBV £
Fixed Assets			
Office premises	172,000	24,300	147,700
Office furniture & fittings	57,140	34,284	22,856
	229,140	58,584	170,556
Current Assets			
Work in progress at 31.12.99		30,800	
Client debtors		10,012	
Client's bank—on cur a/c	46,854		
—on dep recpt.	329,000	375,854	
Cash in hand		100	
Prepaid expenses		3,000	
		419,766	
Less: Current Liabilities			
Client creditors (Note 1)		372,846	
Firm's bank		36,296	
Accrued expenses		1,642	
		(410,784)	
Net Current Assets			8,982
			179,538

Represented by:

	A. Jefferson £	P. McEnroy £	Total £
Capital Accounts	90,000	44,000	134,000
Current Accounts (Note 2)	32,492	13,046	45,538
	122,492	57,046	179,538

Notes to the accounts

Note 1: Clients Funds[1]

	£
Funds held on behalf of Clients	
—on current account	46,854
—on deposit receipt	329,000
	375,854
Less: Total of Clients' credit balances	(372,846)
Amount over-deposited in Clients' Account	3,008

Note 2: Partners' Current Accounts

	A. Jefferson £	P. McEnroy £	Total £
Opening balance 1.1.99*	(6,540)	(3,686)	(10,226)
Add: Salary	20,000	–	20,000
Interest on capital	4,500	2,200	6,700
Profit Share	34,532	34,532	69,064
	52,492	33,046	85,538
Less: Drawings	(20,000)	(20,000)	(40,000)
Balance at 31.12.99	32,492	13,046	45,538

* In this particular illustration the opening balance on each of the partners' current accounts was a debit balance. Hence the negative figures of £6,540 and £3,686 for Jefferson and McEnroy respectively as at 1 January 1999.

1 See the Solicitors (Scotland) Accounts Rules 1997, rule 4 (1) (a).

QUESTIONS[1]

1. Annan and Wyllie are in a trading partnership. They share profits in the ratio A:60%; W:40%. They have agreed that partnership accounts be drawn up as at 30 April each year. At 30 April 19-3 the following trial balance was extracted:

		Dr £	Cr £
Buildings		50,000	
Office Equipment at cost		7,500	
Motor Vehicles at cost		15,000	
Depreciation provision at 1.5.-2:			
Buildings			7,000
Office Equipment			2,250
Motor Vehicles			9,375
Stock at 1.5.-2		31,420	
Debtors		35,600	
Bank Account			20,775
Cash in Hand		780	
Creditors			27,340
Capital Accounts:	Annan		40,000
	Wyllie		25,000
Current Accounts at 1.5.-2:	Annan		3,750
	Wyllie		2,025
Sales			143,680
Purchases		83,575	
Salaries		17,570	
Office Overheads		6,250	
Drawings:	Annan	18,500	
	Wyllie	15,000	
		281,195	281,195

You have been asked to prepare a set of final accounts for the year ended 30 April, 19-3 for the partnership. Discussions with Annan have revealed the following:

(a) Provision for depreciation has still to be made. Buildings at 2% of cost, office equipment at 20% reducing balance, and motor vehicles at 25% of cost.

(b) Stock at 30 April 19-3 was £35,200.

(c) An invoice for office overheads of £225 has still to be included.

(d) Interest is allowable on the partners' capital account balances at a rate of 10% p.a.

(e) Annan has calculated that interest to be charged on drawings is: Annan £775, Wyllie £595. This is to be incorporated in the accounts.

---

1 For suggested solutions see p 301.

2. Taylor Rodger & Paton are in partnership, sharing profits and losses in the ratio 2:2:1 respectively. In addition Paton is to be given a salary of £5,000. The partners have also agreed that interest is to be allowed on each partner's capital account balance at the rate of 7% per annum. On 31 May 19-4 the following trial balance was extracted from the partnership records:

		£	£
Capital Accounts:	Taylor		35,000
	Rodger		35,000
	Paton		20,000
Current Accounts:	Taylor		17,750
	Rodger		19,200
	Paton		13,050
Drawings:	Taylor	18,000	
	Rodger	16,250	
	Paton	10,750	
Sales			347,650
Purchases		260,326	
Rent and Rates		10,761	
Heat and Light		1,112	
Salaries and Wages		39,615	
Bad Debts		650	
Insurance		988	
General Expenses		4,153	
Provision for Doubtful Debts at 1.6.-3			1,560
Debtors		42,619	
Stock at 1.6.-3		51,720	
Motor Vehicles		27,500	
Provision for Depreciation of Motor Vehicles at 1.6.-3			16,530
Motor Vehicle Running Expenses		5,296	
Gain on sale of Motor Vehicle			1,258
Cash in Hand		726	
Creditors			46,246
Bank account		10,428	
Freehold Premises at cost		52,350	
		553,244	553,244

The following information has still to be taken into account:
1. Stock was valued at £53,462 at 31 May 19-4.
2. Rates and insurance had both been paid in advance—£531 and £125 respectively.
3. A bill for heat and light came in on 6 June 19-4 relating to April and May 19-4. The bill was for £210.
4. The provision for doubtful debts has to be increased to £1,630.
5. Insurance for building contents of £300 has been included in general expenses. This is to be transferred into the insurances account.
6. Depreciation on Motor Vehicles for the year has still to be charged. This is normally charged at 20% of cost.
7. Having prepared the bank reconciliation you discover that £175 of bank charges has not been included in the records at all.

Prepare the Trading, Profit and Loss and Appropriation Account for the year ended 31 May 19-4 and the Balance Sheet as at that date.

3. Munro Graham and Harris have been trading together in partnership for some years. Their partnership agreement stipulates that profits are to be shared in the ratio 4:3:3 after awarding salaries to Graham and Harris of £5,000 each, and interest on capital balances at 7½% p.a. Interest is also to be charged on drawings. The following trial balance has been extracted at 30 June 19-5:

		£	£
Capital Accounts—	Munro		26,000
	Graham		17,000
	Harris		22,000
Current Accounts at 1.7.-4—	Munro		13,258
	Graham		16,177
	Harris		12,265
Freehold land and buildings		47,000	
Plant and Equipment		45,490	
Office fixtures and fittings		8,320	
Motor Vehicles		27,680	
Cumulative depreciation at 1 July 19-4:			
Plant and Equipment			11,716
Office fixtures and fittings			3,170
Motor Vehicles			10,230
Stock in trade at 1 July 19-4		92,316	
Debtors		80,671	
Cash in hand		923	
Bank account			11,557
Creditors			98,708
Long term loan			30,000
Sales			502,618
Purchases		349,833	
Discounts allowed on sales		5,416	
Motor vehicle running costs		7,915	
Repairs and renewals		4,338	
Rent and rates		3,960	
Heat and light		3,274	
Telephone		1,506	
Advertising and stationery		2,750	
Bank interest and charges		3,419	
Insurance		2,521	
General expenses		5,493	
Wages and salaries		38,724	
Drawings account:	Munro	15,000	
	Graham	13,250	
	Harris	14,900	
		774,699	774,699

In drawing up the trial balance the partners were unsure how to account for the following:

(a) Depreciation is at the following rates:

    Plant and equipment   —20% of cost

    Office fixtures and fittings—10% of net book value

    Motor vehicles   —25% of cost

(b) Stock in trade at 30 June 19-5 was £97,409.

(c) A debtor has gone into liquidation owing the partnership £2,617. The liquidator has intimated that there is unlikely to be any payout.

(d) Interest is due on the long term loan annually on 30 June. The £3,000 charge has not been accrued yet.

(e) Rent and rates paid in advance amount to £750.

(f) The telephone bill for the quarter to 31 July 19-5 was £480.

(g) Interest to be charged on the partners' drawings is:

    Munro —£426

    Graham—£375

    Harris   —£412

Prepare the Trading, Profit and Loss and Appropriation Account for the year ended 30 June 19-5, and the Balance Sheet as at that date, taking into account the above items.

4. Innes and Moran are in partnership as solicitors. Their financial year end is 31 July 19-6. The partners have asked you to prepare a Profit and Loss and Appropriation Account for the year then ended, together with a Balance Sheet as at that date. They have presented you with the following information:

Innes Moran & Co., Solicitors
Trial Balance as at 31 July 19-6

	£	£
Partners' capital accounts 1 August 19-5—Innes		75,000
—Moran		62,000
Partners' current accounts 1 August 19-5—Innes		13,219
—Moran		10,625
Partners' drawings—Innes	20,000	
—Moran	20,000	
Office premises—cost	95,000	
—accumulated depreciation to 1 August 19-5		10,890
Office furniture and fittings—cost	37,250	
—accumulated depreciation to 1 August 19-5		14,890
Work in Progress (including fees not yet rendered) at 1 August 19-5	22,620	
Debtors	42,195	
Fees rendered		231,454
Creditors		2,516
Cash in hand	250	
Firm's bank account	22,971	
Clients' bank accounts:—on current account	36,500	
—on deposit receipt	185,000	
Clients' ledger		219,540

Wages and salaries	113,040
Rates and insurance	13,157
Stationery	8,615
Telephone, fax and postages	14,836
Bank interest and charges	1,250
Sundry office expenses	7,450
	640,134 640,134

Notes:

(a)   Depreciation is to be provided on fixed assets each year as follows:
Office premises 2% of cost.
Office furniture and fittings—15% reducing balance method.

(b)   Work-in-progress (including fees not rendered) at 31 July 19-6 was valued by the partners at £25,715. This is to be incorporated into the accounts.

(c)   The partnership agreement stipulates the following:
   (i)   Profits are to be shared equally between the partners.
   (ii)   Interest on partners capital accounts is to be calculated at 5% of the balance at the start of each year.
   (iii)   Innes and Moran are both to receive a salary of £18,500 each year.
   (iv)   Drawings made by the partners are not subject to interest charges.

(d)   On subsequent review of the Client's ledger you find that one client who has a debit balance of £375 has been netted against the credit balances which should actually total £219,915.

(e)   Other accounting adjustments are required as follows:
   (i)   The rates bill has been paid in advance by £1,576.
   (ii)   A telephone bill for £3,141 was received on 31 August 19-6. It related to the three months up to that date.
   (iii)   Sundry office expenses totalling £615 have to be accrued at the year end.

5.   (a)   Keegan, Gilmorton and McNaughton decide to set up in partnership as solicitors under the name of Keegan & Co. They have discussed the financing of the partnership and have decided that £110,000 will be required to establish an office and vehicles and provide sufficient working capital until the fees start to come in.

   Keegan has agreed that property he owns valued at £50,000 would be his capital input, Gilmorton has £10,000 available in cash, and McNaughton can supply furniture and office equipment valued at £7,500 plus £5,000 in cash. Each partner agrees that their car will be brought into the partnership and the cars have been valued at £10,000 each. The remainder of the funds required is to be borrowed from the bank as a short term loan.

   You are required to prepare the balance sheet as it would stand on the first day of their business after each partner and the bank has made their contribution, assuming a start date of 1 September 19-7.

   (b)   Keegan & Co., Solicitors have drawn up their Profit and Loss Account for the year ended 31st August 19-8. This shows a net profit of £36,000 for the year. They are unsure how they should allocate this profit and have decided that they would adopt the rules laid down by section 24 of the Partnership Act 1890.

   They have asked you to prepare the Appropriation account on this basis, and show their Capital account position at 31 August 19-8 bearing in mind the following:

(i) Further capital was input by Keegan during the year, this amounted to £6,250. It was agreed that this would be treated as a further capital contribution and not a loan to the partnership.

(ii) Drawings were made by each partner:

Keegan	£13,250
Gilmorton	£11,750
McNaughton	£12,300

(iii) The partners have decided to use single fluctuating capital accounts instead of using a Capital account and a Current account.

6. Neilsen, Chalmers & Pryce have been in partnership as solicitors for a few years. Their financial year end is 30 April. Salaries of £13,500, £18,500 and £21,000 are payable to Neilsen, Chalmers & Pryce respectively. In addition, the balance of the partners' capital accounts at the beginning of the year attract interest at a rate of 10% per annum. Remaining profits/losses are thereafter shared equally. The firm has provided you with the following information:

Neilsen, Chalmers & Pryce, Solicitors
Trial Balance as at 30 April 19-9

	£	£
Office Premises—Cost	120,000	
—Accumulated Depreciation		7,325
Office Furniture & Fittings—Cost	55,140	
—Accumulated Depreciation		22,866
Motor Vehicles—Cost	54,000	
—Accumulated Depreciation		13,500
Partners' Capital Accounts as at 1 May 19-8—Neilsen		51,000
—Chalmers		51,000
—Pryce		35,000
Partners' Current Accounts—Neilsen	17,500	
—Chalmers	16,726	
—Pryce	15,000	
Client Ledger		371,727
Client Bank—on deposit receipt	332,500	
—on current account	43,354	
Outstanding Fees/Debtors	12,037	
Cash in Hand	100	
Fees rendered		330,175
Work in Progress at 1 May 19-8	33,970	
Office wages and salaries	137,259	
General expenses	15,275	
Rates and insurance	16,350	
Telephone and postages	11,421	
Staff travel expenses	12,129	
Heat and light	14,615	
Stationery	11,717	
Bank overdraft		39,250
Bank interest and charges	2,750	
	921,843	921,843

Mrs. Neilsen has provided more details for your information:

(i)   The firm provides depreciation on its fixed assets as follows:

Office premises; 4% charge per annum using the reducing balance method.

Motor vehicles; 25% charge per annum using the reducing balance method.

Office furniture and fittings; 15% charge per annum using the straight line method.

(ii)   The firm has calculated the value of its Work in Progress (including fees not yet rendered) as at 30 April 19-9 to be £29,500.

(iii)   Accounting adjustments should be included to reflect the following:

(a)   A rates bill arrived at the end of March for the quarter to 30 June 19-9. The bill totalled £3,000 and was paid on 1 April 19-9.

(b)   Insurance premiums paid in respect of the office premises included £1,250 for the month of May 19-9.

(c)   One of the staff delayed lodging an expense claim for travelling on office business. The claim amounted to £163 and related to travel in March and April.

(d)   An invoice from British Telecom totalling £473 arrived in the office shortly after the financial year end and related to telephone charges to 30 April 19-9. This amount has not yet been included in the firm's records.

(iv)   The Clients Ledger balance comprised:

	£
Total Credit balances	377,254
Total Debit balances	5,527
	371,727

After the balances had been extracted from the records and included in the Trial Balance, the partners reviewed the debit balances and decided that a total of £625 should be written off as irrecoverable client outlays.

(v)   The partners' current account balances at 30 April 19-9 are shown after deduction of partners drawings for the year. Each partner had drawings of £13,500 during the year.

Required:

Prepare a Profit and Loss Statement for the year to 30 April 19-9 and a Balance Sheet as at that date using the above information.

7. Queen and Rice are in partnership, practising under the name of Queen & Co., Solicitors. You have been presented with the following information and are required to prepare the Profit and Loss and Appropriation Account for the year to 30 November 19-2 and the Balance Sheet at that date.

Queen & Co., Solicitors
Trial Balance as at 30 November 19-2

		£	£
Partners Capital Accounts	—Queen		25,000
	—Rice		36,000
Partners Current Accounts	—Queen		7,258
	—Rice		13,124
Drawings	—Queen	30,000	
	—Rice	30,000	
Firm's bank			51,320
Cash in Hand		250	
Clients' bank	—on current account	43,176	
	—on deposit receipt	233,000	
Clients' ledger			275,540
Fees rendered			273,641
Work in Progress at 1 December 19-1		33,800	
Outstanding fees not yet paid		50,175	
Creditors			5,790
Office wages and salaries		143,760	
Rates, rent and common charges		35,960	
Staff travelling expenses		5,371	
Insurance		7,250	
Telephone, fax, postage and couriers		9,102	
Heat and Light		1,960	
Repairs and renewals		8,240	
Printing, stationery and advertising		7,320	
Overdraft interest and charges		6,419	
Commission received			7,167
Equipment leasing		4,773	
Office cleaning		1,350	
General expenses		5,690	
Office furniture and equipment	—Cost	17,320	
	—Accum. depreciation		10,390
Motor vehicles	—Cost	29,370	
	—Accum. depreciation		13,559
Vehicle running costs		9,503	
Staff training costs		5,000	
		718,789	718,789

Notes:

(i)   Work in Progress at 30 November 19-2 was £39,500.

(ii) Depreciation has still to be charged on office furniture and equipment at 10% reducing balance, and motor vehicles at 20% of cost.

(iii) Interest is to be permitted on partners capital accounts at 7.5% p.a.

and interest is to be charged on drawings. Mr Queen has calculated this to be: Queen £372, Rice £360.

(iv) Upon examination of the Clients' Ledger it was found that credit balances amounted to £279,450 with debit balances of £3,910 in respect of recoverable client disbursements.

(v) Profits are to be shared equally between Queen and Rice, after a salary of £17,500 has been allocated to Rice, and £10,000 to Queen.

Queen & Co., Solicitors
Profit and Loss Account for the year ended 30th November 19-1
Extract

	£	£
Total income		280,713
Less Expenses:		
Office wages and salaries	120,390	
Staff travelling expenses	5,280	
Staff training costs	4,850	
Rates, rent and common charges	29,618	
Insurance	7,100	
Telephone, fax, postage and couriers	7,061	
Heat and light	1,790	
Repairs and renewals	3,647	
Printing stationery and advertising	4,650	
Equipment leasing	–	
Vehicle running costs	9,139	
Office cleaning	1,275	
General expenses	2,418	
Overdraft interest and charges	1,425	
Depreciation	6,570	
		205,213
Net profit		75,500

Queen & Co., Solicitors
Balance Sheet as at 30 November 19-1
Extract

	£	£
Fixed Assets		
At net book value		20,740
Current Assets		
Work in Progress	33,800	
Outstanding fees	35,270	
Recoverable client disbursements	3,900	
Amount over deposited in clients' funds account	1,500	
Cash in Hand	250	
	74,720	
Current Liabilities		
Creditors	5,420	
Firm's bank	8,658	
	14,078	
Net Current Assets		60,642
Total Assets		81,382

8. Jim Short and Sam Thweet recently decided to set up a solicitors firm which specialised in commercial law. Both partners had acquired the relevant experience in large firms in Glasgow, and were enthusiastic about setting up on their own. The partnership commenced trading on 1 June 1999 when the partners purchased their freehold office property for £175,000, two cars for £48,000 and office furniture and equipment for £27,000. The partners had agreed to contribute capital as follows:

	Capital Accounts £	Current Accounts £
Short	100,000	46,500
Thweet	75,000	40,000

Short also agreed to make a loan to the partnership of £20,000, with a fixed rate of interest of 10% per annum. The loan is repayable in full in five years time. The balance in the firm's bank account after all of these transactions is £31,500.

(a) You are required to prepare the first balance sheet of Short and Thweet at 1 June 1999 taking into consideration the above information.

The business went well in the first year of trading, with the firm taking on many new and interesting clients to the extent that additional staff were employed. Unfortunately the firm's book-keeper/cashier left on the 4 June 2000 and was unable to prepare the trial balance. She did however manage to write up the cash books and other records so that the partners were able to summarise the business transactions to 31 May 2000 as follows:

Staff salaries (excluding partners' salaries) totalled £164,900; Postage and telephone costs were £11,300; Motor vehicle expenses totalled £7,600; Stationery costs were £9,400; Office expenses were £7,300; Rates and Insurance costs were £7,100; Heat and light cost £4,700; Repairs and Maintenance for the office property were £3,200 and Interest paid to J. Short on 30 May 2000 was £2,000. Fees rendered during the year amounted to £315,750.

In addition, the partners managed to find out the following balances:

Cash in hand—£500; General creditors—£7,300; Client creditors—£362,250; Client debtors—£33,000; Client bank balance, current account—£35,200 and deposit receipts—£329,000.

Finally, the balance on the firm's account per the cash book was £101,600 at 31 May 2000.

(b)   You are required to prepare a trial balance at 31 May 2000 for the firm, taking into account all of the information so far disclosed.

After the preparation of the trial balance, the following information has come to your attention:

(i)   The bank reconciliation shows that the book-keeper did not take partners drawings into account when preparing the cash book. Short withdrew £35,000 during the year and Thweet £31,000. These have therefore still to be deducted from the firm's bank balance.

(ii)   The partners agreed to charge interest at 5% per annum on the balances on their fixed capital accounts.

(iii)   They agreed to share profit/losses in the ratio of Short ⅓, Thweet ⅔ after deduction of salaries and interest on capital. The salaries payable were £37,500 each.

(iv)   Depreciation for the year is to be provided on Motor vehicles at 25% of cost and on Office furniture and equipment at 20% of cost.

(v)   Partners valued work in progress on 31 May 2000 at £20,000.

(vi)   The postage and telephone expenses excluded an unpaid bill of £750 for the fax machine, and other unpaid invoices discovered by the partners were as follows:

	£
Office expenses	350
Rates	450

(vii)   Insurance premiums paid during the year were paid in advance. The last payment, made in May, was for the quarter to 31 July 2000 and totalled £750.

(c)   Using all of the information above, you are required to prepare the Profit and Loss and Appropriation Account for the year to 31 May 2000 and the balance sheet at that date.

Chapter Eight: Accounting for partnership changes

Solicitors' partnerships are commercial entities that exist in a changing business environment. It can be expected that on occasion certain changes will occur within the partnership itself. Existing partners may want to alter the way in which profits/losses are shared among them, or a new partner may have been admitted to the partnership, or an existing partner may have left the firm. When any such change happens, it is important for the good order of the business that the event is recorded in the accounting records of the firm.

In the first instance it may appear that the accounting procedures necessary to record the effects of a particular event, such as a change in the partners' profit sharing arrangements, are straightforward. That is, apportion profits or losses among the individuals in relation to arrangements in place at the time the profit/loss was earned by the business. However, if one considers the ramifications of partnership changes in greater depth, it will become clear that other factors must be considered and steps taken to account for them, assuming that it would be appropriate in the circumstances to do so.

Matters such as the *true value of the assets and liabilities* of the firm and the intangible asset of *Goodwill* should be examined in the event of a partnership change to ensure that each of the partners is being fairly treated both at the time of the change and, perhaps more importantly, afterwards.

It is the intention in this section to look first at the main types of changes which can happen within a partnership and how to account for them. At this stage the consideration of the accounting processes involved will be simplified to the extent of only looking at the allocation of *revenue profits/losses* between the partners (that is, the trading profits or losses that have been generated by a partnership in the normal course of its business). Once the principles have been charted, the further complications caused by *changes in the value of assets and liabilities* and the existence of *Goodwill* will be examined and consideration given to the accounting treatment each should receive in the context of the events considered earlier.

REVENUE PROFITS/LOSSES

Changes in the profit/loss sharing arrangements between existing partners

From time to time it may be necessary for a partnership to adjust the profit/loss sharing arrangements which operate within the firm. This may be to reflect changing circumstances such as partners' relative contributions to the business. For example, a large and prestigious new client may have been secured by the endeavours of one particular partner who has in turn requested that an adjustment be made to the firm's profit sharing arrangements in his favour. If this change happens at the start of a firm's financial year, it is a straight-forward task to appropriate subsequent profits/losses among the partners using the revised basis. If the change to the profit/loss sharing arrangements is made at some stage during a financial year, then a slightly more involved accounting process is required.

Firstly it is necessary to split the firm's profit/loss into two periods—(i) from the start of the financial year to the date of change of the profit/loss sharing ratios, and; (ii) from this later date until the end of the financial year in question. In the absence of any information to the contrary, this can be done simply on a time basis. The assumption here, therefore, is that profits/losses have been earned at a constant rate throughout the year.

Next the profit/loss attributable to each of the above periods should be appropriated to the partners using the relevant profit/loss sharing ratios.

Finally, in order to calculate the earnings of each partner over the financial year in which the change occurred, all that remains is to add together the appropriated profit/loss for each period.

ILLUSTRATION 8.1

Assumptions:
- (i)   The financial year of ABC Partnership is from 1 January until 31 December each year.
- (ii)   Profits earned during the year to 31 December 1999 amounted to £120,000.
- (iii) Profits/losses are shared—   A: 3/6
                                          B: 2/6
                                          C: 1/6
- (iv) On 1 October 1999 the partners decided to change the basis on which the firm's profits/losses are allocated. Under the new arrangements, all profits and losses are shared equally.

Required:

Calculate the profits which each partner would receive in 1999.

Solution:

ABC Partnership
1999 Financial Year

1 Jan	1 Apr	1 July	1 Oct	31 Dec

Profit for the year:

←————————————————£120,000————————————————→

Profit split:

Period 1	Period 2
←————————£90,000————————→	←——£30,000——→

Profits appropriated:

	Period 1		Period 2		Total
A receives (3/6)	£45,000	+ (2/6)	£10,000	=	£55,000
B receives (2/6)	£30,000	+ (2/6)	£10,000	=	£40,000
C receives (1/6)	£15,000	+ (2/6)	£10,000	=	£25,000
	£90,000		£30,000	=	£120,000

Admission of a new partner

Another event which can happen frequently in the context of partnerships is when a new partner is admitted. The reason(s) behind existing partners assuming new partners into their firm will obviously vary depending on the circumstances but may include the following:

(1) Individuals may have been with the firm for a number of years in junior roles, know how it operates, know the clients, fit in well with the existing partners in that they have complimentary skills and are of suitable character generally, and the existing partners believe that the promotion to status of partner is reward for all of their hard work to date;

(2) the existing partners feel that a new appointment at senior level is necessary because of the firm's workload. In other words, the existing partners are struggling to cope with the sheer volume of work and feel that simply delegating more work to subordinate staff is not the answer;

(3) the firm wishes to expand into a new area of work (eg develop a department dedicated to the provision of services relating to environmental law) but existing partners lack the required expertise;

(4) the firm would like to assume a particular individual as partner because of the additional work in the form of new clients which they are likely to bring with them;

(5) the firm needs a fresh injection of new capital to expand, to upgrade its facilities (eg computerise the office), or simply to survive if it is experiencing cash flow or any other financial problems (prospective partners beware!).

In normal circumstances when a new partner joins a partnership the profit sharing arrangements will need to be amended since, predictably, the individual will wish to share in the future profits of the business. The accounting procedures necessary will be very similar to those adopted in **Illustration 8.1** above and will depend on the timing of the new partner's arrival in relation to the firm's financial year. If an appointment is at the start of a financial year, the firm's profit for that year will simply be allocated on the basis of the new profit sharing arrangements.

If, on the other hand, the new partner joins the partnership at some point during a financial year, it will again be necessary to split the firm's profits into two periods before apportioning such profits among the partners using the relevant profit sharing ratios.

ILLUSTRATION 8.2

Assumptions:

(i) The financial year of the DEF Partnership is from 1 January until 31 December each year.

(ii) Profits earned from normal trading activities during the year to 31 December 1999 came to £140,000.

(iii) Profits/losses are shared equally.

(iv) On 1 July 1999 a new partner G was admitted. The partners agreed that profits/losses should continue to be shared equally and that profits in respect of the year to 31 December 1999 should be split as follows:

   Period 1: 1 January to 30 June, £60,000

   Period 2: 1 July to 31 December, £80,000

Required:

Calculate each partners' share of the firm's trading profit in respect of the year to 31 December 1999.

Solution:

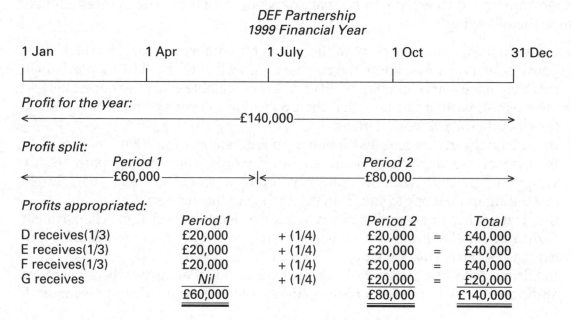

DEF Partnership
1999 Financial Year

1 Jan	1 Apr	1 July	1 Oct	31 Dec

Profit for the year:

←————————————————£140,000————————————————→

Profit split:

Period 1	Period 2
←————£60,000————→	←————£80,000————→

Profits appropriated:

	Period 1		Period 2		Total
D receives(1/3)	£20,000	+ (1/4)	£20,000	=	£40,000
E receives(1/3)	£20,000	+ (1/4)	£20,000	=	£40,000
F receives(1/3)	£20,000	+ (1/4)	£20,000	=	£40,000
G receives	*Nil*	+ (1/4)	£20,000	=	£20,000
	£60,000		£80,000		£140,000

Outgoing Partners

In accounting for the normal trading profits of a partnership when one of the partners leaves the business, be it for reasons of retirement, death or where the partner simply wishes to move on, once again similar procedures to those used in **Illustrations 8.1** and **8.2** above would be followed.

ILLUSTRATION 8.3(a)

Assumptions:

   (i)   HIJ is a three partner firm of solicitors with an accounting year 1 January to 31 December.

  (ii)   Profits generated by the partnership in the 1999 financial year totalled £100,000.

 (iii)   Profits/losses are shared equally.

 (iv)   Partner H retired from the firm on 1 October 1999. It was agreed at that time that a profit of £90,000 should be attributed to the period running from 1 January to the date of his departure.

Required:

Calculate each partner's entitlement with respect to the firm's 1999 trading profits.

Solution:

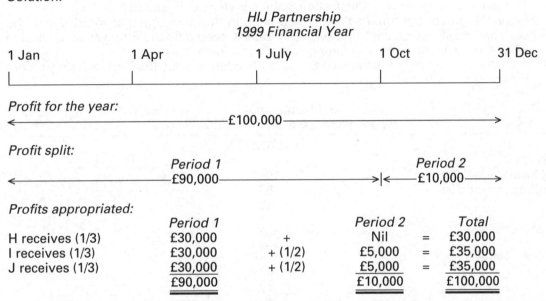

Profits appropriated:

	Period 1		Period 2		Total
H receives (1/3)	£30,000	+	Nil	=	£30,000
I receives (1/3)	£30,000	+ (1/2)	£5,000	=	£35,000
J receives (1/3)	£30,000	+ (1/2)	£5,000	=	£35,000
	£90,000		£10,000		£100,000

If on the other hand H had left the business at the beginning of 1999, it would be reasonable to assume that the profits of the partnership for this year should simply be shared out by the remaining partners, I and J.

In **Illustration 8.3(a)**, it should be appreciated that £30,000 will probably not be the total amount to which the outgoing partner H will be entitled, this sum only being representative of his share of the firm's profits in the year of his retirement. He will almost certainly be looking for the return of his capital as well. The difficulty here is in quantifying just how much the partner is due from the firm.

REVALUATION OF PARTNERSHIP ASSETS AND LIABILITIES

Outgoing Partners

At its simplest, in addition to an appropriate share of the trading profits in the year of departure as well as any profits from previous years that were not taken as drawings, outgoing partners would also expect the return of the balance of their original capital accounts together with interest thereon (assuming of course that the partnership agreement so provided). It would be a straightforward task to calculate this amount.

It is reasonable to assume that outgoing partners will also expect full reward for their participation in the business in a general sense. If the firm has gone through a period of expansion or growth which has resulted in an increase in its value, any partner who is leaving will wish an appropriate share of this increase. Similarly, it is also possible that the assets and liabilities of the partnership will see changes in their values over time. If such changes are ignored, it is quite probable that some partners will experience windfall gains whilst others lose out.

ILLUSTRATION 8.3(b)

Assumptions:
   (i)   The same facts apply as in **Illustration 8.3(a)** above, and, in addition,
   (ii) Before H retired, the three solicitors had been in business together for 20 years and each had equal capital contributions. All property owned by the firm was purchased in 1970 and is shown in the accounting records at original cost.
   (iii) An extract from the firm's Balance Sheet as at 30 September 1999, immediately before H retired, appears as follows:

HIJ Partnership
Balance Sheet Extract as at 30/9/99

	£'000
Assets	
Office Property, at cost	100
Other Property, at cost	50
Bank	89
Cash	1
	240
Partners' Capital	
H	80
I	80
J	80
	240

[ignore depreciation]

Required:

On the basis of the above information state (a) the amount of capital repayment to which 'H' would be entitled upon leaving the business on 1 October 1999, and (b) show a Balance Sheet extract immediately after his departure.

Solution:

   (a)   H capital repayment = £80,000.
   (b)   The firm's Balance Sheet would now appear as follows:

HIJ Partnership
Balance Sheet Extract as at 1/10/99

	£'000
Assets	
Office Property, at cost	100
Other Property, at cost	50
Bank	9*
Cash	1
	160
Partners' Capital	
I	80
J	80
	160

[*Note—it has been assumed that the remaining partners have simply met the repayment of H's capital from funds held at the bank]

However, it was mentioned above that the firm has existed for many years and that assets are valued at cost. Consider the following additional points:

(iv)   One week after H retires, I and J sell the firm's Other Property, which had a cost price of £50,000 in 1970, for £110,000. Furthermore, the market value of the remaining Office Property at 8 October 1999 was estimated at £220,000. I and J decide that their Office Property should be shown in the Balance Sheet at its revalued figure.

(v)   The partners agree that any surplus or deficit created by revaluations of this nature should be shared equally.

Required:

Draft the Balance Sheet extract of the firm as at 8 October 1999.

Solution:

HIJ Partnership
Balance Sheet Extract as at 8/10/99

	£'000
Assets	
Office Property, at current market value	220
Other Property	–
Bank	119*
Cash	1
	340
Partners' Capital	
I	170
J	170
	340

[*Note—this figure comprises the £9,000 balance remaining after H has withdrawn his £80,000, plus £110,000 being the proceeds from the sale of the property]

It is clear that I and J have benefited at the expense of H since they have 'inherited' his share of the gains on the property which have probably been building up over many years. In fairness to the outgoing partner, it would have been desirable to revalue all the partnership assets at the date of his departure and to base his capital repayment on the revalued amounts. If this had happened, H would have been in the following position:

HIJ Partnership
Balance Sheet Extract as at 1/10/99

	£'000
Assets	
Office Property, at current market value	220
Other Property, at current market value	110
Bank	89
Cash	1
	420
Partners' Capital	
H	140
I	140
J	140
	420

In other words, H should receive a total of £140,000 from the partnership and not only £80,000 as shown earlier[1].

This illustration also conveniently highlights another area of which partners should be aware. Namely the manner in which capital is returned to an outgoing partner. In the above case, although H is entitled to a payment of £140,000, it can be seen from the Balance Sheet that the maximum amount available is only £90,000 (of which £89,000 is held at the bank with the remaining £1,000 being cash). The problem would be even more marked had the outgoing partner possessed a greater share of the firm's capital.

One possible solution here is for the partners I and J to borrow the necessary money from a bank, for example, to repay H his capital, which may or may not be appropriate in the circumstances. Alternatively, the partners may have provided for capital to be repaid in instalments to an outgoing individual over a number of years. If the latter approach was adopted, it is possible for the remaining partners to minimise borrowings since the repayments would be funded, at least in part, out of the future profits of the business[2].

Other Partnership Changes

The revaluation of a firm's assets may also be appropriate when there is either a change in the profit/loss sharing ratios among the existing partners or a new partner is introduced. The determining factor is the basis on which partners share revaluation gains or losses and whether or not this basis is affected by the changes envisaged here[3].

If partners share the gains or losses arising upon the revaluation of assets on an identical basis to the method of sharing normal trading profits or losses, then where there is a change in the latter it will be necessary to revalue assets and account for any

---

1   The £140,000 is assumed to include H's share of the 1999 profits, being £30,000, which has already been credited to his capital account. Similarly the other partners capital account balances will also include their shares of the profits to 1 October 1999.

2   If an outgoing partner does not receive the full amount due on departure, any outstanding balance is usually transferred to a loan account in the outgoing partner's name, appearing as such in future Balance Sheets. Interest payable on the loan will be charged to the Profit and Loss account as a normal trading expense.

3   The existence of various income streams was identified in the previous chapter. See the section dealing with the definition of income in the partnership agreement.

gains or losses among the partners. As has been seen earlier, normal trading profit or loss sharing ratios are of course affected when a new partner is admitted. Again, therefore, this situation will require an asset revaluation together with adjustments to partners' capital accounts.

If revaluation surpluses or deficits are distributed among partners using some other basis, for example by reference to the relative balances on the partners' capital accounts, then it could be argued that an asset revaluation will only be necessary when this particular basis itself is altered. Thus a change in the way in which trading profits/losses are shared is not in itself compelling grounds for an asset revaluation. In contrast, the arrival of a new partner may necessitate a revaluation, depending upon the terms of his appointment. Where the new partner is to be entitled to a share of all forms of partnership income, irrespective of source, it follows that the basis of apportionment of revaluation gains or losses is being adjusted. On such occasions assets should be revalued and the partners' capital accounts amended appropriately to protect the interests of all concerned. If on the other hand the new partner is precluded from sharing in gains or losses attributable to assets which were purchased before his arrival, then there is no real need for an asset revaluation at this stage[1].

Accounting treatment of asset revaluations

The revaluation of the fixed assets of any business will be recorded through its *Revaluation account*. The corresponding entries to those made in this account will appear in the relevant asset account. Upon completion of the revaluation process for each of the assets involved, the balance on the revaluation account is transferred to the partners capital accounts using an agreed basis of apportionment.

More specifically, the first step is to open the revaluation account and then –

(1)   for each asset showing a *gain* on revaluation,
        Dr the asset account
        Cr the revaluation account
        with the gain; and
(2)   for each asset showing a *loss* on revaluation,
        Dr the revaluation account
        Cr the asset account
        with the loss.
        Once this process has been completed—
(3)   if there is an *increase* in the total value of the assets under review (that is, if there is an overall profit on revaluation),
        Dr the revaluation account with an amount equal to that of the total profit
        Cr each partners' capital account with an appropriate share of the profit
        Or alternatively,
(4)   if there is an overall *loss* experienced,
        Dr each partners' capital account with an appropriate share of the loss
        Cr the revaluation account with an amount equal to that of the total loss.

If the revaluation of assets produces neither an overall gain nor loss, that is where there is a zero balance on the revaluation account, no further action is required.

---

1   It should be noted however that partners are normally free to revalue their firm's assets at any time, provided that such action is not contrary to generally accepted accounting practice.

138   *Accounting for partnership changes*

ILLUSTRATION 8.4

Assumptions:

  (i)   K, L and M have been together in partnership for a number of years sharing all profits or losses in the ratio:
         K 5/10
         L 3/10
         M 2/10.

 (ii)   Their accounting year runs from 1 January until 31 December.

(iii)   In view of certain forthcoming changes to the partnership structure, the partners have decided to revalue the firm's assets. The following revaluation figures are to be applied:

Office property	£26,250
Motor vehicles	£3,900
Stock	£2,835
Fixtures & fittings	£1,635

(iv)   The Balance Sheet of KLM as at 31 December 1999 was as follows.

KLM Partnership
Balance Sheet as at 31 December 1999

	£	£
Fixed Assets		
Office property, at cost		12,000
Motor vehicles, at cost *less* depreciation		5,325
Fixtures & fittings, at cost *less* depreciation		1,965
		19,290
Current Assets		
Stock	3,060	
Trade debtors	6,795	
Bank	2,085	
		11,940
		31,230
Partners Capital		
K		14,340
L		9,630
M		7,260
		31,230

Required:

 (a)   Show all of the accounts necessary to record the above revaluation of the partnership's assets, and

 (b)   draw up the firm's revised Balance Sheet as at 1 January 2000.

Solution (a):

OFFICE PROPERTY

	£		£
Balance b/d	12,000		
Revaluation (increase)	14,250	Balance c/d	26,250
	26,250		26,250

MOTOR VEHICLES

	£		£
Balance b/d	5,325	Revaluation (decrease)	1,425
		Balance c/d	3,900
	5,325		5,325

FIXTURES & FITTINGS

	£		£
Balance b/d	1,965	Revaluation (decrease)	330
		Balance c/d	1,635
	1,965		1,965

STOCK

	£		£
Balance b/d	3,060	Revaluation (decrease)	225
		Balance c/d	2,835
	3,060		3,060

REVALUATION

		£		£
Motor vehicles		1,425	Office property	14,250
Stock		225		
Fixtures & fittings		330		
Profit on revaluation:				
K	6,135			
L	3,681			
M	2,454	12,270		
		14,250		14,250

CAPITALS

	K £	L £	M £		K £	L £	M £
				Balances b/d	14,340	9,630	7,260
				Profit on			
Balances c/d	20,475	13,311	9,714	Revaluation	6,135	3,681	2,454
	20,475	13,311	9,714		20,475	13,311	9,714

Solution (b):

KLM Partnership
Balance Sheet as at 1 January 2000

	£	£
Fixed Assets		
Office property, at valuation		26,250
Motor vehicles, at valuation		3,900
Fixtures & fittings, at valuation		1,635
		31,785
Current Assets		
Stock	2,835	
Trade debtors	6,795	
Bank	2,085	
		11,715
		43,500
Partners Capital		
K		20,475
L		13,311
M		9,714
		43,500

GOODWILL

Assets in the nature of property, motor vehicles, office fixtures and fittings for example, clearly have a physical presence which assists in the valuation process. It is easy to see when a vehicle is new or old, in good or poor condition and to assign a reasonable value accordingly. In contrast it is a much more difficult and subjective exercise when attempting to ascertain a correct valuation for intangible assets. Goodwill falls into this latter category.

The existence of goodwill is perhaps seen most readily in the case where a business is sold as a going concern and the selling price appears to be higher than one would expect when reference is made to the total value of identifiable assets. For example, a business may comprise the following list of assets:

	£'000
Office property	450
Machinery	150
Trade debtors	120
Stock	80
	800

The business may have been sold for £900,000. The difference between the two prices reflects the premium which the buyer has willingly paid for the business as a going concern. In this case, goodwill has been valued at (£900,000 – 800,000) £100,000[1].

Goodwill may exist for any one or a combination of different reason(s). For example, a firm may have:

(1)   a sound customer or client base which carries with it the prospect of future work;

(2)   a highly skilled, efficient, reliable and contented workforce, including a management team of similar standing;

(3)   an excellent geographical location for a business of its type; and,

(4)   in the case of trading concerns, excellent supplier contacts[2].

It would appear reasonable that a prospective purchaser of a business should pay for such factors under the general heading of goodwill given the potential influence which they would have on future profitability. The buyer may choose instead to start afresh, but it is most unlikely that the new business will immediately enjoy all, or even a majority, of the above advantages.

The significance of goodwill in any situation besides being influenced by the existence or otherwise of any of the above factors, will also depend to a great extent on the general nature of the entity's activities. Where repeat business from customers or clients is commonplace, it may be harder to ignore the importance of goodwill than where one-off transactions are more frequent.

It can be argued that the work of a solicitor's practice falls into the latter category. Indeed this assertion can be substantiated by the fact that many legal firms specifically exclude goodwill in the partnership agreement. Even if it is accepted that goodwill is of limited direct relevance to a solicitor in terms of its effects within their own business, it is still important that solicitors are aware of goodwill and its implications owing to its potential significance in client matters. The same can also be said of many other accountancy related issues in general.

Valuation of goodwill

It was mentioned above that it is more difficult to place a proper valuation on an asset like goodwill because of its intangible nature. In the simplistic situation where there is an individual selling a business as a going concern to a willing buyer, market

---

1   The assumption has been made that the assets were shown at a realistic market value and that none of the £100,000 could be attributed to gains on their sale.

2   It can be gathered from the items listed here that the concept of goodwill cannot be said to be unique to partnership accounting. For example, the treatment of goodwill in the books and records of limited companies is the subject of ongoing debate within the accountancy profession. See the contents of SSAP 22 'Accounting for Goodwill'.

forces will help determine the value of any goodwill—the seller will want as high a price as possible but the buyer will want to acquire the business as cheaply as possible. The actual selling price will largely be determined through negotiation between the two parties.

Even negotiations of this sort will require a starting point. Different industries or occupations have their own ways of calculating goodwill valuations, but commonly used techniques have been identified as follows:[1]

(1) With retail businesses, it is possible to value goodwill as average weekly sales over a certain period (say, one year) multiplied by a given figure. The latter figure will vary depending on the type of business involved. It will also probably change gradually over time in any sector of industry or commerce, taking into account developments in the general business environment.

(2) Professional firms, for example like accountants, can value goodwill as a multiple of gross annual fees[2].

(3) Rather than basing the calculation on sales or turnover as in (1) and (2) above, an alternative method is to use the average annual net profit over a number of years multiplied by a given figure.

(4) It is also possible to use the 'super-profits' method. In the case of a sole proprietor business, the owner does not deduct a salary from the profit and loss account. Any remuneration taken from the business will appear as a drawing in the capital account. Similarly there will be no charge to the profit and loss account for interest on capital. In such respects the net profit of a sole trader's business does not represent its true profit figure. 'Super-profit' is the amount of profit remaining after an adjustment has been made to reflect the contributions of the owner, both in terms of effort and capital used.

Super-profit may be calculated:

	£	£
Net profit		50,000
Less:—a salary which the proprietor would receive for similar work elsewhere	15,000	
—interest on capital at a rate commensurate with the risk involved	5,000	20,000
Super-profit		30,000

The super-profit figure would then be multiplied by a given figure to provide a valuation in respect of the goodwill.

It should be stressed that irrespective of which of the above methods is adopted, the final value attached to goodwill will of course depend on what a buyer of a business is willing to pay and how much the seller is prepared to accept.

The valuation of partnership goodwill is complicated in many instances by the absence of an independent, open-market force acting on the valuation process—that is, very often it is only the partners themselves who are interested in the value of goodwill and no-one external to the firm. If partners cannot agree on a valuation figure, there is a danger of a stalemate situation developing. A solution to this difficulty can usually be found by seeking appropriate professional assistance (eg from a firm of accountants experienced in this area).

---

1 See F Wood *Business Accounting 1* (6th edn, Pitman Publishing, 1993) p 332.
2 This is commonly referred to as an 'x' year's purchase of a firm's gross fees.

Accounting for partnership goodwill

It is usual to address the issue of goodwill in the context of partnerships when an event occurs which affects the way goodwill is allocated among the partners. Considering the nature of goodwill and its direct association with the future profits of a business, then to a great extent, when there is a change in the partnership of a kind previously considered (that is, the admission of a new partner, the departure of an existing partner, etc), the partners should review goodwill. This review will involve financial adjustments among the partners to compensate any individual losing goodwill and to charge anyone acquiring a greater share of goodwill as a result of the change.

ILLUSTRATION 8.5(a)

Assumptions:

   (i)   N and O have been in partnership together for some years now, running a profitable business. They have decided to admit a new partner, P, to benefit from his management experience.

  (ii)   At the date of the change goodwill was valued by the partners at £60,000.

 (iii)   The partners have always shared all profits and losses equally in the past and will continue to do so after P is admitted.

Required:

Show the effects which the partnership change has on each partner's share of the firm's goodwill.

Solution:

Partner	Old profit shares	Share of goodwill BEFORE 'P' is admitted	New profit shares	Share of goodwill AFTER 'P' is admitted	Difference
N	1/2	£30,000	1/3	£20,000	(£10,000)
O	1/2	£30,000	1/3	£20,000	(£10,000)
P	Nil	Nil	1/3	£20,000	+£20,000

It is clear that as a result of P joining the firm, N and O have each lost £10,000 of the partnership's goodwill. P on the other hand has gained £20,000. It is reasonable to assume therefore that both N and O should receive some form of payment or compensation from P.

There are various possible ways to account for goodwill, some more involved than others. The accounting treatment adopted will depend on the degree to which the partners want goodwill shown in the records of the business. If the partners wish the process to be as simple as possible, the adjustment could consist of nothing more than sums of money passing between the partners in a private capacity. That is, in terms of the NOP illustration above, P would make direct payments to N and O of £10,000 each for his right to a share of the partnership goodwill, with no note of the transaction appearing in the partnership's accounting records[1].

Alternatively, it is possible to open a *Goodwill account* and to process the adjustment in respect of goodwill through this account, with corresponding entries to the partners' capital accounts. After the adjustment had been carried out, the partners could then decide whether to retain a value for goodwill in the accounting

---

1   Tax implications of such transactions should not be ignored.

records (ultimately to appear in the Balance Sheet), or to close the account off. If the latter option is selected, the corresponding entries to those in the goodwill account would be made once more to the partners' capital accounts.

ILLUSTRATION 8.5(b)

Assumptions:

    (i)   The same facts apply as in Illustration 8.5(a) above, and in addition,

    (ii)   P pays in £95,000 as his capital contribution

    (iii) An extract of the firm's Balance Sheet immediately before P was admitted appears as follows:

NO Partnership
Balance Sheet Extract (Before P admitted)

	£'000
Assets	
Property	100
Vehicles	30
Bank	20
	150
Partners' Capital	
N	75
O	75
	150

[ignore depreciation]

Required:

Describe the sequence of entries in the firm's accounts which would be necessary to record an adjustment for goodwill among the partners (a) by using and retaining a goodwill account, and (b) by using a goodwill account but thereafter closing it off. In addition, show an extract of the firm's Balance Sheet in each case.

Solution:

    (a)   Goodwill account opened and retained.

The sequence of accounting entries would be as follows:

    (i)   apportion the goodwill of £60,000 between the original partners using the old profit and loss sharing ratios;

    (ii)   record the £95,000 capital contribution from 'P' being paid into the partnership's bank;

    (iii) balance off the accounts and draft the Balance Sheet.

That is:

GOODWILL

		£		£
(i) Capital:	N 30,000			
	O 30,000	60,000	Bal c/d	60,000
		60,000		60,000

BANK

		£		£
Bal b/d		20,000		
(ii) Capital:	P	95,000	Bal c/d	115,000
		115,000		115,000

PARTNERS' CAPITAL

	N £	O £	P £		N £	O £	P £
				Bal b/d	75,000	75,000	–
				(i) Goodwill	30,000	30,000	–
Bal c/d	105,000	105,000	95,000	(ii) Bank			95,000
	105,000	105,000	95,000		105,000	105,000	95,000

NOP Partnership
Balance Sheet Extract (After P admitted)
(Goodwill a/c retained)

	£'000
Assets	
Property	100
Vehicles	30
Goodwill	60
Bank	115
	305
Partners' Capital	
N	105
O	105
P	95
	305

If there is a further partnership change at some future date and this involves a goodwill revaluation, the revaluation surplus or loss will be shared among the three partners in accordance with the profit and loss sharing ratios operating at that date. No action would be required if the goodwill value continued at £60,000.

Solution:

(b) Goodwill account closed off after adjustments processed.
The accounting sequence would be as follows:

(i) apportion the goodwill of £60,000 between the original partners using the old profit and loss sharing ratios;

(ii) re-apportion goodwill among all of the partners using the new profit and loss sharing ratios, closing off the goodwill account.

(iii) record the £95,000 capital contribution from P being paid into the partnership's bank;

(iv) balance off the accounts and draft the Balance Sheet.
That is;

GOODWILL

			£				£
(i) Capital:	N	30,000		(ii) Capital:	N	20,000	
	O	30,000			O	20,000	
	P	–	60,000		P	20,000	60,000
			60,000				60,000

BANK

	£		£
Bal b/d	20,000		
(iii) Capital: P	95,000		115,000
	115,000		115,000

PARTNERS' CAPITAL

	N £	O £	P £		N £	O £	P £
				Bal b/d	75,000	75,000	–
(ii) Goodwill	20,000	20,000	20,000	(i) Goodwill	30,000	30,000	–
Bal c/d	85,000	85,000	75,000	(iii) Bank	–	–	95,000
	105,000	105,000	95,000		105,000	105,000	95,000

NOP Partnership
Balance Sheet Extract (After P admitted)

	(No Goodwill a/c retained) £'000
Assets	
Property	100
Vehicles	30
Bank	115
	245
Partners' Capital	
N	85
O	85
P	75
	245

The NOP illustration above concentrated on the treatment of goodwill upon the arrival of a new partner. If there had been a change in the way profits and losses were distributed among existing partners, then similar accounting procedures would have to be followed so that partners who have experienced a reduction in their share of goodwill are compensated by those gaining. The same general rules apply where a partner leaves a firm.

PARTNERSHIP DISSOLUTION

The final main area in partnership accounting to be considered is in relation to the *dissolution of a partnership*.

The reasons behind any particular dissolution will obviously vary, but some of the more common explanations will include the following:

(1) the firm was established to meet a specific business objective which has since been achieved;
(2) the firm was established for a fixed term and that term has expired;
(3) a partner has given notice of his intention to dissolve the partnership;
(4) the business is simply no longer profitable;
(5) a partner has been declared bankrupt or has died.

The occurrence of an event in the nature of any of the above does not in itself mean that a partnership would automatically be dissolved. It may well be the case that the relevant partnership agreement contains provisions which stipulate an alternative course of action to that of dissolution.

It should also be mentioned at this stage that the Partnership Act 1890 provides for the Court to dissolve partnerships in certain situations. For example where a partner is certified insane, or where there has been a 'wilful and persistent breach of the partnership agreement' by one or more of the partners[1].

Besides any partnership agreement in existence, the provisions contained within the Partnership Act should also be given due cognisance when a dissolution is

---

1 See Partnership Act 1890, s 35.

inevitable since it directly addresses the process involved[1]. As a result, partnership dissolutions will generally tend to follow a similar pattern.

First of all the partnership assets will be disposed of[2]. Next all the liabilities of the firm will be settled, with those attributable to parties other than partners being dealt with first. Where a partner has made a loan or advance to the firm in excess of the agreed capital contribution, this too can be properly classified as a debt of the partnership and as such it should be repaid before the return of partners' capital. Any favourable balance on a partner's current account (net of drawings) may also be dealt with in this way, assuming that the amount standing at credit in that partner's capital account is consistent with the requirements of the partnership agreement.

The final main stage in the process is to return the partners' outstanding capital. Depending on the outcome of the dissolution, partners may receive more or less capital than expected.

It is unlikely that the net sum of cash finally available for transfer to the partners will be exactly equal to the total of the balances on their capital accounts since very often either a profit or loss is realised. A profit on dissolution will, therefore, have the effect of increasing the capital paid to each of the partners, with a loss on dissolution having the reverse effect. If the loss is a severe one and it results in a partner's capital account being forced into an overall deficit position, the partner will be obliged to pay a further sum into the firm's bank account to make good the deficit.

Accounting for a dissolution

The accounting procedures adopted in the event of a partnership dissolution largely reflect the above process. The key account used will be the *Realisation account*.

---

1   Partnership Act 1890, s 44.
2   The disposal of partnership assets does not necessarily mean that they will be sold to persons outwith the firm. It is possible for a partner to take over an asset at a value agreed with the other partners. Furthermore, payment in respect of the asset might be made by way of an adjustment against the partner's capital account rather than through the exchange of cash.

ILLUSTRATION 8.6

Assumptions:

(i) The Balance Sheet of the Q and R partnership at 31 July 1999 appears as follows:

QR Partnership
Balance Sheet as at 31 July 1999
(all figures in £'000's)

	Cost	Acc. Depr'n	
	£	£	£
Fixed assets:			
Office property	75	—	75
Motor vehicles	25	10	15
Office equipment	15	5	10
	115	15	100
Current assets:			
Stock of stationery		3	
Debtors	20		
Less: Provision for bad debts	(2)	18	
Bank		13	
		34	
Less: Current liabilities:			
Creditors		(4)	30
			130

Represented by:	Q	R	Total
	£	£	£
Partners' capital accounts	75	25	100
Partners' current accounts	20	10	30
	95	35	130

(ii) The two partners decided to dissolve the partnership on 31 July 1999, with the proceeds from the sale of the firm's assets as follows:

	£
Office property	95,000
Motor vehicles	17,000
Office equipment	9,000
Stationery	3,000

(iii) Costs of the dissolution amounted to £8,000.
(iv) The partners have agreed to share any dissolution profit or loss equally.

Required:

(a) Describe the various steps involved in the dissolution of the Q R partnership, and (b) show the various entries in the firm's accounts which would be necessary to record this entire process. Also, (c) state the amount of any profit or loss which arises. Finally, (d) state the amounts which Q and R would each receive after the completion of the dissolution.

Solution (a):

(i) Transfer the balances on any provision account to the relevant asset account. For example:
   Dr Provision for bad debts account
   Cr Debtors account.
(ii) Transfer the balances on the asset accounts to the Realisation account. For example:
   Dr Realisation account
   Cr Office property account.
(iii) Dispose of the assets, recording the transactions in the firm's Bank account and the realisation account. For example:
   With respect to the sale of the Office property
   Dr Bank account, £95,000
   Cr Realisation account, £95,000.

(iv)   Settle any liabilities (including the costs of the dissolution), recording any such payment in the firm's Bank account as well as directly to the liability account itself. For example:

Dr Creditors account
Cr Bank account.

(v)   Calculate any resulting profit or loss on dissolution and share this among the partners on the agreed basis.

(vi)   Transfer the balances on the partners' current accounts to their capital accounts.

(vii)   Pay the partners what they are due. This should result in all the firm's accounts being closed off.

Solution (b):

The various entries needed in the accounts of the firm to record the dissolution are as follows: (Note: All figures are in £'000's)

PROVISION FOR BAD DEBTS

	£		£
(i) Debtors	2	Bal b/d	2

DEBTOR

	£		£
Bal b/d	20	(i) Prov. for Bad Debts	2
		(ii) Realisation	18
	20		20

PROVISION FOR DEPRECIATION: MOTOR VEHICLES

	£		£
(i) Motor Vehicles	10	Bal b/d	10

MOTOR VEHICLES

	£		£
Bal b/d	25	(i) Prov. for Depreciation: Motor Vehicles	10
		(ii) Realisation	15
	25		25

PROVISION FOR DEPRECIATION: OFFICE EQUIPMENT

	£		£
(i) Office Equipment	5	Bal b/d	5

OFFICE EQUIPMENT

	£		£
Bal b/d	15	(i) Prov for Depreciation: Office Equipment	5
		(ii) Realisation	10
	15		15

OFFICE PROPERTY

	£		£
Bal b/d	75	Realisation	75

STATIONERY

	£		£
Bal b/d	3	Realisation	3

BANK

	£		£
Bal b/d	13	(iv) Creditors	4
		(iv) Realisation: costs	8
(iii) Realisation: Sale of assets	141	Bal c/d	142
	154		154
Bal b/d	142	(vii) Capital: Q	101
		R	41
	142		142

CREDITORS

	£		£
(iv) Bank	4	Bal b/d	4

REALISATION

	£		£
(ii) Debtors	18	Bank: Sale of assets	
(ii) Motor Vehicles	15	(iii) Motor Vehicles	17
(ii) Office Equipment	10	(iii) Office Equipment	9
(ii) Office Property	75	(iii) Office Property	95
(ii) Stationery	3	(iii) Stationery	3
(iv) Bank: costs	8	(iii) Debtors	17
Bal c/d	12		
	141		141
(v) Capital: Q	6	Bal b/d	12
R	6		
	12		12

CURRENT ACCOUNT: Q

	£		£
(vi) Capital: Q	20	Bal b/d	20

CURRENT ACCOUNT: R

	£		£
(vi) Capital: R	10	Bal b/d	10

CAPITAL ACCOUNT: Q

	£		£
Bal c/d	101	Bal b/d	75
		(v) Realisation	6
		(vi) Current a/c: Q	20
	101		101
(vii) Bank	101	Bal b/d	101

CAPITAL ACCOUNT: R

	£		£
Bal c/d	41	Bal b/d	25
		(v) Realisation	6
		(vi) Current a/c: R	10
	41		41
(vii) Bank	41	Bal b/d	41

Solution (c):

The QR Partnership made a profit of £12,000 upon dissolution and this amount was shared equally between the partners.

Solution (d):

Partner Q received £101,000 and R received £41,000.

QUESTIONS[1]

1. Allan and Bryce admitted Campbell as junior partner to their solicitor's practice five years ago, and agreed to share profits in the ratio 2:2:1 respectively. Campbell is now handling more difficult cases and recently introduced a significant new client to the firm. All three partners agreed to share profits equally from 1 July 1999. The firm's year end is 30 September. Profits for the year ended 30 September 1999 were £115,000 and it was agreed that of that sum £70,000 relates to the period from 1 October 1998 to 30 June 1999.

Required:

Show the allocation of profits among the partners for the year to 30 September 1999.

2. Davidson and Evans have been practising in partnership for some years sharing profits equally. On 31 January 1999 they decided to admit Fraser, a well deserving employee, to the partnership. Profits were to be shared 2:2:1 respectively. Unfortunately by September 1999 Evans' health had deteriorated so badly that the family doctor advised that Evans should give up work. Evans withdrew from the partnership on 30 September 1999. Davidson and Fraser then agreed to share profits in the ratio 3:2 thereafter.

Required:

Show the allocation of profits among the partners for the year to 31 December 1999 assuming that the profits for the year were £95,000, split:

	£
Period to 31 January	6,000
1 February to 30 September	74,000
1 October to 31 December	15,000

3. Geddes Harris and Irons are in partnership as solicitors. The partnership started in a small office which cost £20,000 ten years ago. They still have this office (now rented out to an insurance broker) but two years ago purchased and moved into a larger office costing £75,000 in the town centre. Both are carried in the balance sheet at cost. The balance sheet also shows office furniture with a written down value of £6,500 and cash at bank £16,000.

The partners' capital accounts are as follows:

	£
G	75,000
H	35,000
I	38,000

Geddes has decided that the time is right to retire from the partnership. The partnership agreement states that revaluation gains should be split in the ratio 3:2:2 respectively. The properties were revalued at £50,000 for the small office and £70,000 for the town centre office. The partners agreed that the office furniture be valued at £6,000.

1   For suggested solutions see p 321.

Required:

(a) How much is Geddes entitled to withdraw on retiring from the partnership?
(b) What problems are likely to arise on the withdrawal of this capital from the partnership and what steps might the remaining partners take to reduce the impact?

4. Jack and King have been in partnership as solicitors for many years. An extract of the firm's accounts at 31 March 1999 showed the following:

JK Partnership
Balance Sheet at 31 March 1999

	£'000	£'000
Fixed Assets		
Office property—cost		40
Office furniture & equipment—net book value		7
Vehicles—net book value		10
		57
Current Assets		
Work in progress	15	
Debtors	40	
Bank	6	
Surplus in clients funds	3	
	64	
Current Liabilities		
Creditors	8	
Net Current Assets		56
		113
Represented by:		
Partners capital—J		65
—K		48
		113

Jack and King have decided to admit a new partner, Lewis, to the partnership to provide expertise in corporate law. They have been offered £100,000 for the office because of its development potential. They also feel that both the furniture and the vehicles are overvalued by £1,000 and £3,000 respectively. The office will be sold in around six months time, but Lewis is to be admitted to the partnership now and they do not think that Lewis should be entitled to benefit from the gain on the office. Equally Lewis does not want to bear the loss on the furniture and vehicles after joining the partnership.

Required:

Show the balance sheet after the admission of Lewis to the partnership so that Lewis will not be affected by the above revaluations. Jack and King currently share all profits equally. Lewis will be entitled to an equal share of all profits after admission. Lewis will pay £25,000 capital contribution to the firm on 1 April 1999.

5. Mento and Nairn have been in partnership sharing all profits equally. They decide to appoint a new partner, Opal, provided that Opal makes a £75,000 capital contribution. This capital input will entitle Opal to share profits equally in the future. Goodwill is to be valued at £90,000, but the partners do not wish it to appear on the balance sheet.

The balance sheet, before the change occurred, was summarised as follows:

		£,000
Fixed Assets		170
Current Assets		80
Current Liabilities		(50)
		200
Represented by:		
Partner's capital M		100
N		100
		200

Required:

Show the balance sheet immediately after Opal was admitted. In addition, show the movements which take place in the partners' capital accounts as a result of the goodwill adjustment.

6. Roxburgh Stevens and Taylor have been in partnership for several years sharing all profits equally. Roxburgh has decided to retire from the partnership on 1 January 2000 and feels that as well as the capital repayment, an amount for goodwill should also be paid out. The partners agree that goodwill should be valued at £48,000, with the partners having an equal share thereon. The two remaining partners do not want to carry goodwill in the accounts. The balance sheet before the transaction was as follows:

RST Partnership
Balance Sheet at 31 December 1999

	£'000	£'000
Fixed Assets		
Property		40
Office furniture & equipment		10
Vehicles		15
		65
Current Assets		
Work in progress	16	
Debtors	25	
Bank	48	
Cash in hand	1	
	90	
Current Liabilities		
Creditors	10	
Net Current Assets		80
		145
Represented by:		
Partners capital—R		35
S		65
T		45
		145

R is taking the capital and goodwill payout by way of a car and computer (shown in the balance sheet at £5,000 and £1,000 respectively) a loan of £20,000 to be paid by the partnership in one year's time and the remainder in cash.

Required:

Show the balance sheet on 1 January 2000, together with a full explanatory note on the movements in the partners' capital accounts. Show the movement in the partners' capital accounts after the above events have taken place together with a balance sheet on 11 January 2000.

7. Utov and Velsky have decided that the purpose of their partnership has been achieved and therefore aim to dissolve the partnership on 1 January 2000. The balance sheet at 31 December 1999 was as follows:

UV Partnership
Balance Sheet at 31 December 1999

Fixed Assets	£'000	£'000	£'000
Property—cost			50
Office furniture & equipment—net book value			5
Vehicles—net book value			7
			62
Current Assets			
Work in progress		7	
Debtors		26	
Bank		17	
Cash in hand		1	
		51	
Current Liabilities			
Loan		7	
Creditors		18	
		25	
Net Current Assets			26
			88
Represented by:			
Partners capital—Fixed	40	20	60
Current	12	16	28
	52	36	88

The two partners have agreed that as with all other profits, they will share any gains or losses on realisation equally. They estimate the cost of dissolution will be £8,000. On realisation, the property sold for £87,000, the office furniture and equipment for £2,000 and the cars £8,000. In total they realised £30,000 from customers in respect of invoices outstanding and work in progress at 31 December 1999.

Required:

Show the entries which will be made in the realisation account, together with the corresponding entries in the other accounts affected, to record the partnership dissolution. State the amounts which Utov and Velsky will each receive as a result of the dissolution.

Chapter Nine: Organisation of business records in a legal firm

Every business must keep accurate and complete records that fully reflect its transactions over a period of time. This basic rule applies to all types of business whether in manufacturing, engineering, education or the service sector such as a firm of solicitors. Business records are required for many reasons. The most important reasons are: to let the owners see how well (or badly) the business is performing; to let potential investors decide whether to put money into the business; and to establish how much tax the business has to pay on its profits.

The records must be as reliable as possible. Accuracy of records can be helped by ensuring that they are arranged and maintained in an orderly manner. The record keeping process should be simple, easy to follow and must include all business transactions. Controls should be incorporated into the accounting system to pick up any errors or omissions which, once detected, can then be corrected.

This chapter introduces how records can be organised for businesses in general. It will also show that, with only slight modification, the same basic recording framework can be applied to a solicitor's practice. The chapter is split into three main sections, being, (1) an overview of accounting systems; (2) consideration of a few basic transactions of a legal practice; and (3) a review of the regulatory environment affecting a solicitor's business records.

The Solicitors (Scotland) Accounts Rules 1997 have a significant effect on the style and content of a solicitor's business records. Hence reference will frequently be made to the Accounts Rules both in this chapter and in the one following. Furthermore in the third section of this chapter, once the impact of the Accounts Rules have been considered, there will also be a brief insight into the effects of three other sources of influence on a legal firm's records. Namely, the Solicitors (Scotland) Accounts Certificate Rules 1997, the Solicitors (Scotland)(Conduct of Investment Business) Practice Rules 1997 and the Money Laundering Regulations 1993.

ACCOUNTING SYSTEM OVERVIEW

General Business

There are several distinct stages in the structure of business records which can be categorised as follows:

(1) source documents;
(2) books of original entry;
(3) summarising and classifying the information;
(4) communication.

The stages, as well as their components, can be shown by the use of a flowchart, as in **Illustration 9.1**.

ILLUSTRATION 9.1

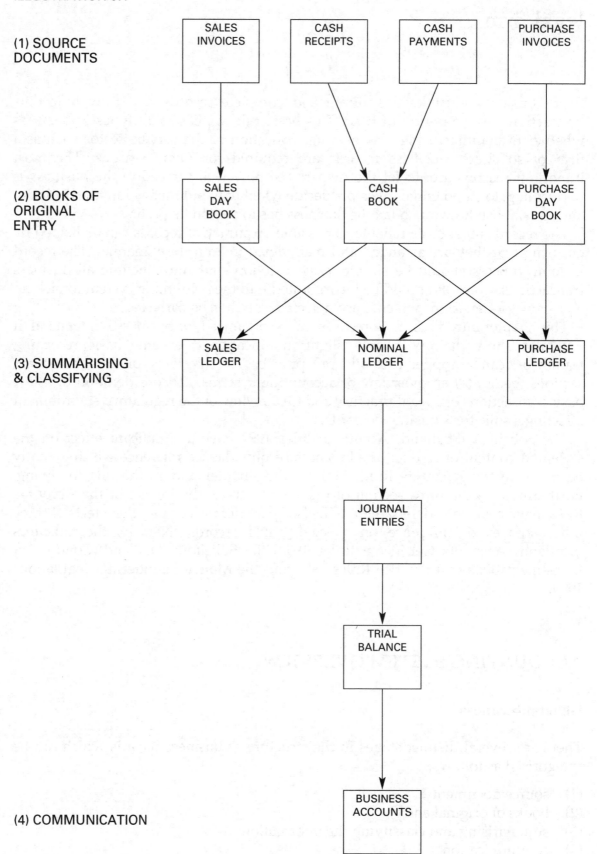

(1) SOURCE
DOCUMENTS

(2) BOOKS OF
ORIGINAL
ENTRY

(3) SUMMARISING
& CLASSIFYING

(4) COMMUNICATION

(1) Source documents

The sales and purchase invoices along with cash receipts and cash payments can all be termed source documents. These represent the initial transactions that need to be fed into the record keeping process.

(2) Books of original entry

The sales daybook, cash book and purchase daybook are the books of original entry into which the data from the source documents is recorded.

(3) Summarising and classifying

The next stage in the process will result in the information in the books of original entry being summarised and classified into different parts of the nominal ledger, depending upon the general nature of the original transactions involved. The nominal ledger comprises a number of different T accounts, each of which is used as a collection point to record transactions of a similar nature.

The sales ledger and purchase ledger are subsidiary records which show in more detail some of the information contained in the nominal ledger. For example, the sales ledger analyses the individual debtors making up the total debtors figure in the nominal ledger, and the purchase ledger does the same for creditors.

The Journal, which is not a formal part of the double-entry system, is simply a diary used to record more unusual events not readily covered by some other part of the accounting system. Each Journal entry will normally show (i) the account and amount to be debited, (ii) the account and amount to be credited and, (iii) a very brief description of the matter being recorded.

(4) Communication

A trial balance can be extracted from the nominal ledger and financial statements prepared. The latter event represents the communication stage of the accounting system.

Legal practices

The principles outlined so far will apply equally to the business of a solicitor. But there is a significant difference between the records of a legal practice and those of a general business. Since the former frequently handles funds belonging to clients, solicitors must as a consequence have an extra dimension to their accounting system enabling them to record all transactions relating to their clients' funds. Not only that, but the solicitor's accounting system must also be capable of maintaining a clear distinction at all times between client funds and those of the firm itself.

The Law Society of Scotland recognised the above need to have the two categories of funds kept apart. Rule 4 of the Accounts Rules makes it a compulsory requirement for solicitors handling money belonging to clients to keep a separate record of all such transactions affecting clients' funds. In essence, therefore, solicitors will have two separate sets of records: those for recording office matters and those for recording transactions involving clients' funds.

Using the same basic flowchart as before, but modified in order that the solicitor's records comply with the provisions of the Accounts Rules, results in **Illustration 9.2**.

ILLUSTRATION 9.2

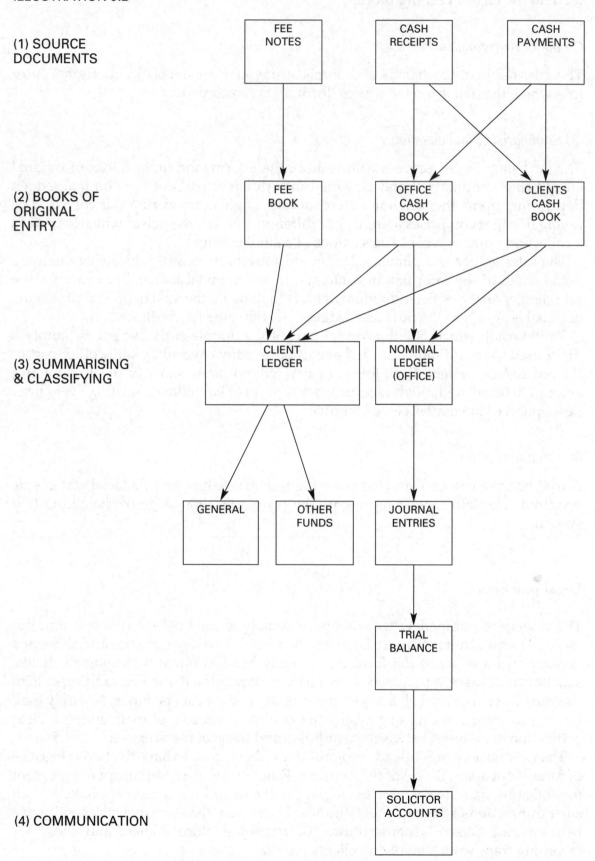

If this flowchart is compared to that of a general business as shown in **Illustration 9.1**, then certain differences will be apparent.

(1) Source documents

Sales invoices are issued to customers in a general business. In the service sector, fee notes are sent instead. This slight difference in terminology is reflected in **Illustration 9.2** above.

Another difference between the two flowcharts can be seen in relation to purchase invoices. In the solicitor's flowchart, there is no box for purchase invoices. The reason for this omission stems from the fact that it is common practice for solicitors to incorporate this information into their records only once such invoices are actually paid. Hence it will be dealt with under cash payments. The reason for this approach is that it helps ensure the correct treatment of recoverable outlays paid by the solicitor on behalf of clients. It is worth mentioning at this point that solicitors can only charge clients for outlays once they have been incurred.

On another related matter, although both flowcharts may appear similar in that they both have boxes for cash receipts and cash payments, the legal business has to deal with a more complicated situation. This stems from the fact that solicitors are generally handling clients funds in addition to their own. Solicitors, as a result, will have a more onerous task when recording such information if they are to comply with Law Society requirements.

(2) Books of original entry

The effect of the different treatment of purchase invoices in a legal firm extends into the next couple of stages of the flowchart. Thus there will be no purchase day book and no purchase ledger in the accounting system of solicitors.

Similarly a legal accounting system does not normally have a sales day book nor a sales ledger. Solicitors will use a fee book to record details of all fees due to the firm. The fee book is also important for the purposes of accounting for Value Added Tax (VAT). It should be noted that fees information at this stage is not yet part of the double-entry system, becoming so only once payment has been received from the clients.

The most significant difference in the books of original entry of a solicitor is the inclusion of a clients cash book. This is to allow the separate recording of client transactions, keeping them apart from office transactions.

(3) Summarising and classifying

The stage of summarising and classifying in a solicitor's system includes a separate client ledger. The client ledger is essentially divided into two sub-ledgers. One of the sub-ledgers is used to record all the detailed transactions relating to individual clients and whether amounts are owed to or from clients at a given time.

To help ensure a proper record of fees issued to clients is maintained, there is normally a column in this part of the client ledger headed *fee memo* which acts as an aide memoir to the solicitor that fees are outstanding.

It is worth emphasising that fees raised by the solicitor and first recorded in the firm's fee book (being a simple diary system in effect) and only become part of the double-entry records when paid by the clients. This method of accounting for fees is known as a *payment request system*[1]. Under this system the solicitor will issue a request for payment to a client. When the client pays the amount due, the solicitors will then issue a VAT invoice/fee note at which point all the relevant accounting double-entries will arise. A benefit of this system is that VAT on fee notes is only paid to Customs & Excise after the money has actually been received from the client, so there is an obvious cash flow advantage to the firm. Another advantage is that it will avoid the need for VAT bad debt relief claims to be made where fees are not paid by the client.

A further sub-ledger of the client ledger exists called *other funds* and is used to record clients money that has been lodged in a specific bank account in the name of a client.

(4) Communication

The records required for communicating financial information are basically the same for a legal practice as they are for a general business.

In summary, it is worth stressing that a solicitor's practice must be sure that its records are organised in such a way as to separately identify office and client transactions. The firm's system must also have adequate accounting controls in place to ensure compliance with all regulatory provisions.

Against this background to a solicitor's accounting system, it will now be useful to consider a few basic transactions commonly encountered by legal firms and how these may be recorded.

BASIC TRANSACTIONS OVERVIEW

There are four basic transactions a solicitor's practice will have to record:

(1)   Receipt of office money
(2)   Receipt of client money
(3)   Payment of office money
(4)   Payment of client money

Journal entries are used below to describe the various bookkeeping steps necessary to record each of the four basic transactions.

It should also be noted that in some cases the accounting entries have been simplified as an aid to clarity at this stage. The following chapter, although still following the principles outlined here, will be more akin to what happens in practice.

(1) Receipt of office money

If a solicitor receives a fee payment of £100 from a client for work done, the double-entry process to record this transaction in the solicitor's records will be:

---

1   The payment request system is commonly encountered in practice. However, some firms may adopt a slightly different accounting treatment.

		Dr £	Cr £
(a)	Client bank	100	
	Client ledger		100
	Being receipt of outstanding fee		
(b)	Client ledger	100	
	Fees		100
	Being recording of fee in accounting records		
(c)	Office bank	100	
	Client bank		100
	Being transfer of funds between client and firm		

There are three main stages to record this single transaction: (a) money received from the client is recorded in the client bank account and client ledger; (b) the solicitor enters the fee in the office records and charges the client ledger account accordingly (the fee memo column in the client ledger would also be updated at this stage since the fee has been settled), and; (c) funds are finally transferred from the clients' bank account to the firm's bank account.

(2) Receipt of client money

If a solicitor receives £400 in advance from a client to be used to settle future costs in an ongoing conveyancing transaction, the double-entry to record this transaction in the solicitor's records is:

		Dr £	Cr £
(a)	Client bank	400	
	Client ledger		400
	Being receipt from client in advance		

It should be noted that the money received still belongs to the client and consequently it must be held in trust by the solicitor until such times as it is used to settle future expenses of that client.

(3) Payment of office money

If a solicitor pays £300 in respect of expenses of the firm, eg insurance renewal, the double entry to record this transaction in the solicitor's records is:

		Dr £	Cr £
(a)	Expenses—insurance	300	
	Office bank		300
	Being payment of office insurance		

Note that the payment is for expenses of the firm and hence it is made from the office bank account. This transaction has nothing at all to do with money held in the clients' bank account at this time and so client funds remain unaffected by this type of business transaction.

(4) Payment of client money

The final basic transaction of a legal practice is the payment of client money. If a solicitor pays £200 in respect of expenses of a client in the ongoing conveyancing transaction mentioned above, the double-entry to record this aspect of the transaction in the solicitors' records is:

		Dr £	Cr £
(a)	Client ledger	200	
	Client bank		200
	Being payment of client expenses		

Since the payment is in respect of client business, it is charged directly to the clients' bank account.

It is important to note that if an advance had not been received earlier from the client sufficient to cover such expenses, then it would have been necessary for the firm to pay the outlays from its office bank account in the first instance.

One of the principal cornerstones of the Accounts Rules is that broadly, at any point in time, the funds held by the firm at its bank in trust for its clients must never fall below the total level of claims by its clients against such funds. The firm should always be in a position to repay all of the funds owed to clients.

To a significant extent, regulations imposed by the Law Society of Scotland will shape the accounting function within legal practices.

REGULATORY ENVIRONMENT AFFECTING A SOLICITOR'S BUSINESS RECORDS

The Solicitors (Scotland) Accounts Rules 1997

The Solicitors (Scotland) Accounts Rules 1997 [SAR] are important regulations with which every solicitor must comply. The regulations are onerous and require solicitors to keep substantial amounts of information as part of their business records.

The most obvious impact of the Rules on the records is the need to keep office and client money completely separate. This requires either a completely separate client cash book to be maintained or if the firm operates with only a single cash book, then this must at least contain separate analysis columns to record client transactions.

The solicitor also has to use a separate client ledger or, again, at least separate clients' columns in the firm's general ledger. It will be recalled that **Illustration 9.2** showed the interaction of a separate client cash book and separate client ledger with other parts of the solicitor's accounting system.

The Accounts Rules also require a solicitor's firm to maintain a record of any transfers between the accounts of its clients [SAR 12(3)], although these can usually be recorded in the client ledger accounts themselves.

The solicitor has at all times to keep the business records written up-to-date which show all clients' money held, received or paid or other money held by the solicitor in a separately named client account [SAR 12(1)].

The solicitor must also keep the business records up-to-date at all times to show the true financial position of the practice and must balance the records every month [SAR 12(4)].

Most well-run solicitor practices will have fully computerised records which not only save time and effort but also include tighter controls to minimise errors in the processing of information. The Accounts Rules require any computerised system to have the facility to produce an immediate printout of any account [SAR 12(6)].

One further area where the Accounts Rules impact on the records is the need for regular reconciliations to be performed and retained [SAR 13 and 14]. Reconciliations are required in a number of areas:

(1)   Client bank account reconciliation.
(2)   Client ledger/ Client bank account comparison.
(3)   Client deposit account reconciliation.
(4)   Client ledger/ Client deposit account comparison.

The reconciliations and comparisons in (1) and (2) above have to be performed on a monthly basis with records of these retained by the solicitor for three years from the date they were prepared.

The reconciliations and comparisons in (3) and (4) must be performed once every three months and at the firms' year-end with records of these retained by the solicitor for three years from the date they were prepared.

The Solicitors (Scotland) Accounts Certificate Rules 1997

It will be clear from the earlier discussions that the Accounts Rules require some additional business records to be maintained by the solicitor that a normal business would otherwise not have to keep. However, the Accounts Rules can only be effective and have force if they are properly monitored to ensure that solicitors are complying with their contents. With this in mind, there are provisions in the Rules [SAR 17] which give the Law Society of Scotland powers of investigation. Every firm of solicitors can expect, therefore, to receive an inspection visit on a cyclical basis.

Owing to the fact that there are a large number of practices in the country which fall within the scope of the Accounts Rules, there may be several years between each inspection visit by Law Society accountants. It is very important that all the provisions of the Accounts Rules are followed consistently and not only when an inspection is due. To ensure this is the case, a solicitor is required to complete a certificate every six months (within one month of the period end) confirming that the Solicitors (Scotland) Accounts Rules have been followed. This certificate is delivered to the Society. The detailed regulations for the completion of a certificate are contained in the Solicitors (Scotland) Accounts Certificate Rules 1997.

The requirement for a solicitor to prepare reconciliations as part of the business records was seen earlier and the Certificate Rules use this information as part of the monitoring process by the Law Society of Scotland. The certificate will contain details of the comparison between the client ledger balances and the client bank account reconciliation. This comparison checks that there is sufficient client money in the client bank account to pay all amounts owed to clients as recorded in the client ledger. Any breach of this requirement where there is a shortfall is very serious and is regarded as such by the Law Society.

Solicitors (Scotland) (Conduct of Investment Business) Practice Rules 1997

An important role carried out by many firms of solicitors is in the provision of financial services advice. Clients frequently consult their solicitors on such financial matters and, as one might consequently expect, it is a further area covered by regulation. Inappropriate advice by solicitors may prove to be expensive to the unfortunate client. With such a wide range of so many similar products on the market, the solicitor must keep up-to-date with developments and changes if best advice is to be consistently offered to clients.

Regulations have been put in place by the Law Society of Scotland to help protect clients from inappropriate advice and these are contained in the Solicitors (Scotland) (Conduct of Investment Business) Practice Rules 1997. Unfortunately for the solicitor in practice, with regulation comes the added burden of additional information and records which have to be maintained. The additional records to be kept in this case include:

(1)   Client agreements.
(2)   Client fact sheets.
(3)   Details of execution only transactions.
(4)   Details of investment advice.

The provision of financial service advice should be covered by a client agreement which will detail the nature of the services to be provided and the solicitor should maintain a record of all such agreements.

Appropriate advice can only be given if the solicitor has sufficient background knowledge of that particular client. This can easily be achieved by completing a fact sheet for each client to obtain all the relevant information on which to base subsequent financial services advice. The solicitor should retain client fact sheets both as an aid to future advice and as a source of proof that steps have been taken by the solicitor to provide best advice.

There are two principal types of transaction a solicitor can enter into when providing financial services: *execution only* or *investment advice*.

Execution only simply means the solicitor does not provide advice or an opinion on the merits of a particular transaction and only executes the wishes of the client. The solicitor should ensure that the client agreement for such cases is properly set up and makes this arrangement clear.

In contrast, transactions involving investment advice are more onerous and require the solicitor to maintain detailed records. Suitable records will again help show that best advice has been given – that is, that the solicitor knows the client and that *best execution* has been achieved. Best execution basically means that transactions are carried out on a timely basis and there is a history of the transaction. The transaction history should show when instructions were received, how they were dealt with and the basis for the advice given to the client.

Financial services work may result in the solicitor keeping documents of title received on behalf of clients. Documents will arise where, for example, investments have been made in stocks and shares. These are important legal documents and the solicitor is required to maintain a record of those held that distinguishes between investments belonging to clients and those belonging to the firm.

The records to be kept by the solicitor when carrying out investment business must be retained for at least ten years.

Just as solicitors are required to submit a certificate of compliance with respect to the Accounts Rules on a regular basis, a similar obligation exists if they also provide investment advice to clients. The Solicitors (Scotland) Investment Business Compliance Certificate Rules 1997 necessitates firms to make regular declarations to the Law Society of Scotland that they have acted in accordance with the Conduct of Investment Business Practice Rules.

The general compliance and reporting framework applicable to investment business is very similar in nature to that of the Accounts Rules[1].

Money Laundering Regulations 1993

Solicitors are also obliged by law to observe the Money Laundering Regulations 1993. Failure to comply with the regulations is a criminal offence punishable by a fine and/or imprisonment for a term of up to two years.

The principal purpose of the regulations is to prevent the proceeds of unlawful activities being legitimised by applying them to lawful transactions. The regulations apply to every one-off transaction involving the payment by or to a client of an amount of ECU 15,000 (approximately £12,000) or more. Where the transaction is of a lesser amount but is associated with other transactions which in aggregate exceed ECU 15,000 this would also be caught. The regulations also apply to every case where the solicitor forms a business relationship or where the solicitor suspects the client is engaged in money laundering either directly or indirectly.

In the present overview of the regulatory environment in which solicitors must carry out their business, the Money Laundering Regulations impose yet more demands both on a firm's business records and indeed on its internal reporting structures.

For example, solicitors are required to verify the identity of every person with whom a business relationship is to be established or for whom a one-off transaction will be executed and to retain the relevant records for a period of at least five years from the date the first step in this process was taken.

Identifying new clients is largely a matter of common-sense. If satisfactory evidence cannot be obtained by the solicitor, the business relationship or transaction should not proceed any further. The evidence of identity should be reasonably capable of confirming that the client is who they claim to be and the solicitor must be satisfied that true identity has been established.

For individual clients, it is suggested that the following details should be ascertained in practice: names used; current permanent address and post code; date and place of birth; and a document with a photograph of the applicant (eg passport or national identity card).

---

1   The Law Society of Scotland has provided advice for its members with respect to investment business. See Law Society Guidance on the Investment Business Rules and Regulations 1997.

Alternatively in the case of corporate clients, a copy of a Certificate of Incorporation as well as of the latest report and accounts of the company involved should be sufficient to meet the demands of the Money Laundering Regulations. If the company is unquoted or if the organisation is a partnership and none of the directors of the company or partners in the partnership are already known, then they should be identified as if individual clients (see above).

Solicitors are not required to undertake identification checks on their clients in some situations. For example, if they are dealing with existing clients, or if the client is a listed company or subsidiary of a listed company, or if the client is a private company or partnership and at least one of the directors or partners is already known to the firm.

On a similar token there are a few matters that are exempt from the regulations. For example where notice is received from other solicitors who confirm they have complied with the regulations, or where there is a cheque drawn on the client's own UK bank account, or in instances involving certain types of legal work (eg criminal work, wills, licensing and gaming work, insurance claims, certain matrimonial matters etc).

The Money Laundering Regulations also directly impact on the internal reporting structures within a solicitor's practice. The aim of the relevant provisions is to make sure that the firm's staff are aware of the need to be watchful for money laundering operations and that they know the correct procedures to follow if they believe that they have encountered such an event. It follows that solicitors will have to train their staff accordingly. As part of this process, firms will have to appoint a suitable person to act as the focus within the firm for the detection of money laundering schemes. All matters of suspicion have to be reported to this key individual who will then decide if further action is necessary. This may involve reporting the matter to the National Criminal Intelligence Service (NCIS). The firm also has a duty to retain suitable records of all events that may be associated with a money laundering scheme.

In conclusion, it will be clear from the above discussion that there are many factors that help shape the general business records of solicitors. It is not difficult to imagine, therefore, that with such a burden falling on the firm a properly organised record system is essential for most solicitors.

QUESTIONS[1]

1. Name the books of original entry you would find in a business and explain how these would be different in a solicitors' practice.

2. Show the journal entries to record the following transactions in the accounting records of a solicitor.
   (a) Receipt of a £5,000 deposit from a client.
   (b) Payment of the firm's telephone bill of £150.
   (c) Payment by the firm of search dues of £25 on behalf of a client.
   (d) Payment of monthly salaries of £70,000 of the solicitors' practice.
   (e) Receipt of £1,500 from a client in settlement of a firm's fee note.

1   For suggested solutions see p 327.

(f)   Receipt of £200,000 mortgage monies from a building society on behalf of a client in respect of a property transaction.

(g)   Refund to client of £3,500 being monies held by the solicitor in the client bank account.

(h)   Payment, by the firm, of a client's survey fee of £450.

(i)   Payment in respect of partners monthly drawings of £9,000.

(j)   Receipt of £200 from a client requested by solicitor to settle some outstanding bills.

3.   Solicitors have to comply with the Solicitors (Scotland) Accounts Rules 1997 and the Solicitors (Scotland) Accounts Certificate Rules 1997.

(a)   Briefly describe the primary objectives of each set of Rules.

(b)   Also, for the Accounts Rules, describe the records that a solicitor has to keep and how current such records need to be to ensure compliance.

Chapter Ten: Recording transactions in a solicitor's practice

The importance of good business records is difficult to over-stress. Although it may not seem vital at the outset of a new commercial venture to get this part of the business running smoothly, the honeymoon period of starting up and earning the first fees will be short lived if such an important area is ignored. In a brief space of time cash flow will almost certainly become an issue. Clients owing fees will have to be chased—but will the records be reliable enough to tell who they are, how much they owe and the nature of the work carried out on their behalf if (when) queried? Expenses of the business will have to be met—is there enough cash to meet such costs and are there any bills being overlooked now that will reappear at some future date when they are least expected or wanted? Payments for tax and VAT will soon arise—are the records sufficiently accurate both to calculate the amounts payable and to avoid penalties by making the correct payments by their due dates? The first Certificate will shortly be due to the Law Society—have breaches of the Accounts Rules been avoided and is there sufficient information available to complete the certificate?

Unless time has been taken to set up a proper system of business records then unfortunately the answers to some or all of the above questions will probably be "NO". Invariably it will be far more expensive to rectify such deficiencies retrospectively than if a suitable system had been in place and used consistently from the outset.

This chapter builds on the basics introduced in the previous chapter and looks at practical procedures for establishing good business records for a solicitor that will help to ensure compliance with, principally, the Solicitors (Scotland) Accounts Rules. There are several identifiable areas in the process of establishing good business records for a solicitor, which can be categorised as follows:

(1)   Setting up the system.
(2)   Transactions.
(3)   Control of the information.
(4)   Compliance and reporting.

Each of the above areas will be examined in turn.

The chapter will conclude with a worked example to illustrate a few simple transactions being recorded in an accounting system and to highlight key information that has to be produced to meet Law Society of Scotland requirements.

SETTING UP THE SYSTEM

It was mentioned in the previous chapter that it is advisable when setting up any new business records system to try to keep it as simple as possible. This will make the system easy to follow with less chance of things going wrong. Solicitors are given guidance in the Accounts Rules on the types of records to be kept and this should be built into the system of record keeping to ensure compliance.

Broadly, if a solicitor comes into contact with client funds either directly or indirectly, the records must show details of such transactions both for individual clients and collectively for all clients.

More specifically, the records should reflect all transactions with clients' money or any other money that is processed through a client account, or any borrowings in the solicitor's name on behalf of clients, or any other money held by the solicitor in a named client deposit account [SAR 12(1a)]. The record system should be capable of providing such details separately for an individual client, as well as producing summary information in respect of all clients funds falling under each of the above headings [SAR 12(1b)].

The Accounts Rules specify that the solicitor's practice should maintain certain records to capture the necessary financial details of client transactions [SAR 12(3)]. Namely (a) a client cash book (or if the firm operates with a single cash book, the latter must have separate columns for client transactions), (b) a record of inter-account transfers between clients and (c) a client ledger (or again as mentioned in the preceding chapter, if the firm operates with a single ledger then this must contain separate columns dedicated to client matters).

The Accounts Rules also contain provisions requiring the solicitor to maintain up-to-date records both in relation to clients and for the actual practice itself. Furthermore in relation to the practice, the Rules stipulate that its record system must be capable at all times of showing its true financial position [SAR 12 (1),(4)].

The Accounts Rules, therefore, leave no doubts that certain minimum standards are required of solicitors' record systems.

In the case of a new business start-up, one of the first decisions to face the solicitor will be the choice between (1) a manual or (2) a computerised accounting system.

(1) Manual Accounting System

As discussed in the preceding chapter, business records need to capture source documentation and record it in a logical manner. The books of original entry of a solicitor's practice, as first outlined in **Illustration 9.2**, are threefold and comprise: (a) a fee book; (b) an office cash book; and (c) a client cash book.

Books of original entry

Fee book. The fee book is used very much as a diary to record information relating to fees and should provide a reference of all work carried out and billed. The fee book will contain details of fee notes issued to clients and for which payment has still to be received. It is also used by the firm for VAT accounting purposes.

A typical fee book might appear as follows:

ILLUSTRATION 10.1

Peter Martin, Solicitors

Fee Book (Extract)

Date	Ref	Description	Total (£)	VAT(£)	Fees (£)	Sundry (£)
5/2/00	J001	Fee no. 321	1762.50	262.50	1500.00	
15/7/00	A023	Sale of car – Reg. No.A1 DRW	3500.00			3500.00
30/11/00	M009	Fee no. 322	1057.50	157.50	900.00	

Cash books. A typical cash book will have two sides to it; namely a left-hand side and a right-hand side. Traditionally the left-hand side is used to record information relating to income with the right-hand side reserved for matters of expenditure. In practical terms, the latter side generally contains more information.

If the legal practice uses two cash books, one for client matters and the other for office transactions, each cash book will still be broadly consistent with this layout. The same general rule is again applicable if the firm uses only a single cash book (where there will also be different columns for client and office transaction details).

The fundamental point about a solicitor's cash book is of course the need to retain a clear distinction between transactions relating to clients' funds and those of the firm itself.

Illustration 10.2 below shows an example of a solicitor's cash book. In this case a single cash book with separate client/office columns is used.

In a practical context it is not difficult to imagine that income and expenditure transactions can relate to a whole variety of different matters. To assist in summarising and classifying such information there is usually some analysis of the transactions in the cash book which attempts to group like income and expenditure items together. In order to avoid too many analysis columns in the cash book only the most commonly arising transactions will have their own separate heading. For example it can be seen in **illustration 10.2** that the expenses of *Salaries*, *Telephone* and *Insurance* command their own columns. There will be a *Sundry* column to act as a collection point for less significant and/or more infrequent items of expenditure. From time-to-time the total figure at the foot of each of these columns will be picked out and incorporated into the firm's double-entry system, appearing within separate T accounts in the nominal ledger.

The cash book will be the firm's principal record of money received and paid.

Bank accounts

Solicitors will also have to establish separate office and client bank accounts in which to physically deposit the money both for safekeeping and to generate interest. The statements received from the bank on a regular basis are third party business records that should mirror those of the solicitor. The two sets of records are subject to regular reconciliations as a control mechanism to help ensure all is in order [SAR 13].

A legal firm will commonly operate with one general client bank account through which day-to-day client monies are deposited and withdrawn. Although this bank account will be in the name of the firm, under the terms of the Accounts Rules the account title must contain the words 'client', 'trustee' or 'trust' [SAR 2(1)]. It is normally the case that bank interest earned on the balance in the general client account will be retained legitimately by the firm as its own income.

Solicitors, however, must be conscious of the situations outlined in the Accounts

ILLUSTRATION 10.2

Tuffnel & Tuffnel, Solicitors

Cash Book (Extract)

INCOME

Date	Ref	Description	Total (£)	VAT (£)	Client Ledger (£)	Sundry (£)
1/1/00	A010	D Anderson	4000.00		4000.00	
3/1/00	G021	A Gordon	1500.00		1500.00	
24/1/00	–	Asset sale	117.50	17.50		100.00
18/2/00	S001	P Simpson	800.00		800.00	
20/2/00	V100	R Vance	25.00		25.00	
28/2/00	C222	K Cohen	5100.00		5100.00	

EXPENDITURE

Date	Ref	Description	Total (£)	VAT (£)	Client Ledger (£)	Salaries (£)	Telephone (£)	Insurance (£)	Sundry (£)
5/1/00	B100	Phone	70.50	10.50			60.00		
7/1/00	S001	Insurance	840.00					840.00	
20/1/00	S002	Payroll	5500.00			5500.00			
1/2/00	A010	D Anderson	2500.00		2500.00				
9/2/00	V100	R Vance	25.00		25.00				
11/2/00	G101	Sundries	141.00	21.00					120.00

Rules [SAR 15] where interest earned on clients' funds should actually be passed on to clients. The two key determinants of whether a client's money should attract interest whilst under the control of the solicitor are the amount involved and the length of time it is anticipated that the funds will be held.

Besides a general client account, solicitors may also need to set up a number of other bank accounts in the name of the solicitor in trust for individually named clients, often referred to as *other funds*. It will be the solicitor who operates these individual accounts and only on the written authority of the client may such accounts be overdrawn.

Summarising and classifying

As outlined in **Illustration 9.2** in the preceding chapter, the next stage in setting up effective business records is the summarising and classifying of information contained in the books of original entry. This is achieved by processing the information into a further set of records.

(1) *Primary records:*   Nominal Ledger
(2) *Subsidiary records:*   Clients Ledger

The primary records summarise and classify all the information from the books of original entry and this is the first time in the business records that double-entry bookkeeping becomes applicable. The subsidiary records are not subject to the rules of double-entry accounting. They merely provide further information and analysis for some of the figures which appear in the firm's nominal ledger.

Primary records The nominal ledger will contain T accounts into which are recorded like transactions from the books of original entry. A nominal ledger may look similar to that shown in **illustration 10.3**.

ILLUSTRATION 10.3

K. Allen, Solicitors
Nominal ledger (Extract):

FEES				SALARIES		
		£				£
	31/1/00 cashbook	5,000			31/1/00 cashbook	8,000
	28/2/00 cashbook	1,500			28/2/00 cashbook	8,500

INSURANCES				CLIENTS LEDGER			
	£				£		£
31/1/00 cashbook	600			31/1/00 cashbook	8,000	1/1/00 bal b/f	14,000
				28/2/00 cashbook	1,500	31/1/00 cashbook	4,000

OFFICE BANK					CLIENTS BANK			
	£			£		£		£
1/1/00 bal b/f	10,000	31/1/00 cashbook		7,200	1/1/00 bal b/f	18,000	31/1/00 cashbook	3,000
31/1/00 cashbook	5,000				31/1/00 cashbook	1,500		

Subsidiary records One of the T accounts appearing in the firm's nominal ledger will be titled the *clients ledger* account. The clients ledger account will have subsidiary records providing a detailed analysis of the individual balances making up the totals shown in it.

An example of the usual format of this particular subsidiary record is shown in **illustration 10.4** below. It will be recalled from the commentary following on from **illustration 9.2** in the previous chapter, that the subsidiary client ledger is usually split into two sub-ledgers, called *general* and *other funds*. The former sub-section will show details of all transactions relating to clients and which will have been processed through the general client bank account. The latter sub-section provides details of client transactions recorded through individually named accounts held in trust for specific clients. The two parts of the client ledger can be seen in **illustration 10.4**.

The columns for *fee memo* and *o/s fee* act simply as aide memoirs for the solicitor that a fee has been issued and there is a balance outstanding from the client. It should be remembered that these entries do not form part of the double-entry records until such times as the client settles the outstanding fee note and the fee transaction is thereafter recorded in the normal way.

Communication

The final stage in setting up the business records is to ensure the information can be communicated effectively and there should be a system for producing the trial balance and putting the figures into final accounts format. As seen earlier in Chapter Two of this book the trial balance is a listing of the net balance on each T account held in the nominal ledger. Producing a trial balance is a mechanical process normally

ILLUSTRATION 10.4

Michael Jones Associates, Solicitors
Client Ledger (Extract)

Account	Date	Ref	Description	General Ledger					Other Funds Ledger		
				Dr (£)	Cr (£)	Cum Bal (£)	Fee Memo (£)	O/S Fees (£)	Dr (£)	Cr (£)	Cum Bal (£)
A010	7/1/00	AJS	From XYZ building society Mortgage loan funds		125000.00	125000.00					
A010	15/1/00	AJS	To PQR selling agents	119000.00		6000.00					
A010	20/1/00	AJS	Mr Anderson Fee no. 118/00 Fee 2500.00 VAT 437.50 Total 2937.50	2937.50			2937.50	2937.50			
A010	31/1/00	AJS	Selves—firm account transfer from client account to pay fees	2937.50		3062.50	-2937.50	0.00			
A010	3/2/00	AJS	Transfer of funds to specific deposit account	3062.50		0.00				3062.50	3062.50
S117	23/2/00	JRE	Funds from client Mrs. Smart		450.00	450.00					
S117	28/2/00	JRE	Settlement of survey fee on behalf of client—paid from firm bank	575.00		-125.00					

carried out on a monthly basis. Examples of trial balances for solicitors' firms were seen earlier in Chapter Seven.

(2) Computerised System

As an alternative to a manual accounting system, a solicitor may choose to implement a computerised system. A computerised system will follow the same basic principles previously described for the manual system. The significant difference will be the appearance of the records.

In a computerised system the cash book will show a listing of transactions allocated to an income or an expenditure column. There is no need for detailed analysis columns within a computerised accounts system because a nominal ledger account code will be allocated to the transaction when it is processed. Thereafter the press of a button will achieve the summarising and classifying of information to the nominal ledger. For each account in a computerised system there will be a listing of all relevant transactions allocated to a debit or credit column as appropriate. Consequently there will be no visible T account formats in the nominal ledger.

In summary, simple and effective business records will reduce the time and effort involved in recording basic transactions of the business and will help to minimise the number of errors that may arise. These principles apply whether a manual or computerised system is used. The choice of system will be dependent on a variety of factors, not least the demands that are likely to be made upon it and the personal preference of the solicitor involved.

TRANSACTIONS

Every business needs to ensure that source information is properly processed for accurate reporting. In a solicitor's practice this is vitally important.

A legal firm must of course record all business transactions relevant to its day-to-day running. But the firm must also keep records of many client transactions, most notably those relating to clients' funds. The Law Society of Scotland is fairly specific when instructing its members as to the nature of client transactions that must be adequately documented in their records, doing so chiefly through the Accounts Rules.

As stated on several previous occasions, the principal rule solicitors have to follow is to keep firms and clients' money separate both in terms of the recording of information in the accounting records and physically in separate bank accounts.

If a solicitor receives monies in excess of £50 from a client it must be paid into a separate client bank account without delay [SAR 4(1b)]. The transaction has to be noted in the solicitor's records with the receipt of money being entered into the client cash book (or in the client column of the firm's main cash book if only one is in use).

There are a number of situations where funds received from a client do not have to be paid in physically to a client bank account [SAR 7]. For example, if the funds are:

(1)   received in the form of cash which is paid in cash to the client or their representative;

(2)   received in the form of a cheque endorsed to the client or their representative and not passed through a bank account;

(3)   received in payment of a debt due to the solicitor or reimbursement for client expenses paid by the solicitor;

(4)   received in settlement of a rendered fee of the solicitor;

(5)   received in the form of a cheque as consideration for a heritable property transaction;

(6)   paid into a separate bank account in the client's or their representative's name;

(7)   not paid into the client account at the request of the client.

It should be stressed that even although the clients' funds are not actually paid into the client account at the bank, the transactions themselves must still be recorded in the records of the solicitor.

Another aspect of transactions involving client funds that often appear in solicitors' records relates to interest. A solicitor commonly handles sizeable sums of money on behalf of individual clients and given the often protracted nature of legal transactions it would seem reasonable for such clients not to be losing interest on their funds whilst they are in the hands of their solicitor.

The Accounts Rules address this matter directly. As a form of benchmark to assist solicitors decide the point at which interest becomes payable to clients, the Rules state that interest will be payable on balances of £500 or more that are likely to be held for at least two months [SAR 15(2)]. The Rules also contain a more general clause, based on reasonableness, which may override the last provision—for example if a solicitor receives £1,000 from a client and it is likely that the money will be held for only one month, then the inference of Rules is that interest would again be payable to the client [SAR 15(1)].

A practical way for the solicitor to deal with situations where a client will be due to receive interest is to place the funds in an individual interest bearing client bank account in the client's name. By doing so the amount of interest payable to the client will be clear and readily attributable. If the solicitor neglects this aspect of stewardship over clients funds, then it will be the firm itself that will have to reimburse any client affected [SAR 15(1)].

Although seemingly in contrast with the general requirement of the Accounts Rules to keep client and office funds completely separate, there may be occasions when office funds appear in the general client account. For example, when a solicitor initially sets up the client bank account there is often a requirement to pay in a deposit when a new account is opened. If this is the case then the deposit will be paid out of the firm's money, with the necessary entries being processed in the records via the firm's and clients' cash books.

Another example of office money being paid into the client bank account could arise if it was discovered that the funds held in the client account were insufficient to meet the total sums due to clients. If such a situation arose, the firm would be obliged to immediately make up any shortfall from its own funds. It would also be in the solicitor's best interests to retain full explanatory records of the event. Given that this would be a glaring breach of the Accounts Rules [SAR 4(1)(a)] and one likely to incur the wrath of the accounts inspection team from the Law Society, hopefully such occasions would be extremely rare.

Clients' money over a certain amount must be paid into a client bank account (with a few exceptions), but obviously it must also be capable of withdrawal. A client bank account should have a withdrawal notice period of no longer than one month but can be longer with the client's agreement [SAR 4(3a)]. Monies paid into the client bank account may be withdrawn for specific reasons and these are clearly defined by the Rules (see later). Again these transactions must be recorded in the solicitor's records.

Furthermore, where clients' monies have been withdrawn by cheque and paid to another bank account, the entries in the records must show the name or account number of the person who is receiving payment. For example if a client's funds held by the firm are passed on to the vendor's agent in a conveyancing transaction, the firm must ensure that the name or account number of the cheque's recipient is recorded in its client cash book and client ledger as well as being marked on the actual cheque itself [SAR 6(3)].

The following withdrawals can legitimately be made by the firm from the client bank account [SAR 6]:

(1)   Where payment is being made to the client or their representative.
(2)   Where the solicitor has incurred expenses of the client or there is an outstanding debt due from the client. This also applies to settlement of the solicitor's professional fees. The important point to note here is that before payment is taken the fee should be debited to the clients ledger account and the fee note must have been sent to the client.
(3)   Where the client has given the solicitor authority to withdraw money from the client account (provided there are sufficient funds belonging to that client to cover the request).
(4)   Where in seeking to generate interest on a client's funds the solicitor transfers the requisite amount from the general client account to a deposit account in the name of the client.
(5)   Where an error is being corrected.
(6)   Where the firm is recovering surplus funds previously held in the account as a float in excess of the amounts actually owed to a client [SAR 6].

Each of the transactions above should be shown in the firm's records.

Finally with respect to withdrawals from the client account, it should be noted that a client's money cannot be withdrawn to meet the payments of another client unless the solicitor has the written agreement of the former. Although there is a pool of clients' money and a variety of client transactions, care should be taken to consider each transaction on a client by client basis.

There is another type of transaction with which solicitors commonly deal. A client may often require a bridging loan as part of a conveyancing transaction. The general presumption here is that the solicitor cannot arrange the loan or overdraft facility if it means drawing down money in their name on behalf of the client. It is largely common-sense for solicitors to avoid placing themselves in such a position that they become liable for repayment of the money. With this situation in mind, the Accounts Rules require solicitors to state in writing to the lender, prior to any funds being drawn, (a) the client's name and address, (b) how the money will be repaid, and (c) that the solicitor accepts no personal liability as regards repayment [SAR 8]. Proper records of this type of transaction would have to be kept by the solicitor involved.

It is also worth noting at this stage that, for borrowing in general, a solicitor must not borrow from clients unless the client is in the business of lending money or unless the client has received independent advice to the making of the loan [SAR 9].

The review of transactions has so far concentrated principally on matters relating to clients. The emphasis is now changed in the next couple of sections more towards general business transactions and the effects of value added tax as well as the costs of employing staff.

Value added tax (VAT)

Value added tax (VAT) is a flat rate tax (standard rate is currently 17.5%) charged on goods and services supplied by businesses. Some goods and services are exempt from the tax and others, although not exempt, are charged at zero per cent. Solicitors provide legal and professional services to clients and VAT has to be added to the fee when it is invoiced. Businesses with annual turnover or fee income in excess of a given level (currently £52,000) must be VAT registered and apply the tax on their services.

ILLUSTRATION 10.5

A firm of solicitors registered for VAT has completed work for a client and will charge a fee of £4,500 before (or net of) VAT. The fee note will show a charge of £4,500, plus VAT of £787.50 (being 17.5% of £4,500) to make the total amount payable by the client come to £5,287.50.

If the firm's turnover was below the VAT threshold level of £52,000 then VAT could have been ignored and the client would only have been due to pay £4,500. From the perspective of those clients who have no means of recovering VAT paid (which will be the majority of private clients) this could mean a substantial saving.

It is open to businesses with a turnover falling below the VAT threshold to elect to register. If a business is likely to be in a situation where it pays more VAT on purchases than it adds on to the value of its sales, this would appear to be a sensible course of action.

It should be noted that VAT is a *self administered* tax, meaning it is calculated, charged and collected by all VAT registered businesses on behalf of the Government. This has an impact on the way the tax is processed within the business records. For registered businesses the VAT on sales/fees and expenses should be recorded in a separate VAT account within the business records. Consequently in such cases, sales/fees and expenses are recorded in the accounts at amounts excluding any VAT element. In contrast, where the business is not VAT registered, these items are recorded including VAT.

The tax charged on sales/fees is called *output* VAT. In **Illustration 10.5** above, the output VAT on the transaction was £787.50. Output VAT is payable to the Government with the solicitor having to pass this amount on to Customs and Excise in due course.

VAT paid by the business on purchases and expenses is called *input* VAT. Input VAT can be recovered from the Government.

When businesses are completing their monthly or quarterly VAT returns, any input VAT paid during the period is set off against output VAT and the net figure due or payable is calculated.

ILLUSTRATION 10.6

Assuming the same basic facts as in **Illustration 10.5**, it is further assumed that the legal firm had incurred VAT inclusive expenses of £1,762.50 during the period. Input VAT paid was £262.50. When preparing the VAT return for the period the output VAT on fees and input VAT on expenses are netted:

	£
Outputs	787.50
Inputs	262.50
Payable to Customs & Excise	525.00

If a purchase includes VAT, the cost of the item exclusive of tax can be found by dividing the gross figure by 1.175. In the above illustration the net cost of purchases was therefore £1,762.50 / 1.175 = £1,500.

The actual processing of transactions which include VAT is relatively straightforward. That said, VAT is an extremely complex tax and advice should be sought whenever there is any uncertainty as to the correct VAT treatment of a transaction[1].

Employee Costs

Another potential source of administrative complication arises when people are employed by the business. This will apply to most firms of solicitors and refers to the full costs of employing staff.

A business has to calculate the amount of personal tax each employee will pay on their salary and deduct this tax from earnings before payment is made to a member of staff. Again the business is acting as a collector of taxes (unpaid) on behalf of the Government. The deductions represent income tax and National Insurance contributions and are made under a system called *Pay As You Earn* (PAYE).

ILLUSTRATION 10.7

It is assumed that an employee earns £2,000 per month. In the normal course of events the member of staff concerned will not receive this full amount, since taxes are first deducted under PAYE:

	£
Gross monthly salary	2,000
Less: Income Tax	(420)
Employees NIC	(200)
Net amount payable to staff member	1,380

(**Note:** all figures assumed)

Similar to VAT, the PAYE system is self administered by the employer and any tax deducted from the payroll costs must be paid over to the Government on a monthly basis. In addition to the employee National Insurance contributions (NIC) deducted from staff wages and salaries, the employer also has to pay *employers'* National Insurance contributions on the total payroll. Employers' NIC will be paid to the Government at the same time as the PAYE deductions.

---

1 Customs and Excise offer a helpline service, the telephone number of which can be obtained from directory enquiries. Advice can be received anonymously!

Once more such transactions have to be recorded in the business records of the legal firm and again the procedure for doing so is relatively straightforward. The total payroll cost including all associated taxes will be recorded against employee costs. The other aspect to the accounting entry will appear against (a) the firm's bank account for the net amounts paid to the employees, and (b) the PAYE account for the amounts to be paid over to the Government. The liability to the Government as reflected by the balance in the PAYE account will remain until such times as the firm makes payment.

ILLUSTRATION 10.8

A legal firm has a monthly gross salary cost of £15,000, analysed as follows (all figures have been assumed):

	£
Net salaries paid to employees	10,350
Tax deducted from salaries	3,150
Employees NIC deducted from salaries	1,500
	15,000
Employers NIC charge	1,500

Although the employees are paid £10,350, the total cost to the employing firm is £16,500 (ie £15,000 gross salaries plus employers NIC of £1,500). The difference of £6,150 represents the PAYE, employers and employees NIC charges, which will be paid separately to the Inland Revenue by the firm in the following month.

It will be clear by this stage that the costs of employing staff can be very significant to a business. If the firm also makes pension contributions to its staff, the total bill will increase still further.

CONTROL OF THE INFORMATION

If the business has spent sufficient time at the outset setting up a good record system with clear guidance on how to record the many transactions that will arise, then this side of the business should operate well.

There are always pressures in any business and sometimes the first casualty is the amount of time devoted to record keeping. Errors and omissions may be the result. Hopefully it is apparent that this cannot be permitted to happen especially for solicitors dealing with clients' money. There are a number of control procedures that should be implemented as part of the business records of a legal practice to minimise such risks. The controls will help identify errors or potential Accounts Rules breaches at an early stage and allow them to be remedied.

It was mentioned earlier in this chapter that the Accounts Rules require solicitors to keep their firm's books and records up-to-date at all times [SAR 12(4)]. This will allow the financial position of the practice to be determined. As part of this control process, the books must be balanced at least monthly as well as on the last day of the accounting period.

The benefit of maintaining computerised business records will be evident in such situations, as the ability to produce financial information will be greatly improved if the system is fully automated. However, if computerised records are used, then an additional control mechanism is required under the Accounts Rules [SAR 12(6)]. The solicitor must be capable of immediately obtaining a visual record of any part of the system's contents. The same also applies to information which has been removed from the system for storage.

Solicitors must keep books and records of the business for tax purposes covering the last seven years. The Solicitors (Scotland) Accounts Rules extend this requirement to ten years [SAR 12(7)] which is another example of the significant controls applicable to legal firms.

Most transactions will at some point pass through the cash book when money is either received or paid. The cash book is without doubt one of the most important records of any business. As a consequence, there must be adequate safeguards over the large number of transactions that will be recorded there.

The bank reconciliation is the most obvious control to be used. It will be recalled from Chapter Six that the bank reconciliation process compares the information in the practice's cash book with the information in the statements received from the bank. In an ideal world the transactions in the cash book will be mirrored by those in the bank statements. Very often this will not be the case in which case further explanations should be sought and the differences explained.

Bank reconciliations should be prepared for all bank accounts operated by the solicitor whether an office or client account. The Solicitors Accounts Rules make provision for a regular client bank account reconciliation to be performed. Every month the solicitor is required to reconcile the balance on the client cash book with the balance on the client bank statements. The reconciliation requires to be kept as part of the business records for a period of three years from the date the reconciliation was prepared [SAR 13(1)].

In addition to the general clients' bank account, it has been seen that solicitors may have a number of other bank accounts held by the firm in the name of individual clients (ie other funds). These too require reconciliation under the Rules but only once every three months. The solicitor has to agree the balance of funds deposited as recorded in the cash book with the client account passbooks, deposit account certificates, etc. The reconciliation should be retained for three years from when it was prepared [SAR 14(1)].

Another example of a control mechanism affecting legal practices is evident with respect to the fundamental requirement of the Accounts Rules that solicitors must at all times ensure amounts owed to clients by the firm are not more than the funds actually held on their behalf in the client bank accounts. To ensure this is the case solicitors must undertake certain comparisons which have to be retained as part of the business records.

For example, on a monthly basis the solicitor should list all credit balances appearing in the client ledger (ie, all amounts owed to clients—debit balances are specifically ignored) and compare the list to the reconciled balance on the client bank account [SAR 13(2)]. If there is insufficient money in the client bank account to cover all amounts owed to clients then the solicitor is in breach of the rules and, as intimated earlier, office money should immediately be paid into the clients' account to clear the shortfall.

Furthermore on a quarterly basis the solicitor should extract a list from the client ledger of all funds invested for specified clients (ie, other funds) and compare this with the balance on the deposited funds reconciliation. Once more any differences should be investigated immediately and remedied [SAR 14(2)].

Comparisons of the nature outlined above, both require to be kept for a minimum of three years.

The Law Society of Scotland regards the safekeeping of clients funds by its members as a very important matter. If something should go wrong in this respect, the Society will want to know what went wrong and who is responsible. With the latter issue in mind, the Accounts Rules require legal practices to appoint at least one *Designated Cashroom Partner* to be responsible for the supervision of the staff, systems and controls used by the firm to ensure compliance with the Rules. It is interesting to note that although at least one partner is given the title of the Designated Cashroom Partner, all partners in a firm are responsible for securing compliance with the Rules [SAR 18]. There can be no escape.

COMPLIANCE AND REPORTING

Any effective system of record keeping should have in-built control mechanisms to ensure that the system consistently operates as planned. Normal businesses that are well run will have such facilities embedded in their daily routines. The same applies to legal firms. But human nature dictates that there will always be some individuals in business who regard record keeping as a non-essential chore to be avoided if possible. It can be confidently predicted that the legal profession is no different in this respect.

To prevent sloppy business practices developing within the legal profession, the Law Society of Scotland polices its members to a fairly significant extent. There is a formal compliance and reporting structure in existence to ensure that firms observe the various regulatory provisions which exist.

For example the Law Society can inspect the books and records of a solicitor at any time provided written notice has been given. The main purpose behind an inspection is to ensure that the firm has been complying with the Accounts Rules. If there has been evidence of a breach of the Rules, the firm will usually be given a period of time to rectify the situation which will vary in length depending upon the severity of the breach involved. The Law Society inspection team will plan subsequent visits to a firm with which they are concerned until such times as they are satisfied that all matters are under control.

Furthermore under the provisions of the Solicitors (Scotland) Accounts Certificate Rules 1997, a solicitor must formally confirm with the Law Society that the firm has complied with the Accounts Rules. Every six-month period the solicitor will complete a certificate to be submitted to the Society within one month of the period end. The provision applies whether or not the solicitor has held clients' money during the period. If the solicitor has held no clients' money, the form of the certificate merely confirms this fact. Where clients' money has been held, the certificate confirms a number of matters including: the period covered by the certificate; the addresses of all places of business from which the firm practices; confirmation that proper books and records have been kept and that the accounting records are up-to-date and balanced at the last day of the accounting period; that the records are in accordance with the Solicitors (Scotland) Accounts Rules; that any reconciling entries in the bank reconciliation are confirmed as correct; details of all Powers of Attorney held during the period, and; details of the Designated Cashroom Partner(s) during the period.

Besides the above, other important information is also required for inclusion in the certificate. With respect to the stewardship of clients' funds, the solicitor has to include summarised details of the client account reconciliation at the two quarterly dates within the six-month period of the certificate. The information will highlight to the Law Society if there have been any breaches in this area.

Information on the firm's account balances is also necessary for inclusion in the certificate as are details of any assistance received from an external accountant in preparing the certificate. The certificate also has a section in which any other relevant matters should be reported. It would be in this latter section that the firm would be obliged to report any breaches of the Accounts Rules that have occurred during the period.

For several years, the most common breaches of the Accounts Rules have fallen into one of the following categories:

(1) Failure to properly reconcile the funds invested for named clients and correct the client ledger accounts for any adjustments [SAR 14].
(2) In cases where a cheque is used to draw money from a client account, failure to record on the cheque the name or account number of the person whose account is to receive the funds [SAR 6(3)].
(3) Failure to render a fee note to the client and process the transaction through the records before monies are transferred from the clients' to the firm's bank account [SAR 6(1d)].
(4) Failure to balance the firm's books on a monthly basis [SAR 12(4)].
(5) Failure to maintain a surplus of clients' money over amounts owed to clients; although this breach tends to be for very short periods and is often caused by administrative errors [SAR 4(1)].
(6) Failure to provide sufficient evidence that procedures are in place for identifying clients under the Money Laundering Regulations [SAR 16].

It is important for the firm to disclose all known breaches in the certificate no matter how minor they may seem, as the Law Society will be dissatisfied if such breaches are only picked up by its inspection team during a subsequent visit.

When completing the certificate it should be noted that if the firm has more than one office and each office has separate books and records then separate compliance certificates must be prepared.

Certificates should be signed by two partners of the firm (unless a sole practitioner), one of which will be the Designated Cashroom Partner.

Where a solicitor conducts investment business this too will carry a compliance burden. The firm will need to maintain its records in a manner consistent with the relevant regulatory provisions affecting this area of activity. It must also submit an appropriate compliance certificate to the Law Society of Scotland approximately once every six months in much the same way as it does for the Accounts Rules.

In summary, proper completion of the accounts certificate and of the conduct of investment business certificate are important elements of the compliance and reporting structure affecting solicitors. Also playing an important role in this respect are the cyclical visits by the Law Society of Scotland's inspection team and the duty incumbent upon solicitors to have proper regard to the regulatory environment within which they conduct business. It should be appreciated that the Law Society of Scotland has very significant powers over its members with respect to the options it may exercise in cases of wayward office procedures and errant solicitors. Solicitors would be advised to studiously observe all regulatory provisions affecting the practice since it is most certainly the route of least pain for all concerned.

WORKED EXAMPLE

It has been seen that the development of the accounting record system of a solicitor's practice can be considered in several parts. A worked example will now be used to illustrate the operation of a typical system. The example will begin with background information about a firm's accounting records. A selection of basic transactions that solicitors' commonly encounter in practice will then be incorporated into the records. Next, control procedures will be applied. The example will end with the production of information necessary for the submission of the related certificate to the Law Society of Scotland.

Background information

At the beginning of its new accounting year, the following balances exist in the records of Masterton & Reid, solicitors:

	Dr £	Cr £
Fixed Assets	50,000	
WIP	14,000	
Firm's Bank	12,500	
Client Bank	16,000	
Client Ledger		10,000
Creditors		13,750
Loan		30,000
Capital Accounts		38,750
	92,500	92,500

The client ledger account shows a credit balance of £10,000. A review of the firm's detailed client ledger on the same date revealed the following:

	Dr £	Cr £
Mr Roseburn		100
Mr Oswald		10,000
Miss Young	1,600	
Mrs Gibson		400
Mr Blue		1,100
	1,600	11,600

During the first month of the new financial period the following transactions occurred:

(1) Valuation and survey fee incurred in respect of a property purchase, paid by the firm on behalf of a client Mr Roseburn for £250 on 1 January 2000.
(2) Deposit received from a client, Mr Roseburn on 3 January 2000 for £5,000.
(3) Mortgage funds received from building society on behalf of Mr Roseburn for £240,000 on 5 January 2000.

(4)   Payment of firm's rates bill on 5 January 2000 for £700.

(5)   Received payment from a debtor, Miss Young on 7 January 2000 for £1,600.

(6)   Payment, on behalf of client Mr Roseburn, on 10 January 2000 to selling agents, Rainbow & Co. for £243,000.

(7)   Received deposit from Mrs Gibson on 13 January 2000 for £1,500—this is likely to be held for more than two months.

(8)   Monthly loan repayment by firm on 20 January 2000 for £2,000.

(9)   Fees in respect of work carried out for Mr Roseburn £1,560 plus VAT of £273 was rendered on 21 January 2000, with payment being received on 28 January 2000.

(10)   Balance of funds held for Mr Blue were repaid to him on 31 January 2000.

Required:

(a)   Show double-entry journal entries for each transaction.

(b)   Record the transactions in the books of original entry. Use separate cash books for the firm and its clients.

(c)   Provide the updated trial balance of the practice after summarising and classifying the various transactions.

(d)   As far as possible, show the information necessary for inclusion in the Solicitors Accounts Rules Certificate that has to be submitted to the Law Society of Scotland.

Masterton & Reid; suggested solution

(a) Journal Entries

		Dr £	Cr £
1	Client ledger—Mr Roseburn	250	
	Firm bank		250
	Being client expenses for Mr Roseburn paid by firm		
2	Client bank	5,000	
	Client ledger—Mr Roseburn		5,000
	Being client funds received from Mr Roseburn		
3	Client bank	240,000	
	Client ledger—Mr Roseburn		240,000
	Being mortgage funds received on behalf of Mr Roseburn		
4	Expenses—Rates	700	
	Firm bank		700
	Being payment of firm expense re electricity		
5(a)	Client bank	1,600	
	Client ledger—Miss Young		1,600
	Being receipts from debtor Miss Young		
(b)	Firm bank	1,600	
	Client bank		1,600
	Being transfer of funds in settlement		
6	Client ledger—Mr Roseburn	243,000	
	Client bank		243,000
	Being settlement of client's (Mr Roseburn's) house purchase		

		Dr £	Cr £
7(a)	Client bank	1,500	
	Client ledger—Mrs Gibson		1,500
	Being client funds received from Mrs Gibson		
(b)	Client ledger—Mrs Gibson	1,900	
	Client bank		1,900
	Being client funds being transferred to specific a/c		

(**Note:** The sum of £1,900 that has been transferred here is made up of the original £400 balance in Mrs Gibson's account at the start of the period, plus £1,500 received on 13 January).

		Dr £	Cr £
(c)	Specific deposit account	1,900	
	Client ledger other funds—Mrs Gibson		1,900
	Being deposit of client funds in named account		
8	Loan	2,000	
	Firm bank		2,000
	Being firm's monthly loan repayment		
9(a)	Client ledger—Mr Roseburn	1,833	
	Fees		1,833
	Being fee raised for work done for Mr Roseburn		
(b)	Firm bank	1,833	
	Client bank		1,833
	Being transfer of funds from client to firm's account		
10	Client ledger—Mr Blue	1,100	
	Client bank		1,100
	Being repayment of client funds to Mr Blue		

(**Note:** These journal entries demonstrate which accounts will be affected by each transaction. Remember that the transactions still require to be recorded in the first instance in the books of original entry. This process is shown in the next section. Where possible the journal numbers have been cross referenced to the daybooks and ledgers.)

(b) Books of Original Entry

CASH BOOK—(FIRM)

INCOME					EXPENDITURE						
Date	Description	Bank	VAT	Transfers	Date	Description	Bank	VAT	Client Ledger	Rates	Loan
1/1/00	Opening Balance	12,500			1/1/00	Survey Fee Mr Roseburn (Journal 1)	250		250		
11/1/00	Settlement Miss Young (Journal 5b)	1,600		1,600	5/1/00	Rates (Journal 4)	700			700	
28/1/00	Taking Payment for fee Mr Roseburn (Journal 9b)	1,833		1,833	20/1/00	Loan repayment (Journal 8)	2,000				2,000
Total for month		3,433		3,433			2,950		250	700	2,000

CASH BOOK—(CLIENTS)

INCOME						EXPENDITURE					
Date	Description	Bank	VAT	Client Ledger		Date	Description	Bank	VAT	Client Ledger	Transfers
1/1/00	Opening Balance	16,000				10/1/00	Mr Roseburn purchase (Journal 6)	243,000		243,000	
3/1/00	Mr Roseburn (Journal 2)	5,000		5,000		11/1/00	Transfer funds (Debt-Young) (Journal 5b)	1,600			1,600
5/1/00	Mortgage Funds (Journal 3)	240,000		240,000		16/1/00	Mrs Gibson transfer to deposit account (Journal 7b)	1,900		1,900	
7/1/00	Receipt Miss Young (Journal 5a)	1,600		1,600		28/1/00	Fee Mr Roseburn (Journal 9b)	1,833			1,833
13/1/00	Mrs Gibson (Journal 7a)	1,500		1,500		31/1/00	Client refund of monies— Mr Blue (Journal 10)	1,100		1,100	
Total for month		248,100		248,100				249,433		246,000	3,433

FEE BOOK

Date	Ref.	Description	Total	VAT	Fees
21/1/00	999 (Journal 9a)	Fee Mr Roseburn	1,833	273	1,560

(c) Summarising and Classifying

Detailed client ledger:
JANUARY 2000

		CLIENT LEDGER	Dr(£)	Cr(£)	Bal(£)	Other Funds(£)
		Mr Roseburn				
		Ref				
1st		Opening balance		100	(100)	
1st	Jnl 1	Survey fee paid by firm	250		150	
3rd	Jnl 2	Deposit from client		5,000	(4,850)	
5th	Jnl 3	Mortgage funds		240,000	(244,850)	
10th	Jnl 6	House purchase	243,000		(1,850)	
21st	Jnl 9a	Fee note	1,833		(17)	
31st		Closing balance			(17)	
		Mr Oswald				
		Ref				
1st		Opening balance		10,000	(10,000)	
31st		Closing balance			(10,000)	
		Miss Young				
		Ref				
1st		Opening balance	1,600		1,600	
7th	Jnl 5a	Receipt from client		1,600	—	
31st		Closing balance			—	
		Mrs Gibson				
		Ref				
1st		Opening balance		400	(400)	
13th	Jnl 7a	Deposit from client		1,500	(1,900)	
16th	Jnl 7b&c	Transfer to deposit a/c	1,900		—	1,900
31st		Closing balance			—	1,900

Mr Blue					
Ref					
1st		Opening balance		1,100	(1,100)
31st	Jnl 10	Repayment to client	1,100		—
31st		Closing balance			—

Extracts from the firm's nominal ledger:

(**Note:** Remember that the information posted in the nominal ledger T accounts has been extracted from the day books. In the case of a solicitor this will be predominantly from the cash book and fee book. The totals of each analysis column in the cash book are posted to the relevant T account. Try to think about the double entry when posting the cash book information to the nominal ledger. For example, on the income side of the cash book the total of the bank column will be a debit to the bank account in the nominal ledger with the other analysis columns on the income side representing the credit side of the double entry. The reverse applies to the expenditure in the cash book where the bank column will be credited to the bank account with the analysis columns on the expenditure side representing the debit of the double entry.)

FIXED ASSETS			
Op bal b/f	50,000	bal c/f	50,000
bal b/f	50,000		

WIP			
Op bal b/f	14,000	bal c/f	14,000
bal b/f	14,000		

BANK—FIRM			
Op bal b/f	12,500	expenditure	2,950
Income from		from cash book	
cash book	3,433	bal c/f	12,983
	15,933		15,933
bal b/f	12,983		

BANK—CLIENT			
Op bal b/f	16,000	expenditure	249,433
Income from		from cash book	
cash book	248,100	bal c/f	14,667
	264,100		264,100
bal b/f	14,667		

(**Note:** The total income and expenditure amounts shown in the firm's and client's banks are taken from the books of original entry—ie the cash books. It is important that the opening balances in the cash book are not double counted as these are already recorded in the T accounts.)

CLIENT LEDGER			
Fee book	1,833	Op bal b/f	10,000
Expend from		Income from	
client cash book	246,000	client cash book	248,100
Expend from			
firm cash book	250		
bal c/f	10,017		
	258,100		258,100
		bal b/f	10,017

CREDITORS			
bal c/f	13,750	Op bal b/f	13,750
		bal b/f	13,750

(**Note:** The total income and expenditure amounts through the client ledger are taken from the client ledger analysis columns in the client and firm cash books.)

LOAN			
Expenditure	2,000	Op bal b/f	30,000
from cash book			
bal c/f	28,000		
	30,000		30,000
		bal b/f	28,000

CAPITAL			
bal c/f	38,750	Op bal b/f	38,750
		bal b/f	38,750

FEES			
		Fee Book	1,560

VAT			
		Fees per	273
		Fee book	

RATES			
Expenditure from cash book	700		

OTHER FUNDS LEDGER			
bal c/f	1,900	Transfers	1,900
		bal b/f	1,900

CLIENT DEPOSIT ACCOUNT			
Deposit		bal c/f	1,900
Transfer	1,900		
bal b/f	1,900		

(**Note:** The 'other funds ledger' T account is a sub-ledger of the main client ledger. The 'other funds ledger' represents the liability due to clients and the 'client deposit account' represents the asset of physical money held on behalf of clients.)

Firm's revised trial balance:

	Dr £	Cr £
Fixed assets	50,000	
WIP	14,000	
Bank—firm	12,983	
Bank—clients	14,667	
Deposit accounts – clients	1,900	
Client ledger		10,017
Creditors		13,750
Loan		28,000
Capital		38,750
Fees		1,560
VAT		273
Rates	700	
Other funds		1,900
	94,250	94,250

(**Note:** Remember that the trial balance simply takes the closing balance of each T account and restates the information in a tabular format.)

(d) Certificate Information

		£
Balances per client bank account		14,667
Analysis of client ledger	Dr/(Cr) £	
Mr Roseburn	(17)	
Mr Oswald	(10,000)	
Miss Young	—	
Mrs Gibson	—	
Mr Blue	—	
	10,017	10,017
Surplus of funds		4,650

The certificate prepared under the Solicitors (Scotland) Accounts Certificate Rules would include the information on client ledger balances and funds held in the client bank accounts. As an extract from the certificate and based on the information in this example the section on 'additional matters' would appear as follows:

			31 Jan 00
			£
1	Client account reconciliations as at		
(i)	(a)	Monies held on general client account	14,667
	(b)	Monies due to clients	10,017
	(c)	Surplus or deficit	4,650
(ii)	(a)	Funds held for named clients	1,900
	(b)	Monies due to named clients	1,900
2	Firm's account balances		
	Due to the firm		12,983
	Due by the firm		nil

QUESTIONS[1]

1. All businesses incur transactions and these must be recorded into the accounting records. The information is captured and initially recorded in the books of original entry. Describe the books of original entry found in a solicitor's practice and explain briefly the principal purposes of each one.

2. Business records must be properly organised to allow accurate and efficient production of accounts and other information.

   Describe how transactions flow through the business records to the stage of finally appearing in the accounts.

3. One of the Solicitors (Scotland) Accounts Rules states that clients' money received in excess of £50 must be paid into a client bank account. Describe the situations where this rule does not apply.

4. The Solicitors (Scotland) Accounts Rules sets out very clearly the situations where withdrawals can be made from the client's bank account. Describe each of them.

5. A solicitors' practice had the following transactions in the quarter to 31 December 2000:

   (1) Issue of firm's fee note number 223 to a client for £1,500 plus VAT.
   (2) Issue of firm's fee note number 220 to a client for £550 plus VAT.
   (3) Payment of office wages and salaries of £18,500 net.
   (4) Payment of office telephone bill, £250 plus VAT.
   (5) Payment of general expenses totalling £275 plus VAT.

   Calculate the VAT liability/reclaim for the quarter ended 31 December 2000 assuming a VAT rate of 17.5%.

6. McGowans, solicitors, are in the process of preparing their monthly client account bank reconciliation and comparison with amounts owed to clients as required by the Solicitors (Scotland) Accounts Rules.

---

1   For suggested solutions see p 329.

You have been given the following information.

At 31 March 2000 the client account bank statements showed a balance of £600 due by the bank to the practice. The firm's client cash book showed they had a balance of £175 at the bank.

Two receipts have not yet been processed through the bank statements: one on 28 March 2000 for £300 and another on 30 March 2000 for £550. The following cheques have still to be paid out of the bank account: cheque number 055 for £720, cheque number 057 for £440 and cheque number 058 for £115.

The client ledger balance at 31 March 2000 was £105 and analysed as follows:

	Dr £	Cr £
Mr Black		20
Miss Roberts	45	
Miss Ash		100
Miss Phillips		25
Mr Veitch		5

Prepare the bank reconciliation at the above date and prepare a statement comparing the list of client ledger balances with the client bank reconciliation to ensure that the client account has sufficient funds.

7. A solicitors' practice, Norris and Peters, are updating their accounting records to reflect various business transactions.

The opening balances in the firm's nominal ledger are:

	Dr £	Cr £
Fixed assets	35,000	
WIP	18,000	
Firms bank	10,000	
Client bank	15,000	
Client ledger		11,000
Creditors		7,500
Loan		19,000
Capital accounts		40,500
	78,000	78,000

The detailed client ledger is as follows:

	Dr £	Cr £
Mrs Stark		7,500
Mr Plane	3,500	
Miss Aster		3,000
Mr Gormley		4,000

During the period the following transactions have occurred:

(1) Deposit received from a client Mrs Stark £500 on 3 July 2000.
(2) Mortgage funds received from building society on behalf of Miss Aster for £150,000 on 10 July 2000.
(3) Received payment from Mr Plane for £3,500 on 15 July 2000 in respect of debt due to the solicitor.
(4) Payment of firms indemnity insurance, for £3,750, on 22 July 2000.
(5) Balance of funds held on behalf of Mr Gormley was repaid on 23 July 2000.

Required:

(a) Prepare the journal entries required to process the transactions.
(b) Record the transactions in the books of original entry.
(c) Show the updated trial balance of the practice.
(d) Show the Solicitors Accounts Certificate Rules extract for ensuring sufficient funds to cover amounts due to clients.

Chapter Eleven: Introduction to corporate accounting reports—Part one

From time to time solicitors will come into contact with the accounting statements of limited companies. It should be appreciated that what follows in both this chapter and in the next will serve only as a brief overview of what is undoubtedly a very complex and technical area of accountancy. It is an area subject to almost constant change, especially in recent years. The objective, therefore, is only to give the reader a broad appreciation of the style and content of corporate accounting statements. As a result comments and observations are confined to generalisations.

The accounting reports of a company are in essence very similar to what has already been considered earlier in the book in relation to partnerships and sole proprietorships. The core financial statements of corporate accounting remain the Profit and Loss Account and the Balance Sheet, but a company will often have to produce additional statements relating to its financial affairs. Furthermore company accounts tend to be much more detailed than for, say, partnerships and sole traders in order that they meet various regulatory requirements.

LIMITED LIABILITY COMPANIES AND THE SEPARATION OF OWNERSHIP FROM CONTROL

The concept of *limited liability* is well known in the business community. In the normal course of events, the owners of a limited liability company are able to limit the extent of financial risk to an agreed amount invested in the company. There is no danger of members (ie shareholders) being forced into a position of personal bankruptcy as a consequence of their company running into financial difficulties[1].

The liability of a company's members can either be limited *by shares* or *by guarantee*. Where liability is limited by shares, if the shares are *fully paid*, the liability of an individual shareholder is restricted to the total amount of money invested in the company's shares. In the case of *partly paid shares*, a member can be called upon to provide funds in addition to those already subscribed to cover some or all of the unpaid part of their shareholding, but no more than that. Where liability is limited by guarantee, the extent of a shareholder's liability is determined by reference to the amount personally guaranteed in terms of the company's Memorandum of Association. In the event of a company liquidation, this amount will be the maximum contribution which a shareholder will be required to pay.

In the UK, it is the former method that is the one normally used by companies to limit the liability of members. The latter is adopted mainly by charities and other such organisations.

---

1   The concept of limited liability was first recognised by the Limited Liability Act 1855. Prior to this Act coming into force, investors faced financial ruin if their businesses failed owing to the debts due to third parties.

There are two classes of limited company, the *public company* and the *private company*. In terms of the number of UK companies in existence, the latter heavily outweighs the former. The main characteristics of a public limited company are as follows:

(1)   its Memorandum of Association states that it is a public company and has been registered as such;

(2)   its name must end with the words 'public limited company' or its abbreviation 'plc';

(3)   the company is limited either by shares or by guarantee and has a minimum authorised[1] and issued (or allotted) share capital of £50,000, with the shares being at least 25% paid up[2]; and,

(4)   the minimum number of members is two.

Many plc's have their shares *listed* (or *quoted*) on the Stock Exchange and are, logically, known as '*listed companies*' (or '*quoted companies*'). Listed companies must comply with the requirements of the Stock Exchange. Some public companies are not listed, either through choice or through prohibition[3].

A private company, on the other hand, is defined as one which is not a public company. It is, therefore, a residual class of company. A private company need only have one member as well as an authorised share capital, although no minimum amount is prescribed by legislation in contrast with the position of a public company. Another difference between a private and a public company is that the former cannot make a general offer of its shares to the public at large, unlike the latter.

A private company though, like a public company, must openly declare to those likely to have any dealings with it that it has limited liability. Hence a private limited company, with very few exceptions[4], must display the word 'limited' after its name (or the abbreviation 'LTD').

The larger an organisation grows then the greater the need for its owners to delegate increasing amounts of work to employees. In the context of a typical large plc, shareholders will delegate responsibility for running the company to *directors*. Directors are voted on to the board of the company by its shareholders and represent the top-tier of the corporate management structure[5]. It is the board of directors that controls the operation of the company, both in terms of day-to-day matters as well as at a strategic level, although it is of course still answerable to shareholders. This fact is evidenced from the requirement imposed on directors to report to shareholders at the company's Annual General Meeting (AGM) and to present a set of final accounts for the year and, most forcibly, by the provisions of the Companies Act[6] which allows shareholders to remove a director by a majority vote.

The combined effect of the concept of limited liability and the separation of ownership from control, particularly in the case of larger companies, has resulted in the accounting practices of all companies being subjected to a far higher degree of

---

1   The authorised share capital of a registered company is stated in its Memorandum. It is the maximum amount of capital that the company plans to raise in the foreseeable future. A company is under no obligation to actually issue shares up to this amount.

2   A plc can exist without the £12,500 paid up share capital but it cannot trade.

3   It may be the case that a plc is not allowed to be listed on the Stock Exchange by reason that it fails to meet certain criteria as contained within *The Listing Book, Financial Services Authority* (FSA, London, April 2000).

4   For exceptions, see Companies Act 1985, s 30.

5   In normal circumstances, directors are employees of the company and any remuneration paid to them in this capacity is a legitimate business expense and can be charged as such in the profit and loss account.

6   See Companies Act 1985, s 303.

regulation than for, say, a partnership or sole proprietor's business. Companies are compelled to be more open with the disclosure of financial information than non-incorporated organisations. Besides being told 'what' to disclose, companies are also instructed 'how', 'when' and 'to whom' to disclose the information in question. The bigger and more complex the company, as a general rule, the more it is forced to disclose.

In order to appreciate the regulatory forces acting on the corporate accounting process more fully, it would be useful to identify the main groups external to the company which use the annual accounts of companies and to briefly consider the nature of some of their information requirements.

USER GROUPS OF THE ANNUAL CORPORATE ACCOUNTING REPORTS

The categories of external users having a reasonable right to information on the company can be summarised as follows:

(1)   the equity investor group (ie shareholders);
(2)   the loan-creditor group (eg banks and other lending institutions);
(3)   the analyst-advisor group (eg solicitors, stockbrokers and others who give
        investment advice to clients);
(4)   the business contact group (eg customers/clients, suppliers);
(5)   the government (or more specifically, various government agencies like
        Customs and Excise, or Inland Revenue, etc);
(6)   the public; and,
(7)   employees[1].

The information requirements of each of the above groups is wide and varied. For example the customers of a company (as part of the business contact group) would probably require information showing how stable the company is, especially in the case of larger contracts. To illustrate, when a new stretch of motorway is being built, the roads authority assigning the work would need reassurance that the company successful in the tendering process is capable of completing the contract works in a financial sense as well as with respect to its organisational capabilities. It would be very disruptive (and probably costly in terms of time and expense) if the company encountered financial difficulties before the new motorway was complete.

A member of the loan-creditor group would also require certain financial information from the prospective borrowing company—for example, again that the company is financially stable, but furthermore, that it will be able to meet its future loan repayments as they fall due. Employees, on the other hand, would probably be interested in the type of financial information which would reassure them of their long-term employment prospects with the company. Details on the level of profitability of the company would also be useful when negotiating wage and salary increases as well as other general improvements in their employment package.

1   The various user groups of corporate annual reports shown here were identified in a report produced by the Institute of Chartered Accountants of Scotland in 1988 in the publication 'Making Corporate Reports Valuable' (Kogan Page). This important publication underpins many of the recent changes in corporate reporting and heavily influenced the Cadbury Committee when it looked at corporate governance, more of which later on.

The group with perhaps the most powerful argument for financial information from a company is its shareholders. The owners of a company require financial information which allows them to check that their funds have been properly looked after by the officers of the company. Information produced to satisfy this requirement is concerned with the *stewardship* function. The other main requirement of equity investors is to obtain financial information to assist with *investment decision making*.

In a broad sense as far as the regulatory forces affecting the corporate accounting process are concerned, the principal motivation in the past has undoubtedly been the need to ensure the proper stewardship of shareholder funds. The need to 'encourage' companies to adopt practices which, for example, result in the production of information for investment decision making purposes, has been clearly subordinate. The information needs of other groups of external users have also been similarly ignored to varying degrees. Notwithstanding this fact, such deficiencies in the corporate accounting process have been recognised and steps are being taken to rectify them[1].

It still remains however, given that the costs of producing financial and other information is so high (to say nothing of the fact that the competitiveness of UK companies may be damaged by the disclosure of sensitive information to rival companies on a global scale), most unlikely that the corporate accounting process could ever meet the information needs of all the external user groups.

FACTORS WHICH SHAPE THE STYLE AND CONTENT OF ANNUAL PUBLISHED ACCOUNTS

The overall process whereby companies provide various financial statements together with supporting notes and other related reports can be referred to as *financial reporting*. Financial reporting, basically because of its importance in a developed economy such as that of the UK, is subject to a fairly onerous level of regulation and supervision. It would be incorrect to assume that the regulation of financial reporting emanates solely from the Government. Rather, it is the joint responsibility of the Government and the private sector, the latter including organisations such as the Stock Exchange and the accountancy profession.

There are in effect therefore several regulatory and supervisory sources with respect to financial reporting in the UK. Before briefly considering the different sources, it is worth mentioning at this stage that the guiding light for many regulatory and supervisory provisions is the need to give a 'true and fair view' of the company's financial position at the end of an accounting period and of its profit or loss for that period. This is an *overriding consideration* incumbent upon companies and, in fact, is set down in statute[2].

The need for accounts to give a true and fair view, being an overriding consideration, means that, for example, even information not demanded by law must be provided by the company if it is necessary in order for the accounts to show

---

1 See the work of the Cadbury Committee on Corporate Governance, 1992. Also, in most recent times the Turnbull Committee Report on Corporate Governance is becoming the central focus of developments in corporate governance.
2 See Companies Act 1985, ss 226–227.

a true and fair view. Furthermore it is possible to depart from specific legal requirements in situations where such compliance would prevent a true and fair view of the company's profitability and financial position being reflected. In the latter instance where there is such a departure, a full explanation must be given of the nature of the departure, the reasons for it and its effects on the reported results.

FINANCIAL REPORTING: REGULATION AND SUPERVISION

The main regulatory and supervisory sources in the UK can be summarised as follows.

The accountancy profession

The accountancy profession helps to regulate itself through such bodies as, for example, the Accounting Standards Board (ASB), the Urgent Issues Task Force (UITF), the Financial Reporting Review Panel, and the Financial Reporting Council (FRC).

Such organisations help guide members of the accountancy profession by setting out accounting standards and guidelines which reflect sound, acceptable accounting practice. For example, see the contents of the various Statements of Standard Accounting Practice (SSAPs), Financial Reporting Standards (FRSs), together with associated exposure drafts and pronouncements by the UITF. It is the normal expectation that for a company's accounts to provide a true and fair view, they should be produced in full compliance with all such standards as may be applicable. If exceptional circumstances dictate departure from compliance with an accounting standard, then this fact must be disclosed by the company concerned and full explanation given, both on the reasons for departure and its effects on the reported results.

The Stock Exchange

The Stock Exchange has its own set of rules to regulate the financial disclosures of quoted companies. The rules are contained within the 'The Listing Book' by the Financial Services Authority (FSA). This book sets out additional disclosure requirements that a plc would otherwise not have to give by virtue of company law or accounting standard. For example, quoted companies are required by Stock Exchange rules to publish interim accounting reports during their financial year.

Parliament and the Government

Although it is Parliament that is responsible for creating the legislation which directly affects financial reporting, it is the Government that is largely responsible for initiating this process. The Government is also able to exert considerable influence on the corporate reporting process at Departmental level, for example, through the

Department of Trade and Industry. The legislation which is of primary importance to company financial reporting are the Companies Acts of 1985 and 1989[1]. The influence of the European Community on the content of such domestic legislation is also evident. The EC's Fourth Directive adopted the concept of true and fair and confirmed that it should be an overriding consideration. The provisions of the Fourth Directive, which are generally regarded as the EC directive with the greatest impact on financial reporting, were implemented in the UK through the Companies Act 1981.

Other influences

There are many other influences which help regulate financial reporting. Contributions from employer organisations (like the Confederation of British Industry and the Institute of Directors), various pressure groups and individuals as well as from other professional bodies (such as the various Law Societies in the UK) all have some influence on the content of Companies Acts, to varying degrees.

Finally, it would be an omission not to point out that sometimes companies will provide more information in their statements than that demanded by the various authorities. It is claimed by some that this shows a pride by such companies in the reporting process and a desire to be seen to be reputable and decent organisations, willing to inform interested parties about the business(es) they are in. Sceptics, on the other hand, will counter-argue that such actions are simply public relations exercises, designed to forestall criticism or pressure on environmental or social issues. No doubt there is some truth to be found in either camp.

CONTENTS OF ANNUAL ACCOUNTS

For the majority of companies, especially smaller private companies, the publication of the annual report and accounts is an exercise in providing as little information as possible on the company's affairs simply because there is little incentive to do otherwise. That said, the main financial reports produced annually by larger plc's are still reasonably informative.

The common perception of a plc's published annual report and set of accounts is of a large, A4 sized, glossy booklet. Besides having complex and detailed financial information about the company's affairs, it will also contain promotional material including plenty of eye-catching illustrations and photographs of company personnel and activities. It is an event in the corporate calendar which provides the opportunity for senior officers to show the company off in the best possible light to shareholders and others, and it is rarely overlooked. Users of those statements would be wise to bear this in mind.

Typically the published financial reports of a quoted company will contain information relating to a *group* of companies. It would be worthwhile taking a few

---

1   The Companies Act 1985 consolidates the provisions of the earlier Companies Acts 1948, 1967, 1976, 1980 and 1981, and was amended by the Companies Act 1989. This effectively constitutes the overall legal framework regulating the corporate financial reporting process.

moments to examine company group structure before moving on to examine the contents of a set of financial reports in more depth.

Group accounts

A group of companies is basically like a family, with the head of the household being the *parent* or *holding undertaking* and its offspring known as *subsidiary* or *associated undertakings* dependent upon the extent of the parent's ownership or control. Group ownership structure may be illustrated diagrammatically as follows (the percentage figures shown just above the different company names represents the shares owned by the company higher up the hierarchy. The remaining shares in such companies are assumed to be owned by organisations external to the group):

GROUP OWNERSHIP STRUCTURE

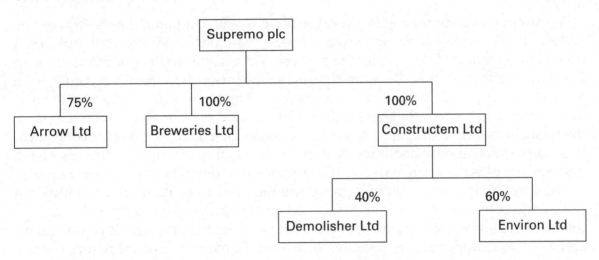

In order for a true and fair view of the group's affairs to be obtained it is necessary to *consolidate* the results from all of the undertakings that make up the group structure, effectively treating them as a single entity for reporting purposes[1]. The *consolidated accounts* of the group should disclose the overall results of the companies (and other organisations) that comprise the group.

It is a common occurrence for a company forming part of a group not to be wholly owned by the ultimate parent company either directly or indirectly through other subsidiaries. In such cases the results of the constituent company will, eventually, be shown in the group accounts in proportion to the extent of ownership belonging to the parent company.

In the case of the subsidiary company Arrow Ltd (see above) where 75% of its shares are controlled by Supremo Plc, there would be a deduction of 25% from the group's profit figure to reflect the extent of outside ownership in Arrow Ltd. The inference here is that although Arrow Ltd's entire profit is absorbed into the group in the first instance, a deduction of 25% is made later on in the consolidated profit and loss account. Such a deduction will be attributed to *minority interests* and will usually

---

1 The term 'undertakings' is used in the 1985 and 1989 Companies Acts rather than the narrower term 'companies' in order to have group accounting provisions apply to *all* organisations which comprise the group. Previously it was suspected that some groups used non-incorporated entities to help manipulate the information being disclosed in the group accounts.

appear in the group's profit statement immediately after the sub-total 'Profit on ordinary activities after taxation'[1].

There is a similar treatment of minority interests in relation to the consolidated balance sheet. The total proportion of the net assets of subsidiaries owned by shareholders falling outside the group will, in effect, be deducted from the total net assets of the group. Minority interests in this respect can be shown after 'Capital and reserves' in the group's consolidated balance sheet[2].

The group accounting treatment of entities part-owned by the group is largely determined by degree of ownership or control. Whether the constituent entity is classified as a 'subsidiary undertaking' or as an 'associated undertaking' will, for example, affect the group's accounting treatment of it. Leaving aside precise legal definitions, an entity can be categorised as a subsidiary undertaking if a parent company holds more than 50% of the voting rights or can otherwise control its activities. Arrow Ltd can therefore be regarded as a subsidiary undertaking of Supremo Plc and the general accounting treatment with respect to the group is as above.

An associated undertaking on the other hand is where a parent has a *participating interest* in the undertaking and over whose operational and financial policies it exercises a significant influence for the purpose of the parent securing a contribution to its own activities over the long term. A participating interest is normally assumed to be a shareholding of 20% or more in an undertaking. The group's consolidated profit and loss account will disclose the share of the profits of all of its associated undertakings for the financial period in question. As far as the consolidated balance sheet is concerned, this statement will only show the cost of the original investment in the associated undertaking plus the group's share of the associated undertakings subsequent profits[3].

The consolidated accounts of a group are required to contain certain additional information on all subsidiary and associated undertakings. For example, the notes to the main accounting statements will contain such details as the names of subsidiary and associated undertakings together with a brief description of the nature of their business. The type of shareholding by the parent, together with the extent thereof, will also be shown.

Finally in this respect, it is worth noting that subsidiary and associated companies still have to publish individual accounts in the same way as any other similarly sized independent companies, irrespective of what is contained in the reports and accounts relating to the group[4].

Layout of the principal accounting statements

In an attempt to standardise the appearance of annual accounts and, by so doing, assist users of such statements in the understanding of them as well as to aid year-

1 See the extract of published accounts in the following Chapter. Also refer to Appendix 5 showing the Companies Act Format 1, Profit and Loss account.
2 See the illustration on published accounts in the following Chapter. See also Appendix 5 showing the Companies Act Format 1 Balance Sheet.
3 For a more detailed definition of 'subsidiary' and 'associated undertakings' refer to Companies Act 1985, ss 258–260, and Sch 4A, para 20.
4 There are certain exceptions to the need to prepare group accounts. If a group is deemed 'small' or 'medium-sized', by reference to the level of gross sales, total assets and number of employees, then such groups are not required to prepare group accounts for their shareholders or the Registrar of Companies. See Companies Act 1985, s 248.

on-year comparisons of a company's results, the Companies Act 1985 provides skeletal formats of the main financial statements. Reporting companies should select the account layouts most appropriate to their activities and, once adopted, apply them consistently over subsequent years.

There are two alternative formats for the balance sheet, allowing companies the choice to present their results in either a vertical (or columnar) style or a horizontal style. **Format 1**, being the vertical method of presentation and the one most commonly used by UK companies, has been reproduced in Appendix 5 later in this book.

In contrast, there are four alternative formats available with respect to the layout of the profit and loss account. Besides allowing for the choice between vertical and horizontal presentation methods, companies also have discretion to disclose profit and loss account items on an 'operational' or 'expenditure' basis. Again the most popular layout used in the UK is the vertical presentation method, with the majority of larger companies choosing to show their results on an operational basis, being the simpler method of the two. It is the profit and loss account **Format 1** which is the most commonly used style, therefore, and again this is shown in Appendix 5[1].

It should be noted that for all formats specified by the Companies Act 1985, the order in which items appear and the various headings and sub-headings used to describe them, are strictly delineated. So long as the statutory requirements are met, however, companies may exercise a degree of discretion as to the content and style of their published accounts. For example companies may choose to provide more details with respect to certain items, or to combine smaller and more insignificant items together, or to introduce new headings into their accounts. Furthermore, some items may be relegated from the face of the main financial statements and shown in the notes to the accounts.

Between the two principal accounting statements, it is fair to say that the above comments are more applicable to the profit and loss account. The Companies Act formats list the items to appear in the financial statements and differentiates the relative importance of such items by a system of coding, using letters (eg A, B, C etc), Roman numerals (eg I, II, III etc) and Arabic numbers (1, 2, 3, etc). Items which are assigned letters or Roman numerals must be shown in the order and under the headings and sub-headings given[2]. In contrast, where Arabic numbers are used, there is more flexibility in the way their items are included in the accounts. The statutory profit and loss account assigns **only** Arabic numbers to items, making this statement more adaptable in nature than the statutory balance sheet which contains many items earmarked with a letter or Roman numeral.

Besides setting out the format for a company's profit and loss account and balance sheet, the Companies Act 1985 also states that the results of the previous financial year must be shown alongside the current year's figures[3]. Although this particular requirement adds to the weight of information contained within a company's annual accounts, having comparative figures immediately to hand should assist users of the financial statements in their analysis of them.

1 The vertical formats for both the 'operational' and 'expenditure' based accounts are shown in Appendix 5 in order that the distinctions between the two can be seen.
2 A fairly obvious exception to this requirement is where there are nil amounts for certain items, both in the present and previous financial years. Such items can safely be omitted.
3 Companies Act 1985, Sch 4, Part I, section A, paras 4(1)–(3).

Disclosure of underlying reasons for levels of business activity

A professional reporting requirement which also affects the layout and content of a company's accounts is that imposed by FRS 3 'Reporting financial performance'. This particular Financial Reporting Standard requires many profit and loss account items to be analysed on the basis of the underlying nature of business activity; that is, whether matters are the result of *continuing operations* or *discontinued operations*. Continuing operations is further sub-divided into *acquisitions* and *others*[1]. The minimum disclosure requirement on the face of the profit and loss account is the analysis of the items, 'turnover' and 'operating profit'. For those format items falling between 'turnover' and 'operating profit', if they are not analysed on the face of the accounts, they should appear so in the notes to the accounts. A similar analysis of the comparative figures from the previous year is also required by the standard, although all of the latter details can be confined to the notes.

This type of information would be beneficial where, for example, the likely future performance of a company is being assessed. If much of the recent success of a particular organisation can be attributed to discontinued operations for example then, in the absence of compensating developments on the ongoing operations side of things, it may be wiser for investors to channel their resources elsewhere.

In so far as a company's turnover figure is concerned, the Companies Act 1985 also imposes a requirement to disclose what has been achieved by each substantially different class of business conducted by the company. A similar disclosure requirement also exists with respect to each geographical area in which the company operates. As a general rule, the relevant amount of turnover contributed by each class of business or geographical segment should be reported if it is significant to the company as a whole. For larger companies, SSAP 25 requires this type of analysis for operating profit and net assets as well as that for turnover. Once again, though, this information is not without its cost in terms of the volume of information contained within the annual accounts.

Company share capital

The share capital of a company represents the stake which the owners have committed to the business. In an analysis of company accounts there are several terms which appear frequently in this respect. Some have already been considered earlier in this chapter when the concept of limited liability was addressed; for example, *authorised* and *issued share capital*, *partly* and *fully paid shares*. Others worthy of note which appear frequently in published accounts include the following.

Ordinary and preference shares

Although the share capital of a company may comprise a mixture of many different types of shares, ordinary shares and preference shares are two of the main categories. Ordinary shares generally tend to form the financial backbone of most companies. Ordinary shares, unlike many types of preference shares, do not carry rights for shareholders to receive a fixed rate of return in the form of dividend payments.

---

1 See FRS 3, para 14.

Dividends receivable by ordinary shareholders can be variable down to zero. However, ordinary shares are residual shares in the sense that in the event of a company winding up, ordinary shareholders are entitled to any surplus funds remaining after debts to third parties and obligations to most other shareholder classes have been met.

The general nature of preference shares is largely clear from the name given to them. The rights of a preference shareholder will be superior to those of an ordinary shareholder in respect of dividends or capital or indeed both. Besides typically attracting the right to a fixed rate of dividend, which is paid out before dividend payments to ordinary shareholders, preference share dividends may also be *cumulative* in nature—this means that a company building up arrears of dividends owing to preference shareholders will not be able to pay its ordinary shareholders a dividend until the arrears to the former shareholder category have been paid off. In some cases, ordinary shareholders could face a long wait for a return on the money invested in the company. Similarly in the case of a winding up, preference shareholders will have a prior claim on capital relative to holders of ordinary shares.

Shares of any class may also be *redeemable*[1]. This means that at some future date the company will have to buy back such shares from its shareholders[2]. Where a company has redeemable shares in issue, its accounts should provide details of redemption dates as well as a note of any amounts payable in addition to the face value of the shares. It is worth bearing in mind the financial implications for a company which is bound to redeem shares in the near future since this could place great demands on its cash resources. In many ways redeemable shares are similar to loans.

Share premium

Shares issued by a company will have a *nominal* or face value attached to them such as 25 pence, 50 pence or £1 for example. If a company issues shares at a price in excess of their nominal value, the difference between the nominal and issue price is referred to as the *share premium*. Companies are obliged by company law to retain this excess in a *non-distributable reserve* known as the *share premium account*. If a company has a share premium account, users of its financial statements can expect to see relevant details of it in the balance sheet[3].

In direct contrast to distributable reserves, the contents of non-distributable reserves cannot be given out to shareholders as cash dividends. The share premium account, as has been seen, is one example of a non-distributable reserve[4]. Another example is a *revaluation reserve*, which would be created if a company asset was revalued. Any surplus arising out of a valuation of a company asset must be credited to the revaluation reserve. The reason why a surplus of this nature should not be distributed to shareholders as a cash dividend is simply because a revaluation surplus is an unrealised profit.

---

1 Assuming it is permitted by the company's Articles of Association.
2 The redemption of a company's shares may be mandatory or, alternatively, at the discretion of the company or shareholders.
3 See the section in a company's balance sheet which deals with shareholders' funds.
4 Once established, the contents of a share premium account can only be used for certain purposes specified by the Companies Act; for example, to fund a bonus issue of shares to existing shareholders. See Companies Act 1985, s 130.

Debentures

A *debenture* is a bond which acknowledges a loan to a company. It carries a fixed rate of interest which is chargeable against a company's profit for the year. The debenture's repayment date may or may not be specified; irredeemable debentures are normally only repaid on the liquidation of the company. A debenture loan may be secured on a certain asset (for example a building) or a class of assets (for example debtors or stock) with the risk that the company could lose the asset(s) in the event of a debenture holder exercising the right to sell them in order to recover any amounts due[1]. Debentures are tradable in the sense that they can be bought or sold on the Stock Exchange, like shares for example. Unlike shareholders, holders of debentures have no voting rights in the affairs of the company.

Taxation

There are many aspects of taxation which appear frequently in companies accounts. Some of the main ones are as follows.

Corporation tax

UK corporation tax is the tax which companies have to pay to the Inland Revenue on their profits. The profit disclosed by a company in its annual accounts, however, will not usually be the figure on which the liability for corporation tax is directly calculated. The accounting profit will first need adjustment before the tax computation can take place owing to the fact that some items have differing accounting and tax treatments (for example, writing off the costs of fixed assets). Any liability for corporation tax arising on a company's profits will fall due for payment nine months after the accounting year end, unless the taxable profits are in excess of £1.5m, in which case payment will fall sooner on an instalment basis.

Deferred tax

Consistent with the above, a company's profits may be recognised in the accounts of one period but not assessed to tax, in part, until a later period. Taking a much simplified example, if a company experienced a gain on an asset as the result of a revaluation, the gain is shown in the accounts of the period in which the revaluation occurred. Being an unrealised gain, no related tax would fall to be assessed in this period. Any tax liability would arise subsequent to the actual sale of the asset, once the gain has in fact been realised.

This is an example of a *timing difference*. Timing differences are differences between profits or losses as computed for tax purposes and the results as stated in financial statements. Deferred tax is the 'notional' tax attributable to timing differences. In the above example, the accounts of the earlier period (that is when the revaluation was carried out) could include a charge for deferred taxation to reflect the tax charge which is fully expected to arise in the future when the asset is sold[2]. The inclusion of

---

1   Where the loan is secured on a specific asset this is known as a *fixed charge*. A *floating charge* means that security for the loan floats over a number of assets belonging to the company.
2   As mentioned in the text, this is a much simplified illustration. In a strict sense, deferred tax would not be provided on revalued assets unless it was likely that they were going to be sold.

deferred tax in the accounts can be regarded as the application of the Matching convention, where the tax charge is being matched with the accounting profits[1]. Besides appearing in the profit and loss account, deferred tax will also feature in the liabilities section of a company's balance sheet.

Double taxation relief

If a company has links abroad which have given rise to foreign taxes, double taxation relief can be obtained against UK corporation tax with respect to that part of the company's income on which foreign taxes have already been paid. Companies are, however, obliged to disclose the full extent of overseas taxation in their accounts, irrespective of whether such relief has been obtained or not.

UK income tax

UK companies do not pay income tax, but income tax may still feature in company accounts. This is the result of companies acting as tax collectors on behalf of the Inland Revenue. Where a company makes debenture interest or royalty payments, for example, it must deduct income tax. The recipients will, therefore, receive their debenture interest, etc net of basic rate tax. The company will then pass on the tax collected to the Inland Revenue, after first netting off any such tax it may itself have suffered on investment income received.

Exemptions for small- and medium-sized companies

Disclosure of accounting information

All companies are required to supply a copy of their annual accounts to shareholders and to file accounts with the Registrar of Companies at Companies House[2]. The information which is held at Companies House is open to public inspection upon payment of a small fee.

There are certain exemptions available to small- and medium-sized private companies with respect to accounting information which has to be lodged with the Registrar. If a private company can satisfy at least two out of three of the criteria shown below for both the financial year in question and the year prior to that, then it would have the option to submit *modified* or *abbreviated accounts*[3].

CRITERIA FOR MODIFIED ACCOUNTS

[Matter]	Small [company]	Medium-sized [company]
(1) annualised turnover	≤ £2.8m	≤ £11.2m
(2) balance sheet total	≤ £1.4m	≤ £5.6m
(3) average weekly number of employees	≤ 50	≤ 250

1 See SSAP 15 'Accounting for Deferred Tax', FRED 19, and the Companies Act 1985, Sch 4 para 47.
2 The Registrar of Companies is situated in Edinburgh for Scottish companies. English and Welsh companies file accounts at the Companies Registration Office in Cardiff. Copies of the latter records are also held at Companies House in London. Companies registered in Northern Ireland file accounts in Belfast.
3 Companies Act 1985, s 248, General Note, as inserted by Companies Act 1989. Assuming that the company, or the group of which it is a part, is not ineligible through the Companies Act.

Where a private company falls within the definition of a 'small company', then it need only supply a balance sheet[1] together with a few other details to the Registrar. There is no compulsion to submit a profit and loss account nor a directors' report for example.

'Medium-sized companies' are permitted to lodge an abridged profit and loss account, where some of the standard information required can be condensed. Apart from that, medium-sized companies must file all other details as normal[2].

Audit requirements

Besides the above exemptions available to smaller companies with respect to the information to be filed at Companies House, they may also be entitled to some latitude when it comes to the requirement for an annual audit by an independent accountant. Normally the financial statements of all limited companies must be audited annually. But if a company meets certain conditions, it may be permitted to avoid such scrutiny either totally or at least in part.

Broadly, small private companies will be completely free from the need for an annual audit if their turnover is less than £350,000[3].

1   See Companies Act, s 248 for the requirements of qualification as a 'small' or 'medium-sized' company. The balance sheet which is filed at Companies House is, even then, not a comprehensive one since much information is summarised and restricted.
2   It should be noted that these disclosure allowances apply only to the accounting information to be sent to the Registrar of Companies. Shareholders of small- and medium-sized companies will normally receive a full set of accounts which have been prepared in accordance with the Companies Act and other relevant authority. However, directors of small companies may prepare accounts for shareholders which, although containing less information than full accounts, still contain more information than the accounts filed with the Registrar.
3   The DTI is presently revising the audit exemption level for small companies. It is expected that the turnover threshold will be significantly increased, probably to circa £1m.

Chapter Twelve: Introduction to corporate accounting reports—Part two

The previous chapter largely provided introductory information on corporate accounting. In particular it contained observations on matters of general layout as well as highlighting some of the more common or important items which frequently appear in a company's annual report. It would now be an appropriate stage to look at each of the main constituent parts of a company's published financial report.

On a purely practical note, it is useful to consider a financial report of a large group of companies in preference to that of, say, a small private company simply because of the more thorough coverage the former will achieve.

CONTENTS OF A PUBLISHED FINANCIAL REPORT

Although there is no compulsory format for plc's to use when drafting their annual financial report, typically it will be made up as follows:

(1) the chairman's statement;
(2) the directors' report;
(3) the group profit and loss account;
(4) the group balance sheet (and the holding company balance sheet);
(5) the group cash flow statement;
(6) the group statement of total recognised gains and losses;
(7) notes to the accounts and statement of accounting policies;
(8) the statement of directors' responsibilities in respect of the accounts; and
(9) the auditors' report.

Other supplementary reports and financial statements are also produced as part of a group's annual published financial report, including a note of historical cost profits and losses and a reconciliation of movements in shareholders funds[1].

Some of the above items are statutory requirements whereas others are provided to satisfy professional requirements, including the listing rules of the London Stock Exchange. The main statutory requirements are contained within the profit and loss account, the balance sheet, the auditors' report and the directors' report.

It is intended now to briefly consider the main contents of each of the principal sections in a group's published financial reports.

---

1 The latter reports mentioned have to be disclosed by some companies as a result of professional requirements. See Financial Reporting Standard 3 'Reporting financial performance'.

The chairman's statement

The chairman's statement is usually found near the front of the annual financial report of a plc. It is normally addressed to the company's shareholders and it should represent the collective view of the board of directors. The chairman is really given a significant level of freedom as to the contents of the statement, given that it is very much free from legislative and regulatory forces. However, that said, the company's auditors may review the contents of the chairman's statement to ensure that it is neither misleading nor incompatible with the information contained elsewhere in the company's financial statements[1].

A chairman's statement ranges in length from about half a page to almost ten pages. In general its contents are not specific since it doesn't usually attempt to quantify matters (in £s), preferring instead to address various issues in a broad and strategic sense. Topics which a chairman's statement considers may include a mixture of the following:

(1) a review of the business's key profit figures, especially the 'bottom-line' profit figures, both in this period and the last, including some observations on the state of the general trading environment faced by the company together with any other factor which has significantly influenced its performance;

(2) a commentary on any major corporate event which has occurred—for example, company acquisitions, disposals, mergers and/or demergers;

(3) a review of the main areas of growth in the company;

(4) comments on share issues, rights issues and bonus issues together with a reference to the level of the company's paid and proposed dividends for the year;

(5) comments on the composition of the senior management team;

(6) comments on the performance and productivity of the workforce;

(7) comments on the effects on the company's fortunes of some aspect of Government policy or of the corporate taxation regime and, very often, a plea for change therein. For example, the whisky industry continuously claims that the extent of excise duty levied on its products is unduly burdensome and that there should be an easing of such taxes;

(8) other comments on what can be done by both company management and others to improve the company's lot.

Perhaps the most important aspect of the chairman's statement is in relation to the likely future prospects of the business. Other statements contained within a plc's financial report are very much focused on historical information and it is principally the chairman's statement which contains an indication of what the future holds in store for the business.

Along a similar vein, very often this statement will mention successful products or services provided by the company with which readers of its financial report will be able to identify. To help form a picture of a company's prospects therefore, besides considering what the chairman has to say on the matter, it is also useful to look closely at the company's products and/or services and to assess whether or not they offer sound, commercial potential. This is likely to be much more indicative of future performance than can be gleaned from the historical financial information contained

---

1 The auditors' review of the chairman's statement sometimes arises because many companies choose to meet some statutory reporting requirements via this statement in preference to including the relevant information in another report, like the Directors' Report for example.

in other statements (for example the profit and loss account and balance sheet). However, a couple of cautionary points should be considered:

(1) chairmen are generally competent politicians by nature and invariably focus on the more upbeat sides of the business, often at the expense of other less attractive aspects which are potentially of equal, if not greater, significance to the overall fortunes of the company; and

(2) some company products or services, although very strong in terms of image and perceived quality, may represent only a small part of the company's activities. It does not necessarily follow, therefore, that simply because a company produces some well-known or desirable article that the company is guaranteed to be financially successful well into the future.

It remains, however, that analysts still regard the chairman's statement as a valuable tool to assess the future success or otherwise of the company in question. It will be possible to form an opinion over time as to how accurate the chairman's statement tends to be. Once a particular individual has a track record in this sense, users of the statement will generally know how much credibility to attach to that chairman's comments.

The directors' report

The directors' report normally follows the chairman's statement in the annual financial report. A directors' report is a statutory requirement designed to provide a narrative supplement to the financial information contained elsewhere in the financial report. The directors' report can be regarded as a catalogue of compulsory details in that its contents are determined by reference to applicable Companies Acts[1], the 'Listing Book' (for quoted companies only) and the requirements imposed by the accountancy profession. Companies should also follow the recommendations of the Turnbull Committee. The directors' report is a convenient medium through which to show the company's compliance with such recommendations[2]. Company directors may also report voluntarily through their report on any matter which they feel to be of interest to external users.

Although many different items fall to be addressed by the directors' report in the first instance, it is common practice for companies to deal with some matters in other parts of the financial report. For example, directors should conduct a fair review of the company's business during the financial period and on its position at the end as well as to comment on likely future business development. More often than not, large quoted companies will use the chairman's statement (and/or the report of its chief executive, if there is one) to satisfy these obligations. This practice is perfectly acceptable so long as the directors' report makes mention of it. Indeed many of the matters raised above as examples of topics commonly dealt with in the chairman's statement are initially the responsibility of the directors' report.

The external auditors of the company will review the directors' report to ensure that it is neither misleading nor inconsistent with information contained within the

---

1 See chiefly Schedule 7 of the Companies Act 1985 as amended.
2 Turnbull provides guidance to directors on implementing the Combined Code of Corporate Governance. The Combined Code consolidates two former pronouncements on corporate governance, namely, the Cadbury Committee's pronouncements on standards of governance, and those of the Greenbury Committee on directors' remuneration. Compliance with this authority is in fact also a requirement of the Listing Book.

company's accounting statements. A ramification of directors using other statements to report on compulsory details is that the auditors' duties as above will then extend to the other statements.

It was mentioned earlier that all companies are required by law to present a directors' report. The contents of a typical directors' report can be summarised as follows[1].

General

The directors of a company are required:

(1) to disclose the principal activities of the company (and its subsidiary undertakings) as well as any significant changes to them during the financial period;

(2) to give a fair review of the development of the business over the period and of the position at its end, as well as to give an indication of likely future business developments;

(3) to comment on research and development activities;

(4) to state the amount of any recommended dividend;

(5) to highlight any important event that has occurred during the period covered by their report.

Directors and their interests

Certain information on directors themselves also have to be disclosed in the report to the shareholders. For example:

(1) the name of any individual who has been a director during the financial period;

(2) for all directors in office at the end of the period, details of their interests (for example in shares, debentures or options relating to the company) both at the end of the period and at the beginning (or at the date of their appointment as a director, if later). The interests of directors' close relatives may also fall to be considered here; and,

(3) if applicable, it should be confirmed that there has been no changes to directors' interests over the period from the end of the financial period and a date not more than one month before the date of notice of the AGM[2]. If there have been any changes, details should be given[3].

Many analysts when reviewing a company's results will automatically look first to changes which have occurred to the financial interests of its directors over a period of time, in order to get a feel for the general direction of the business. It should be mentioned that this particular 'weather vane' to a company's future prospects has its limitations due not least to the existence of insider dealing provisions.

Fixed assets

Directors are required to highlight significant variances between the open market value of fixed assets and the value at which they are shown in the company's records.

---

1   This list of contents of a directors' report is merely illustrative and not intended to be exhaustive.

2   This particular requirement applies only to listed companies.

3   Besides information of this nature being included in the directors' report, other details relating to directors must also be disclosed elsewhere in the financial report. For example, certain information on the level of directors' emoluments within listed companies will normally be contained in the 'Report of the Directors on Remuneration' as required by the Listing Book.

This type of information can be useful when attempting to ascertain the real asset value of a business. That is, land and buildings bought many years ago and shown in the accounts at original cost are likely to be heavily under-valued in real terms, especially in times of a property boom.

Share capital

Under requirements imposed by the Listing Book, the directors' report must give particulars of substantial share holdings in any class of the company's voting capital, other than those belonging to the directors[1].

This type of disclosure by directors should help keep members generally informed of movements in the company's shares and possibly signal a potential major build-up of shares by a particular external party, potentially culminating in a company take-over.

Political and charitable donations

Where a company has made political and charitable contributions to UK organisations totalling more than £200 in the year, separate totals for each category of donation have to be included in the directors' report. Furthermore, where a single political donation exceeds £200, the amount of the donation plus the name of the recipient must be disclosed.

Employment policy

In the case of companies employing more than 250 employees, the directors' report must also include details on certain matters affecting employees. For example:

(1) the company's policy on the employment of disabled people; and,
(2) to what extent the company involves employees in business affairs, etc.

Post-balance sheet events

Directors must state the nature of any important events affecting the business which have occurred after the balance sheet date and before the date the accounts are approved by the board.

Acquisitions of a company's own shares

The Companies Acts also provide that the directors' report should furnish details of acquisitions by the company of its own shares during the year.

Re-appointment of auditors

It is customary for the directors' report to point out that the auditors wish to be re-appointed or alternatively if there are any proposals for changes in the company's auditing arrangements (for example the appointment of a new firm of auditors).

---

1   See para 12.43(1) of the Listing Agreement of the Stock Exchange and also Companies Act 1985, s 199.

There are various other matters which would often appear in a directors' report, but the above is a fair summary of the main items.

The group profit and loss account

It was mentioned in the previous chapter that most larger companies produce their profit and loss accounts in accordance with Format 1, Schedule 4 of the Companies Act 1985. An example of such a profit and loss account can be seen below. This is by no means intended to be a fully comprehensive statement but one merely to illustrate the main points. It should also be noted that the example used here also shows certain items analysed by reference to continuing operations, acquisitions and discontinued operations, as required by FRS 3. Again this relates to a presentational aspect in published accounting reports of large plc's that is so fundamental that it should not be ignored, hence its inclusion in **Illustration 12.1**.

ILLUSTRATION 12.1

(*Note:* The numbers shown in parenthesis refer to commentary notes following the illustrations)

Wonderworld Products Plc
Group Profit and Loss account for the year to 31 March 1999

	1999	1999	1998
	£M	£M	£M
Turnover (1)			
Continuing operations	150		135
Acquisitions	22		—
	172		135
Discontinued operations	42		46
		214	181
Cost of sales (2)		(170)	(145)
Gross profit (3)		44	36
Distribution costs (4)	17		(14)
Administrative expenses (5)	16		(13)
		(33)	(27)
		11	9
Other operating income (6)		1	2
Operating profit (7)			
Continuing operations	11		11
Acquisitions	2		—
	13		11
Discontinued operations	(1)		(1)
		12	10
Provisions for loss on operations to be discontinued (8)		(1)	—
Profit on ordinary activities before interest (9)		11	10
Other interest receivable and other income		2	1.5
Interest payable and similar charges		(1.5)	(2)
Profit on ordinary activities before taxation (10)		11.5	9.5
Tax on profit on ordinary activities (11)		(3)	(3)
Profit on ordinary activities after taxation		8.5	6.5
Minority interests (12)		(0.5)	(0.5)
Profit for the financial year (13)		8	6
Dividends paid and proposed (14)		(2)	(2)
Retained profit for the financial year		6	4
Earnings per share (15)—basic		61.2p	59.8p
—diluted		59.6p	57.5p

Explanatory Notes

(1) Turnover

This figure usually represents the sales which the company has made to its customers outside the group for goods and/or services falling within its ordinary activities. The turnover figure is stated net of VAT and trade discounts. Further details as to how a company computes its turnover figure will appear in the notes on accounting policy located elsewhere in the company's annual financial report. FRS 3 necessitates that turnover be analysed between continuing operations, acquisitions and discontinued operations as shown. This is also true of the results of the immediately preceding year, although these can be shown in the notes to the accounts. The notes will also often give segmental information on the company's turnover, depending on circumstances—that is, turnover may be analysed on the basis of the class of business responsible for its generation, and/or on a geographical basis.

(2) Cost of sales

The cost of sales figure, although required by virtue of the Companies Act 1985, is not defined in the Act. Furthermore there is no specific professional requirement to disclose its detailed calculation. In essence, cost of sales is calculated in a way seen earlier in Chapter Three. As with turnover, the cost of sales figure is net of any VAT.

(3) Gross profit

Again as seen earlier, gross profit is found by deducting the cost of goods sold from the sales or turnover figure. A company's gross profit is often used as a basis of assessment as to how well it is doing relative to the results of previous years and/or competitors.

(4) Distribution costs

Once more, the Companies Act requires a figure to be disclosed for an item but does not define it. However, it would normally be expected for a company to include in this figure charges such as the costs of storing the goods before sale, marketing costs and the costs of transporting the goods to customers.

(5) Administrative expenses

Broadly, if a company cannot allocate costs elsewhere it will show them under 'administrative expenses'. Directors of plc's are conscious of the possible adverse reaction of shareholders and others to an excessively high figure being shown here. If company accountants can avoid assigning costs to this particular heading then as a general rule they will. If the choice exists to show a charge under 'distribution costs' or 'administrative expenses', it will normally be shown under the former heading, which appears a much more productive use of shareholders' money!

(6) Other operating income

If income cannot be classified under 'turnover' or some other defined income category (for example interest receivable) then it will be shown at this point, assuming that it is associated with a company's ordinary activities. An example of income which could be disclosed under 'other operating income' could be rental income from surplus premises. Royalty income may likewise appear here.

(7) Operating profit

A company's operating profit is normally taken as the profit before any exceptional income or expenses of a non-operating nature are considered and before interest and tax charges. FRS 3 requires operating profit to be broken down into operating profit from continuing operations, acquisitions and discontinued operations. As with the turnover figure, this analysis appears on the face of the profit and loss account.

(8) Exceptional items

Exceptional items should always be disclosed. Some exceptional items must be shown on the face of the profit and loss account[1], whereas others can be consigned to the notes to the

---

1 See FRS 3, para 20.

accounts. Once again such items require to be analysed by reference to continuing operations, acquisitions and discontinued operations. In the illustration it can be seen that a loss provision has been made with respect to some operation to be discontinued.

(9) Profit on ordinary activities before interest

This sub-total will show, in effect, the trading profit of the business after any exceptional items have been considered.

(10) Profit on ordinary activities before taxation

This item in particular should be considered with reference to the associated details appearing in the company's notes to the accounts. It is a formal requirement that the notes provide information on charges such as: auditors' costs, the costs of additional non-audit accountancy work carried out by the auditors or their associates (eg tax or general management advice), directors' emoluments, employees' wages and salaries, depreciation charges etc.

(11) Tax on profit on ordinary activities

The figure shown under this heading represents the total amount of tax which the group will have to pay in relation to the profit made on its ordinary activities over the financial period. The figure will normally be analysed into its different components (for example into corporation tax, deferred tax, UK income tax etc) in the notes to the accounts.

(12) Minority interests

The charge in respect of minority interests reflects the share of the group's after tax profit which belongs to external, part-owners of group subsidiary undertakings.

(13) Profit for the financial year

The profit for the financial year represents the profit remaining for the period after provision has been made for all costs and taxes. It is the amount which could be distributed to shareholders[1].

(14) Dividends

Where a company makes a profit over a financial year, the directors will normally recommend that at least some of the profits are paid to shareholders in the form of a dividend[2]. It is not unusual for plc's to pay shareholders an interim dividend during the financial period with the balance at the end, once the final level of dividend payment has been confirmed. Any profit not paid out to shareholders will be retained by the company in its profit and loss reserve and shown in its balance sheet.

(15) Earnings per share

FRS 14 'Earnings per share' imposes a requirement on quoted companies to show figures for earnings per share (EPS) on the face of the profit and loss account. Full explanatory details of how the calculation was made must also be given in the notes to the accounts. Although the precise definition is fairly complex, EPS is found as follows:

$$EPS = \frac{\text{Profit on ordinary activities after tax, minority interests, extraordinary items and any preference dividends}}{\text{Average number of ordinary shares in issue *}}$$

* Diluted EPS takes account of potential ordinary shares. These shares will not have been issued at the year end but may appear at some future date. For example this would include share options held by directors or employees that might subsequently be converted into shares.

1 It should be noted that before directors can distribute all, or even some, of the profits of any one financial year to shareholders, the Companies Act first requires consideration to be given to the cumulative profit and loss position. It may be that the current year's profit is outweighed by the profit and loss deficit brought forward at the beginning of the period. In this situation the company would not be able to make a dividend payment.
2 Assuming that the company is not in the position of having a cumulative deficit. See footnote 1 above.

The group balance sheet

The second major accounting statement in a set of published accounts is the balance sheet. In the case of a group of companies there is a requirement to show both a consolidated statement for the group as a whole as well as a balance sheet for the holding company on its own. This can be achieved by either publishing two separate balance sheets or alternatively by showing the necessary details in the one statement. It is the latter approach that has been adopted in **Illustration 12.2**[1]. As with **Illustration 12.1** of a profit and loss account, the following balance sheet seeks only to highlight some of the more important items and is not intended to be a comprehensive example of a published balance sheet.

It will be worthwhile to bear the following general points in mind in order that the illustration may be considered in its proper perspective:

(1)   the balance sheet is a document which shows the financial position of an organisation at a given point in time. That is, it shows what it owns and what it owes at the balance sheet date;

(2)   the values assigned to all of the business's assets and liabilities are obtained from its books and records at the balance sheet date. It follows, therefore, that the bases on which such items are valued are of crucial importance

(3)   businesses generally prepare accounts under the historic cost convention. This means that asset values shown in the balance sheet are based on their original cost as depreciated to date. Some assets, however, may have been revalued with the revaluation figure being shown in the balance sheet.

(4)   a published balance sheet will provide only a skeleton of the company's financial position; the 'meat' is very often hidden away in the accompanying notes to the accounts.

---

1   Again Format 1 of the Companies Act 1985 has been chosen to provide the necessary balance sheet framework, given that it is the one most often used by UK companies. See Appendix 5: The Companies Act 1985 Company Accounts Formats.

ILLUSTRATION 12.2

Zizi Products Plc
Group Balance Sheet as at 31 March 1999

	The Group		The Company	
	1999 £M	1998 £M	1999 £M	1998 £M
Fixed Assets (1)				
Intangible assets (2)	2	1.5	—	—
Tangible assets (3)	34	30	29	22
Investments (4)	5	4.5	4	2
	41	36	33	24
Current Assets (5)				
Stocks (6)	26	20	12	7
Debtors (7)	15	12	12	11
Investments (8)	5	5	3	3
Cash at bank and in hand	9	6	5	2
	55	43	32	23
Current Liabilities				
Creditors : Amounts falling due within one year (9)	(25)	(25)	(13)	(9)
Net Current Assets (10)	30	18	19	14
Total Assets Less Current Liabilities (11)	71	54	52	38
Creditors : Amounts falling due after more than one year	(14)	(10)	(11)	(9)
Provisions for liabilities and charges (12)	(1)	(1)	—	—
Net Assets (13)	56	43	41	29
Capital and Reserves (14)				
Called up share capital (15)	15	12.5	15	12.5
Share premium account (16)	0.5	0.5	0.5	0.5
Revaluation reserve (17)	6	6	3	3
Other reserves	5	0.5	4	—
Profit and loss account (18)	29	23	18.5	13
Shareholders' Funds (19)	55.5	42.5	41	29
Minority interests (20)	0.5	0.5	—	—
Total Capital Employed (21)	56	43	41	29

Approved by the Board, 22 May 1999
Sir Leslie Oakes, Managing Director (22)

Explanatory Notes

(1) Fixed assets

Under the prescribed format laid down by the Companies Act, fixed assets must be sub-divided into three groups, namely Intangible assets, Tangible assets and Investments. The notes to the accounts should disclose further information in a standard format relating to the cost (or revaluation) of the asset at the beginning and end of the financial period, details of any movements in fixed assets (for example with respect to acquisitions, disposals, etc of fixed assets) and details of depreciation charges.

(2) Intangible assets

This category will provide a value for those assets which are not of a physical nature. For example patents, trademarks, development costs, goodwill etc.

(3) Tangible assets

Tangible assets are assets having a physical presence. Included here, for example, would be land and buildings, plant and machinery, fixtures and fittings.

(4) Investments

Investments shown under the general heading of fixed assets are assumed to be held for the long term, which is generally taken as being more than a year.

(5) Current assets

Like fixed assets, current assets have to be analysed into predetermined categories.

(6) Stocks

Although the face of the balance sheet will disclose the total value of stock at the balance sheet date, the notes to the accounts are obliged to show values for each constituent stock category. For example, the notes would show details of stocks of raw materials and consumables, work in progress, finished goods, etc.

(7) Debtors

Again as with stocks, debtors are also analysed in the notes to the accounts. The latter could be expected to provide information such as the extent of trade debtors, the amounts owed by group undertakings, details of prepayments and accrued income.

(8) Investments

Current asset investments are those held for the short term (ie less than a year).

(9) Creditors

Creditors must be split into those falling due within 12 months, and those due to be paid in more than 12 months. Both short and long-term creditors are subject to analysis into specific sub-categories in the notes to the accounts.

(10) Net current assets

This sub-total represents current assets, less, current liabilities/creditors: amounts falling due within one year. As a general rule, financially healthy companies would be expected to have a safe excess of the former over the latter.

(11) Total assets less current liabilities

This is a sub-total comprising the figures for fixed assets, plus, net current assets.

(12) Provisions for liabilities and charges

The figure shown here will consist of provisions for pensions and similar obligations, deferred taxation and other provisions. Taxation, other than deferred taxation, is included in creditors: amounts falling due within one year.

(13) Net assets

Another sub-total found by deducting the combined value of long-term creditors and provisions for liabilities and charges from the figure per note 11 above. The net assets figure represents the balance sheet total.

(14) Capital and reserves

The capital and reserves section of the balance sheet is an important part of the document in that it helps explain how the business (as shown by the net asset figure, note 13 above) has been funded. Again as with many other parts of the balance sheet, there are normally comprehensive back-up details on each sub-section shown in the notes to the accounts.

(15) Called up share capital

This figure shows the total nominal (or face value) of the company's shares which have been issued.

(16) Share premium account

The share premium account figure reflects the excess of what shareholders actually paid for their shares over the nominal value of the shares when they were issued.

(17) Revaluation reserve

Where a fixed asset has been revalued to a new figure in excess of the asset's previous net book value the surplus would be held in a revaluation reserve. Losses on revaluation are generally charged to this reserve. Like the contents of the share premium reserve, any amount held in a revaluation reserve should be considered as non-distributable to shareholders in the form of cash dividends.

(18) Profit and loss account

Any amount not distributed to shareholders nor assigned to some other special reserve will be held in the profit and loss (reserve) account.

(19) Shareholders' funds

Shareholders' funds can be regarded as a measure of the claim which shareholders have on the business.

(20) Minority interests

The figure shown as minority interests in the group balance sheet will highlight the extent of net assets of subsidiaries owned by shareholders outside the group. It shows to what extent the group is dependent on outside shareholders for the funding of its activities.

(21) Total capital employed

This total should be the same as in note 13 above.

(22) The balance sheet has to be signed by at least one director on behalf of the board of directors.

Group cash flow statement

All larger companies are required to include a cash flow statement within their published financial report. This particular disclosure requirement is not a statutory one but a professional one by virtue of FRS 1 'Cash Flow Statements'. The basic purpose of any cash flow statement is to state the cash receipts and cash payments for a particular accounting period. Building on this notion, in order to make the published cash flow statement more informative, FRS 1 sets out a framework whereby cash flows are classified under standard headings. Namely:

(1)   operating activities;
(2)   dividends received from joint ventures and associates;
(3)   returns on investments and servicing of finance;
(4)   taxation;
(5)   capital expenditure and financial investment;
(6)   acquisitions and disposals;
(7)   equity dividends paid;
(8)   management of liquid resources;
(9)   financing.

A company presenting a cash flow statement should follow the above sequence.

    Much of the detail of the cash flow can be shown in the notes accompanying the main statement. Besides specific notes to explain the composition of the (net) figures shown on the face of the cash flow statement, there will also be other more general notes. The purpose of the latter is to show the relationships existing between figures contained in the cash flow statement and figures contained elsewhere in the company's annual financial report. For example, companies are obliged to show a reconciliation of the operating profit figure (as contained within the profit and loss account) to the figure depicting the cash flow from 'operating activities' (per the cash flow statement).

A typical company cash flow statement can be illustrated as follows[1].

ILLUSTRATION 12.3

Dastardly Creations Plc
Group cash flow statement for the year ended 31 March 1999

		1999		*1998*
(1)	*£M*	*£M*		*£M*
Cash flow from operating activities (2)		(30.0)		28.0
Dividends from joint ventures and associate (3)				
Dividends from joint ventures		1.5		1.25
Dividends from associate		0.5		0.75
		2.0		2.0
Returns on investments and servicing of finance (4)		(4.5)		(2.5)
Taxation (5)		(5.8)		(5.4)
Capital expenditure and financial investment (6)		(1.7)		(0.6)
Acquisitions and disposals (7)		(35.7)		(27.0)
Equity dividends paid (8)		(5.1)		(4.8)
Cash outflow before use of liquid resources and financing		(20.8)		(10.3)
Management of liquid resources (9)		1.4		1.2
Financing—issue of shares	1.2			
—increase in debt (10)	4.7	5.9		3.0
Decrease in cash in the period (11)		(13.5)		(6.1)

Explanatory Notes

(1) General

Ilustration 12.3 shows the cash flow statement of a group and should, therefore, reflect the cash inflows and outflows of the group as a whole. Any internal cash flows (between companies belonging to the group, for example) are eliminated. With respect to the format of the cash flow statement in general, it can be seen that the information shown on the face of the illustrative statement has been restricted on this occasion to the net cash flow relating to each of the standard headings. As mentioned previously, companies are still required to provide additional notes giving details of the individual categories of cash inflows and outflows falling under each of the standard headings. This can be achieved either by showing the relevant details on the face of the statement or by providing additional notes to accompany the cash flow statement.

(2) Cash flow from operating activities

The starting point for the statement is with the cash generated from operating activities. However, this figure will not be the same as the profit per the profit and loss account, since the latter figure will first need some adjustment to remove the effects of non-cash transactions— for example, depreciation charges, unsettled credit purchases and sales in relation to trading activities, changes in stock levels, etc.

(3) Dividends from joint venture and associate

Any dividends that have been received from a joint venture or from an associate have to be detailed seperately in the cash flow statement.

1 Figures shown in published cash flow statements will be shown net of VAT or other sales tax unless the tax is irrecoverable by the reporting entity.

(4) Returns on investments and servicing of finance

The purpose of this section is to highlight the cash flows that have resulted from previous investments by the entity as well as to show the cash payments made to parties who have provided finance. With respect to the latter category, this will include cash payments to non-equity and minority shareholders but it will exclude payments to equity shareholders in the parent company (owing to the fact that details of the latter appear elsewhere in the cash flow statement).

(5) Taxation

The cash flows shown under this heading are those to and from the tax authorities in respect of capital or revenue profits. Cash flows relating to VAT, for example, are normally not included under this heading.

(6) Capital expenditure and financial investment

Items which would fall to be considered under this part of the statement will include cash flows arising upon the acquisition or disposal of fixed assets and investments.

(7) Acquisitions and disposals

Where an organisation has acquired or disposed of any subsidiary, trade, business, joint venture etc, details of the resulting cash flows will be found here.

(8) Equity dividends paid

The cash outflow in the form of dividends to shareholders of equity shares in the parent company are highlighted under this heading[1].

(9) Management of liquid resources

A reporting entity is required to explain its policy on 'liquid resources'. It would be expected that cash flows associated with the purchase or sale of government securities, or corporate bonds, for example, would be shown here. Liquid resources are stated as being 'current asset investments held as readily disposable stores of value' by FRS 1.

(10) Financing

Cash flows falling in this category are receipts from and payments to all external providers of finance to the company. It should be noted that it is only the principal amounts involved in such activities that are included in this section—cash flows relating to the servicing of finance are dealt with under note 4 above. That is, although the receipts from, say, the issue of debentures would be shown as a cash inflow in the 'Financing' section, subsequently arising debenture interest payments would appear in the 'Returns on investment and servicing of finance' section as outflows.

Where a principal sum of money has been received from or repaid to an external provider of finance, the relevant cash flow will be detailed in this section of the statement. It could be expected to find cash flow information on receipts from share issues or on the issue of debentures, for example, falling under the 'Financing' heading.

(11) Increase/decrease in cash in the period

FRS 1 now requires reporting entities to reconcile the change in cash experienced over the period to the movement in its net debt position as reflected in the balance sheet. It would be normal therefore to find a reconciliation statement to this effect also contained within the financial report[2].

---

1   Dividend payments to minority shareholders were seen to fall within the earlier section dealing with 'Returns on investment and servicing of finance' rather than under the present heading. The reason for this classification is clear if it is considered from the perspective of the shareholders in the parent company—ie the cash is not accruing to them.

2   Net debt comprises borrowings less cash and liquid resources. Definitions of each of these terms can be found in FRS 1, para 2.

It is important to appreciate that the company's cash flow statement, having been prepared on a strict cash in/cash out basis, is as a result fundamentally different from the other more traditional accounting statements like the profit and loss account and balance sheet, given that the latter will be prepared on the historic cost basis involving the Matching convention. The cash flow statement should really be considered as bringing a new dimension to the type of information available to external users of corporate financial reports.

Typical practical uses of the cash flow statement can be summarised as follows:

(1)   The cash flow statement can be used to help assess the financial liquidity of the company. That is, is the company generating sufficient cash to meet its immediate liabilities?

(2)   It can also help assess the organisation's ability to meet debts as they fall due. In other words, it provides an indication of solvency.

(3)   Simply by reading the cash flow statement from top to toe should give the user an idea of how much cash has been generated from trading activities, the net costs of servicing the company's borrowings and capital, the amount of taxation paid, the net amount of investments in fixed assets and changes in the long-term financing structure of the company.

(4)   By re-arranging the information provided in the cash flow statement it may make it easier to answer questions such as:

(a)   where does all the cash come from? Is it generated internally through trading activities or has the company relied on cash injections from the issue of new share capital or through further commitments to long-term borrowing to prop up its cash balances?

(b)   where does the company spend its cash? Is it investing significant proportions of its cash for the future (eg in fixed assets), or does it channel most of its cash resources merely into the servicing of borrowings or capital?

(5)   It can also be worthwhile to review the reconciliation between the figure representing cash flow from operating activities in the cash flow statement with the operating profit figure in the profit and loss account. Is there a difference between these figures and, if so, how big is that difference? A company may appear very profitable as evidenced by the level of profit in its profit and loss account, but it may still be under-performing in terms of its ability to generate hard cash. An alternative picture may also emerge—although a business may appear only modestly profitable, it still might be producing reasonable and steady net cash flows. Where a comparison between the cash flow statement and the profit and loss account provides a consistent impression of the company's performance, this will serve to reassure. If there is a lack of consistency, then it may be prudent to dig deeper—especially in cases where the business is declaring healthy profits on the one hand, but may in fact be experiencing net cash outflows on the other. It is important to understand the causes of this latter type of situation.

It cannot be over-emphasised that the control of cash is vital in any business, not only in companies. On a wider plane, it is of no use, for example, for the staff of a legal firm to work all the hours of the day providing valuable services to their clients if the paper profit as reflected by the firm's profit and loss account is not turned into hard cash through strict control of WIP, feeing and debtors. Similarly, the careful regulation of payments to creditors to at least coincide with cash receipts from debtors can also help the cash position of a firm. This in itself may slightly improve actual profitability through lower bank borrowing charges if the firm is in overdraft.

Group statement of total recognised gains and losses

Some company profits and losses are not reported in the published profit and loss account, for example, surpluses from the revaluation of property or some foreign currency gains or losses. Previously, items of this nature could have been hidden away in the notes to the accounts. The aim of the statement of total recognised gains and losses is to highlight such items collectively in a formal report.

The statement of total recognised gains and losses is the fourth of the so-called *primary statements* contained within the annual report, the others being the profit and loss account, the balance sheet and the cash flow statement. It is usually much smaller than the other primary statements and generally consists of only a few lines.

A typical example of such a statement can be shown as follows:

ILLUSTRATION 12.4

Amtex Plc
Group statement of total recognised gains and losses
for the year ended 31 March 1999

	1999 £M	1998 £M
Profit for the financial year	15	12
Surplus on revaluation of investment property	1	—
Surplus on revaluation by associated undertaking	—	2.5
Exchange differences on foreign currency transactions	0.7	(2.7)
Total recognised gains and losses relating to the financial year	16.7	11.8

Notes to the accounts and statement of accounting policies

One of the largest sections in an annual financial report is the notes to the accounts. The notes to the accounts are exactly that. For example, much of the detailed statutory and professional disclosure requirements are achieved by inclusion of the relevant information in the notes rather than cluttering the profit and loss account or balance sheet.

The notes to the accounts of a company may include details on some, or indeed all, of the following matters:

(1) turnover, analysed on the basis of different classes of business and/or geographical markets;

(2) employees, where, for example, the average number of staff employed during the year (analysed over appropriate categories—eg between manufacturing and administration) and the costs of employing them are given;

(3) directors' emoluments, where the rewards received by the directors are stated. This will include information on such things as salaries, pension contributions, benefits in kind, compensation paid to former directors, etc. It is useful to read this type of information whilst bearing in mind the results of the business. It would be reasonable to expect that there will be some correlation between payments to directors and the level of success enjoyed by the company;

(4) depreciation charges on fixed assets;
(5) interest payable and receivable;
(6) auditors' remuneration;
(7) income from investments;
(8) taxation, and so on.

Companies will also normally make a declaration of their accounting policies which have been applied in formulating the results reported in the annual financial statements. Again this could be included in the notes to the accounts or alternatively it may appear as an independent statement in its own right. In either case, the user of the report could expect information on matters such as:

(1) whether the company conforms to the historic cost convention in reporting its results;
(2) the basis on which fixed assets are depreciated;
(3) the method used to value stocks;
(4) how the company accounts for items such as profits on long-term contracts, or transactions in foreign currencies or income from government grants, etc.

In general, companies should disclose accounting policies relating to matters which have a material influence on the reported profitability or financial position of the organisation.

Statement of directors' responsibilities in respect of the accounts

Until fairly recently, annual financial reports of companies were somewhat ambiguous on the extent of the duties and responsibilities of directors. In many ways this had the effect of confusing the lay-user of accounting reports, particularly with respect to the relative responsibilities of directors and auditors of the company. Thankfully, directors now normally include a formal statement of their responsibilities in the annual report. Where the directors do not act in accordance with best practice in this respect and such a statement is not made, then the extent of the directors' responsibilities must be detailed in the auditors' report instead[1].

The statement of directors' responsibilities will address the following points:

(1) it should state that the directors are responsible for:
    (a) maintaining suitable accounting records;
    (b) taking reasonable steps to prevent and detect fraud and other irregularities;
    (c) safeguarding the company's assets;
    (d) preparing accounts for each financial period and ensuring that such accounts give a true and fair view of the state of affairs of the company at the end of that period and of its profit or loss for the same financial period.
(2) it should also confirm that all applicable accounting standards have been followed[2] and that appropriate accounting policies have been adopted and consistently applied; and

---

1 See Statement of Auditing Standard 600, para 4. However, in situations where a small company is exempt from audit requirements, there will be no compulsion to provide a statement of directors' responsibilities as per SAS 600. In the latter situation directors have to do no more than make a brief statement dealing with this matter on the face of the balance sheet.
2 Subject to a full explanation of any departures from such standards as contained within the notes to the accounts.

(3)   the statement should also highlight the fact that the directors, being responsible for the preparation of the company's accounts as above, have made judgements and estimates that they consider to be prudent and reasonable.

The statement of directors' responsibilities in respect of the accounts will normally appear just before the auditors' report.

The auditors' report

The basic purpose of the auditors' report is for the auditors to confirm whether or not the accounts:

(1)   give a true and fair view of:
   (a)   the state of affairs of the company at the end of the financial period; and
   (b)   of its profit or loss for the same period; and
(2)   have been prepared in accordance with the Companies Act.

It was mentioned earlier in the present chapter in the section dealing with the directors' report that directors of listed companies should state the extent to which the company has complied with the Combined Code of Corporate Governance during the financial period. Thus in addition to the above core duties, and as a direct consequence of directors having this obligation imposed upon them, auditors have a further spin-off duty to review any such disclosure[1].

It is a statutory requirement for companies to include an audit report within the annual financial report[2]. *It should be noted, however, that not all parts of the annual report are in fact subjected to the audit process with many parts falling outwith its remit.* The audit report should clearly state which parts of the main report have been audited. Audits of limited companies will be performed by an independent accountancy firm, by staff who are suitably qualified for this type of work. Auditors are not, therefore, simply paid employees of the company who are bound to agree with company management. On the contrary, they should more properly be regarded as the 'watchdogs' of the company.

Besides being qualified accountants and consequently having to meet certain professional standards, auditors are further regulated by the Auditing Practices Board. Amongst other things, this body issues Statements of Auditing Standards (SASs) with which auditors must also comply when performing company and other audits in the United Kingdom. With this type of self-regulatory environment, there should be little difference in the quality and thoroughness of audits performed by the different audit firms that exist in the UK, at least in theory.

The audit process

Auditors are appointed (or re-appointed) at the Company's AGM, with the period of appointment lasting until the next AGM. Auditors will normally visit the company's office(s) when conducting the audit. They have freedom of access to *all* of the company's books and records and, similarly, have the legal right to demand that

---

1   The Listing Book specifically requires auditors to undertake this work.
2   If a company is exempt from the requirement to have an annual audit, it follows that it need not include an auditor's report as part of its annual financial statements.

directors and employees of the company provide them with whatever information or explanations are necessary in order for a proper audit of the accounts to be achieved. It would be illegal for directors of a company to withhold information from the auditors or to otherwise prevent them from carrying out any test or examination that they wished to perform.

Auditors will carry out their duties on a *test basis* only—that is, they do not check every transaction that a company makes during a year. By reviewing the internal control systems of the company and combining this review with an examination of various sample transactions to ensure that the systems work as they should, the auditor can be reasonably confident in the accuracy of the accounting records and of the financial statements derived from them.

When performing their various tests and checks, auditors will be conscious of the relative importance that different areas of the audit will have on their overall conclusion. As a consequence, the concept of *materiality* will be applied throughout an audit. This means that areas where there is a greater probability of errors occurring (on the part of the client company) or, where the results of some aspect of the audit will have a significant effect on the overall outcome of the audit process, will attract more of the auditors' time and efforts. On a practical working level materiality will be defined in £s, with the amount being variable dependent upon the matter under investigation within a company. Materiality levels will also vary between different companies.

In spite of the fact that an audit of a company is carried out on a limited test basis, the entire audit will still have been planned and executed in such a way that the auditors can achieve a reasonable level of assurance that the accounts are free from material mis-statement, whether this has been caused by error, fraud or some other irregularity.

The audit process will also involve auditors assessing any significant judgements and estimates which were made by directors in preparing the accounts. This will include looking at whether the accounting policies adopted by management are appropriate, that such policies have in fact been consistently applied and that they have been adequately detailed in the accounts.

At the conclusion of the audit, the auditors will give their opinion as part of their formal report, which will be addressed to the shareholders and included within the company's annual financial report.

Audit opinions

The most common opinion given by auditors is an *unqualified opinion*. This means that in the opinion of the auditors, and without reservation, the accounts give a true and fair view and have been properly prepared with due regard to relevant authority.

Occasionally, some matters on which directors have had to make judgements and estimates are so important that if they were not specifically disclosed and explained in the accounts, then the accounts could be seriously misleading. For example, consider the situation where a company's long-term borrowing requirements are under review by its financiers and if a satisfactory outcome is not forthcoming the company's future is cast into doubt. In such situations, so long as the matter is fully disclosed and its potential effects stated in the accounts, the auditors could still issue an unqualified opinion, so long as (a) the *fundamental uncertainty* is highlighted and (b) there are no other matters which lead to the accounts failing to show a true and fair view.

Auditors may from time to time express *qualified opinions*. Auditors may qualify their opinion if, for example, they disagree with the accounting treatment used by the directors with respect to some matter. In extreme cases where the auditors consider that the point on which they disagree is so material and fundamental as to undermine the validity of the accounts making them misleading to users, the auditors will issue an *adverse opinion*. This is the severest qualification possible— basically it means that the accounts are an unreliable source of information about the company.

Another factor which might result in a qualified opinion is where there have been limitations imposed on the scope of the audit. For example, there might have been a flood or fire at the company's office resulting in the destruction of some of the business records. Where a limitation on the scope of the audit is of such a magnitude that the auditors are prevented from reaching reasonable conclusions, then they will issue a *disclaimer of opinion*. In this instance the auditors are stating that it has not been possible for them to form an opinion as to whether the accounts are true and fair[1].

Auditors' duty of care

As mentioned above, the auditors' report is addressed to the shareholders and it is to this group, and to the company itself, that the auditors owe a duty of care when carrying out their work. The case of *Caparo Industries plc v Dickman and Others*[2] provided some much needed guidance on the extent of the auditors' duty of care. In this case it was held that, unless special features exist, auditors do not have a duty of care to prevent loss to anyone relying on their report except (a) the shareholders as a body and, (b) the company. Thus in normal circumstances, auditors will have no responsibility to creditors or lenders to the company, to individuals or organisations who subscribe for the company's shares on the basis of the audit report, nor to individual shareholders who may have been mislead by the accounts that were the subject of the audit report.

The outcome of the *Caparo* case has been widely accepted on the basis that it adopts a fairly pragmatic approach in determining the extent of the auditors' liability. In all types of business it is important that risk equates to the level of return. This is no different for firms of auditors. If the judgement had not placed restrictions, auditors may have been liable to anyone relying on their audit report, which seems an unduly onerous burden relative to the size of audit fees. Furthermore, given that it is the duty of company's directors to produce accounts which give a true and fair view, it would appear to be somewhat harsh to make the auditors assume complete responsibility by virtue solely of the fact that they conducted an independent audit[3].

However, the existence of 'special features' in a given situation may lead to an extension of the auditors' duty of care. So, for example, it may be that an auditor's duty of care could extend to a third party if it can be shown that the auditor knew, or might reasonably have known, that reliance would be placed on the audit report by the third party in relation to some specific matter. In this type of situation the House of Lords decision in the *Caparo* case could be affected.

---

1   Examples of the styles of wording which could be used by the auditors for each of the audit opinions mentioned can be found in SAS 600 'Auditors Report on Financial Statements'.
2   [1990] 1 All ER 568.
3   The Cadbury Committee also accepted that the outcome of the *Caparo* case was fair and reasonable.

Audited v unaudited financial reports

Finally in this section, and as a general observation going beyond the present discussion on the contents of a company's annual financial report, it is important to be aware that not all financial statements with which solicitors come into contact in their daily work will be audited. On the contrary, many will be *unaudited* and as such will not have been scrutinised by an independent accountant. (For example, partnership accounts.)

Unaudited financial statements should always be handled with care since for a variety of reasons many will not fairly reflect the true financial health of an organisation. Unaudited financial statements may have been produced by someone who is incompetent or otherwise unsuitable. In extreme instances, they may have been deliberately designed to mislead the people using them. Either way, the extent of reliance which can be placed upon unaudited financial reports should be carefully considered.

Supplementary reports and other financial statements

Although the preceding commentary to date is a fair review of the principal contents of a group's annual financial report, additional supporting reports are also often found. Some of the more common ones are as follows.

Reconciliation of movements in shareholders' funds

This statement reconciles the financial period's opening and closing figures for shareholders' funds, showing the factors that have contributed to changes in the size of the shareholders' stake in the company. The statement would show the effect on shareholders' funds of items such as those included in the statement of recognised gains and losses, the profit or loss for the period, dividends paid, etc.

Note of historical cost profits and losses

The note of historical cost profits and losses will only normally appear where a company's accounts have not been prepared on a pure historical cost basis. Therefore where the value of some of the company assets have been reported at revalued amounts, a note of historical cost profits will appear. This note, in effect, attempts to restate the traditional profit and loss account in summary form as it would have appeared had there been no asset revaluations.

Operating and financial review

It is considered good practice for listed companies to provide an operating and financial review within their annual report. The review should be a balanced and objective analysis and explanation of the main features which underlie the results and financial position of a company. The review may appear as part of some other statement within the main annual report (for example within the chairman's statement) or it could be shown separately.

Five year summary

If a listed company adopts good practice, it will provide a five-year summary of its results. So, for example, profit and loss account items such as turnover, operating profit, profit after taxation and retained profit for the year, will all be analysed over a five-year period. Details of certain balance sheet items will also be given in this form and likewise for some key statistics (eg EPS, dividends per share, etc). One benefit of having access to this type of information is that it helps put the results of the most recent financial period into perspective.

Finally, the Cadbury Committee made a general recommendation that, where appropriate, companies should establish a committee structure in an attempt to achieve higher standards of corporate governance. It is relatively common, therefore, to see the annual financial reports of companies making mention of audit, remuneration, nomination and management committees as a result. Indeed, some of the aforementioned committees may in fact present a formal report within the main financial report.

CONCLUSION

This chapter and the previous one have jointly served to introduce and briefly explain the type of information that might be found in a set of annual company accounts. Armed with this basic knowledge, it is suggested that the reader obtain copies of actual company reports and review them in order that at least a measure of familiarity can be achieved with this type of accounting information. In this respect, Marks and Spencer plc has a reputation for producing relatively clear and informative annual reports.

In closing, it should be remembered that the main purpose here has been to give readers a very brief insight into corporate reports, not to try and create instant experts!

Chapter Thirteen: Financial management and control of a legal practice

The purpose of this chapter is to highlight the importance of sound financial management and control in a legal business. Finance is the lifeblood of the business. A solicitor must get to know the main pressure points and be able to control the flow. This chapter will outline some of the steps that can be taken to improve the financial management procedures operating within the firm. The focus of the chapter is on the legal business itself. Matters relating to the control of clients' money which, although obviously linked to the present discussion, will largely have been covered earlier in this book so only attracting fleeting comment in the current chapter.

Sound financial management and control of a legal business is essential in the present economic climate if a firm is to be capable of surviving into the foreseeable future. An important aspect of accountancy is the recording function—that is, the actual writing up of the business records. The records must be maintained in an organised manner. They must also be accurate and up-to-date. Good accounting records are a pre-requisite to sound financial management.

In a small legal firm the solicitor will probably perform the recording function personally. One advantage of this essential chore is that the solicitor will have first-hand knowledge of the accounting system and the contents of the records. In larger organisations the solicitor will probably delegate this task to an employee, *but* the well known business saying 'you can delegate work but you cannot delegate responsibility. . .' certainly applies in the context of a legal firm. If things go wrong and the firm breaches the Accounts Rules for example, it will be the solicitor who will be called to account. It is essential that the solicitor remains in full control of the finances of the firm and of its clients at all times. In the context of a partnership, a partner should be nominated to perform this function, although all partners will still share responsibility.

If the accounting system is capable of meeting the requirements of bodies like the Law Society, the Inland Revenue, Customs and Excise for example, then it should also be possible to derive all sorts of additional reports and management information to assist solicitors in the financial management and control function of running their business. However, it must be appreciated that there will be an economic cost involved in obtaining this information. It is always important to consider the cost of producing such reports relative to the benefits which will be gained from them.

THE PROFIT AND LOSS ACCOUNT AND BALANCE SHEET

A firm's management should have ready access to a recent set of annual accounts comprising the firm's profit and loss account and balance sheet. To an extent, the partners of a firm might use these traditional annual reports for the purpose of financial management and control. With respect to the profit and loss account, this particular statement will give internal management a broad appreciation of the overall profitability of the business. It shows amongst other things, the firm's turnover for the year, the amount of expenses incurred, the net profit and, if the appropriation account is included, how much each profit-sharing partner has received.

The balance sheet also provides useful information. It shows the financial position of the firm at a given date by providing details of the amount of capital the partners have invested, as well as information on assets and liabilities, both long- and short-term in nature. It highlights what the business owns (fixed and current assets) relative to the claims against it (both by partners and other parties). From the information provided in the balance sheet, it is possible to gain an impression of the general health of the business at a particular date.

The information contained in the profit and loss account and in the balance sheet will be enhanced still further if comparative information from earlier years is available.

Unfortunately, on their own, the traditional annual accounts will be insufficient to provide the partners of a firm with all the information necessary for effective financial management and control purposes. First of all the annual accounts are historic in nature and do not look sufficiently to the future and secondly, a firm's management will need far more detailed and up-to-date information than these reports are capable of ever delivering.

Although the following discussion is primarily intended to outline the type of additional information that a firm's management might call upon to assist them in this respect, it will also indirectly highlight deficiencies of the profit and loss account and balance sheet when used for this purpose. Matters to be considered are as follows:

(1) Fees.
(2) Work in progress (WIP).
(3) Control of expenses.
(4) Client debtors (credit control).
(5) Outlays on behalf of clients.
(6) Cash.
(7) Working capital management.
(8) Effective use of clients' funds.
(9) Financial ratios and statistical information.

ADDITIONAL INFORMATION NECESSARY FOR FINANCIAL MANAGEMENT AND CONTROL PURPOSES

Management accounting is essentially bespoke accounting for the benefit of the internal management of the business. Management accounts drafted to suit the partners of one particular firm may not be ideal for the management of another. Therefore the style of presentation used in the following illustrations should not be regarded as being set down in tablets of stone. They should instead be considered more of a starting point from which legal firms may customise their own reports.

(1) Fees

It will be simple to find the amount of fees rendered by the firm over the course of the year by referring to its profit and loss account. In attempting to assess whether the extent of the current year's fees are 'good' or 'bad', partners could refer to the results of previous years and/or the budgeted figure for the present year which was forecast in advance and/or the contents of the firm's business plan[1].

In order to ensure that the business is optimising fees rendered, other additional information is still required. It would be useful for a firm's management to obtain further details of fees rendered as follows:

(a)   the extent of fees generated by each partner and/or fee earner;
(b)   the extent of fees generated for each different work category. That is, what are the gross fees attributable over the period to conveyancing, criminal, matrimonial, legal aid, reparation work, etc?

and in the case of larger legal firms:

(c)   the extent of fees generated by each department, each branch office or other definable organisational unit.

It was mentioned above that using comparative information such as the results of previous years is a useful way of assessing feeing performance for the firm as a whole. The same is also true at this more detailed level. It will be a relatively straightforward task to calculate the fees rendered by each of the individual partners in the current financial year to date (YTD) and to compare the figures with the extent of fees rendered by each partner over the same period in earlier years. In this way it would be possible to identify any patterns or trends that are developing.

The type of information referred to above can readily be shown in a tabular form, making it more easily assimilated by its users, namely the firm's management:

ILLUSTRATION 13.1

FIRM NAME: WALLACE, WATSON AND WILSON, SOLICITORS   *FINANCIAL YEAR: 1997*

Date of Report: – –/– –/– –

Management Report: Fees Rendered, Analysed by Fee Earner

Fee Earner/ Partner	(i) Fees Rendered in current month £'000	(ii) Fees Rendered YTD (including current month) £'000	(iii) Fees Rendered over same period in previous years 1996 £'000	(iv) 1995 £'000	(v) 1994 £'000
Wallace, K	12	48	45	42	39
Watson, P	10	38	etc	etc	etc
Wilson, A	13	etc	etc	etc	
Totals	35	etc	etc		

---

1   *Variance analysis* is a technique commonly used by business managers. Basically the technique involves comparing actual and forecast results for a period. If a significant variance emerges between the two figures, further endeavours would follow to discover the reason(s) behind the difference. If necessary, action would subsequently be taken by management. Just as fees might be treated in this way, other figures could also be subject to this form of scrutiny, for example, all the different categories of business expense.

This type of table would allow each partner to see at a glance how much they have contributed to the firm in terms of fees rendered relative to each other and relative to the performance of themselves or others in previous years.

As an alternative it would also be possible to benchmark their present performance against, say, budgeted figures for the period rather than the fees rendered in previous years as shown above in columns (iii)-(v) inclusive, if the partners believe it to be more appropriate. This would obviously be the case where a firm has only just started trading, or where a new partner has recently joined and no previous periods' figures are available. It might also apply if there has been a significant change in the work that the firm has been handling, etc.

Irrespective of what comparative information is selected, partners should be continually aware of the state of the firm in terms of its gross fee income. It also helps to know how productive each partner has been in terms of fees[1].

A slightly more sophisticated version of the above table can also prove useful for a firm's management. The focus this time is on the fees rendered by each fee earner for each category of work.

ILLUSTRATION 13.2

FIRM NAME: MacDONALD FRASER, WS   *FINANCIAL YEAR: 1997*

Date of Report: – –/– –/– –

Management Report: Fees Rendered, Analysed by Fee Earner and Work Category
(Year to Date (YTD))

Fee Earner	Conveyancing £'000	Matrimonial £'000	Criminal £'000	Legal Aid £'000	Reparation £'000	Other £'000	Totals £'000
A	12	6	—	—	6	1	25 *1
B	—	—	18	18	—	—	36
C	—	9	—	etc	etc	etc	etc
D	—	—	etc	etc	etc		
E	6	—	etc	etc			
F	—	—	etc				
Other	—	—					
Totals	18 *2	15					*3

Work Category (column group header over Conveyancing through Other)

Explanatory notes

*1 To find A's contributions to fees rendered, add across the columns.
*2 To find the extent of fees rendered in respect of, say, conveyancing matters, add down through the different rows.
*3 This figure will represent the grand total of fees rendered for the period under review.

This table, besides showing the extent to which each partner has rendered fees, would also provide a ready means of assessing the fees rendered under each of the different work headings.

---

1 The broader picture should be borne in mind when assessing the performance of fee earner/partners. For example, how much general administration each person carries, how much voluntary work each individual does, are they good at finding new clients, etc. The existence of such factors will reduce the amount of time available to fee earners to spend on chargeable client work.

Information of this nature would be more useful, and hence more valuable, if, for example it can be compared to the results of previous years.

ILLUSTRATION 13.3

FIRM NAME: MacDONALD FRASER ,WS *FINANCIAL YEAR : 1997*

Date of Report: – –/– –/– –

Management Report: Fees Rendered, Analysed by Fee Earner and Work Category (Year to Date) with Comparatives

	Work Category							*Comparative Totals*			
Fee Earner	*Conv £'000*	*Matrim £'000*	*Crim £'000*	*Legal Aid £'000*	*Repar £'000*	*Other £'000*	**Totals** *(1997) £'000*	*1996 £'000*	*1995 £'000*	*1994 £'000*	
A	12	6	—	—	6	1	25	28	32	32	*1
B	—	—	18	18	—	—	36	34	34	31	
C	—	9	—	—	etc	etc	etc	etc	etc	etc	
D	—	—	etc	etc	etc						
E	6	—	etc	etc							
F	—	—	etc								
Other	—	—	etc								
Totals	18	15	etc				*3	*3	*3	*3	
Comparatives 1996	20	15	etc								
1995	26	13	etc								
1994	27	12	etc								
	*2										

Explanatory notes

*1 To review A's current feeing performance relative to previous years, the figures contained in the final four columns should be compared.

*2 To find the contribution that, say, conveyancing business has made relative to previous years, the last four rows of the first column should be considered.

*3 To see how the firm's overall feeing has changed over time, the figures as indicated should be compared.

Any significant deviations from past (or planned) performance should be analysed further by the firm's management, with subsequent appropriate action taken.

It is possible to amend the presentational format of **Illustrations 13.1** and **13.2** to highlight the relative performance of a separate department or work groups, or branch offices, etc. Likewise, the same general format can be altered to include general fees and commission earned by including additional rows/columns where appropriate.

Cost of time

It is all very well knowing the value of gross fees rendered by a firm, as well as the sectional gross contributions made by the different fee earners or work categories over a period of time, but it would be short sighted and potentially dangerous for a firm's management to be unaware of the costs of running the business generally and, more specifically, the costs attributable to the different fee earners and/or categories of work. After all, if a solicitor does not know how much the work has cost to produce, how can it be known that the work has been profitable? A solicitor could be about to commence a lengthy and involved piece of work for a client that may simply not be profitable and may, in fact, cost the business money once all direct and indirect (often hidden) expenses are considered. In actual fact the solicitor may be better letting the work go and concentrating on other more profitable business.

A legal firm's management must be familiar with the true costs of performing legal work if the business is to survive and thrive. Indeed, *all* fee earners in a firm should be aware of costs for the same reasons and not be left to conduct their business in an economic information vacuum. If staff are unaware of costs, it is likely that inefficient work practices will develop. People may simply fail to appreciate the implications of commercial constraints and the importance of sound time management practice.

The cost of time has been addressed by the Law Society[1] and its publications on the matter should be considered essential reading for all solicitors, but especially the management of any law firm. Before progressing further, it would be beneficial to define a few key terms which are synonymous with discussions on cost of time.

The following definitions are as stated in the Fees Supplement 1999 of the Scottish Law Directory (emphasis authors own).

'*Fee-earners*
Fee-earners are those members of staff in an office who perform legal work directly attributable and chargeable to specific clients as opposed to staff members such as typists, receptionists, clerks and juniors who perform general work which cannot be charged directly to any specific client and whose cost is recovered as a general overhead.

Chargeable hours
Chargeable hours are the hours in the year worked during normal working hours during which the fee-earner is actually and directly engaged on work for clients for which a charge will be made.

Hourly cost rate
The *hourly cost rate* is the amount per chargeable hour which each fee-earner requires to earn in the course of undertaking work for clients in order to meet the firm's overheads and salaries (including notional salaries of profit-sharing partners).

Notional salary
In order to calculate the basic cost of time for each fee-earner, it is necessary to assign to each profit-sharing partner a *notional salary*. This is not the anticipated income of the partner, but represents a reasonable level of professional remuneration before full account is taken of such factors as responsibility, commercial risk, pension provision, and interest on capital. The level of notional salary is a matter of judgement and may depend upon the age, experience, and ability of each partner.'

It is normally possible to calculate with a fair degree of accuracy the hourly cost rate for fee-earners in any legal firm. Without going into the matter in great depth, crudely, this involves taking the total costs of running the business and dividing this figure by the number of chargeable hours it is expected that the fee-earners will be able to achieve in the same period.

The 'total costs' referred to here will include:

(1) the full cost of employing staff (that is, salaries, employers' pension contributions, any pensions payable, employers' National Insurance Contributions, etc);

---

1 *The Scottish Law Directory Fees Supplement 1999* (T & T Clark, 1999).

(2) the full cost of salaried partners (who are in effect treated as employees in the present sense since their salaries are often assured, courtesy of the full profit-sharing partners);

(3) with respect to the profit-sharing partners, allowances will be included for their notional salaries, pension contributions, interest on their capital tied up in the business, etc;

(4) property costs of the office(s) and all other general business running expenses.

Assuming for the moment that the rates actually charged to clients equate to cost rates, if the fee-earners of the firm can meet their collective chargeable hours target then it will follow that the costs of the firm will have been recovered.

If their target is exceeded, this will be welcomed at least by all profit-sharing partners who will benefit by sharing in the additional profit generated. The additional profit share attributable to each profit-sharing partner will help compensate such individuals, if nothing else, for the risks and stresses of being in business.

However, just as they would gain in this latter situation, should the actual chargeable hours billed fall below target, they would be facing a cut to their basic notional salaries, assuming they wished to avoid the firm's financial position deteriorating beyond its position at the start of the financial year when the fees targets were established. To be profitable, a firm's management must try to ensure amongst other things that all fee-earners achieve their chargeable hour targets for the period.

The hourly cost rate will usually vary fairly considerably in a legal practice, dependent on factors such as the size of firm, its location (city centre or country) etc.

Equally important to ensure an efficient operation, legal work must be handled by an appropriate grade of staff. Within a given firm the hourly cost rate will change across the different grades of fee-earners. Senior partners or partners with specialist knowledge will have a much higher cost rate than an unqualified assistant. Qualified assistants, trainees, associates and salaried partners for example, will fall at various rates between these two poles. By applying the appropriate grade of staff, the firm can remain competitive in terms of the final bill that a client will have to face. Effective delegation is an important business skill.

Cost rate v charge rate

In order to illustrate a point above, the assumption was made that the hourly charge rate actually applied to clients equated with the hourly cost rate in respect of the work undertaken. Although this can be the case in practice, it is a very common occurrence for the two rates to vary. Ideally from the firm's perspective, the final bill payable by the client should exceed its economic cost. If a firm can consistently apply charge rates to its clients which are above its cost rates and still retain happy clients, this firm will be in a healthier position than another firm which has to regularly discount its charge rates to below cost rates in order to win work. In the latter case, all else being equal, the staff will have to achieve more chargeable hours to meet the firm's costs over the financial period.

The final fee payable by a client in respect of work has been identified by the Law Society as consisting of two principal parts; the *base factor* and the *supplementary factor*[1].

---

1 *The Scottish Law Directory Fees Supplement 1999.*

'Base factor

The *base factor* is the cost of the time spent on a particular piece of business for a client. It is calculated from the hourly cost rates for the fee-earners involved.

Supplementary factor

The *supplementary factor* is a supplement or weighting added in appropriate circumstances to the time cost of a piece of legal work in order to produce a fair and reasonable fee for such work after taking into account all the circumstances affecting it.'

Solicitors in practice should, in the main, attempt to maximise fee income from each client, (that is, maximise the supplementary factor). The final fee payable by a client must be fair and reasonable having regard to all the circumstances. When setting the final fee for a client, the solicitor should refer to the 'seven pillars of wisdom', namely:

(1)   the time spent on the matter;
(2)   the number and importance of the documents perused or prepared;
(3)   the circumstances surrounding the work carried out and the place(s) at which this was done;
(4)   the complexity, difficulty or novelty of the subject matter;
(5)   the responsibility, specialist knowledge and skills involved;
(6)   the value of the subject matter;
(7)   the importance of the matter to the client.

A solicitor charging enhanced rates for work carried out must be able to justify the fee by reference to some or all of the above criteria.

Time recording and cost recovery

Much of the foregoing discussion on the cost of time will, by necessity, involve an appropriate *time recording system* being operational within the legal practice. The actual method employed to record the time spent on client matters will vary dependent on the needs of a particular firm. The time recording system adopted might simply involve the sole practitioner making a hand-written note on the client file, or alternatively, more progressive firms may employ highly sophisticated and complex systems prepared by a specialised commercial supplier.

Ultimately the firm's management should know how the fee-earners are spending their time in order that areas of inefficiency can be highlighted. Time recording should help achieve this objective. An appropriate system will also allow all fee-earners to have accurate and reliable information for client feeing purposes. The accuracy of the firm's budgets and forecasts in this respect should similarly benefit.

Besides recording time spent on individual client matters, it is also important for the overall profitability of the firm that care should be taken to record, in so far as it is reasonable and practical to do so, all expenses that can be directly attributed to the client matter in hand in order that they can (properly) be recovered as disbursements.

By identifying the true cost of particular forms of legal work, the firm should benefit from knowing with more accuracy the relative rewards which are generated from its different work categories.

Profit margins

Once the firm's management is in possession of all the relevant cost information, it should be possible to apply this to the value of the fees rendered in order to highlight how much profit is generated by each fee-earner/partner, each work category, etc.

Again this information could be tabulated on a regular basis for management purposes as follows in **Illustration 13.4**.

ILLUSTRATION 13.4

FIRM NAME: MacDONALD FRASER ,WS   *FINANCIAL YEAR: 1997*

Date of Report: – –/– –/– –

Management Report : Contribution to Profit by Fee Earner and Work Category
(Year to Date)

Fee Earner	Conv. £'000	Matri. £'000	Crim. £'000	Legal Aid £'000	Repar. £'000	Other £'000	Total (i) £'000	Share of costs (ii) £'000	Contribution to Profit (iii) £'000	
A	12	6	—	—	6	1	25	12	13	*1
B	—	—	18	18	—	—	36	14	22	
C	—	9	—	—	etc	etc	etc	etc	etc	
D	—	—	etc	etc	etc	etc				
E	6	—	etc	etc	etc					
F	—	—	etc	etc						
Other	—	—	etc	etc						
Total (iv)	18	15	etc	etc						
Less Share of costs (v)	11	9	etc							
Contribution (vi)	7	6	etc							

*2

Explanatory notes

*1   The contribution which A has made to the profitability of the firm (column (iii)) is found by deducting the 'Share of costs' figure in column (ii), from the 'Total' fees rendered shown in column (i) in A's row.

*2   The contribution made to the success of the firm by 'Conveyancing', is seen in row (vi) and is found by deducting the figure in row (v) from that shown in row (iv).

This type of information will allow a firm's management to see the relative importance to overall profitability of each partner or work category. Armed with such information, it should be possible for the firm thereafter to concentrate its efforts on generating and completing higher profit margin legal work.

By the same token, areas of work which are simply unprofitable should be sacrificed if resources can be effectively utilised elsewhere on more profitable business. It should be appreciated though that some business costs will be fixed and largely independent of work volume or type (eg office rental costs). If a firm ceases a particular line of business, it should be borne in mind that the fixed costs previously apportioned to, and at least partially met by, the discontinued business will now fall to be met by the remaining work categories. For this reason it may still be worthwhile continuing marginally profitable work if only to help recover some of the business's fixed costs.

With reference to all of the above discussions relating to fees rendered, it is clear that if a firm's management is to monitor and successfully control their fees over time, additional information way beyond that shown in the firm's profit and loss account is necessary.

(2) Work in progress

One of the key pressure points in the control of a firm's finances is *work in progress* (WIP). WIP is the value of work carried out on behalf of a client prior to the stage when an invoice can be raised.

More often than not a particular piece of legal work will extend over many weeks, months or even years. As the case progresses, the solicitor will be incurring more and more expense on behalf of the client. Some expenses will be direct—for example, staff time charged to the particular client matter—others will be indirect—for example, the portion of office overheads which each case is expected to bear. As time passes and the case continues without an invoice being raised against the client, then the greater the WIP figure. Unless arrangements exist to the contrary, it will be *the solicitor* who will have to finance WIP until it can be turned into cash (ie, when the client is invoiced and pays). This represents an actual cost to the solicitor which may never be recovered from the client.

Also worth noting is that the higher the level of WIP, then the greater the business risk to the solicitor should the client subsequently default on payment.

Good financial management will mean that a solicitor should attempt to minimise the level of WIP outstanding for the firm as a whole as well as with respect to individual clients. Ideally, a solicitor should attempt to obtain payment in advance or at least get a sizeable deposit from clients before work and outlays on their behalf commence, particularly so if the ability and/or willingness of the client to pay is in any doubt. This approach may not be appropriate for all clients as there is a danger of causing offence, especially to long-standing quality clients.

Where payment in advance is not possible, the solicitor should insist on interim invoices, which is a reasonable compromise for reasonable clients. Thus when work gets to a pre-determined stage (falling short of outright work completion), an interim invoice will be sent to the client. The continuation of the work will be dependent upon timeous settlement of all interim invoices.

Besides reducing the exposure to any one client, interim invoicing also minimises the financial outlays (including payments to staff, overheads, direct recoverable outlays, etc) which a solicitor will have to make on a client's behalf. Control of WIP levels is an essential part of sound financial management in a legal practice. It is a useful discipline for the firm's management to review WIP levels on a regular basis. At the very least a monthly statement should be drafted for management control purposes which shows each partner's attributable WIP totals. The statement could be drafted along similar lines as the pro-forma used earlier for fees rendered, suitably amended.

Firms carrying out Legal Aid work should be familiar with the threshold figures at which point it is possible to request an interim payment. Again this should help minimise WIP.

(3) Control of expenses

Turning to an earlier illustration, when reviewing the profit and loss account of Jefferson MacInroy & Co.[1], the amounts attributable to expenses is readily apparent.

---

1   See Chapter Seven for full details of this illustration.

At an initial level, total expenses for the period (in this case £235,136) can be assessed relative to the firm's turnover (£330,900) and the net profit figures (£95,764) to see if the relationships are generally reasonable. Looking at budgeted figures or the results of previous years will help to form an opinion on how well the firm has done in its most recent financial period in terms of cost control.

At a more detailed level, it is also good practice to compile further, more specific expense analysis reports. At the end of a financial year for example, it would be a relatively straightforward task to draft a report in tabular form which shows details of the different forms of expenditure that the firm has incurred over, say, the past five years, including the present year's results. This could appear as follows in **Illustration 13.5**.

ILLUSTRATION 13.5

FIRM NAME: JEFFERSON, MACINROY & CO., (SOLICITORS)

Date of Report: – –/– –/– –

Management Report : Expense Analysis for the five year period, 1995-1999 inclusive

Expenses Category	Year to: 31.12.99 £	31.12.98 £	31.12.97 £	31.12.96 £	31.12.95 £
Office wages & salaries	161,572	150,250	146,150	140,200	135,210
Rates and Insurance	13,250	13,100	12,900	12,900	12,850
Stationery	11,432	11,300	11,350	11,250	10,100
Sundry expenses	9,256	9,220	9,120	9,000	8,950
Telephone and postages	16,710	15,000	14,200	13,800	13,500
Bank interest and charges	6,500	5,500	4,750	4,500	4,450
Bad debts, written off	420	400	350	350	300
Depreciation—office premises	4,568	4,568	4,568	4,568	4,568
—office furniture & fittings	11,428	12,400	14,000	7,000	8,000
Totals	235,136	221,738	217,388	203,568	197,928

For each expense it is possible to see how costs have changed over the five-year period. If the trends appear reasonable, bearing in mind the general inflation rate, levels of business activity, etc, then this will provide reassurance to the firm's management.

If, however, certain expenses appear to have risen at a disproportionate rate, it will be a sign to trigger further detailed investigation into the reasons behind the adverse changes.

As an alternative or even in addition to the report in **Illustration 13.5**, present year costs could again be analysed relative to the budgeted figures for that year with variances being highlighted, as detailed in **Illustration 13.6**.

ILLUSTRATION 13.6

FIRM NAME: JEFFERSON, MACINROY & CO, SOLICITORS

Date of Report: – –/– –/– –

Management Report: Actual v Budgeted Expense Levels
For the year to 31/12/99

Expenses Category	Actual Out-turn £	Budgeted for year £	Variance £	%'age change
Office wages & salaries	161,572	155,000	6,572	4.2%
Rates and Insurance	13,250	13,000	250	2%
Stationery	11,432	12,000	(568)	(4.7%)
Sundry expenses	9,256	10,000	(744)	(7.4%)
Telephone and postages	16,710	15,000	1,710	11.4%
Bank interest and charges	6,500	2,000	4,500	225%
Bad debts, written off	420	500	(80)	(16%)
Depreciation—office premises	4,568	4,500	68	1.5%
—office furniture & fittings	11,428	11,500	(72)	(0.6%)
Totals	235,136	223,500	11,636	5.2%

It can be seen that the actual costs incurred vary relative to the estimated figures, which would have presumably been produced around the beginning of the financial year. Where the variances are significant, explanations should be obtained. If further action is required to improve the situation, the firm's management should ensure that it is in fact done.

Insignificant variances can be ignored, assuming that the partners are happy with the original budgeted figure, of course. The final column in **Illustration 13.6**, showing the size of the variance in percentage terms, may help users in their assessment[1].

Although the above statements have been examined in the context of a financial year end procedure, such reports could be prepared at more regular intervals. A firm's management may wish to examine this type of information on a monthly basis as it progresses through a financial year. There should be little difficulty in drafting the above reports to work on a 'year to date' basis accordingly.

Regular checks on the nature and levels of the firm's expenses are a necessary and important part of the proper financial control of the practice.

(4) Client debtors (credit control)

The discussion on matters of financial control has until now concentrated on items that might first be referred to at a summary level in the firm's profit and loss account.

---

1 To calculate the percentage variance for say 'Office wages and salaries'; $\dfrac{£6,572}{£155,000} \times \dfrac{100}{1} = 4.2\%$ increase over budget. This is obviously an unfavourable variance given that the out-turn figure is higher than that forecast. Out of all the figures analysed, 'Bank interest and charges' must attract attention given that the out-turn figure is so far in excess of the budget.

A consideration of Jefferson MacInroy & Co's balance sheet also reveals areas which must be examined in greater detail by the firm's management if a tight rein on its finances is to be achieved. This is certainly the case with the level of client debtors.

Once work has been done for a client and the fee note raised, it would be easy for a solicitor to feel that the job is finished. Unfortunately, clients delaying and defaulting on payments to their solicitors is an all too common experience. Solicitors must take precautionary measures to minimise such occurrences.

A review of the debtors figure as contained in the firm's balance sheet at the end of the year should be conducted to determine whether or not it appears reasonable relative to, say, the total fees rendered over the period and/or the closing debtors balances from the balance sheets of previous years. As a rule, debtors levels should be kept as low as possible, both to minimise financial risk to the firm through client non-payment and to minimise the amount of the firm's resources which are tied up in uncollected bills. It is worth remembering that it is *the firm* that has to finance its debtors level until the debts are recovered from clients, just as it has to finance the prior stage of WIP (ie work done but not yet invoiced). The greater the debtors' figure and level of work in progress, the more finance is required to meet the working capital requirement of the firm[1], which means the more cash the partners must find to keep the business running.

A firm's management will need more information relating to debtors than simply the total figure shown in the balance sheet. They will also need this information far more frequently than once a year. At the very least a legal firm should review outstanding debtors once a month. By keeping debtors under constant review and by taking action at appropriate stages to recover fees, cash flows into the firm are maximised and the risks of bad debts occurring are minimised.

A *debtors ageing schedule*, where outstanding client debts to the firm are analysed on the basis of the length of time the debts have remained unpaid with reference to the partner/fee earner responsible, is a useful management report. A debtors ageing schedule can be shown as in **Illustration 13.7**.

---

1 Working capital management is considered later at point (7) in this chapter.

ILLUSTRATION 13.7

FIRM NAME: CROSBY, WEIR AND CLELLAND (SOLICITORS)   *FINANCIAL YEAR: 1996/97*

Date of Report: – –/– –/– –

Management Report: Summary Debtors Ageing Schedule

Level of fees invoiced and outstanding:

Partner/ Fee Earner	Less than 30 days £	Between 30 and 60 days £	Between 60 and 90 days £	More than 90 days £	TOTAL £
A	15,000	24,000	7,000	—	46,000
B	6,000	13,000	3,000	—	22,000
C	12,000	22,000	5,000	2,500	41,500
D	12,000	21,000	2,000	500	35,500
E	8,000	15,000	2,000	—	25,000
F	12,000	25,000	11,000	5,000	53,000
Totals	65,000	120,000	30,000	8,000	223,000

A further management report, giving full details of all debts which are over say, 60 days can also be used to augment the above schedule. This may include an outline of the steps which have already been taken to recover the individual debts as well as the planned future action. The objectives here are to accelerate the recovery of debts and to identify and minimise possible bad debts.

Even although the above reports have an important function as part of the firm's overall credit control system, the efficiency of this side of the business will be much improved if appropriate procedures are in place *before* the solicitor commences work for the client. It will be easier to recover fees if the firm's terms of business have been clearly stated to the client at the outset. The initial *letter of engagement* issued to clients should deal with all relevant matters in this respect including the level and timing of fees to be rendered, the recovery of disbursements and the time within which it is expected that debts are paid, for example. The firm's staff should follow a clear credit control pattern (which obviously has to be consistent with the terms of the letter of engagement) and follow pre-determined courses of action as time progresses and the firm's invoices remain unpaid.

The fact should also not be overlooked that it will be a difficult task to obtain settlement of an invoice if the client cannot be found! Basic risk management procedures should involve establishing full details of the client, including the rather obvious matters such as name, address(es), telephone number(s), employer, bank details, company address if relevant, etc. It would also be advisable to routinely seek references (trade, bank and/or credit agencies) as background information on new (and in some cases, established) clients. This type of information will help the solicitor to determine and hence minimise the likelihood of bad debts arising in the future[1].

---

1   This type of information is virtually compulsory if regard is paid to the solicitors' money laundering regulations where the handling of substantial clients' funds occurs.

(5) Outlays on behalf of clients

The same comments raised above with respect to treatment of WIP and client debtors apply to disbursements on behalf of clients. The firm must avoid as far as possible building up balances of recoverable outlays on behalf of its clients. Outlays should be recovered from clients (or the Scottish Legal Aid Board) at the earliest possible date.

Again as with outstanding invoices, the level of recoverable outlays per partner/fee earner should be regularly monitored.

(6) Cash

It is a sobering thought that one of the main reasons for business failure is *liquidity* or *cash flow problems*. A firm can appear profitable but if money is not coming in at a rate at least equal to the rate of outflow, the business will be building up a pit of debt from which it may not escape. In the context of a partnership this may mean personal bankruptcy for some or all of the partners. Sound financial control of a legal practice, by necessity, demands strict cash management.

It is normal in a legal practice for some months of the financial year to place heavier demands on the firm's cash position than others. This may be as a result of:

(1) low cash income in certain months (eg July/August being holiday months, or January when the smaller, private clients are recovering from the expense of the Festive Season); or
(2) because certain periodic cash outgoings fall due (eg VAT payments to Customs and Excise, payment of partnership taxes to the Inland Revenue, property costs such as a quarterly rent payment, etc); or
(3) a combination of both of the above.

The cash demands on the practice will not normally be constant throughout any financial year, appearing more as a series of peaks and troughs if presented in a graph.

Partners must be aware of such major fluctuations and plan ahead accordingly. Management should attempt to smooth out the peaks and troughs into a more plateau-like profile. If certain months are identified in advance as likely cash flow problem areas, partners might consider some or all of the following courses of action.

(1) delay major forms of cash outflows to some other time, so giving the opportunity for more cash to come into the business before it has to go back out again. If the firm is planning to purchase new fixed assets for example, this expenditure may have to be delayed or the method of acquisition reviewed; ie, lease or hire-purchase the asset in preference to an outright, immediate purchase[1];
(2) accelerate the rate of cash flowing into the business; for example by adopting more rigorous credit control procedures with respect to slow payment by clients of the firm's invoices and/or the recovery of outlays on behalf of clients. Also, WIP could be reviewed to see if some clients could be sent an interim invoice.

---

1 Tax implications should not be ignored in such matters.

Even if the latter can be achieved, there will be a time delay before the invoice turns into a cash receipt;

(3)   Reduce the extent of regular cash outflows. For example partners may reduce the level of their drawings (at least temporarily) to ease the net cash flow position of the business. Also, and rather obviously so, try and minimise business expenses generally.

If the firm is in the healthy and extremely fortunate position of having a positive cash balance at all times, the cost of having inefficient cash flow management practices might only be the interest foregone on the cash it might otherwise have in the bank were it not for this problem. Very commonly, however, legal firms operate on the basis of a bank overdraft. An overdraft is an expensive, short-term financing method, especially if the agreed overdraft limit is breached, if in fact going above the borrowing limit is permitted by the bank. It is not hard to imagine the detriment caused to a legal firm, or any business for that matter, if the bank blocks expenditure permanently or even temporarily.

The greater the level of overdraft required by a firm then obviously the more it will be paying to the bank in interest and charges. Good cash flow management is essential if such dangers and costs are to be minimised.

Using a *cash flow statement* is a recognised technique employed by all sorts of businesses in this area of financial control. A cash flow statement is prepared in advance of, say, a financial year and shows the monthly cash inflows and outflows expected throughout that period. It will also show the net cash flow each month (ie inflows less outflows) as well as the running, cumulative cash balance at the end of each month. A cash flow statement can be illustrated as follows in **Illustration 13.8**.

ILLUSTRATION 13.8

Date: --/--/--

McGrowther James and Co (Solicitors)
Forecast Cash Flow Statement for the Period 1 January to 31 December 2000

	Explanatory Notes	Jan £	Feb £	March £	April £	May £	June £	July £	Aug £	Sept £	Oct £	Nov £	Dec £
CASH INFLOWS													
Fees recovered	(1)	20,000	23,000	30,000	32,000	32,000	30,000	28,000	25,000	34,000	32,000	28,000	25,000
VAT on fees recovered	(2)	3,500	4,025	5,250	5,600	5,600	5,250	4,900	4,375	5,950	5,600	4,900	4,375
Other cash inflows (VAT exempt)	(3)	2,500	1,575	1,250	3,400	1,400	1,750	4,100	1,625	1,550	4,000	1,600	1,625
Total cash inflows		26,000	28,600	36,500	41,000	39,000	37,000	37,000	31,000	41,500	41,600	34,500	31,000
Less: CASH OUTFLOWS													
Wages and salaries	(4)	15,600	15,600	16,000	16,250	16,250	16,000	15,600	15,600	16,500	16,250	15,600	18,000
Property costs		3,500	—	—	3,500	—	—	3,500	—	—	4,000	—	—
Other office running costs		1,500	1,500	1,500	1,500	1,500	1,500	1,550	1,550	1,550	1,550	1,550	1,550
VAT paid on expenses	(5)	825	225	225	825	225	225	835	235	235	835	235	235
Disbursements	(6)	100	100	100	100	100	100	100	100	100	100	100	100
Cash outflows, sub-total (i)		21,525	17,425	17,825	22,175	18,075	17,825	21,585	17,485	18,385	22,735	17,485	19,885
TAXES													
Quarterly VAT payment	(7)	14,000	—	—	11,500	—	—	15,175	—	—	13,920	—	—
Bi-annual tax payment	(8)	15,500	—	—	—	—	—	15,500	—	—	—	—	—
Cash outflows, sub-total (ii)		29,500	—	—	11,500	—	—	30,675	—	—	13,920	—	—
NET CASH FLOW BEFORE PARTNERS' DRAWINGS	(9)	(25,025)	11,175	18,675	7,325	20,925	19,175	(15,260)	13,515	23,115	4,945	17,015	11,115
Less: Partners' drawings		8,000	8,000	8,000	8,000	8,000	8,000	8,000	8,000	8,000	8,000	8,000	8,000
NET CASH FLOW AFTER PARTNERS' DRAWINGS		(33,025)	3,175	10,675	(675)	12,925	11,175	(23,260)	5,515	15,115	(3,055)	9,015	3,115
CUMULATIVE CASH POSITION	(10)												
Opening bank/cash		5,000	(28,025)	(24,850)	(14,175)	(14,850)	(1,925)	9,250	(14,010)	(8,495)	6,620	3,565	12,580
Net cash flow for the month		(33,025)	3,175	10,675	(675)	12,925	11,175	(23,260)	5,515	15,115	(3,055)	9,015	3,115
Closing bank/cash		(28,025)	(24,850)	(14,175)	(14,850)	(1,925)	9,250	(14,010)	(8,495)	6,620	3,565	12,580	15,695

Explanatory notes

(1) Fees recovered

Work will be done for clients and the related invoices rendered. This section will show an estimate of the cash expected to be received from clients each month as the invoices are settled. The fees recovered figure should be shown net of any VAT which will be paid by the clients since this is considered elsewhere in the cash flow statement. Likewise outlays paid by the firm and subsequently repaid by clients should be excluded at this stage.

(2) VAT on fees recovered

Most legal practices will be registered for VAT and will add on 17.5% VAT to client invoices. When the clients settle their invoices, that part of the total cash received attributable to VAT should be separated and shown independently in the cash flow statement so removing its potentially distorting effects. For the purposes of a forecast cash flow statement, an estimate for this item can be found by applying 17.5% to the expected monthly 'fees recovered' figures, as has been done in this example.

(3) Other cash inflows (VAT exempt)

This section will include forecasts of the cash expected to be generated by referrals of clients to Building Societies, insurance companies etc. The estimated cash receipts from such commissions would be identified here as would any bank interest generated on the clients' account which can legitimately be retained by the firm. Cash inflows of this nature will be free from VAT.

(4) Wages and salaries

It would be possible to construct a forecast cash flow statement showing a single monthly cash outflow figure which covers all the different forms of business expenses. The other extreme is to show all the payments under their separate headings as they are shown in the profit and loss account for example. A reasonable compromise for the purposes of inclusion in the forecast cash flow statement is to separately identify the major forms of cash expenditure and group together the lesser expense categories. In the present illustration, monthly forecast figures for 'wages and salaries' and 'property costs' are used to highlight the major expense items. 'Other office running costs' will include forecasts of the bills to be paid in respect of heating and lighting, postages, stationery, staff travel, vehicle running costs, etc.

(5) VAT paid on expenses

When the firm pays an electricity bill, for example, the portion attributable to recoverable VAT should be separated and displayed under 'VAT paid on expenses'.

(6) Disbursements

It was mentioned earlier that a firm's management should attempt to minimise the levels of outlays incurred on behalf of its clients. It is reasonable to assume when considering cash flow matters that as some outlays are paid by the firm, others will be recovered. If the general level of disbursements is not anticipated to change significantly over the year, or in any one month, this item could virtually be ignored. On the other hand, if it is forecast that the total disbursements figure will rise over the period, some allowance should be made in the outflows section of the cash flow statement to accommodate the change in the general level. Given that it is well nigh impossible to predict such outlays in any one month, probably the best approach is to estimate the annual rise expected and divide this by twelve to find the monthly cash outflow figure[1].

(7) Quarterly VAT payment

For a legal practice it can be assumed that at the end of each VAT period (being three months in this illustration, ending 31 March, 30 June, 30 September and 31 December) the firm will be faced with having to account to the Customs and Excise for the difference between the VAT

---

1 If a general decrease in the level of disbursements was predicted on the other hand, this would translate to positive effect on the forecast cash flow statement with 1/12 of the forecast annual decrease being shown in the monthly cash inflow section of the statement.

collected on invoices paid by clients and the VAT paid on its expenses. This 'quarterly VAT payment' is a cash outflow for the firm in the months in which it is made (in this case, April, July, October and the following January), although the firm will of course be able to use this money up to the point it is transferred to the Customs and Excise.

Firms have a reasonable amount of discretion when initially choosing their VAT periods. When making this particular decision, a legal firm should attempt to avoid the end of a VAT period clashing with those times of the year when cash flows are under pressure from other factors. It would not appear sensible to plan a VAT payment to fall in the same month as the quarterly office rental payment or in the months when the partnership is facing a demand for cash from the Inland Revenue. Where possible, firms should plan major cash outflows so that they do not compound each other to the detriment of the firm's cash position.

(8) Bi-annual taxes payment

It is assumed that taxes on partners' income from the business will generally be paid in two equal instalments each year, falling in January and July.

(9) Net cash flow before partners' drawings

It is reasonable to assume that consideration should first be given to the firm's forecast cash position throughout a period before the level of partners drawings is determined. The 'net cash flow before partners' drawings' figure in the statement will highlight the amount of cash available on a month-to-month basis from which the partners can make a draw on account of profits. Although the level of partner drawings will normally be calculated for a financial year based on the profit expectations for that period, the effect of drawings on the firm's cash flow position should not be ignored[1].

(10) Cumulative cash position

The purpose of this section in the cash flow statement is to chart the cumulative cash position as the firm progresses through the year. By examining the 'closing bank/cash' figure it will be possible to see the firm's cash requirements at different stages throughout the year. Used as a working document, partners can take corrective measures before the problems actually arise in order to minimise the cash demands falling at any one time. Once all practical steps have been taken and the forecast cash flow statement finalised, if the predicted cash flow pattern is such that the firm will still have to review its overdraft limit (upwards), an approach should be made to the firm's bank in good time. If the bank is satisfied that the increased level of borrowings falls within reasonable limits and the cash flow statement shows that the cash demand is only temporary, the firm can be confident of its immediate future. A firm's management that does not plan ahead in this way, with the partners finding themselves called before the banker after the overdraft limit has been breached without prior notification, will be in a much weaker negotiating position. This will probably result in excessive bank interest and other charges, increased bank involvement in the firm's affairs, less autonomy by the partners in the running of their business and increased levels of stress generally.

Once the partners of a legal practice become familiar with the basic content and layout of the forecast cash flow statement, it will prove an extremely valuable tool in terms of the increased quality of the financial management and control that they exert over the business. When formulating such a forecast statement, solicitors should try to be as objective and realistic as possible. A healthy degree of pessimism being incorporated into the figures as to the firm's future will not be misplaced. Are staff likely to expect or demand a high wage rise this year? Is a rent review on the office property due to occur in the near future with the prospect of higher rental charges a distinct possibility? How are other office expenses likely to change this year? Are any business assets (like motor vehicles, IT equipment, office furniture, etc) needing replacement? What are the future market expectations for the type of

---

1 See also the section dealing with partners' drawings as contained within Chapter Seven which looked at partnership agreements.

legal services provided by the firm? Is a partner due to retire soon with consequential pressure being placed on the firm's cash? Will partners be required to inject more equity into the business?

All of the above types of questions and more should be addressed when considering the future of the firm in general, as well as when the firm's management are drafting the forecast statements such as the cash flow.

The cash flow statement should be updated as the business progresses through the financial period and the facts become known if the usefulness of the statement to management is to be maintained.

(7) Working capital management

The *working capital* of a legal firm is basically the amount of money and other assets which are available for the day-to-day operation of the business. It can be found by deducting the value of current liabilities from current assets. Controlling working capital and cash flow are probably the two most important financial management functions that the partners of the firm will perform.

Many matters which are directly relevant to effective working capital management have already been discussed. However, it is important to appreciate the collective and interactive nature of the levels of a firm's debtors and recoverable outlays, its WIP and creditors levels, for example. If a firm is to operate efficiently, its *working capital requirement* should be minimised so ensuring that both partners' funds and borrowed funds are not unnecessarily locked into the business. Thus the amount of WIP a firm is carrying at any one time should be kept as low as possible by billing clients as regularly as possible, within reason. The greater the level of WIP, the more finance a firm has tied up. Likewise for debtors and outlays. The more finance committed to such items, the less that is freely available to the owners of the business whether to draw out or to channel into some other business area.

It is possible to reduce the working capital requirement of the business by slowing payments to creditors and allowing the overall level of creditors to increase. But a firm's management should be extremely careful if tempted to use this tactic since it is all too easy to obtain a bad reputation in this respect, making subsequent trading more difficult and potentially more costly as suppliers adopt counter measures.

(8) Effective use of clients' funds

It can be seen from the balance sheet of the Jefferson MacInroy & Co practice that the firm has £3,008 over-deposited in the clients' account. This is the firm's money. Although many firms like the reassurance of having a 'float' in the clients' account, care needs to be taken to ensure that it does not become excessive since in all probability it could be used more effectively elsewhere. The firm may well be paying bank interest at overdraft rates on its own business account which will be greater than the amount being received in return for the amount over-deposited in the clients' account.

It is also possible that at least some of the interest earned on the clients' account is legitimately attributable to the firm. For example, prudent solicitors will ensure the availability of cleared funds in order that a conveyancing transaction can be settled on the date of entry. This means that the related building society loan received on behalf of the client can, in effect, be held by the firm for three full days earning interest for the firm. However, it is common practice for firms to cash such cheques either on the day before or on the actual date of settlement. This will save the client a modest amount of interest but there is a danger of dishonoured cheques arising if the same procedure is applied when dealing with a client's personal cheque. To remove this particular form of risk, personal cheques should be cashed five days before the date of settlement. Observing this strategy will result in an increase in interest to the firm.

Benefits may also accrue to a legal practice simply on the strength of having a substantial clients' account. This is probably the principal reason why banks want to handle the affairs of a legal firm. It is important that banks are assessed objectively by solicitors before final selection, to maximise the benefits which will accrue to the firm as well as its clients. For example:

(1) What interest rates are offered on the clients' account?
(2) Is interest credited monthly by the bank or quarterly? The former is generally more desirable owing to the compounding effect.
(3) What interest rates will be paid on the firm's money; or more likely, what interest rates and other bank charges will be levied on the firm when in deficit with the bank?
(4) How close is the bank to the solicitor's office? Convenience can save time and hence money.
(5) What prospects are there for the bank referring new business on to the firm? Again the proximity of the bank to the firm's offices may be important in this respect.

Even once a bank has been selected, it is wise to periodically review the interest rates being offered (and charged) by the firm's bank to ensure that it remains competitive.

(9) Financial ratios and statistical information

Without doubt *financial ratios* and *statistical information* have an important and valuable contribution to make in the management and control of a legal practice. Used properly, financial ratios and statistics can be applied to help a firm's management analyse and interpret accounting data which in turn, when coupled to their in-depth knowledge of the business, assists them in measuring the firm's progress, in diagnosing its weaknesses and in planning its future.

One of the benefits of this type of approach is that it can be used to help summarise large amounts of financial data, particularly with respect to the results of different accounting periods. Financial ratios and statistics can be used to highlight the changes which have occurred between financial periods so providing the partners of a legal firm with valuable financial management information. For example, when comparing the current year's results of a legal practice with those of the previous year, it is a useful discipline to add an additional column to the statement to express, on a line by line basis, the percentage change which has occurred to the different items.

ILLUSTRATION 13.9

Frederickson and McCarthy, (Solicitors)
Profit and Loss Account for the year ended 31 December 1997

	1997 £'000	1996 £'000	%'age change
Income			
Fees rendered	1,350	1,250	8% *1
Commission	304	270	12.6%
Other income	30	25	20%
	1,684	1,545	9%
Less: Expenses			
Staff costs: Associates	215	193	11.4%
: Other fee earners	261	209	24.9%
: Other staff	349	309	12.9%
Office rent and rates	75	73	2.7%
Heat and light	20	17	17.6%
Office repairs and maintenance	27	28	(3.6%) *2
Library, stationery and postages	86	81	6.2%
Insurances	44	42	4.8%
Repair of computer and office equipment	76	71	7%
Travelling expenses	46	43	7%
Telephone and related expenses	39	36	8.3%
Bank interest and charges	28	25	12%
Bad debts w/o	25	7	257%
Miscellaneous expenses	73	71	2.8%
	1,364	1,205	13.2%
Net profit, before appropriation to profit-sharing partners	320	340	(5.9%)

Explanatory notes

*1   The percentage change is calculated thus: $\dfrac{1350-1250}{1250} \times \dfrac{100}{1} = 8\%$
with the result subject to rounding.

*2   The 1997 figure in respect of 'Office repairs and maintenance' charges is the only expense that has decreased compared to 1996, as shown by the use of parenthesis.

By glancing at the '*Percentage change*' column in the above profit and loss account, it is readily apparent that the firm has experienced a reduction of 5.9% in its net profit figure over 1997. Although its income has increased by 9%, an overall increase of 13.2% in its expenses has more than wiped out the beneficial effect of the former. Further line-by-line analysis reveals where the most significant changes have occurred. This statement would be a valuable starting point for the partners of Frederickson and McCarthy in their endeavours to identify the causes of their decline in fortune and in their subsequent attempts to remedy the situation.

Trend analysis

Although year-on-year change expressed in percentage terms as shown in **Illustration 13.9** is a useful financial management device, potentially of more benefit is where financial results of, say, 4-5 years are converted to a common statistical base and compared in terms of the changes which have occurred in each item over the years relative to the earliest year. That is, relative to the *base year*.

To illustrate, consider the results of Frederickson and McCarthy from 1997 back to 1993 which have been summarised in **Illustration 13.10**.

ILLUSTRATION 13.10

Frederickson and McCarthy, (Solicitors)
Profit and Loss Account Summary for the years 1993 to 1997 inclusive

	1997 £'000	1996 £'000	1995 £'000	1994 £'000	1993 £'000
Income					
Fees rendered	1,350	1,250	1,250	1,000	975
Commission	304	270	250	250	150
Other income	30	25	25	24	24
	1,684	1,545	1,525	1,274	1,149
Less: Expenditure					
Staff costs: Associates	215	193	193	190	190
: Other fee earners	261	209	207	205	205
: Other staff	349	309	309	305	221
Office rent and rates	75	73	71	70	68
Heat and light	20	17	17	15	14
Office repairs and maintenance	27	28	28	25	25
Library, stationery and postages	86	81	80	75	72
Insurances	44	42	42	39	39
Repair of computer and office equipment	76	71	70	68	64
Travelling expenses	46	43	43	38	35
Telephone and related expenses	39	36	36	32	29
Bank interest and charges	28	25	24	20	19
Bad debts w/o	25	7	5	4	4
Miscellaneous expenses, including depreciation	73	71	71	65	62
	1,364	1,205	1,196	1,151	1,047
Net profit, before appropriations	320	340	329	123	102

Converting the financial information in **Illustration 13.10** into a new statement, in which 1993 is taken as the base year with subsequent changes to any item being expressed in terms of how it has altered relative to 1993, reveals the analysis contained within **Illustration 13.11**.

ILLUSTRATION 13.11

Frederickson and McCarthy, (Solicitors)
5-Year Analysis of Results, 1993 to 1997 inclusive, using 1993 as the Base Year

	1997 %'age	1996 %'age	1995 %'age	1994 %'age	1993 %'age
Income					
Fees rendered	138.5	128.2	128.2	102.6	100
Commission	202.7	180.0	166.7	166.7	100
Other income	125.0	104.2	104.2	100.0	100
	146.6	134.5	132.7	110.9	100
Less: Expenditure					
Staff costs: Associates	113.2	101.6	101.6	100.0	100
: Other fee earners	127.3	102.0	101.0	100.0	100
: Other staff	157.9	139.8	139.8	138.0	100
Office rent and rates	110.3	107.4	104.4	102.9	100
Heat and light	142.9	121.4	121.4	107.1	100
Office repairs and maintenance	108.0	112.0	112.0	100.0	100
Library, stationery and postages	119.4	112.5	111.1	104.2	100
Insurances	112.8	107.7	107.7	100.0	100
Repair of computer and office equipment	118.8	110.9	109.4	106.3	100
Travelling expenses	131.4	122.9	122.9	108.6	100
Telephone and related expenses	134.5	124.1	124.1	110.3	100
Bank interest and charges	147.4	131.6	126.3	105.3	100
Bad debts w/o	625.0	175.0	125.0	100.0	100
Miscellaneous expenses	117.7	114.5	114.5	104.8	100
	130.3	115.1	114.2	109.9	100
Net profit, before appropriations	313.7	333.3	322.6	120.6	100

Illustration 13.11, where the financial results of Frederickson and McCarthy have been converted for the purposes of statistical analysis, shows the extent of change within the different Income/Expenditure categories over the period 1993 to 1997[1].

Although a few solicitors will approach this form of statistical analysis with some trepidation (to say the least), once mastered, it is a useful aid for financial control and management purposes. The same is also true of *business ratios*.

Business ratios

Business ratios often portray, as a single figure, the relationship(s) that exist between other figures which may appear in a firm's profit and loss account and in its balance sheet. The proper use of ratios demands that they should be interpreted with full regard to all other available facts about the business. It would be dangerous practice to reach a conclusion over some facet of the business purely on the basis of a few ratios considered in isolation. Ratios should be considered as pieces of a jigsaw culminating in the full appreciation of the firm's financial affairs.

The value of ratios calculated in any one period is undoubtedly enhanced if other benchmark results are to hand. The firm's ratios from earlier financial periods

---

1   It is a relatively straightforward task to convert financial information into this format. For example, to find the percentage change in 'Staff costs : Other staff' which has occurred in 1995 relative to 1993, the following calculation is used : $\left\{ \dfrac{309-221}{221} \right\} \times \dfrac{100}{1} + 100 = 139.8\%$

and/or the results of other firms[1], for example, will help management put the present period's ratios into perspective.

To assist in the explanation of ratios and how they are calculated, the balance sheet detailed in **Illustration 13.12** has been prepared in respect of the hypothetical legal firm of Frederickson and McCarthy.

ILLUSTRATION 13.12

Frederickson and McCarthy (Solicitors)
Balance sheet as at 31 December 1997

	1997 £'000	1996 £'000
Fixed Assets		
Improvements to leasehold property	50	—
Motor vehicles	110	100
Office furniture and fittings	80	114
Computer equipment	45	35
	285	249
Current Assets		
Work in progress	465	465
Client debtors	324	284
Cash in hand and at bank	27	51
	816	800
Less: Current Liabilities		
Creditors	112	100
Bank overdraft	429	353
	541	453
Net Current Assets	275	347
	560	596
Represented by:		
Partners' capital	560	596

Further assumptions :

(i)   Frederickson and McCarthy is a 5-partner firm.
(ii) Notional salaries payable to each partner per annum are:

	£
A Frederickson	40,000
K Frederickson	40,000
E McCarthy	40,000
B Little	30,000
S McGuire	30,000
	180,000

(iii) Ignore clients' funds.
(iv) There are 10 other fee earners in the practice and a further 20 clerical staff.
(v)   All of the above assumptions apply to both 1997 and 1996.

A selection of the more commonly used business ratios within a legal context can be summarised as follows:-

---

1   The Law Society of Scotland conducts a financial survey of its members firms from time to time. By participating in this inter-firm survey, members get access to the results in return. The results can be considered as the 'industry averages'.

Return On Capital Employed (ROCE). This ratio reflects the level of profitability enjoyed by the business and also the amount of return the proprietors receive on their investment in the business. It can be calculated in basically two different ways.

(a) *Partners' notional salaries are excluded from the computation*

$$\text{ROCE} = \frac{\text{Net profit, before deduction of tax and partners' drawings}}{\text{Capital employed}} \times \frac{100}{1}$$

Applying this ratio to the 1997 results of Frederickson and McCarthy produces the following result:

$$\text{ROCE} = \frac{£320,000}{£560,000} \times \frac{100}{1}$$
$$= 57.1\%$$

(b) *Partners' notional salaries are included in the computation, by deducting their total value before recognising the net profit figure of the business*

$$\text{ROCE} = \frac{\text{Net profit, after deduction of partner's notional salaries}}{\text{Capital employed}} \times \frac{100}{1}$$

$$\text{ROCE} = \frac{£320,000 - £180,000}{£560,000} \times \frac{100}{1}$$
$$= 25\% \text{ per annum}$$

Either of the two different approaches may be adopted. However, it is probably preferable to use method '(a)' if the relative profitabilities of different legal firms is under consideration in order that a truer comparison can be achieved. In contrast, where a firm is comparing its current performance with that achieved in a previous financial period, it may be argued that method '(b)' is more appropriate. This will reflect the fact that the partners are fully employed in the business of the firm and that by using the net profit figure after deduction of their notional salaries, this should give a fairer reflection of the level of reward attracted by their capital invested in the business.

Frederickson and McCarthy's results look healthy and in all probability, the results show levels of return considerably above what the partners could expect to earn on their money if invested in the Stock Exchange or building society, for example.

If the ROCE figure had appeared low relative to other forms of investment carrying a similar level of risk or relative to the firm's own performance in previous years, the partners would have to consider taking steps to (i) increase the net profit, or (ii) decrease the level of capital employed in the firm (for example, by reducing debtors and/or WIP in order that the firm is in a position to release some of the partners' capital) or (iii) both of the above[1].

Net Profit Percentage. Another ratio used to assess the level of profitability is the *Net Profit Percentage*. In so far as a legal firm is concerned, again the option exists as to whether the firm determines its net profit figure before or after deduction of

---

1 When calculating ROCE, the figure used in respect of capital employed should be the average capital employed during the year. It is normal, however, to use the capital employed at the end of the period, unless there has been some major change.

partners' notional salaries or drawings as was also the case in the ROCE calculation above. For the present purpose it will be assumed that partners' notional salaries have been deducted. So.

$$\text{Net Profit Percentage} = \frac{\text{Net profit}}{\text{Turnover}} \times \frac{100}{1}$$

$$= \frac{£140,000}{£1,684,000} \times \frac{100}{1}$$

$$= 8.3\%$$

The net profit percentage is also a measurement of a firm's vulnerability to a decline in turnover and/or in increase in expenditure.

Again, as with the ROCE figure and indeed for virtually all business ratios, the firm's management would have to look at the other available benchmark information before arriving at a conclusion as to the merits of this year's net profit percentage.

If the partners of a legal firm are concerned at the level of its profitability, there are additional ratios and measures relating to *average fees rendered* and *expenses as a percentage of turnover* which can be used to gain a higher level of insight into the business.

Average fees per partner. The *average fees per partner* is found quite simply by dividing the fees rendered figure by the number of partners engaged in the business. In the case of Frederickson and McCarthy, this works out at:

$$\frac{£1,350,000}{5} = £270,000$$

Average fees per fee earner. Found;

$$= \frac{\text{Fees rendered}}{\text{No of fee earners (including partners)}}$$

$$= \frac{£1,350,000}{15} = £90,000$$

Expenses as a percentage of turnover. It is probably a fairer assessment to exclude partners' notional salaries from this particular calculation. Assuming this to be the case, Frederickson and McCarthy's figure in respect of *expenses as a percentage of turnover* is calculated thus:

$$= \frac{\text{Total expenses (excluding partners' notional salaries)}}{\text{Turnover}} \times \frac{100}{1}$$

$$= \frac{£1,364,000}{£1,684,000} \times \frac{100}{1}$$

$$= 81\%$$

Basically this means that 81% of the firm's turnover is used to meet business expenses. The remaining 19% is used to meet the partners' notional salaries and to recognise a bottom-line net profit figure.

If further detail is required to analyse expenses, the figures in respect of individual expense categories can of course be computed.

For example, if management wished to find *Office rent and rates as a percentage of turnover*:

$$= \frac{£75,000}{£1,684,000} \times \frac{100}{1} = 4.45\%$$

Likewise, *Staff costs as a percentage of turnover* is found;

$$= \frac{\text{Staff costs}}{\text{Turnover}} \times \frac{100}{1}$$

$$= \frac{(£215,000 + £261,000 + £349,000)}{£1,684,000} \times \frac{100}{1}$$

$$= \underline{\underline{49\%}}$$

By analysing the above type of results over a period of, say, 4-5 years, this should help assist the firm's management to assess its profitability and to identify any necessary steps which will have to be taken either to correct undesirable trends or to encourage favourable ones.

Turnover per employee, and, net profit per employee. Another couple of useful ratios are *Turnover per employee* and *Net profit per employee*. The trend they exhibit over time will give an indication of changes in productivity. Frederickson and McCarthy's 1997 ratios will be:

(i)   Turnover per employee $= \dfrac{\text{Turnover}}{\text{No. of employees}}$

$$= \frac{£1,684,000}{30}$$

$$= \underline{\underline{£56,133}}$$

A variation on this ratio could be to focus purely on fees rendered, rather than on turnover.

(ii)   Net profit per employee $= \dfrac{\text{Net profit (before deduction of partners' notional salaries)}}{\text{No. of employees}}$

$$= \frac{£320,000}{30}$$

$$= \underline{\underline{£10,667}}$$

The latter ratio besides giving a measure of productivity, also provides another indication of profitability.

Partnership solvency test/capital adequacy test. The *Partnership solvency test* provides an assessment of the firm's financial position. It is calculated as follows:

$$\text{Partnership solvency test} = \frac{\text{Partners' Capital}}{\text{Total Assets}} \times \frac{100}{1}$$

Applying this test to Frederickson and McCarthy's 1997 balance sheet results gives:

$$\text{Partnership solvency test} = \frac{£560,000}{£1,101,000} \times \frac{100}{1}$$

$$= \underline{50.86\%}$$

If this calculation had revealed a negative score, then the practice will be in a serious position given that it will be insolvent. Where a firm's liabilities are greater than its assets, its management should seek immediate assistance since the business will be on the verge of failure.

Assuming all to be well, with a firm's solvency test ratio at least being positive, this score can also be used as a measure of the adequacy of the partners' capital. It would normally be expected that a firm should have a ratio of greater than 20%. Frederickson and McCarthy appear therefore to be in a healthy state in this respect. The Law Society of Scotland has produced Guidance Notes on this subject which have been reproduced in appendix 3. Given the importance of the matter, a thorough understanding of the Guidance Notes is highly desirable.

Current ratio. It was mentioned earlier that careful financial management of a practice will entail keeping the firm's liquidity position under almost constant review. The *current ratio* provides a means by which this can be done. This technique assesses the firm's ability to meet its short-term commitments by comparing its current assets to its current liabilities. The liquidity position[1] of Frederickson and McCarthy is calculated as follows:

$$\text{Current ratio} = \frac{\text{Current assets}}{\text{Current liabilities}}$$

$$= \frac{£816,000}{£541,000}$$

$$= \underline{1.51}$$

By giving a result of greater than 1, this ratio suggests that the firm's liquidity position is reasonably healthy. However, it could be argued that WIP is not readily turned into cash. In Frederickson and McCarthy's case, if this argument is accepted and WIP omitted from the calculation, its position will appear much more vulnerable. Indeed it could be in trouble if its short-term creditors (including the bank) sought immediate repayment of their outstanding debts. That is:

---

1 'Solvency', or, 'short-term viability' are alternative terms for liquidity.

$$\frac{\text{Cash} + \text{Debtors}}{\text{Current liabilities}}$$

$$= \frac{£351,000}{£541,000}$$

$$= \underline{\underline{0.65}}$$

The ratio immediately above is sometimes known as the *Acid Test* Ratio.

The firm's management will presumably be best placed to judge the likelihood of such short-term difficulties arising given their knowledge of the business. Whether or not a problem is identified by the partners in this respect, the firm might still be advised to, for example, avoid further investments in fixed assets, and/or, to reduce its WIP level, and/or, to tighten its credit control procedures to ensure clients pay more promptly.

Debtor days. Another measurement which can help in the assessment of liquidity is to calculate the average time taken for clients to pay invoices rendered by the firm. This can be termed the calculation of *debtor days* and can be found as follows:

$$\text{Debtor days} = \frac{\text{Outstanding fees at year end}}{\text{Total fees rendered during the year}} \times \text{Number of days in the year}$$

$$= \frac{£324,000}{£1,350,000} \times 365 \text{ days}$$

$$= \underline{\underline{87.6 \text{ days}}}$$

In other words, Frederickson and McCarthy's clients take on average almost three months to settle their invoices. In normal practice, it is expected that clients meet their debts to the firm with 1-2 months, so Frederickson and McCarthy's clients seem to be taking excessive periods of credit or there was a high level of invoicing activity by the firm at its financial year end. The WIP and credit control process should be reviewed as appropriate.

Interest cover. The last few measurements mentioned above are helpful in assessing the liquidity or short-term viability of a legal practice. Its longer-term viability should also be considered from time to time. A firm's *interest cover* provides such an indication of its financial strength:

$$\text{Interest cover} = \frac{\text{Profit (after deduction of partners' notional salaries)}}{\text{Interest and related charges for the period}}$$

$$= \frac{£140,000}{£28,000}$$

$$= \underline{\underline{5 \text{ times}}}$$

This particular measurement provides an indication of a firm's capabilities of servicing its debts.

A reasonable target for the interest cover figure for legal firms is between 4-6 times. Consequently, the longer-term viability of this particular firm does appear healthy.

It is possible to tabulate all of the above ratios in a formal statement. A basic layout for the results of Frederickson and McCarthy is shown in **Illustration 13.13**.

ILLUSTRATION 13.13

Frederickson and McCarthy (Solicitors)
Management Report : Summary of Key Business Ratios in respect of the 5 year period,
1993 to 1997 inclusive

	Year				
	1997	1996	1995	1994	1993
RATIO					
(i) ROCE—(a) before deduction of partners' notional salaries	57.1%	57%	etc	etc	etc
—(b) after deduction of partners' notional salaries	25%	26.8%	etc	etc	
(ii) Net profit %—(a) before deduction of partners' notional salaries	19%	22%	etc		
—(b) after deduction of partners' notional salaries	8.3%	10.4%			
(iii) Average fees per partner	£270,000	£250,000			
(iv) Average fees per fee earner (incl. partners)	£90,000	£83,333			
(v) Total expenses as a % of turnover	81%	78%			
(vi) Turnover per employee	£56,133	£51,500			
(vii) Net profit per employee	£10,667	£11,333			
(viii) Partnership solvency/capital adequacy test	50.9%	56.8%			
(ix) Current ratio	1.51	1.77			
(x) Acid test ratio	0.65	0.74			
(xi) Debtor days	87.6 days	82.9 days			
(xii) Interest cover	5 times	6.4 times			

By looking back at the results and background information relating to any of the firm's earlier years, it would be possible to calculate all of the ratios and other measurements mentioned above. Once complete the table could be used to help highlight any trends which have been developing with respect to the matters considered in the table. This in turn may trigger further investigative work by the partners before settling on the appropriate courses of action.

To conclude this section, it is worth again stressing that care is needed when using statistical analysis and business ratios to assess a legal business. Unfortunately, although they create the illusion of precision, they are basically fairly crude methods of evaluating a firm's financial health and progress. Even assuming that the figures used in the computations are accurate and have been produced in a consistent manner throughout the period under examination, the results still need to be considered in their true perspective. This demands an in-depth knowledge of the business under review.

The following notes of caution therefore should be borne in mind when applying statistical analysis and ratios:

(1) Ratios and statistical financial analysis do not tell the whole story about a business. Other information and background knowledge is required. For example, peculiarities of practice may mean that a ratio relevant to one small or general practice may be inappropriate for a large or specialised practice. Size, nature and practice location is important information to be borne in mind when conducting this form of analysis.

(2) In comparing such results over time (or between separate businesses) it is vital to ensure that the various figures and calculations employed are consistent with each other. Failure to so ensure will mean that like is not being compared with like.

(3) Care should be taken to avoid information overload. Using too many ratios, for example, may make a situation appear confused and much of the benefit possible from these techniques will be lost. It is much better to select and use a few, fully understood key ratios which are considered to be important for the purpose in hand.

(4) Watch out for the effects of inflation over a period of time if it is running at a significant level.

(5) Ratios are only as good as the raw data used in their calculations. The figure used must, amongst other things, be realistic. If not (for example if the balance sheet figures used are unduly optimistic) they may need adjustment before they can be used. If they are adjusted, bear in mind the comment above on consistency.

CONCLUSION

Finally, although this chapter has focused on fairly specific aspects of a legal business and on how and why it is important that they are addressed by the partners of a legal firm if they are to meet their duties with respect to the proper financial management and control of their practice, it is important that wider issues are not overlooked nor ignored.

From time to time, legal practice managers must detach themselves from the routine matters of business to address the strategic issues affecting the firm. For example, the financial framework of the firm must always be sound. If not, then much of the discussion on specific financial controls almost becomes irrelevant since the firm will probably be destined for failure. Virtually from day one in the life of a legal firm, partners must consider matters such as how the business is to be financed and, in particular, what types of finance should be used? At what level should the mix of borrowings to partners' capital be set? With respect to borrowings, how much of the firm's borrowings should be short-term (eg a bank overdraft) and how much should be long-term (eg a mortgage)[1]? What major future events have to be considered now in order that the firm is well placed to meet its commitments as they fall due? And so on.

The proper financing of a practice is vital and certainly worthy of expert professional advice as and when necessary.

---

1 In general, a business should always attempt to match long-term uses of finance (eg purchase of property) to long-term types of finance (eg a mortgage and/or partners' capital). Similarly, short-term uses should be matched with short-term types of finance.

QUESTIONS[1]

1. The following information has been extracted from the records of McKenzie Kelvin and Co (Solicitors).

McKenzie Kelvin and Company, Solicitors
Income and expenditure statement for the year ending 30 April 1998

	Year to 30.4.98 £'000	Budgeted £'000
Income		
Fees rendered	1,500	1,350
Commission	250	225
Other income	125	100
	1,875	1,675
Less: Expenses		
Staff wages and salaries	925	775
Office rent and rates	80	80
Heating and lighting	35	32
Office maintenance	30	30
Library, stationery and postages	75	68
Telephone and fax	50	45
Insurances	52	51
Professional subscriptions	10	10
Travelling expenses	55	50
Bank interest and charges	37	25
Miscellaneous expenses	63	58
Motor vehicle running costs	21	19
Bad debts w/o	27	17
Office equipment maintenance & repairs	35	36
General expenses	61	50
Depreciation charges: Motor vehicles	20	20
: Office equipment	15	15
: Office fixtures and fittings	10	10
	1,601	1,391
Net profit, before appropriations	274	284

The firm's management has requested that you prepare a statement which highlights the variances which have arisen over the course of the year between the actual results and the original budget figures. Summary comments on the more significant contents of this statement are also required for management use.

Note: The above statement should be drafted in a style similar to that appearing in **Illustration 13.6**.

2. You are the practice manager for the legal firm of Frederickson and McCarthy, Solicitors. Using the information given in **Illustration 13.10**, draft a variance

---

1 For suggested solutions see p 335.

analysis statement which focuses on the changes occurring between the financial years 1993 and 1994 and comment briefly on your findings.

Note: The general style of your statement should be similar to that used above in respect of question 1, although the column expressing the variances in £'000 can be omitted with only the *% change* column being shown.

3.   Refer to **Illustration 13.8**, McGrowther James & Co (Solicitors). After a review of their initial forecast cash flow statement for 1998, the partners have decided that certain steps are necessary to improve the firm's cash flow position. In particular, it has been noted that quarterly property costs and VAT payments fall in the same month. The adverse effects of this are further compounded in January and July when the tax liability in respect of the preceding year falls due for payment in two equal instalments.

In light of the above, the following proposals have been made:

   (i)   The firm should apply to Customs and Excise to alter its VAT period (and hence dates of VAT repayment) as follows:

VAT period	*VAT due for payment:*
1 December–28 February	March
1 March–31 May	June
1 June–31 August	September
1 September–30 November	December

In so doing, the firm's VAT repayments in 1998 will be:

January	=	£14,000, being the final payment due under the old VAT periods
March	=	£6,475, being the net VAT due for January and February 1998
June	=	£15,175, being in keeping with the new VAT period
September	=	£13,230, being in keeping with the new VAT period
December	=	£15,145, being in keeping with the new VAT period

   (ii)   The firm should change the dates on which it pays its quarterly property costs to be one month later than at present. This has been discussed and agreed with the landlord. Property costs in respect of 1998 have been re-scheduled as follows:

Amount (£)	*Payment Due*	*Period*
£1,167	January	January
£2,333	February	February and March
£3,500	May	May, June and July
£3,667	August	August, September and October [The rent increases by £167 per month on 1 October].
£4,000	November	November, December and January (1999)

(iii) Partners' drawings are to be reduced to £6,000 per month from January until June inclusive, reverting back to £8,000 in July until the end of the year. The partners have, reluctantly, agreed to this suggestion.

Required

Draft a revised forecast cash flow statement for McGrowther James & Co for the period to 31 December 1998.

4. MacDonald Evans & Co, Solicitors have been in business for several years. You have been asked by them to prepare a forecast cash flow statement for the 12 month period, 1 January to 31 December 1998. The following information has been provided by them to assist you in this task:

    (i) The partners have estimated that they will receive fees and commissions as follows:

FEES:	January	£10,000
	February	£13,000
	March/April/May/September/ October	£16,000 in each month
	June/July	£12,000 in each month
	August/November	£8,000 in each month
	December	£6,000
COMMISSIONS:	May/June/July	£450 in each month
	All other months of the year	£250

    (ii) The firm is leasing a car for £500 per month. Vehicle running costs and other travel expenses amount to a further £250 per month.

    (iii) The staff wages bill for each month is £1,500. A bonus of a further £1,000 is payable in May and again in December.

    (iv) Office rent and rates are paid quarterly in advance on 1 January, 1 April, 1 July and 1 October. The quarterly cost is £2,550.

    (v) General office expenses have been estimated at £1,200 per month.

    (vi) The partners have received notice that their income tax payable for the previous year will be £30,000. This bill will be paid in two equal instalments—1 January and 1 July 1998.

    (vii) The partners have intimated that they wish total drawings of £4,000 per month. This figure was calculated:

	£
Estimated profit for 1998	90,000
less: Estimated tax liability thereon	(25,000)
	65,000
less: Creation of a reserve - renewal of computer equipment due in 1999	(17,000)
Available funds	48,000
Monthly drawings, £48,000/12 =	£4,000

    (viii) Ignore VAT and disbursements on behalf of clients.
    (ix) Assume overdraft at 1 January is £25,000.

Required

The partners have also asked you to state the maximum overdraft they will need in 1998 and when this will be required.

5. James Smith and Brian Bryce have decided to set up in partnership as solicitors. Through various family connections, the new firm will immediately have an enviable client base. The following information has been obtained from the partners:

(i)   The practice is to be established on 1 January 1997.

(ii)   The partners have agreed to pay £5,000 each as their capital contributions to the business. This money will be used to help meet the initial start-up costs of the firm.

(iii) They have decided to rent office property at a cost of £3,000 + VAT per month, payable quarterly in advance on the following dates:

    1 January, 1 April, 1 July, 1 October.

   A one-off deposit of £1,000 + VAT has also to be paid on 1 January. Recoverable VAT payable at 17.5% on the quarterly rental payments and deposit amounts to £525 and £175 respectively.

(iv)   A secretary will begin work for the firm on 1 January. The total costs of employing this person for the first year will be £12,000, payable in 12 equal monthly instalments. From 1 April, a qualified assistant will join the practice. The new assistant will cost a total of £18,000 per annum, again such costs will be spread equally over the year and payable monthly.

(v)   The partners have forecast fee income for the year, and the related VAT thereon, as below. Further, the firm is expecting to receive other income (which is VAT exempt) again as shown below:

	Jan £	Feb £	March £	April £	May £	June £
Fee income received	—	—	5,000	7,000	10,000	15,000
VAT recovered	—	—	875	1,225	1,750	2,625
Other income	—	—	100	100	250	250

	July £	Aug £	Sept £	Oct £	Nov £	Dec £
Fee income received	15,000	15,000	20,000	25,000	25,000	20,000
VAT recovered	2,625	2,625	3,500	4,375	4,375	3,500
Other income	250	350	350	350	350	350

(vi)   The firm's VAT quarters will run as follows:

VAT Quarter	VAT Payment/Reimbursement due
Dec/Jan/Feb	1 March
March/April/May	1 June
June/July/Aug	1 September
Sept/Oct/Nov	1 December
Dec/Jan/Feb	1 March

(vii) The partners' tax on partnership profits will be calculated on the preceding year basis and payable in two equal instalments on 1 January and 1 July following the year of assessment.

(viii) Although Bryce expects to spend virtually all of his time in the office, Smith will have to travel frequently on office business. It has been agreed that a car be bought for Smith at a total cost of £14,100 (inclusive of non-recoverable VAT, owing to the fact that the car will be subject to private use) on 1 January.

(ix)   The partners estimate other expenses as follows:

Vehicle running and other travel costs	— £250 per month from January to June inclusive, then £350 per month thereafter, excluding VAT
Office expenses	— £750 per month from January to June inclusive, then £950 per month thereafter, excluding VAT
Office fixtures and fittings	— One-off costs of £4,000 + recoverable VAT of £700, payable in January
Office equipment	— One-off costs of £10,000 + recoverable VAT of £1,750, payable in January
Insurances and professional subscriptions	— One-off annual payment of £2,250 due on 1 January each year (Assume such payments are VAT exempt)

(x)   The partners are assuming that they will be able to recover VAT on the majority of the normal running costs of the firm. It is expected that the recoverable VAT paid in relation to 'Vehicle running and other travel costs' and 'Office expenses' will amount to £150 in total for each of the six months to 30 June 1997 and £200 each month thereafter until the end of the year.

(xi)   The partners have agreed to restrict their drawings in the first year to:

Jan/Feb/March	—	NIL
Apr/May/June	—	£1,000 per month each
July/Aug/Sept	—	£2,000 per month each
Oct/Nov/Dec	—	£3,000 per month each

(xii)   The firm has arranged an overdraft facility of £30,000 at its bank for the first year of business.

(xiii)   Ignore disbursements.

Required

(a) Draft a statement which shows the firm's predicted VAT flows for each of the twelve months. The statement should highlight (i) the monthly VAT recovered on fees and (ii) any recoverable VAT which has been paid on the various forms of expenditure. It should also show the amount of VAT the firm will expect to recover from or pay to Customs and Excise at the end of each of its VAT quarters.

(b) Draft a forecast cash flow statement for the firm of Smith and Bryce in respect of the twelve month period ending 31 December 1997. Also, state the maximum overdraft which the firm will require in this period and whether or not the present overdraft facility of £30,000 is sufficient.

6.   Using the information given in **Illustration 13.5** prepare a statement for Jefferson MacInroy Co which shows details of the firm's expenses converted to a common statistical base, with 1988 taken as the base year. Comment on the statement's more significant disclosures.

Note: The layout used in **Illustration 13.11**, Frederickson and McCarthy (Solicitors), suitably amended, may be adopted here.

7. Refer to **Illustrations 13.10** and **13.12** which provide information on the firm of Frederickson and McCarthy. With respect to the firm's balance sheets 1995 to 1997 inclusive, the following information is also available:

Frederickson and McCarthy (Solicitors)
Balance Sheet as at 31 December 1993, 1994 and 1995

	1995 £'000	1994 £'000	1993 £'000
Fixed Assets			
Improvements to leasehold property	—	—	15
Motor vehicles	120	140	100
Office furniture and fittings	120	125	130
Computer equipment	50	65	45
	290	330	290
Current Assets			
Work in progress	465	465	465
Client debtors	250	250	150
Cash in hand and at bank	40	10	5
	755	725	620
Less: Current Liabilities			
Creditors	100	95	95
Bank overdraft	350	320	300
	450	415	395
Net Current Assets	305	310	225
	595	640	515
Represented by:			
Partners' capital	595	640	515

In addition, note that the 'further assumptions' given at the end of **Illustration 13.12** can be taken as applying to the years 1993, 1994 and 1995 except for the following:

(i) **In 1994 and 1993**, partners notional salaries totalled £100,000 per annum.

(ii) **In 1993**, only 15 clerical staff were employed. A further 5 clerical staff were appointed in January **1994.**

Required

With reference to all of the details referred to above, fully complete the summary report shown in abridged form in **Illustration 13.13**, namely the 'Management Report : Summary of Key Business Ratios in respect of the five-year period, 1993 to 1997 inclusive'. Comment on the contents. **Illustration 13.11** may also be used as an aid to interpret the results of Frederickson and McCarthy.

Suggested solutions
Chapter Two: Recording financial information

1. (a) A   (g) A
    (b) A   (h) A
    (c) A
    (d) L
    (e) A
    (f) L

2. (a) A   (g) A   (m) I
    (b) A   (h) A   (n) E
    (c) E   (i) C   (o) L
    (d) L   (j) E   (p) A
    (e) I   (k) E   (q) E
    (f) L   (l) A

3. (a) £ 4,500   (d) £12,000
    (b) £12,000   (e) £15,000
    (c) £ 2,000   (f) £54,400

4. (a) A   (f) L
    (b) L   (g) A
    (c) A   (h) A
    (d) L   (i) L
    (e) A   (j) A

5. Assets   = £3,500 + 10,000 + 2,500 + 250 = £16,250

    Less: Liabilities = £600 + 7,500 + 2,000 + 750   = (£10,850)

    Capital   <u>£5,400</u>

6. (i) + (ii) [Note '+' = increase '–' = decrease]

    (a) Car (A,+);   Cash in Hand (A,–)   (f) Office equipment (A,+);   Creditors (L,+)

    (b) Electricity (E,+); Cash at Bank, (A,–)   (g) Loan-Bloggs (L,–);   Cash in Hand (A,–)

    (c) Debtor (A,–)   Cash in Hand (A,+)   (h) Fees Rendered (I,+);   G & Co(A,+)

    (d) Buildings (A,+); Loan (L,+)   (i) G & Co (A,–);   Cash at Bank (A,+)

    (e) Stock (A,+);   Creditors (L,+)   (j) Cash in Hand (A,–); Cash at Bank (A,+)

7.

	Account to be debited	Account to be credited
(a)	Cash in Hand	Capital
(b)	Cash at Bank	F & Co (Debtors)
(c)	Motor Cars	Cash at Bank
(d)	Electricity	Cash in Hand
(e)	ABC Ltd (Debtors)	Fees rendered
(f)	Cash at Bank	ABC Ltd (Debtors)
(g)	Cash at Bank	Bank loan
(h)	DC Ltd (Creditors)	Cash at Bank
(i)	Petrol	Cash in Hand
(j)	Building	Bank loan

8.

MR A – CAPITAL

		£	JULY		£
			1	Bank	3,000
			2	Motor vehicle	3,500

CASH AT BANK

JULY		£	JULY		£
1	Capital	3,000	3	Cash	100
20	BC Ltd	1,000	4	Office equip	570
			9	Telephone	340
			10	Insurance	200
			28	Car running	190
			30	Compo Ltd	250

MOTOR CAR

JULY		£
2	Capital	3,500

PETTY CASH

JULY		£	JULY		£
3	Bank	100	3	Petrol	20
			21	Sundries	12

PETROL

JULY		£
3	Cash	20

BC LTD

JULY		£	JULY		£
8	Fees	1,000	20	Bank	1,000

OFFICE EQUIPMENT

JULY		£
4	Bank	570

FEES RAISED

			JULY		£
			8	BC Ltd	1,000
			16	CM Ltd	500

TELEPHONE

JULY		£
9	Bank	340

INSURANCE

JULY		£
10	Bank	200

COMPUTER

JULY		£
15	Compo Ltd	1,500

COMPO LTD

JULY		£	JULY		£
30	Bank	250	15	Computer	1,500

CM LTD

JULY		£
16	Fees raised	500

SUNDRIES

JULY		£
21	Cash	12

CAR RUNNING EXPENSES

JULY		£
28	Bank	190

9.(i)

CAPITAL

MAY	£	MAY	£
31 Balance c/f	27,000	1 Bank	27,000
		JUNE	
		1 Balance b/f	27,000

CASH AT BANK

MAY	£	MAY	£
1 Capital	27,000	2 Office premises	15,000
10 Loan	5,000	7 Furniture	1,500
		15 Car	7,500
		20 Cash in Hand	150
		27 Office equipment	450
		31 Balance c/f	7,400
	32,000		32,000
JUNE			
1 Balance b/f	7,400		

OFFICE PREMISES

MAY	£	MAY	£
2 Bank	15,000	31 Balance c/f	15,000
JUNE			
1 Balance b/f	15,000		

OFFICE FURNITURE

MAY	£	MAY	£
7 Bank	1,500		
30 A Supplier	150	31 Balance c/f	1,650
	1,650		1,650
JUNE			
1 Balance b/f	1,650		

LOAN

MAY	£	MAY	£
31 Balance c/f	5,000	10 Bank	5,000
		JUNE	
		1 Balance b/f	5,000

OFFICE EQUIPMENT

MAY	£	MAY	£
27 Bank	450	31 Balance c/f	450
JUNE			
1 Balance b/f	450		

CASH IN HAND

MAY	£	MAY	£
20 Bank	150	31 Balance c/f	150
JUNE			
1 Balance b/f	150		

CAR

MAY	£	MAY	£
15 Bank	7,500	31 Balance c/f	7,500
JUNE			
1 Balance b/f	7,500		

A SUPPLIER

MAY	£	MAY	£
31 Balance c/f	150	30 Office furniture	150
		JUNE	
		1 Balance b/f	150

(ii)

Charlie D
Trial Balance as at 31 May 19-7

	Dr £	Cr £
Capital		27,000
Cash at Bank	7,400	
Office premises	15,000	
Office furniture	1,650	
Office equipment	450	
Car	7,500	
Loan		5,000
Cash in Hand	150	
A Supplier (Creditors)		150
	32,150	32,150

10.

CAPITAL (C)

			£
	1	Bank	3,000
	4	Motor Vehicles	4,500

OFFICE FURNITURE & EQUIPMENT (A)

		£
3	Bank	1,200

MOTOR VEHICLE (A)

		£
4	Capital	4,500

RENT (E)

		£
2	Bank	500

INSURANCE (E)

		£
5	Noinsure Ltd	350

NOINSURE LTD (L)

		£			£
14	Bank	35	5	Insurance	350

CASH AT BANK (A)

		£			£
1	Capital	3,000	2	Rent	500
8	Fees rendered	330	3	Office furniture & equipment	1,200
			9	Petty cash	120
			14	Noinsure Ltd	35

STATIONERY (E)

		£
6	Blueprint	85

BLUEPRINT (L)

		£
6	Stationery	85

FEES RENDERED (I)

		£
7	A Dollar	280
8	Bank	330

A DOLLAR (A)

		£
7	Fees	280

PETTY CASH (A)

		£			£
9	Bank	120	10	Petrol	25
			11	Office sundries	10
			12	Office sundries	7
			13	Cleaning	50
			15	Postage	10

OFFICE SUNDRIES (E)

		£
11	Petty cash	10
12	Petty cash	7

CLEANING (E)

		£
13	Petty cash	50

POSTAGE (E)

		£
15	Petty cash	10

PETROL (E)

		£
10	Petty cash	25

Suggested solutions
Chapter Three – Simple accounting statements

1

P Marwick (Trader)
Trading and Profit and Loss Account for the year ended 31 May 1999

	£	£
Sales		16,000
Less: Cost of Goods Sold		
Purchases		(7,000)
Gross Profit		9,000
Less: Expenses		
General expenses	1,400	
Stall site rental	1,200	
Insurances	450	
		(3,050)
Net Profit		5,950

P Marwick
Balance Sheet as at 31 May 1999

	£	£
Fixed Assets		
Stall, at cost		1,500
Current Assets		
Trade debtors	200	
Bank	7,000	
Cash	550	
	7,750	
Less: Current Liabilities		
Trade creditors	(1,300)	
Net Current Assets		6,450
		7,950
Represented by:		
Capital, 1.6.99		6,500
Add: Net profit	5,950	
Less: Drawings	(4,500)	
		1,450
		7,950

2.

N Goldberger (Jeweller)
Trading and Profit and Loss Account for the year ended 31 December 1999

	£	£
Sales		75,000
Less: Cost of Goods Sold		
Opening stock, 1.1.99	5,000	
Add: purchases	25,000	
	30,000	
Less: closing stock, 31.12.99	(5,000)	
		(25,000)
Gross profit		50,000
Less: Expenses		
Rent and rates	7,500	
Electricity costs	1,250	
Staff wages	9,000	
Insurances	2,500	
Motor vehicle expenses	1,500	
Stationery	500	
Telephone	500	
		(22,750)
		27,250

N Goldberger (Jeweller)
Balance Sheet as at 31 December 1999

	£	£
Fixed Assets (at cost)		
Fixtures and fittings		10,000
Motor vehicle		10,000
Office equipment		2,000
		22,000
Current Assets		
Stock	5,000	
Cash at bank	19,750	
	24,750	
Less: Current Liabilities		
Creditors	(4,000)	
Net Current Assets		20,750
		42,750
Represented by:		
Capital, 1.1.99		40,500
Add: Net profit for year	27,250	
Less: Drawings	(25,000)	
		2,250
		42,750

3.

Gilberts (Solicitors)
Profit and Loss Account for the period ended 30 September 1999

	£	£
Fees rendered		150,000
Less: Expenses		
Office wages	80,000	
Telephone	2,000	
Heating and lighting	3,000	
Insurances	1,500	
Subscriptions to professional journals	250	
Motor vehicle running costs	4,000	
Stationery	1,000	
Property maintenance	2,500	
Office equipment maintenance	250	
Travel expenses	750	
		(95,250)
Net profit		54,750

Gilberts (Solicitors)
Balance Sheet as at 30 September 1999

	£	£
Fixed Assets (at cost)		
Office property		125,000
Office furniture and fittings		10,000
Motor vehicles		30,000
Office equipment		15,000
		180,000
Current Assets		
Debtors	2,500	
Cash at bank	29,750	
	32,250	
Less: Current Liabilities		
Creditors	(1,000)	
Net Current Assets		31,250
		211,250
Represented by:		
Capital, 1.4.99		206,500
Add: Net profit for period	54,750	
Less: Drawings	(50,000)	
		4,750
		211,250

4.

Casper
Trading and Profit and Loss Account for the year ended 30 November 1999

	£	£
Sales		43,000
Less: Cost of goods sold		
Opening stock, 1.12.98	3,250	
Add: Purchases	18,250	
	21,500	
Less: Closing stock, 30.11.99	(4,250)	
		(17,250)
Gross profit		25,750
Less: Expenses		
Rates	2,350	
Gas	900	
Heating and lighting	1,250	
Wages	18,000	
Telephone	1,600	
Postages and stationery	750	
Motor vehicle running costs	1,900	
Loan interest paid	1,300	
		(28,050)
Net loss		(2,300)

Casper
Balance Sheet as at 30 November 1999

	£	£
Fixed Assets (at cost)		
Premises		32,500
Fixtures and fittings		15,000
Motor vehicle		7,500
		55,000
Current Assets		
Stock	4,250	
Debtors	4,500	
	8,750	
Less: Current Liabilities		
Loan : N E Breaker	12,000	
Creditors	10,000	
Bank overdraft	7,800	
	(29,800)	
Net Current Liabilities		(21,050)
		33,950

Represented by:

Capital, 1.12.98		41,750
Less: Net loss	2,300	
Drawings	5,500	
		(7,800)
		33,950

(a) Casper has made a net loss for the year to 30 November 1999 of £2,300.

(b) In an attempt to increase profitability, Casper should look at:

   (i)   increasing the selling price of the goods (but watch pricing relative to competitors);

   (ii) taking steps to drive a harder bargain with suppliers in order to reduce the cost of goods sold;

   (iii) reducing expenses.

(c) With respect to Casper's financial position as shown by the balance sheet as at 30 November 1999:

   (i)   There is a short term liquidity problem given the magnitude of the net current liabilities (£21,050).

   (ii) Casper is due to repay N E Breaker's loan within two months, as well as paying off the bank overdraft of £7,800 and £10,000 worth of creditors. How can this be done? Possible courses of action include:

      (1) Increasing the bank overdraft in the short-term to meet the other short-term debts. This will be difficult to achieve given the loss-making position of the business.

      (2) Casper may be able to take out a mortgage or other long-term loan secured on the premises and use the funds to settle some short-term debts. Again, the long-term profitability of the firm will have to be improved to meet mortgage/loan repayments as they fall due.

      (3) Casper should also consider selling a fixed asset to raise cash. For example, would Casper be better off selling the car to release much needed funds and then leasing another vehicle? Alternatively, Casper could sell the premises and then rent a property.

      (4) Casper could also try to obtain a longer period of credit from his suppliers whilst simultaneously reducing the length of credit offered to customers.

      (5) Ultimately, it may be that the business is now unprofitable and Casper should close the business before losing any more money.

5.

Nature of expenditure:

(a) Capital

(b) Revenue

(c) Revenue

(d) Revenue

(e) Capital

(f) Revenue

(g) Revenue

(h) Revenue

(i) Revenue

(j)   Revenue

(k)   Capital

6.

(a)   *Acquisition cost of microcomputer system:*

	£
Basic purchase price	5,000
Delivery	50
Computer installation and testing costs	250
Supply and installation of specialist wiring	150
Staff training	500
Computer software	750
	6,700

(b)   *Items charged to the period's Profit and Loss account*

	£
Computer insurance	100
Computer maintenance	200
Computer paper	25
Printer toner cartridges (2 @ £90 each)	180

Suggested solutions,
Chapter Four: Accounting adjustments—part one

1.

Straight-line method

$$\text{Annual depreciation charge} = \frac{\text{Cost} - \text{Estimated residual value}}{\text{Working life in years}}$$

$$= \frac{£2,350 - £350}{5}$$

$$= \underline{\underline{£400}}$$

The solicitor's Profit and Loss accounts would show a deprecation charge of £400 for each of Years One - Five inclusive.

2.

Fixed Asset: Office furniture

	Year 1	Year 2	Year 3	Year 4	Year 5
	£	£	£	£	£
Cost	2,350	2,350	2,350	2,350	2,350
Less: Accumulated depreciation	(400)	(800)	(1,200)	(1,600)	(2,000)
NBV	1,950	1,550	1,150	750	350

3.

Reducing balance method

		£
Year One:	Opening NBV (original cost)	16,000
		× 25%
	Depreciation charge for year	4,000
Year Two:	Opening NBV (16,000 – 4,000)	12,000
		× 25%
	Depreciation charge for year	3,000
Year Three:	Opening NBV (12,000 – 3,000)	9,000
		× 25%
	Depreciation charge for year	2,250

4.

Fixed Asset: Motor vehicle

	Year 1 £	Year 2 £	Year 3 £
Cost	16,000	16,000	16,000
Less: Accumulated depreciation	(4,000)	(7,000)	(9,250)
Net book value at end of year	12,000	9,000	6,750

5.

(i) Depreciation charge which will be written-off as an expense in Donaldsons' Profit and Loss account for the year to 31 December 1996:

			£
Office Property:	£100,000 × 2%	=	2,000
Office furniture and fittings:	£5,000 × 10%	=	500
Computer equipment:	£25,000 × 20%	=	5,000
Motor vehicles:	£30,000 × 25%	=	7,500
Total Depreciation Charge on Fixed Assets			15,000

(ii)

Donaldsons (Solicitors)
Balance Sheet (Extract) as at 31 December 1996

Fixed Assets	Cost £	Accumulated Depreciation £	Net Book Value £
Office property	100,000	2,000	98,000
Office furniture & fittings	5,000	500	4,500
Computer equipment	25,000	5,000	20,000
Motor vehicles	30,000	7,500	22,500
	160,000	15,000	145,000

6.

(i) Depreciation charge which will be written off as an expense in Donaldsons' Profit and Loss account for the year to 31 December 1997:

			£
Office Property:	£100,000 × 2%	=	2,000
Office furniture and fittings:	£5,000 × 10%	=	500
Computer equipment:	(£25,000 − £5,000) × 20%	=	4,000
Motor vehicles:	(£30,000 − £7,500) × 25%	=	5,625
Total Depreciation Charge on Fixed Assets			12,125

(ii)

Donaldsons (Solicitors)
Balance Sheet (Extract) as at 31 December 1997

Fixed Assets	Cost	Accumulated Depreciation	Net Book Value
	£	£	£
Office property	100,000	4,000	96,000
Office furniture & fittings	5,000	1,000	4,000
Computer equipment	25,000	9,000	16,000
Motor vehicles	30,000	13,125	16,875
	160,000	27,125	132,875

7.

(a) The depreciation charge on McNamarras' car which would be charged to the Profit and Loss account for the year to 31 December 1995 can be calculated thus:

$$£18,000 \times 20\% = £3,600$$

Also,

McNamarras (Solicitors)
Balance Sheet (Extract) as at 31 December 1995

Fixed Assets	Cost	Accumulated Depreciation	Net Book Value
	£	£	£
Motor vehicle	18,000	3,600	14,400

(b) *Gain/loss on disposal of motor vehicle*

The gain or loss realised on the sale of the vehicle is found by comparing the *cost* of the vehicle with the *sum* of its *net book value* at the date of sale plus the *sale proceeds*.

The cost of the car is known at £18,000, as is the sale price (that is, either £13,000 or £12,000). However, the net book value of the asset at the date of sale must first be found before it is possible to determine whether there has been a gain or loss on disposal.

Net book value of the car at 1.6.96	=	Cost of the car	—	Accumulated depreciation at 1.6.96
	=	£18,000	—	[£3,600 + (£3,600 x 5/12)]
	=	£18,000	—	[£3,600 + £1,500]
	=	£18,000	—	£5,100
	=	£12,900		

Therefore, assuming a selling price of:

(i) £13,000, McNamarras made a gain on disposal of £100. This gain on the sale of the motor vehicle would be detailed as such in the Profit and Loss account for the period in which it occurred, that is, the year to 31 December 1996. A gain on the sale of a fixed asset will appear as a credit entry within Profit and Loss account.

(ii) £12,000, McNamarras made a loss on disposal of £900. This amount will be charged to the Profit and Loss account for the year to 31 December 1996, appearing there as a debit entry in the same way as any other expense incurred during the period.

In either of the above cases, besides the period's Profit and Loss account showing a gain/loss on disposal of the car, given the nature of McNamarras' vehicle depreciation policy (depreciation is charged for each complete month of the car's ownership) it is also necessary for the Profit and Loss account to contain details of the car's depreciation charge for the year to 31 December 1996. The relevant charge, therefore, will be based on 5/12 of a full year's charge, since the asset was only owned for five months in 1996 from 1 January to 1 June:

$$£3,600 \times 5/12 = £1,500$$

In summary, McNamarras' Profit and Loss account for the year to 31 December 1996 will contain a depreciation charge of £1,500 in respect of the car, plus details of the gain/loss realised upon its sale. The balance sheet of McNamarras' business on 31 December 1996 will no longer include information on the car since, quite simply, the firm ceased to own the asset on 1 June of that year.

8.

(a) (i) *1996*

Motor vehicles, depreciation charge for the year to 31 December:

Car	Depreciation charge £	Working
A	5,000	[20,000 × 25%]
B	3,750	[9/12 (20,000 × 25%)]
C	1,250	[6/12 (10,000 × 25%)]
Total depreciation charge on motor vehicles written off to the Profit and Loss account	10,000	

(ii)

Donald and MacGregor (Solicitors)
Balance Sheet (Extract) as at 31 December 1996

Fixed Assets	Cost £	Accumulated Depreciation £	Net Book Value £
Motor vehicles	50,000	10,000	40,000

Note: It should be remembered that the balance sheet of any business is in essence a summary document. Hence, the details relating to the three cars have been pooled and shown under the general heading of 'Motor vehicles'. In this way, the balance sheet is kept clear of cluttering detail whilst at the same time conveying valid summary information to the users of the statement.

(b) (i) *Gain or loss on disposal of car C*

Net book value of car C on 1.10.97	= Cost	–	accumulated depreciation to date of sale
	= £10,000	–	[£1,250 + 9/12 ((£10,000 – £1,250) × 25%)]
	= £10,000	–	[£1,250 + 9/12 (£2,188)]
	= £10,000	–	£2,891
	= £7,109		

Note

To find the accumulated depreciation provided to the date of the sale of car C will involve calculating the depreciation charge provided against car C in 1997 and adding this to car C's depreciation charge in 1996 (the latter figure having been previously worked out as £1,250).

It is now possible to find whether a gain or loss has been made in the disposal of the vehicle by comparing the net book value of car C on 1 October 1997 (£7,109) with its actual selling price (£8,000).

The gain of £891 on the sale of car C will appear in the 1997 Profit and Loss account as a credit entry.

(ii) Total depreciation charge relating to motor vehicles in the year to 31 December 1997:

Car	Depreciation charge £	Working
A	3,750	(£20,000 – £5,000) × 25%
B	4,063	(£20,000 – £3,750) × 25%
C	1,641	9/12 ((£10,000 – £1,250) × 25%)
Total depreciation charge on motor vehicles written off to the Profit and Loss account	9,454	

(iii)

Donald and MacGregor (Solicitors)
Balance Sheet (Extract) as at 31 December 1997

Fixed Assets	Cost £	Accumulated Depreciation £	Net Book Value £
Motor vehicles*	40,000	16,563	23,437

Note

* Given that car C was sold during the year, the balance sheet of the firm as at 31 December 1997 will contain details of only cars A and B.

9.

1996   (i)   *Recording the initial vehicle purchases:*

Motor vehicles

1996		£	1996	£
1.1.96	Bank	20,000		
1.4.96	Bank	20,000		
1.7.96	Bank	10,000		

Note

Assuming all payments are made by cheques the corresponding credit entries for each of the above debit entries in the Motor vehicle account will be in the firm's Bank account which for the purposes of this illustration has been ignored.

(ii)   *Recording the year's depreciation charge*

	DEPRECIATION EXPENSE				ACCUMULATED DEPRECIATION (MOTOR VEHICLE)			
1996		£	1996	£	1996	£	1996	£
31.12.96	Accumulated depreciation (Motor vehicle) 10,000						31.12.96 Depreciation expense	10,000

(iii)   *Transferring the balance on the Depreciation expense account over to the period's Profit and Loss Account*

	DEPRECIATION EXPENSE				PROFIT AND LOSS			
1996		£	1996	£	1996	£	1996	£
31.12.96	Accumulated depreciation [Motor vehicle] 10,000		31.12.96 Profit and Loss	10,000	31.12.96 Depreciation expense	10,000		

Note

At the end of the 1996 financial year, it can be seen that the balances remaining in the Motor vehicles account and its associated Accumulated depreciation account are £50,000 (debit) and £10,000 (credit) respectively. This information will be brought together in the firm's balance sheet in order for the net book value of the cars (£40,000) to be highlighted.

1997   (i)   *Recording the disposal of car C on 1.10.97*

	MOTOR VEHICLES				ACCUMULATED DEPRECIATION (MOTOR VEHICLE)			
1997		£	1997	£	1997	£	1997	£
1.1.97	Bal b/f	50,000	1.10.97 Disposal of Motor vehicle 10,000(a)		(b) 1.10.97 Disposal of Motor vehicle 2,891		1.1.97 Bal b/f	10,000

BANK

1997		£	1997		£
1.1.97	Bal b/f	xxx			
1.10.97	Disposal of Motor vehicle	8,000 (c)			

DISPOSAL OF MOTOR VEHICLE (CAR C)

1997		£	1997		£
(a) 1.10.97	Motor vehicle	10,000	1.10.97	Accumulated depreciation (Motor vehicle)	2,891 (b)
(d) 1.10.97	Profit and Loss	891	1.10.97	Bank	8,000 (c)
		10,891			10,891

Notes

(a), (b) The details relating to car C are transferred from the Motor vehicles account and the Accumulated depreciation (Motor vehicle) account to the Disposal of Motor vehicle account.

(c) The receipt of the £8,000 sale proceeds is recorded in the firm's Bank account with the corresponding credit entry being in the Disposal of Motor vehicle account.

(d) The Disposal of Motor vehicle account is closed off with the balance (that is, the gain on disposal of £891) being transferred to the period's Profit and Loss account.

(ii) *Recording the year's depreciation charge*

DEPRECIATION EXPENSE

1997		£	1997		£
31.12.97	Accumulated depreciation (Motor vehicles)	9,454			

ACCUMULATED DEPRECIATION (MOTOR VEHICLES)

1997		£	1997		£
1.10.97	Disposal of Motor vehicle	2,891	1.1.97	Bal b/f	10,000
			31.12.97	Depreciation expense	9,454

(iii) *Transferring the balance on the Depreciation expense account over to the period's Profit and Loss account*

DEPRECIATION EXPENSE

1997		£	1997		£
31.12.97	Accumulated depreciation (Motor vehicles)	9,454	31.12.97	Profit and Loss	9,454

PROFIT AND LOSS

1997		£	1997		£
31.12.97	Depreciation expense	9,454			

(iv) *Balances remaining in the Motor vehicles account and the Accumulated depreciation (Motor vehicles) account at 31 December 1997 carried forward into 1998*

MOTOR VEHICLES

1997		£	1997		£
1.1.97	Bal b/f	50,000	1.10.97	Disposal of Motor vehicle	10,000
			31.12.97	Bal c/f	40,000
		50,000			50,000
1998					
1.1.98	Bal b/f	40,000			

ACCUMULATED DEPRECIATION (MOTOR VEHICLES)

1997		£	1997		£
1.10.97	Disposal of Motor vehicle	2,891	1.1.97	Bal b/f	10,000
31.12.97	Bal c/f	16,563	31.12.97	Depreciation expense	9,454
		19,454			19,454
			1998		
			1.1.98	Bal b/f	16,563

Suggested solutions,
Chapter Five: Accounting adjustments - part two

1.

  (i) To write off Wilson and Wilson's bad debts, the following entries are necessary:
      (a) *Dr* Bad debts   £400
                 Cr   F Staedtler   £400
      (b) *Dr* Bad debts   £360
                 Cr   Mrs R Patton   £360

  (ii) At the end of the financial year, the balance on the bad debts account (£760) is transferred to the Profit and Loss account along with the other expenses of the period. That is:
      Dr   Profit and Loss   £760
             Cr   Bad debts   £760

  (iii) After the adjustments to record the bad debts have been made, the total Client debtors figure which would appear in the firm's balance sheet at the end of the year would be £11,400 (that is, the total of the client debit balances remaining in the Clients Ledger namely £2,650 + £8,750).

2.

  (i) The amount written off as bad debts to Leggett and Co's Profit and Loss account for the year to 30 June 1997 will be £2,250 + £350 = £2,600.

  (ii) The Provision for doubtful debts account will have a closing credit balance equating to 5% of the year end Client debtors figure. Thus:

                                          £

Client debtors balance at 30 June 1997
after correction of the cashier's omission   24,300   (that is, £24,650 – £350)
                                                   × 5%

Balance on Provision for doubtful debts
   account at 30.6.97   1,215

Given that it has only just been set up, the full cost of establishing the provision (being £1,215) will be charged to the period's Profit and Loss account.

(iii)   *Leggatt and Co*
                   Balance sheet extract as at 30 June 1997

	£	£
Current assets		
Client debtors	24,300	
Less: Provision for doubtful debts	(1,215)	
		23,085

3.

(i)

Leggatt and Company
Amounts charged to the Profit and Loss account for the year to 30 June 1998

		£
(a)	Bad debts written off	2,000
	Increase in Provision for doubtful debts	135*

Note

*At the beginning of the financial period the Provision for doubtful debts had a credit balance of £1,215, being the amount brought forward from the previous accounting year (see Question Two solution). By the end of the year the provision has to be increased to £1,350 to reflect the likelihood of a higher level of debt non-payment associated with the higher end of period Client debtors figure (£27,000). Accordingly, the amount needed to increase the Provision for doubtful debts from £1,215 to its revised balance of £1,350, namely £135, should be charged to the period's Profit and Loss account.

(b)   The total bad debts written off during the year of £2,000 should be charged (that is, debited) to the period's Profit and Loss account.
However, given that the Provision for doubtful debts is being reduced (that is, from £1,215 to £1,000), the amount necessary to reduce the provision to its revised level (that is, £215) should be *credited* to the Profit and Loss account.

(c)   In this situation, since the Provision for doubtful debts at the close of the accounting period is exactly the same as it was on the opening day of the financial period, no adjustment is necessary. Thus, only the £2,000 worth of bad debts written off during the period need be detailed in the Profit and Loss account.

(ii)

Leggatt and Company
Balance Sheet Extract for the year ending 30 June 1998

	(a)	(b)	(c)
Current Assets	£	£	£
Client debtors	27,000	20,000	24,300
Less: Provision for			
doubtful debts	(1,350)	(1,000)	(1,215)
	25,650	19,000	23,085

4.

Business Expense	Amount of Expense Prepaid	Amount of Expense Accrued	Amount of expense charged to the firm's Profit and Loss Account for the year to 30.6.96	Details to be included in the firm's balance sheet as at 30.6.96
	£	£	£	
(i) Office rent	500	—	2,950 – 500 = 2,450	*Current assets* Prepaid expense £500
(ii) Office rates	—	800	4,000+800 = 4,800	*Current liabilities* Accrued expense £800
(iii) Heating and lighting	—	125	1,750+125 = 1,875	*Current liabilities* Accrued expense £125

Note

It would be normal to combine the £800 and £125 accrued expenses in the balance sheet and show as the one total figure of £925.

5.

P Squires (Solicitor), first financial year
Office rent and rates

The figure which would appear in the Profit and Loss account with respect to Office rent and rates expenses is £3,600 – £425 + £300 = £3,475.

The balance sheet drawn up on the last day of the financial year would include the following :

    (a) *Current assets*
          Prepaid expenses   £425
and, (b) *Current liabilities*
          Accrued expenses   £300

A6

(i)   Evans and Bevans, Solicitors

(a)   *Profit and Loss account for the year ended 31 July 1997*

	£	£
Fees rendered		120,000
Add: Increase in Work in Progress		
Work in progress, 31.7.97	30,000	
Less: Work in progress, 1.8.96	NIL	30,000
		150,000

(b)   *Profit and Loss account for the year ended 31 July 1998*

	£	£
Fees rendered		125,000
Add: Increase in Work in Progress		
Work in progress, 31.7.98	32,500	
Less: Work in progress, 1.8.97	(30,000)	2,500
		127,500

(c)   *Profit and Loss account for the year ended 31 July 1999*

	£	£
Fees rendered		130,000
Less: Decrease in Work in Progress		
Work in progress, 31.7.99	28,000	
Less: Work in progress, 1.8.98	(32,500)	(4,500)
		125,500

(ii)   *Evans and Bevans, Solicitors*
       Balance sheet items

It would be normal to expect a figure in respect of *only closing work in progress* to be shown in the firm's balance sheet in the Current assets section. Thus, for each of the three financial years in question :

	(a)	(b)	(c)
	as at 31.7.97	*as at 31.7.98*	*as at 31.7.99*
Current Assets	£	£	£
Work in progress	30,000	32,500	28,000

7.

If closing work in progress was over-valued, this would have the effect of increasing the fee income figure for that period. In turn, this would lead to the over-statement of net profit (or under-statement of net loss, if the firm was in a loss making situation). Finally, the financial position of the firm, as disclosed by the balance sheet would be artificially enhanced as a result.

To elaborate further on the latter point, it will be recalled that generally, the net profit of a firm will be added to the owner's Capital in the balance sheet at the end of the accounting period. If net profit is overstated, say by £5,000, then the balance sheet will in turn show the owner's wealth as being overstated by this amount. The balancing effect will be found in the Current asset section, where the closing value for work in progress is shown, again overstated by £5,000.

8.

Condor (Plastics) Ltd
Profit and Loss account extract for the year ending 31 August ....

	(a) 1997		(b) 1998	
	£	£	£	£
Sales		100,000		125,000
Less: Cost of Goods Sold				
Opening stock	—		15,000	
Add: Purchases	75,000		85,000	
	75,000		100,000	
Less: Closing stock	(15,000)	(60,000)	(20,000)	(80,000)
Gross profit c/f		40,000		45,000

Condor (Plastics) Ltd
Balance sheet extract as at 31 August ....

	(a) 1997	(b) 1998
	£	£
Current assets		
Trading stock, at 31.8.9....	15,000	20,000

9.

The effects of inaccurate valuations on closing stocks were directly considered in section (4) of this chapter.

10.

(i)

WORKSHEET
O.B. Knobe, Solicitor

	Trial Balance DR £	Trial Balance CR £	Adjustments DR £	Adjustments CR £	Profit & Loss A/C DR £	Profit & Loss A/C CR £	Balance Sheet DR £	Balance Sheet CR £
Office premises, at cost	144,000						144,000	
Office fixtures and fittings, at cost	35,140						35,140	
Motor vehicles, at cost	50,000						50,000	
Accumulated depreciation								
: Office premises		13,025		6,549(i)				19,574
: Office fixtures & fittings		17,116		5,271(ii)				22,387
: Motor vehicles		13,550		7,290(iii)				20,840
Debtors	6,037						6,037	
Capital		128,274						128,274
Cash in hand	100						100	
Bank overdraft		29,123						29,123
Fees rendered		305,000				305,000		
Work in progress, 1.7.95	33,970				33,970			
Postages	3,450				3,450			
Rates	12,000			2,000(vii)	10,000			
Insurance	4,625			850(viii)	3,775			
Office wages and salaries	107,084				107,084			
Staff travel expenses	12,100		150(v)		12,250			
General expenses	15,000				15,000			
Telephone	8,000		450(vi)		8,450			
Heating and lighting	14,600				14,600			
Stationery	11,732				11,732			
Bank interest and charges	2,750				2,750			
Bad debts	5,000				5,000			
Drawings — O.B. Knobe	40,500						40,500	
	506,088	506,088						
Depreciation expense								
: Office premises			6,549(i)		6,549			
: Office fixtures & fittings			5,271(ii)		5,271			
: Motor vehicles			7,290(iii)		7,290			
Work in Progress, 30.6.96 c/f			29,500(iv)				29,500	
Work in Progress 30.6.96				29,500(iv)		29,500		
Accrued expenses								
: Staff travel				150(v)				150
: Telephone				450(vi)				450
Prepaid expenses								
: Rates			2,000(vii)				2,000	
: Insurance			850(viii)				850	
Provision for doubtful debts c/f				302(ix)				302
Provision for doubtful debts			302(ix)		302			
			52,362	52,362				
Net profit for year					87,027			87,027
					334,500	334,500	308,127	308,127

(ii)

O B Knobe, Solicitor
Profit and Loss account for the year to 30 June 1996

	£	£
Fees rendered		305,000
Less: Decrease in Work in Progress		
Work in progress, 30.6.96	29,500	
Less: Work in progress, 1.7.95	(33,970)	(4,470)
		300,530
Less: Expenses		
Postages	3,450	
Rates	10,000	
Insurance	3,775	
Office wages and salaries	107,084	
Staff travel	12,250	
General expenses	15,000	
Telephone	8,450	
Heating and lighting	14,600	
Stationery	11,732	
Bank interest and charges	2,750	
Bad debts	5,000	
Depreciation charges:		
Office premises	6,549	
Office furniture & fittings	5,271	
Motor vehicles	7,290	19,110
Increase in Provision for doubtful debts		302
		(213,503)
Net profit for the year		87,027

O B Knobe, Solicitor
Balance sheet as at 30 June 1996

	Cost £	Accumulated Depreciation £	N B V £
Fixed Assets			
Office premises	144,000	19,574	124,426
Office fixtures and fittings	35,140	22,387	12,753
Motor vehicles	50,000	20,840	29,160
	229,140	62,801	166,339
Current Assets			
Work in progress, 30.6.96		29,500	
Debtors	6,037		
Less: Provision for doubtful debts	(302)	5,735	
Prepaid expenses		2,850	
Cash in hand		100	
		38,185	
Less: Current Liabilities			
Accrued expenses		600	
Bank overdraft		29,123	
		(29,723)	
Net Current Assets			8,462
			174,801
Represented thus:			
Capital 1.7.95			128,274
Add: Profit for the year			87,027
			215,301
Less: Drawings			(40,500)
			174,801

11.

T Dimple, Solicitor
Profit and Loss account for the year ended 31 December 1996

	£	£
Fees rendered		162,625
Add: Increase in Work in progress		
Work in progress 31.12.96	22,500	
Less: Work in progress 1.1.96	(21,300)	1,200
		163,825
Add: Commissions received		836
Reduction in Provision for bad debts		307
		164,968
Less: Expenses		
Office wages and salaries	50,531	
Heating and lighting	2,777	
Rates	756	
Sundry office expenses	324	
Postage and telephone	1,488	
Stationery	1,300	
Insurance	700	
Bad debts written off	650	
Staff travel expenses	1,655	
Vehicle running costs	2,750	
Depreciation charges:		
Office furniture & fittings	1,442	
Motor vehicles	4,375	5,817
		(68,748)
Net profit for the year		96,220

T Dimple, Solicitor
Balance Sheet as at 31 December 1996

	Cost £	Accumulated Depreciation £	N B V £
Fixed Assets			
Freehold office premises	99,650	—	99,650
Office furniture & fittings	30,724	17,742	12,982
Motor vehicles	28,500	15,375	13,125
	158,874	33,117	125,757
Current Assets			
Work in progress, 31.12.96		22,500	
Client debtors	4,460		
Less: Provision for bad debts	(223)	4,237	
Prepaid expenses		360	
Bank		23,645	
Cash		186	
		50,928	
Less: Current Liabilities			
Creditors		5,250	
Accrued expenses		750	
		(6,000)	
Net Current Assets			44,928
			170,685
Represented thus:			
Capital, 1.1.96			98,465
Add: Profit for the year			96,220
			194,685
Less: Drawings			(24,000)
			170,685

Suggested solutions
Chapter Six: Bank reconciliations

1.

Maguire Swanson & Co., Solicitors
Bank Reconciliation Statement as on . . . .

	£	£
Balance in hand per bank statement		3,550
Add: Outstanding lodgements		
Cash	950	
Cheques	500	1,450
		5,000
Less: Unpresented cheques		
Cheque No:		
9801	250	
9807	1,150	
9809	100	1,500
Balance in hand per cash book		3,500

2.

F. Muldroch & Co. (Solicitors)

(a) *Adjusted cash book balance:*

Original balance	£2,250
Less SOs and DDs not yet entered (£345 + £455 + £200 + £250)	£1,250
	£1,000
Add credit transfer from SLAB not yet entered	£4,250
	£5,250

(b) *Bank reconciliation Statement as on . . . .*

	£	£
Balance in hand per bank statement		6,400
Add: Outstanding lodgements		850
		7,250
Less: Unpresented cheques		
Cheque No:		
90445	750	
90449	150	
90452	650	
90458	450	(2,000)
Balance in hand per cash book		£5,250

3.

S. & R. Robertson, Solicitors

(a)   *Adjusted cash book balance:*

Original favourable balance	£11,465
Less Direct Debits not yet entered (£550 + £650)	(£1,200)
	£10,265
Less Bank charges not yet entered	(200)
	£10,065
Add credit transfers not yet entered (£2,500 + £325 + £2)	£2,827
Balance in hand per adjusted cash book	£12,892

It would also be possible to arrive at the adjusted cash book balance by redrafting the cash book and making the appropriate entries to update it. This could be done as follows:

S. & R. Robertson, Solicitors
Cash Book (Extract)
May 2000

Debit			Credit			
Date	*Description*	*£*	*Date*	*Description*	*Ch. No.*	*£*
1	Bal b/f	11,465	1	Bank charges		200
„	Bank interest	2	„	Insurances		550
„	Dividends Received	325	„	Insurances		650
	Scot. Legal Aid Bd.	2,500	„	Bal c/f		12,892
		14,292				14,292
1	Bal b/f	12,892				

(b)

S. & R. Robertson, Solicitors
Bank Reconciliation Statement as on 1 May 2000

	£	£
Balance in hand per bank statement		13,022
Add: Outstanding lodgements:		
S. Dicks	350	
Cash	25	375
		13,397
Less: Unpresented cheques:		
Cheque No.		
715	415	
722	90	(505)
Balance in hand per cash book (as adjusted)		12,892

4.

Simpsons, Solicitors
Cash Book (Extract)
February 2000

DR			CR			
Date	*Narrative*	*(£)*	*Date*	*Narrative*	*Cheq.*	*(£)*
1	Dividends Rec'd	850	1	Bal b/f		3,625
„	Bal c/f	3,275	„	Security		500
		4,125				4,125
			„	Bal b/f		3,275

Simpsons, Solicitors
Bank Reconciliation Statement as on 1 February 2000

	£
Overdraft per bank statement	(4,825)
Add: Outstanding lodgement	2,000
	(2,825)
Less: Unpresented cheque:	
Cheque No.	
092	(450)
Deficit per cash book (as adjusted)	(3,275)

5.

Simpsons, Solicitors
Cash Book (Extract)
March 2000

DR			CR			
Date	*Narrative*	*(£)*	*Date*	*Narrative*	*Cheq.*	*(£)*
1	Bal b/f	4,880	1	Security		500
			„	Bal c/f		4,380
		4,880				4,880
„	Bal b/f	4,380				

Simpsons, Solicitors
Bank Reconciliation Statement as on 1 March 2000

	£	£
Balance in hand per bank statement		3,970
Add: Outstanding lodgements:		
G. Sylvestre	900	
Cash	45	945
		4,915
Less: Unpresented cheques:		
Cheque No.		
092	450	
095	85	(535)
Balance in hand per cash book (as adjusted)		4,380

Suggested solutions
Chapter Seven: Partnership accounting

1.

Annan & Wyllie
Trading and Profit and Loss Account for the year ended 30 April 19-3

	£	£	£
Sales			143,680
Less: Cost of Goods Sold			
Opening Stock		31,420	
Add: Purchases		83,575	
		114,995	
Less: Closing Stock		35,200	
			79,795
GROSS PROFIT			63,885
Less: Expenses			
Salaries		17,570	
Office overheads		6,475	
Depreciation: Buildings	1,000		
Motor Vehicles	3,750		
Office Equipment	1,050		
		5,800	
			29,845
NET PROFIT			34,040

Appropriated thus:

	Annan	Wyllie	Total
	£	£	£
Interest on capital	4,000	2,500	6,500
Interest on drawings	(775)	(595)	(1,370)
Profit Share	17,346	11,564	28,910
	20,571	13,469	34,040

Annan & Wyllie
Balance Sheet as at 30 April 19-3

	Cost £	Accumulated Depreciation £	£
Fixed Assets			
Buildings	50,000	8,000	42,000
Office Equipment	7,500	3,300	4,200
Motor Vehicles	15,000	13,125	1,875
	72,500	24,425	48,075
Current Assets			
Stock		35,200	
Debtors		35,600	
Cash in Hand		780	
		71,580	
Less: Current Liabilities			
Creditors	27,340		
Accruals	225		
Bank Overdraft	20,775		
		(48,340)	
Net Current Assets			23,240
Total Assets			71,315

Represented by:

	Annan £	Wyllie £	Total £
Partners' Capital Accounts	40,000	25,000	65,000
Partners' Current Accounts			
Balance at 1.5.-2	3,750	2,025	
Add: Appropriated Profit	20,571	13,469	
	24,321	15,494	
Less: Drawings	(18,500)	(15,000)	
	5,821	494	
			6,315
			71,315

2.

Taylor Rodger & Paton
Trading Profit and Loss Account for the Year ended 31 May 19-4

	£	£
Sales		347,650
Less: Cost of Goods Sold		
Opening Stock	51,720	
Purchases	260,326	
	312,046	
Closing Stock	(53,462)	
		258,584
GROSS PROFIT		89,066
Less: Expenses		
Rent and Rates	10,230	
Heat and Light	1,322	
Salaries and Wages	39,615	
Bad debts	650	
Increase in provision for doubtful debts	70	
Insurance	1,163	
Motor Vehicle Running Expenses	5,296	
Depreciation	5,500	
Bank Charges	175	
General Expenses	3,853	
		(67,874)
Add: Sundry Income		
Gain on sale of motor vehicle		1,258
NET PROFIT		22,450

Appropriated thus:

	Taylor £	Rodger £	Paton £	Total £
Salary—Paton	—	—	5,000	5,000
Interest on Capital	2,450	2,450	1,400	6,300
Profit Share	4,460	4,460	2,230	11,150
	6,910	6,910	8,630	22,450

Taylor Rodger & Paton
Balance Sheet as at 31 May 19-4

	Cost £	Accumulated Depreciation £	£
Fixed Assets			
Freehold Premises	52,350	—	52,350
Motor Vehicles	27,500	22,030	5,470
	79,850	22,030	57,820
Current Assets			
Stock		53,462	
Debtors	42,619		
Provision for Doubtful Debts	(1,630)	40,989	
Prepaid expenses		656	
Bank account		10,253	
Cash in hand		726	
		106,086	
Current Liabilities			
Creditors	46,246		
Accruals	210		
		46,456	
			59,630
Total Assets			117,450

Represented by:

	Taylor £	Rodger £	Paton £	Total £
Partners' Capital Accounts	35,000	35,000	20,000	90,000
Partners' Current Accounts				
Balance at 1.6-3	17,750	19,200	13,050	
Add: Appropriated Profit	6,910	6,910	8,630	
	24,660	26,110	21,680	
Less: Drawings	(18,000)	(16,250)	(10,750)	
	6,660	9,860	10,930	
				27,450
				117,450

3.

Munro Graham and Harris
Trading Profit and Loss Account for the Year ended 30 June 19-5

	£	£
Sales		502,618
Less: Cost of Goods Sold		
Opening stock	92,316	
Purchases	349,833	
	442,149	
Closing stock	(97,409)	
		344,740
GROSS PROFIT		157,878
Less: Expenses		
Rent and Rates	3,210	
Heat and Light	3,274	
Telephone	1,826	
Advertising and stationery	2,750	
Insurance	2,521	
Wages and salaries	38,724	
Motor vehicle running costs	7,915	
Repairs and renewals	4,338	
Discounts allowed	5,416	
General expenses	5,493	
Bank interest and charges	6,419	
Bad debts	2,617	
Depreciation: Plant and equipment	9,098	
Office fixtures and fittings	515	
Motor vehicles	6,920	
		101,036
NET PROFIT		56,842

Appropriated thus:

	Munro £	Graham £	Harris £	Total £
Interest on capital	1,950	1,275	1,650	4,875
Interest on drawings	(426)	(375)	(412)	(1,213)
Salary	—	5,000	5,000	10,000
Profit share	17,272	12,954	12,954	43,180
	18,796	18,854	19,192	56,842

Munro Graham and Harris
Balance Sheet as at 30 June 19-5

	Cost £	Accumulated Depreciation £	£
Fixed Assets			
Freehold land and buildings	47,000	—	47,000
Plant and equipment	45,490	20,814	24,676
Office fixtures and fittings	8,320	3,685	4,635
Motor vehicles	27,680	17,150	10,530
	128,490	41,649	86,841
Current Assets			
Stock		97,409	
Debtors		78,054	
Prepaid expenses		750	
Cash in hand		923	
		177,136	
Current Liabilities			
Bank overdraft	11,557		
Creditors	98,708		
Accrued expenses	3,320		
		113,585	
Net Current Assets			63,551
Long Term Liabilities			
Loan			(30,000)
Total Assets			120,392

Represented by:

	Munro £	Graham £	Harris £	Total £
Capital Accounts	26,000	17,000	22,000	65,000
Current Accounts				
Balance at 1.7.19-4	13,258	16,177	12,265	
Add: Appropriated profit	18,796	18,854	19,192	
	32,054	35,031	31,457	
Less: Drawings	(15,000)	(13,250)	(14,900)	
	17,054	21,781	16,557	55,392
				120,392

4.

Innes Moran & Co., Solicitors
Profit and Loss Account for the year ended 31 July 19-6

	£	£	£
Fees rendered			231,454
Add: Work in Progress at 31 July 19-6			25,715
			257,169
Less: Work in Progress at 1 August 19-5			22,620
			234,549
Less Expenses:			
Wages and salaries		113,040	
Rates and insurance		11,581	
Stationery		8,615	
Telephone, fax, postages		16,930	
Bank interest and charges		1,250	
Sundry office expenses		8,065	
Depreciation: Office premises	1,900		
Office furniture and fittings	3,354	5,254	
			(164,735)
NET PROFIT			69,814

Appropriated thus:

	Innes	Moran	Total
	£	£	£
Interest on capital	3,750	3,100	6,850
Salary	18,500	18,500	37,000
Profit Share	12,982	12,982	25,964
	35,232	34,582	69,814

Innes Moran & Co., Solicitors
Balance Sheet as at 31 July 19-6

	Cost £	Accumulated Depreciation £	£
Fixed Assets			
Office premises	95,000	12,790	82,210
Office furniture and fittings	37,250	18,244	19,006
	132,250	31,034	101,216
Current Assets			
Work in Progress		25,715	
Debtors		42,570	
Clients funds (Note 1)		1,585	
Bank account		22,971	
Cash in Hand		250	
Prepaid expenses		1,576	
		94,667	
Current Liabilities			
Creditors		2,516	
Accrued expenses		2,709	
		5,225	
Net Current Assets			89,442
			190,658

Represented by:

	Innes £	Moran £	Total £
Capital Accounts	75,000	62,000	137,000
Current Accounts (Note 2)	28,451	25,207	53,658
	103,451	87,207	190,658

Innes Moran & Co., Solicitors
Notes to the Accounts at 31 July 19-6

Note 1: Clients Funds

	£
Funds held on behalf of clients	
—on current account	36,500
—on deposit receipt	185,000
	221,500
Less: Total of clients credit balances	(219,915)
Amount over-deposited in clients account	1,585

(This method of presentation is somewhat neater than showing the separate amounts in current assets and current liabilities on the face of the balance sheet and is a perfectly acceptable way of showing the information).

Note 2: Current Accounts

	Innes	*Moran*	*Total*
	£	£	£
Opening balance at 1 August, 19-5	13,219	10,625	23,844
Interest on capital	3,750	3,100	6,850
Salary	18,500	18,500	37,000
Profit Share	12,982	12,982	25,964
	48,451	45,207	93,658
Less: Drawings	(20,000)	(20,000)	(40,000)
Balance as at 31 July 19-6	28,451	25,207	53,658

5.

(a)

Keegan & Co., Solicitors
Balance Sheet as at 1 September 19-7

	£	£
Fixed Assets		
Property		50,000
Office furniture and equipment		7,500
Motor Vehicles		30,000
		87,500
Current Assets		
Cash at bank	22,500	
Current Liabilities		
Short term loan	7,500	
Net Current Assets		15,000
		102,500

Represented by:

	Keegan £	Gilmorton £	McNaughton £	Total £
Partners' Capital Accounts	60,000	20,000	22,500	102,500

(b)

Keegan & Co., Solicitors
Appropriation Account for the year ended 31 August, 19-8

	£
Net Profit	36,000

Appropriated thus:

	Keegan £	Gilmorton £	McNaughton £	Total £
Profit	12,000	12,000	12,000	36,000

Keegan & Co., Solicitors
Capital Accounts as at 31 August 19-8

	Keegan £	Gilmorton £	McNaughton £	Total £
Balance at 1 September 19-7	60,000	20,000	22,500	102,500
Add: Input during year	6,250	—	—	6,250
Profit share	12,000	12,000	12,000	36,000
Less: Drawings	(13,250)	(11,750)	(12,300)	(37,300)
	65,000	20,250	22,200	107,450

6.

Neilsen, Chalmers & Pryce, Solicitors
Profit and Loss Statement for the year ended 30 April 19-9

	£	£	£
Fees rendered			330,175
Add: Work in Progress at 30 April 19-9			29,500
			359,675
Less: Work in Progress at 1 May 19-8			(33,970)
			325,705
Less: Expenses			
Office wages and salaries		137,259	
General expenses		15,275	
Rates and insurance		13,100	
Telephone and postages		11,894	
Staff travel expenses		12,292	
Heating and lighting		14,615	
Stationery		11,717	
Bank interest and charges		2,750	
Depreciation: Motor vehicles	10,125		
Office premises	4,507		
Office furniture and fittings	8,271	22,903	
Bad debt written off		625	
			242,430
NET PROFIT			83,275

Appropriated thus:

	Neilsen £	Chalmers £	Pryce £	Total £
Partner's salary	13,500	18,500	21,000	53,000
Interest on capital	5,100	5,100	3,500	13,700
Share of Profit	5,525	5,525	5,525	16,575
Appropriated Profit	24,125	29,125	30,025	83,275

Neilsen, Chalmers & Pryce, Solicitors
Balance Sheet as at 30 April 19-9

	Cost	Accum. Dep'n	
	£	£	£
Fixed Assets			
Office premises	120,000	11,832	108,168
Office furniture and fittings	55,140	31,137	24,003
Motor vehicles	54,000	23,625	30,375
	229,140	66,594	162,546
Current Assets			
Work in Progress		29,500	
Outstanding fees/debtors		12,037	
Ledger debit balances/recoverable client outlays		4,902	
Prepaid expenses		3,250	
Cash in Hand		100	
		49,789	
Current Liabilities			
Deficit in client account (see note)		1,400	
Bank overdraft		39,250	
Accrued expenses		636	
		41,286	
Net Current Assets			8,503
			171,049

Represented by:

	Neilsen	Chalmers	Pryce	Total
	£	£	£	£
Partners capital	51,000	51,000	35,000	137,000
Partners current accounts				
Balance at 1.5.-8	(4,000)	(3,226)	(1,500)	
Add: Appropriated profits	24,125	29,125	30,025	
	20,125	25,899	28,525	
Less: Drawings	(13,500)	(13,500)	(13,500)	
	6,625	12,399	15,025	34,049
				171,049

Clients Funds

	£
Funds held on behalf of clients	
—on deposit receipt	332,500
—on current account	43,354
	375,854
Less: Client creditors	(377,254)
Deficit in Client account	(1,400)

Breach of Rule 4 Solicitors (Scotland) Accounts Rules 1997.

Firm should immediately make up the shortfall by transferring at least this amount from its own bank account.

7.

Queen & Co., Solicitors
Profit and Loss Account for the year ended 30 November 19-2

	£	£	£
Fees rendered			273,641
Add: Work in Progress at 30 November 19-2			39,500
			313,141
Less: Work in Progress at 1 December 19-1			33,800
			279,341
Commission received			7,167
			286,508
Less: Expenses			
Office wages and salaries		143,760	
Staff travelling expenses		5,371	
Staff training costs		5,000	
Rates, rent, and common charges		35,960	
Insurance		7,250	
Telephone, fax, postage and couriers		9,102	
Heat and light		1,960	
Repairs and renewals		8,240	
Printing stationery and advertising		7,320	
Equipment leasing		4,773	
Vehicle running costs		9,503	
Office cleaning		1,350	
General expenses		5,690	
Overdraft interest and charges		6,419	
Depreciation—office furniture and equipment	693		
—motor vehicles	5,874		
		6,567	258,265
NET PROFIT			28,243

Appropriated thus:

	Queen £	Rice £	Total £
Interest on capital account	1,875	2,700	4,575
Interest on drawings	(372)	(360)	(732)
Salary	10,000	17,500	27,500
Share of deficit	(1,550)	(1,550)	(3,100)
	9,953	18,290	28,243

Queen & Co., Solicitors
Balance Sheet as at 30 November 19-2

	Cost	Accum Dep'n	
	£	£	£
Fixed Assets			
Office furniture and equipment	17,320	11,083	6,237
Motor vehicles	29,370	19,433	9,937
	46,690	30,516	16,174
Current Assets			
Work in Progress		39,500	
Outstanding fees		50,175	
Client outlays recoverable		3,910	
Cash in Hand		250	
		93,835	
Current Liabilities			
Deficit on client funds account (Note 1)		3,274	
Creditors		5,790	
Firms bank		51,320	
		60,384	
Net Current Assets			33,451
			49,625

Represented by:

	Queen	Rice	Total
	£	£	£
Partners' Capital Accounts	25,000	36,000	61,000
Partners' Current Accounts (Note 2)	(12,789)	1,414	(11,375)
	12,211	37,414	49,625

Note 1: Clients Funds

	£
Funds held on behalf of clients:	
on deposit receipt	233,000
on current account	43,176
	276,176
Less: Total clients credit balances	(279,450)
Deficit on clients funds account	(3,274)*

* Breach of Solicitors (Scotland) Accounts Rules 1997, Rule 4. The firm should immediately make good this shortfall.

Note 2: Partners Current Accounts

	Queen £	Rice £	Total £
Opening balance as at 1 December 19-1	7,258	13,124	20,382
Add: Appropriated Profit	9,953	18,290	28,243
	17,211	31,414	48,625
Less: Drawings	(30,000)	(30,000)	(60,000)
Balance as at 30 November 19-2	(12,789)	1,414	(11,375)

8.

(a)

J. Short and S. Thweet, Solicitors
Balance Sheet as at 1 June 1999

	£
Fixed Assets	
Freehold Office Property at cost	175,000
Motor vehicles at cost	48,000
Office furniture and equipment at cost	27,000
	250,000
Current Assets	
Firm's bank	31,500
	281,500
Long Term Liabilities	
Loan from J. Short (10%)	(20,000)
	261,500

Represented by:

	Short £	Thweet £	Total £
Capital Accounts	100,000	75,000	175,000
Current Accounts	46,500	40,000	86,500
	146,500	115,000	261,500

(b)

J. Short and S. Thweet, Solicitors
Trial Balance as at 31 May 2000

		£	£
Capital Accounts, 1 June 1999	—Short		100,000
	—Thweet		75,000
Current Accounts, 1 June 1999	—Short		46,500
	—Thweet		40,000
Long term loan	—Short (10%)		20,000
Freehold office property	—Cost	175,000	
Motor vehicles	—Cost	48,000	
Office equipment	—Cost	27,000	
Firm's bank account		101,600	
Clients' bank	—Current account	35,200	
	—Deposit receipt	329,000	
Client debtors		33,000	
Client creditors			362,250
Fees rendered			315,750
Staff salaries		164,900	
Postages and telephone		11,300	
Motor vehicle expenses		7,600	
Stationery		9,400	
Office expenses		7,300	
Rates and insurance		7,100	
Heat and light		4,700	
Repairs and maintenance		3,200	
General creditors			7,300
Cash in hand		500	
Interest		2,000	
		966,800	966,800

(c)

J. Short and S. Thweet, Solicitors
Profit and Loss Account for the year to 31 May 2000

	£	£
Fees rendered		315,750
Add: Increase in Work in Progress		20,000
		335,750
Less: Expenses		
Staff salaries	164,900	
Postage and telephone	12,050	
Motor vehicle expenses	7,600	
Stationery	9,400	
Office expenses	7,650	
Rates and insurance	7,050	
Heat and light	4,700	
Repairs and maintenance	3,200	
Interest	2,000	
Depreciation: Motor vehicles	12,000	
Office furniture and equipment	5,400	
		235,950
NET PROFIT		99,800

Appropriated thus:

	Short £	Thweet £	Total £
Partner's salary	37,500	37,500	75,000
Interest on partner's capital 5%	5,000	3,750	8,750
Share of Profits	5,350	10,700	16,050
Appropriated Profit	47,850	51,950	99,800

(c)

J. Short and S. Thweet, Solicitors
Balance Sheet as at 31 May 2000

	Cost £	Accumulated Depreciation £	£
Fixed Assets			
Freehold office property	175,000	—	175,000
Motor vehicles	48,000	12,000	36,000
Office furniture and equipment	27,000	5,400	21,600
	250,000	17,400	232,600
Current Assets			
Work in Progress		20,000	
Client debtors		33,000	
Prepaid expenses—insurance		500	
Firm's bank account		35,600	
Surplus on clients' bank accounts (Note 1)		1,950	
Cash in hand		500	
		91,550	
Current Liabilities			
General creditors	7,300		
Accrued expenses	1,550		
		(8,850)	
Net Current Assets			82,700
Total Assets			315,300
Long Term Liabilities			
Loan: J. Short (10%)			(20,000)
			295,300

Represented by:

	Short £	Thweet £	Total £
Partners Capital Accounts	100,000	75,000	175,000
Partners Current Accounts (Note 2)	59,350	60,950	120,300
	159,350	135,950	295,300

(c)
J. Short and S. Thweet, Solicitors
Balance Sheet Notes at 31 May 2000

Note 1: Surplus on Client Bank Accounts

	£
Clients bank accounts—current account	35,200
—deposit receipt	329,000
	364,200
Less: Client ledger credit balances	362,250
Balance in hand	1,950

Note 2: Partners Current Accounts

	Short £	Thweet £	Total £
Balance at 1 June 1999	46,500	40,000	86,500
Add: Appropriated profits	47,850	51,950	99,800
	94,350	91,950	186,300
Less: Drawings	(35,000)	(31,000)	(66,000)
Balance as at 31 May 2000	59,350	60,950	120,300

Suggested solutions
Chapter Eight: Accounting for partnership changes

1.

1/10			30/6			30/9
←		£70,000	→<	£45,000		30/9 →
Split						
A(2/5)	28,000		+ (1/3)	15,000	=	43,000
B(2/5)	28,000		+ (1/3)	15,000	=	43,000
C(1/5)	14,000		+ (1/3)	15,000	=	29,000
	70,000			45,000		115,000

2.

1/1		31/1		30/9		31/12
←	£6,000	→<	£74,000	→<	£15,000	£ →
Split						
D (1/2)	3,000	+ (2/5)	29,600	+ (3/5)	9,000 =	41,600
E (1/2)	3,000	+ (2/5)	29,600		=	32,600
F		+ (1/5)	14,800	+ (2/5)	6,000 =	20,800
	6,000		74,000		15,000	95,000

3. (a)

OLD PROPERTY

Bal b/d	20,000		
Revaluation	30,000	Bal c/d	50,000
	50,000		50,000

NEW PROPERTY

Bal b/d	75,000	Revaluation	5,000
		Bal c/d	70,000
	75,000		75,000

OFFICE FURNITURE

Bal b/d	6,500	Revaluation	500
		Bal c/d	6,000
	6,500		6,500

REVALUATION

New property	5,000	Old Property	30,000
Office furniture	500		
G—Capital	10,500		
H—Capital	7,000		
I—Capital	7,000		
	30,000		30,000

CAPITAL ACCOUNTS

	G	H	I		G	H	I
				Bal b/d	75,000	35,000	38,000
Bal c/d	85,500	42,000	45,000	Reval'n	10,500	7,000	7,000
	85,500	42,000	45,000		85,500	42,000	45,000

Geddes is entitled to withdraw £85,500

(b). If Geddes wants immediate withdrawal of the capital there will be cash flow problems. Cash at bank is only £16,000. Solutions might be some combination of the following:

(a) Stage payments over a period of time.
(b) Bank loan.
(c) Sell one of the offices to raise funds.
(d) Admit a new partner with capital input.
(e) Additional capital input from existing partners.
(f) Use other assets as part of payment (eg car, etc).

4.

PROPERTY

	£		£
Bal b/d	40,000		
Revaluation	60,000	Bal c/d	100,000
	100,000		100,000

OFFICE FURNITURE

Bal b/d	7,000	Revaluation	1,000
		Bal c/d	6,000
	7,000		7,000

VEHICLES

Bal b/d	10,000	Revaluation	3,000
		Bal c/d	7,000
	10,000		10,000

REVALUATION

Vehicles	3,000	Property	60,000
Office furniture	1,000		
Bal c/d	56,000		
	60,000		60,000
J—Capital	28,000	Bal b/d	56,000
K—Capital	28,000		
	56,000		56,000

CAPITAL ACCOUNTS

	J	K	L		J	K	L
				Bal b/d	65,000	48,000	—
				Reval'n	28,000	28,000	—
Bal c/d	93,000	76,000	25,000	Cash in	—	—	25,000
	93,000	76,000	25,000		93,000	76,000	25,000

BANK

Bal b/d	6,000		
Capital input	25,000	Bal c/d	31,000
	31,000		31,000

JK Partnership
Balance Sheet at 1 April 1999

	£'000	£'000
Fixed Assets		
Office property—valuation		100
Office furniture & equipment—valuation		6
Vehicles—valuation		7
		113
Current Assets		
Work in progress	15	
Debtors	40	
Bank	31	
Surplus on clients funds	3	
	89	
Current Liabilities		
Creditors	8	
Net Current Assets		81
		194
Represented by		
Partners capital—J		93
K		76
L		25
		194

5.

MNO Partnership
Balance Sheet Extract

	£,000
Fixed Assets	170
Current Assets	155
Current Liabilities	(50)
	275

Represented by:

Partner's capital—M	115
N	115
O	45
	275

Capital Accounts

	M	N	O
	£'000	£'000	£'000
Bal b/d	100	100	—
Goodwill before admission	45	45	—
Goodwill after admission	(30)	(30)	(30)
Capital input	—	—	75
	115	115	45

6.

RST Partnership
Balance Sheet at 1 January 2000

	£'000	£'000
Fixed Assets		
Property		40
Office furniture & equipment		9
Vehicles		10
		59
Current Assets		
Work in progress	16	
Debtors	25	
Bank	23	
Cash in hand	1	
	65	
Current Liabilities		
Creditors	10	
Loan	20	
	30	
Net Current Assets		35
		94
Represented by:		
Partners capital—S		57
T		37
		94

OFFICE FURNITURE & EQUIPMENT

Bal b/d	10	Capital: R		1
		Bal c/d		9
	10			10

VEHICLES

Bal b/d	15	Capital: R		5
		Bal c/d		10
	15			15

BANK

Bal b/d	48	Capital: R		25
		Bal c/d		23
	48			48

LOAN: R

Bal c/d	20	Capital: R		20
	20			20

CAPITAL ACCOUNTS

	R	S	T		R	S	T
				Bal b/d	35	65	45
Goodwill post	—	24	24	G'dwill pre	16	16	16
Car	5						
Computer	1						
Loan	20						
Bank	25						
Bal c/d	—	57	37				
	51	81	61		51	81	61

7.

PROPERTY

Bal b/d	50	Realisation	50

OFFICE FURNITURE & EQUIPMENT

Bal b/d	5	Realisation	5

VEHICLES

Bal b/d	7	Realisation	7

WORK IN PROGRESS

Bal b/d	7	Realisation	7

DEBTORS

Bal b/d	26	Realisation	26

CASH

Bal b/d	1	Bank	1

BANK

Bal b/d	17	Cost of dissolution	8
Cash	1		
Realisation: Property	87	Loan paid	7
Office equip	2	Creditors paid	18
Vehicles	8	Partners paid—U	64
Debtors/WIP	30	V	48
	145		145

LOAN

Bank paid	7	Bal b/d	7

CREDITORS

Bank	18	Bal b/d	18

CAPITAL ACCOUNTS

	U	V		U	V
			Bal b/d	40	20
			Current A/c	12	16
Cash paid	64	48	Realisation	12	12
	64	48		64	48

REALISATION ACCOUNT

Property	50	Bank—Property	87
Office furniture/Equipment	5	Office items	2
Vehicles	7	Vehicles	8
Debtors	26	Debtors	30
Work in progress	7		
Bank—Cost of dissolution	8		
Bal c/d	24		
	127		127
U—Capital	12	Bal b/d	24
V—Capital	12		
	24		24

Suggested solutions
Chapter Nine: Organisation of business records in a legal firm

1.

The books of original entry are:

(a) Sales Day Book
(b) Purchase Day Book
(c) Cash Book

In a solicitors' practice there would normally be two cash books, one for the firm's transactions and one for client transactions.
Alternatively one cash book may be used with additional analysis columns for client transactions.

The sales day book would be known as a fee book and is operated as a control over fees issued to clients. The information in the fee book will only be recorded into the double entry accounting records when the client pays the fee.

It is common for a solicitor's practice not to operate a purchase day book since such expenses are recorded in the records when paid via the cash book.

2.

		Dr £	Cr £
(a)	Clients' bank	5,000	
	Client ledger		5,000
	Being deposit received from client		
(b)	Expenses — telephone	150	
	Office bank		150
	Being payment of firm's telephone bill		
(c)	Client ledger	25	
	Office bank		25
	Being payments on behalf of client		
(d)	Salaries	70,000	
	Office bank		70,000
	Being payment of salaries		
(e)	(i) Clients' bank	1,500	
	Client ledger		1,500
	Being receipt of outstanding fees		
	(ii) Client ledger	1,500	
	Fees		1,500
	Being payment of fee by client		
	(iii) Office bank	1,500	
	Clients' bank		1,500
	Being transfer of funds to solicitor		

(f)	Clients' bank	200,000	
	Client ledger		200,000
	Being client mortgage monies received		
(g)	Client ledger	3,500	
	Client bank		3,500
	Being refund to client		
(h)	Client ledger	450	
	Office bank		450
	Being survey fee paid on behalf of client		
(i)	Drawings	9,000	
	Office bank		9,000
	Being partners' monthly drawings		
(j)	Client bank	200	
	Client ledger		200
	Being monies received from client		

3(a).

Solicitors (Scotland) Accounts Rules 1997

The main objective of the Accounts Rules is to ensure that clients money held by the solicitor is not used by the solicitor for business purposes. To this end the rules require firms and clients money to be recorded separately and for regular reconciliations to be prepared to ensure that at all times there is sufficient money held in a clients bank account to cover all amounts owed to clients.

Solicitors (Scotland) Accounts Certificate Rules 1997

The Accounts Rules place several obligations on the solicitor and the Law Society must ensure these obligations are being met. The Accounts Certificate Rules require the solicitor to make a six-monthly return to the Law Society confirming they have complied with the rules and to provide details of the reconciliations of clients' money performed during the period. The certificate should be signed by two partners, one of whom must be the Designated Cashroom Partner, unless the solicitor is a sole practitioner. Where an external accountant has been instructed to assist in checking the accounting records, the solicitor is required to indicate the extent of assistance received.

3(b).

(i) Records are required to keep office and client money completely separate.
(ii) A client ledger has to be kept.
(iii) Records of inter-client account transfers have to be maintained.
(iv) All records to be kept fully up-to-date.
(v) If records are computerised then it must be possible to obtain an immediate printout of any account.
(vi) Regular reconciliations are to be performed and kept for specified periods.

Suggested solutions
Chapter Ten: Recording transactions in a solicitor's practice

1.
The books of original entry are:

Sales Day Book/Fee Book

This is used to record all sales invoices or fee notes issued by the business. The information in the fee book would be recorded in the client ledger as a memo item to remind the solicitor that the fee has been issued and is still outstanding. Only when the fee is paid will the fee be recorded through the double entry records.

Cash Book

This is used to record all income and expenditure of the business and in a solicitors practice there will either be a separate cash book for clients or separate client columns in the firm's cash book.

To assist in the summarising and classifying of information in the cash book, transactions are allocated into analysis columns.

Note:

In practice solicitors do not operate a purchase day book. All such items are dealt with on a cash basis and recorded into the cashbook when paid.

2.
The initial transactions will be recorded in the books of original entry being either the sales/fee day book, the purchase day book or the cash book.

From this stage the information is summarised and classified into the nominal ledger where double entry accounts are used. To help in the control of information subsidiary ledgers are also used in a solicitor's practice at this stage which will primarily be the client ledger.

The client ledger is sub-divided into a non-specific (or general) funds section and a specific (or other) funds section. The non-specific section deals with all general transactions relating to clients and the other funds section deals with all transfers of clients' monies to specific accounts for any particular client.

The information from the nominal ledger is extracted and a trial balance is prepared where the debits and credits must be equal.

From the trial balance stage any final adjustments can be made before the business accounts are prepared.

3.
Clients' money does not have to be paid into a client bank account in the following cases [SAR 7]:

(a) In the form of cash which is paid in cash to the client or representative.
(b) In the form of a cheque endorsed to the client or representative.
(c) If paid into a separate bank account in the client's or representative's name.
(d) On the request of the client.
(e) In payment of a debt due to the solicitor or reimbursement for client expenses paid by the solicitor.
(f) In settlement of a rendered fee of the solicitor.
(g) In the form of a cheque as consideration for a heritable property transaction.

4.
Withdrawals can be made from the client account in the following cases [SAR 6]:

(a) Payment being made to the client or their representative.
(b) Where there is an outstanding debt due from the client for expenses settled by the solicitor.
(c) Settlement of the solicitors professional fees.
(d) On the authority of the client.
(e) Transfer of funds from the general client account to a deposit account in the name of the client.
(f) Where monies have been paid into the client bank account by mistake.
(g) Where a surplus is held on the client's account and this is no longer required.

5.
The VAT element of each relevant transaction will first have to be calculated after which the total output VAT collected by the firm will be compared to the input VAT paid during the quarter. This will reveal whether a net payment of VAT is due to Customs and Excise or whether the firm is in a position to reclaim some VAT.

	Output VAT(£)	Input VAT(£)	Net(£)
(1)	262.50	—	
(2)	96.25	—	
(3)	—	—	
(4)	—	43.75	
(5)	—	48.13	
	358.75	91.88	266.87

The practice has a VAT liability of £266.87 for the quarter which will be paid to Customs and Excise.

6.

McGowans, Solicitors.

Client Bank Reconciliation 31 March 2000

	£	£
Balance per client bank statement		600
Add: Outstanding lodgements:		
28.3.00	300	
30.3.00	550	
		850
Less: Unpresented cheques:		
55	720	
57	440	
58	115	
		(1,275)
Balance per client cash book		175

Statement of Client Balances v Client Bank Account.

	£
Total of amounts owed to clients	150
Total of clients bank account per reconciliation	175
Surplus funds held in client bank account	25

7.

(a) Journal entries

		Dr £	Cr £
(1)	Client bank	500	
	Client ledger		500
	Being deposit received from Mrs Stark.		
(2)	Client bank	150,000	
	Client ledger		150,000
	Being mortgage funds received on behalf of Miss Aster		
(3)	(a) Client bank	3,500	
	Client ledger		3,500
	Being payment from Mr Plane		
	(b) Firm bank	3,500	
	Client bank		3,500
	Being transfer of funds to solicitor		
(4)	Insurance	3,750	
	Firm bank		3,750
	Being firm's expense for insurance costs		
(5)	Client ledger	4,000	
	Client bank		4,000
	Being refund of amounts owed to Mr Gormley		

(b) Books of Original Entry

Firm's Cash Book

Income

Date	Description	Bank (£)	VAT (£)	Transfers (£)
	Opening balance	10,000		
19/7/00	Receipt Mr Plane Debt (Jnl 3b)	3,500		3,500
		3,500		3,500

Expenditure

Date	Description	Bank (£)	VAT (£)	Insurance (£)
22/7/00	Insurance expenses	3,750		3,750
		3,750		3,750

Client Cash Book

Income

Date	Description	Bank (£)	VAT (£)	Client Ledger (£)
	Opening balance	15,000		
3/7/00	Deposit from Mrs Stark (Jnl 1)	500		500
10/7/00	Mortgage funds on behalf of Miss Aster (Jnl 2)	150,000		150,000
15/7/00	Monies from Mr Plane (Jnl 3a)	3,500		3,500
		154,000		154,000

Expenditure

Date	Description	Bank (£)	VAT (£)	Client Ledger (£)	Transfers (£)
23/7/00	Refund of monies to Mr Gormley (Jnl 5)	4,000		4,000	
19/7/00	Transfer to firms a/c re Mr Plane debt (Jnl 3b)	3,500			3,500
		7,500		4,000	3,500

(c) Classifying and Summarising/Trial Balance

July 2000
Client Ledger

Ref		Dr £	Cr £	Bal Dr/(Cr) £
Mrs Stark				
	Opening balance			(7,500)
Jnl 1	Deposit received		500	(8,000)
	Closing balance			(8,000)
Mr Plane				
	Opening balance			3,500
Jnl 3	Receipt		3,500	—
	Closing balance			Nil
Miss Aster				
	Opening balance			(3,000)
Jnl 3a	Receipt building society		150,000	(153,000)
	Closing balance			(153,000)
Mr Gormley				
	Opening balance			(4,000)
Jnl 5	Refund to client	4,000		—
	Balance			Nil

FIRMS BANK

	£		£
open bal	10,000	31/7/00 Expenditure from cash book	3,750
Income from cash book	3,500	bal c/f	9,750
	13,500		13,500
bal b/f	9,750		

CLIENTS BANK

	£		£
open bal	15,000	31/7/00 Expenditure from cash	7,500
Income from cash book	154,000	bal c/f	161,500
	169,000		169,000
bal b/f	161,500		

INSURANCE

	£		£
Expenditure from cash book	3,750	bal c/f	3,750
bal b/f	3,750		

CLIENTS LEDGER

	£		£
Expenditure from cash book	4,000	open bal	11,000
bal c/f	161,000	Income from cash book	154,000
	165,000		165,000
		bal b/f	161,000

Updated Trial Balance

	Dr £	Cr £
Fixed assets	35,000	
WIP	18,000	
Firm's bank	9,750	
Client bank	161,500	
Client ledger		161,000
Creditors		7,500
Loan		19,000
Capital accounts		40,500
Insurance	3,750	
	228,000	228,000

(d) Accounts Certificate Information

Analysis of client ledger

	Dr £	Cr £
Mrs Stark		8,000
Mr Plane		Nil
Miss Aster		153,000
Mr Gormley		Nil
		161,000
Balance per client bank		161,500
Amounts owed to clients		161,000
Surplus of funds held		500

Suggested solutions
Chapter Thirteen: Financial management and control of a legal practice

1.

McKenzie Kelvin and Company, Solicitors
Management Report : Income and expenditure statement for the year ending 30 April 1998
: Actual v Budget

	Actual Out-turn £'000	Budgeted £'000	Variance £'000	Variance % change
Income				
Fees rendered	1,500	1,350	150	11.1%
Commission	250	225	25	11.1%
Other income	125	100	25	25%
	1,875	1,675	200	11.9%
Less: Expenses				
Staff wages and salaries	925	775	150	19.4%
Office rent and rates	80	80	—	—
Heating and lighting	35	32	3	9.4%
Office maintenance	30	30	—	—
Library, stationery and postages	75	68	7	10.3%
Telephone and fax	50	45	5	11.1%
Insurances	52	51	1	2.0%
Professional subscriptions	10	10	—	—
Travelling expenses	55	50	5	10%
Bank interest and charges	37	25	12	48%
Miscellaneous expenses	63	58	5	8.6%
Motor vehicle running costs	21	19	2	10.5%
Bad debts w/o	27	17	10	58.8%
Office equipment maintenance & repairs	35	36	(1)	(2.8%)
General expenses	61	50	11	22.0%
Depreciation charges:				
Motor vehicles	20	20	—	—
Office equipment	15	15	—	—
Office fixtures and fittings	10	10	—	—
	1,601	1,391	210	15.1%
Net profit, before appropriations	274	284	(10)	(3.5%)

The report to management should probably include reference to the following:

(1) *Income*

    (a) Overall 'Income' has increased by almost 12% over what was originally anticipated.

    (b) 'Fees rendered' and 'Commissions' have increased by 11.1% over budget expectations.

    (c) 'Other income' has shown the greatest increase, with the actual out-turn being 25% higher than budgeted income from this source.

Assuming the budget was reasonable, all of the above represent favourable variances.

(2) *Expenses*

Overall, 'Expenses' appear to be higher than budgeted. However, the increase experienced within individual expense categories is in many cases broadly consistent with the higher income levels. Indeed the percentage change in the majority of expense categories is actually below the level of increase in income. Even allowing for the favourable change in income, and the upward effects that such an increase would naturally have on expenses, the following expense categories should still be highlighted given the significance of their variances:

Expense categories	Variance—% change on budget
(a) Staff wages and salaries	19.4% increase

    (a) **Staff wages and salaries**   19.4% increase
'Staff wages and salaries' are significantly higher than what was budgeted. Increased feeing activity could explain some of this change but not all. Why this increase? Were new staff taken on during the year and/or was there a general pay increase, neither of which was anticipated? Has there been a drop in staff productivity for some reason? Has the extra income generated simply been unprofitable?

    (b) **Bank interest and charges**   48% increase
There has been a very unfavourable increase in 'bank interest and charges' over the year. Why has this occurred? Has the firm persistently breached any overdraft limit and incurred penalty charges? Is the bank levying higher interest rates and charges generally? Is the bank still competitive? Has there been an error either at the bank or in the firm's budgeting process?

    (c) **Bad debts written off**   58.8% increase
The firm has experienced a serious increase in the amount of bad debts that it is having to write off. Why is this so? Should there be a review of the firm's credit control policy? Are proper risk assessment procedures being applied before work commences? In its drive to increase fee income, have more, riskier clients been taken on? Again in retrospect, was the original figure

budgeted in respect of bad debts reasonable or should
it have been higher?

(d) General expenses   22% increase
Once more this expense category has increased
disproportionately in relation to budget and the higher
income activity. Why has this occurred? Was the
increased income obtained from unprofitable work? Is
there any slackness creeping in to the firm's cost control
practices? Have there been general increases in costs
charged by the firm's suppliers?

(3) *Net profit*

The actual net profit of £274,000 is slightly down on the budgeted figure of
£284,000, being an unfavourable variance of around 3.5%. This in itself will
probably not give cause for concern. However, it is disappointing that the
increased income has not resulted in a similar increase in overall profitability.
Further detective work is necessary to find out the underlying reasons.

2.

Frederickson and McCarthy, Solicitors
Management Report : Income and expenditure statements for the financial years
1994 and 1993
: Year-on-year comparisons

	1994 £'000	1993 £'000	Variance % change
Income			
Fees rendered	1,000	975	2.6%
Commission	250	150	66.7%
Other income	24	24	—
	1,274	1,149	10.9%
Less: Expenditure			
Staff costs: Associates	190	190	—
: Other fee earners	205	205	—
: Other staff	305	221	38%
Office rent and rates	70	68	2.9%
Heating and lighting	15	14	7.1%
Office repairs and maintenance	25	25	—
Library, stationery and postages	75	72	4.2%
Insurances	39	39	—
Repair of computer and office equipment	68	64	6.3%
Travelling expenses	38	35	8.6%
Telephone and related expenses	32	29	10.3%
Bank interest and charges	20	19	5.3%
Bad debts w/o	4	4	—
Miscellaneous expenses, including depreciation	65	62	4.8%
	1,151	1,047	9.9%
Net profit, before appropriations	123	102	20.6%

Commentary

(a)   'Net profit before appropriations to partners' has improved by 20.6% between 1993 and 1994, rising from £102,000 to £123,000 respectively.

(b)   Although total 'Income' has increased by 10.9%, this has largely been due to the substantial increase in commissions which the firm has received. 'Commissions' have increased by approximately 66.7% over the year, from £150,000 in 1993 to £250,000 in 1994. Is this sustainable? Is it possible to improve this income stream still further if the firm commits more resources to generating this type of income. What is the profit margin on this work—have the related costs increased in line/disproportionately with the change in the level of income? 'Fees rendered' has experienced a 2.6% rise between the two periods. What have the general trading conditions been like for the firm? The answer to this question should put the increase of 2.6% into some form of perspective.

(c)   'Other income' has not altered. (Again, a knowledge of the general background trading conditions facing the firm will dictate the true level of achievement of the firm in this respect).

(d)   Total 'Expenditure' has increased by approximately 9.9%, which is broadly consistent with the increase in total income. (Some expenses will be fixed and will be largely independent of fluctuations in business activity. For example, 'office rent and rates'. Other forms of expenditure will tend to vary in a manner consistent with changes in business activity. For example, the costs of telephones, staff travel, stationery and postages etc. All significant changes must be highlighted and their courses investigated, if not readily apparent).

(e)   'Staff costs: other staff' have increased by 38% between the years 1993 and 1994. Is this unexpected? Were more clerical staff recruited? Was the firm understaffed in this respect in 1993 and have recent appointments simply brought such costs up to a more realistic and sustainable level? How has the ratio of 'Clerical Staff:Fee earning staff' changed over a similar time scale? Is the firm now overstaffed with clerical/administrative personnel?

(f)   Are the increases experienced under the other expense categories reasonable, or have there been disproportional, large, and/or unexpected changes which should have their causes investigated further?

Date : --/--/--

3.

McGrowther James and Co (Solicitors)
Revised Forecast Cash Flow Statement for the Period 1 January to 31 December 1998

	Jan £	Feb £	March £	April £	May £	June £	July £	Aug £	Sept £	Oct £	Nov £	Dec £
Cash Inflows												
Fees recovered	20,000	23,000	30,000	32,000	32,000	30,000	28,000	25,000	34,000	32,000	28,000	25,000
VAT on fees recovered	3,500	4,025	5,250	5,600	5,600	5,250	4,900	4,375	5,950	5,600	4,900	4,375
Other cash inflows (VAT exempt)	2,500	1,575	1,250	3,400	1,400	1,750	4,100	1,625	1,550	4,000	1,600	1,625
Total cash inflows	26,000	28,600	36,500	41,000	39,000	37,000	37,000	31,000	41,500	41,600	34,500	31,000
Less: Cash Outflows												
Wages and salaries	15,600	15,600	16,000	16,250	16,250	16,000	15,600	15,600	16,500	16,250	15,600	18,000
Property costs	1,167	2,333	—	—	3,500	—	—	3,667	—	—	4,000	—
Other office running costs	1,500	1,500	1,500	1,500	1,500	1,500	1,550	1,550	1,550	1,550	1,550	1,550
VAT paid on expenses	825	225	225	825	225	225	835	235	235	835	235	235
Disbursements	100	100	100	100	100	100	100	100	100	100	100	100
Cash outflows, sub-total (i)	19,192	19,758	17,825	18,675	21,575	17,825	18,085	21,152	18,385	18,735	21,485	19,885
Taxes												
Quarterly VAT payment	14,000	—	6,475	—	—	15,175	—	—	13,230	—	—	15,145
Bi-annual tax payment	15,500	—	—	—	—	—	15,500	—	—	—	—	—
Cash outflows, sub-total (ii)	29,500	—	6,475	—	—	15,175	15,500	—	13,230	—	—	15,145
Net Cash Flow Before Partners' Drawings	(22,692)	8,842	12,200	22,325	17,425	4,000	3,415	9,848	9,885	22,865	13,015	(4,030)
Less: Partners' drawings	6,000	6,000	6,000	6,000	6,000	6,000	8,000	8,000	8,000	8,000	8,000	8,000
Net Cash Flow After Partners' Drawings	(28,692)	2,842	6,200	16,325	11,425	(2,000)	(4,585)	1,848	1,885	14,865	5,015	(12,030)
Cumulative Cash Position:												
Opening bank/cash	5,000	(23,692)	(20,850)	(14,650)	1,675	13,100	11,100	6,515	8,363	10,248	25,113	30,128
Net cash flow for the month	(28,692)	2,842	6,200	16,325	11,425	(2,000)	(4,585)	1,848	1,885	14,865	5,015	(12,030)
Closing bank/cash	(23,692)	(20,850)	(14,650)	1,675	13,100	11,100	6,515	8,363	10,248	25,113	30,128	18,098

4.

McDonald Evans and Co (Solicitors)
Forecast Cash Flow Statement for the Period 1 January 1998 to 31 December 1998

	Jan £	Feb £	March £	April £	May £	June £	July £	Aug £	Sept £	Oct £	Nov £	Dec £
Cash Inflows												
Fees received	10,000	13,000	16,000	16,000	16,000	12,000	12,000	8,000	16,000	16,000	8,000	6,000
Commissions received	250	250	250	250	450	450	450	250	250	250	250	250
	10,250	13,250	16,250	16,250	16,450	12,450	12,450	8,250	16,250	16,250	8,250	6,250
Less: Cash Outflows												
Staff wages	1,500	1,500	1,500	1,500	2,500	1,500	1,500	1,500	1,500	1,500	1,500	2,500
Office rent and rates	2,550	–	–	2,550	–	–	2,550	–	–	2,550	–	–
Vehicle and other travel expenses	750	750	750	750	750	750	750	750	750	750	750	750
General office expenses	1,200	1,200	1,200	1,200	1,200	1,200	1,200	1,200	1,200	1,200	1,200	1,200
Partners' taxes	15,000	–	–	–	–	–	15,000	–	–	–	–	–
	21,000	3,450	3,450	6,000	4,450	3,450	21,000	3,450	3,450	6,000	3,450	4,450
Net Cash Flow Before Drawings	(10,750)	9,800	12,800	10,250	12,000	9,000	(8,550)	4,800	12,800	10,250	4,800	1,800
Less: Partners' drawings	4,000	4,000	4,000	4,000	4,000	4,000	4,000	4,000	4,000	4,000	4,000	4,000
Net Cash Flow After Drawings	(14,750)	5,800	8,800	6,250	8,000	5,000	(12,550)	800	8,800	6,250	800	(2,200)
Cumulative Cash Position:												
Opening bank/cash	(25,000)	(39,750)	(33,950)	(25,150)	(18,900)	(10,900)	(5,900)	(18,450)	(17,650)	(8,850)	(2,600)	(1,800)
Net Cash Flow for the month	(14,750)	5,800	8,800	6,250	8,000	5,000	(12,550)	800	8,800	6,250	800	(2,200)
Closing bank/cash	(39,750)	(33,950)	(25,150)	(18,900)	(10,900)	(5,900)	(18,450)	(17,650)	(8,850)	(2,600)	(1,800)	(4,000)

5.

(a)

Smith and Bryce, Solicitors
Forecast VAT Flows for the period 1 January to 31 December 1997

	Jan £	Feb £	March £	April £	May £	June £	July £	Aug £	Sept £	Oct £	Nov £	Dec £
VAT Inflow												
VAT recovered on fees	—	—	875	1,225	1,750	2,625	2,625	2,625	3,500	4,375	4,375	3,500
VAT Outflows												
Recoverable VAT paid on :												
Office rental payments	525			525			525			525		
Office deposit	175											
Office fixtures and fittings	700											
Equipment	1,750											
Vehicle running and other travel costs/Office expenses	150	150	150	150	150	150	200	200	200	200	200	200
	3,300	150	150	675	150	150	725	200	200	725	200	200
Net Monthly (Outflow)/Inflow	(3,300)	(150)	725	550	1,600	2,475	1,900	2,425	3,300	3,650	4,175	3,300
Quarterly VAT Receipt/ From/Payment to Customs & Excise	—	—	3,450 Receipt	—	—	2,875 Payment	—	—	6,800 Payment	—	—	11,125 Payment

(b)

Smith and Bryce, Solicitors
Forecast Cash Flow Statement for the period 1 January to 31 December 1997

	Jan £	Feb £	March £	April £	May £	June £	July £	Aug £	Sept £	Oct £	Nov £	Dec £
Cash Inflows												
Income of capital	10,000	—										
Fee income	—	—	5,000	7,000	10,000	15,000	15,000	15,000	20,000	25,000	25,000	20,000
VAT recovered on fees	—	—	875	1,225	1,750	2,625	2,625	2,625	3,500	4,375	4,375	3,500
Other cash income (VAT exempt)	—	—	100	100	250	250	250	350	350	350	350	350
Total Cash Inflow	10,000	—	5,975	8,325	12,000	17,875	17,875	17,975	23,850	29,725	29,725	23,850
Less: Cash Outflows												
Staff wages, total cost	1,000	1,000	1,000	2,500	2,500	2,500	2,500	2,500	2,500	2,500	2,500	2,500
Deposit on office property	1,000	—	—	—	—	—	—	—	—	—	—	—
Quarterly office rental payment	3,000	—	—	3,000	—	—	3,000	—	—	3,000	—	—
Insurances and prof subs	2,250	—	—	—	—	—	—	—	—	—	—	—
Purchase of car	14,100	—	—	—	—	—	—	—	—	—	—	—
Vehicle running and other travel costs/Office expenses	1,000	1,000	1,000	1,000	1,000	1,000	1,300	1,300	1,300	1,300	1,300	1,300
Office fixtures and fittings	4,000	—	—	—	—	—	—	—	—	—	—	—
Purchase of office equipment	10,000	—	—	—	—	—	—	—	—	—	—	—
Recoverable VAT paid	3,300	150	150	675	150	150	725	200	200	725	200	200
Cash outflows, sub-total (i)	39,650	2,150	2,150	7,175	3,650	3,650	7,525	4,000	4,000	7,525	4,000	4,000
Less: Taxes												
Quarterly VAT (receipt)/payment	—	—	(3,450)	—	—	2,875	—	—	6,800	—	—	11,125
Bi-annual tax payment	—	—	—	—	—	—	—	—	—	—	—	—
Cash outflow, sub-total (ii)	—	—	(3,450)	—	—	2,875	—	—	6,800	—	—	11,125
Net Cash Flow Before Drawings	(29,650)	(2,150)	7,275	1,150	8,350	11,350	10,350	13,975	13,050	22,200	25,725	8,725
Less: Drawings	—	—	(2,000)	(2,000)	(2,000)	(2,000)	(4,000)	(4,000)	(4,000)	(6,000)	(6,000)	(6,000)
Net Cash Flow After Drawings	(29,650)	(2,150)	7,275	(850)	6,350	9,350	6,350	9,975	9,050	16,200	19,725	2,725
Cumulative Cash Position:												
Opening bank/cash	NIL	(29,650)	(31,800)	(24,525)	(25,375)	(19,025)	(9,675)	(3,325)	6,650	15,700	31,900	51,625
Net cash flow for the month	(29,650)	(2,150)	7,275	(850)	6,350	9,350	6,350	9,975	9,050	16,200	19,725	2,725
Closing bank/cash	(29,650)	(31,800)	(24,525)	(25,375)	(19,025)	(9,675)	(3,325)	6,650	15,700	31,900	51,625	54,350

The partners should contact their bank and request a slightly higher overdraft than the £30,000 previously arranged. Although it is predicted that the maximum overdraft required will be £31,800 in February, it may be prudent for the firm to request an overdraft facility of, say, £35,000 to allow for unforeseen eventualities.

6.

Jefferson MacInroy & Co, Solicitors
5-Year Summary Analysis of Expenses, 1995 to 1999 inclusive,
Using 1988 as the Base Year

	Year				
Expense category	*1999* %	*1998* %	*1997* %	*1996* %	*1995* **Base Year** %
Office wages and salaries	119.5	111.1	108.1	103.7	100
Rates and insurance	103.1	101.9	100.4	100.4	100
Stationery	113.2	111.9	112.4	111.4	100
Sundry expenses	103.4	103.0	101.9	100.6	100
Telephone and postages	123.8	111.1	105.2	102.2	100
Bank interest and charges	146.1	123.6	106.7	101.1	100
Bad debts, w/o	140.0	133.3	116.7	116.7	100
Depreciation					
—office premises	100.0	100.0	100.0	100.0	100
—office furniture & fittings	142.8	155.0	175.0	87.5	100
Totals	118.8	112.0	109.8	102.8	100

Commentary

(a) 'Office wages and salaries' have seen a fairly steady increase over the period, with the greatest increase between 1998 and 1999. Overall, this cost has increased by 19.5% since 1995. Is this to be expected? If the firm's income was examined for the same period, has the change been consistent with changes in wages and salaries? Has there been a reduction in staff productivity, (or even an increase) once fee income is considered?

(b) 'Stationery' costs have increased over the period by 13.2%. However, since 1996 stationery costs have fluctuated within a reasonable band. The main increase was between 1995 and 1996. Is this explainable?

(c) 'Telephone and postages' has increased by 23.8% since 1988. Again, the rise should be questioned relative to general business activity. The largest rise was between 1998 and 1999. Once more, is this reasonable?

(d) 'Bank interest and charges' has risen by 46.1% since 1995. This item of expense is worthy of further investigation. Is the increase reasonable or is the bank over-charging?

(e) 'Bad debts written off' are now at a level 40% above what they were in 1995. Is this reasonable in the circumstances or is the firm needing to review its credit control, and/or risk management procedures?

(f) 'Depreciation—office furniture and fittings'. This cost has fluctuated considerably since 1995. Has the depreciation policy in respect of this asset been followed consistently over the period under review? If so, this indicates that there must have been new office furniture and fittings purchased around 1997.

Generally, it should be noted that it is difficult to interpret such results in the absence of further information relating to the business and its economic environment.

7.

Frederickson and McCarthy, Solicitors

Management Report : Summary of Key Business Ratios in respect of the 5-year period, 1993 to 1997 inclusive

Ratio	Year				
	1997	1996	1995	1994	1993
(i) ROCE—(a) before deduction of partners' notional salaries	57.1%	57%	55.3%	19.2%	19.8%
(b) after deduction of partners' notional salaries	25%	26.8%	25%	3.6%	0.4%
(ii) Net Profit Percentage— (a) before deduction of partners' notional salaries	19%	22%	21.6%	9.6%	8.9%
(b) after deduction of partners' notional salaries	8.3%	10.4%	9.8%	1.8%	Negligible
(iii) Average fees per partner	£270,000	£250,000	£250,000	£200,000	£195,000
(iv) Average fees per fee earner (including partners)	£90,000	£83,333	£83,333	£66,667	£65,000
(v) Total expenses as percentage of turnover	81%	78%	78.4%	90.3%	91.1%
(vi) Turnover per employee	£56,133	£51,500	£50,833	£42,467	£45,960
(vii) Net profit per employee	£10,667	£11,333	£10,967	£4,100	£4,080
(viii) Partnership solvency/capital adequacy test	50.9%	56.8%	56.9%	60.7%	56.6%
(ix) Current ratio	1.51	1.77	1.68	1.75	1.57
(x) Acid text ratio	0.65	0.74	0.64	0.63	0.39
(xi) Debtor days	87.6 days	82.9 days	73 days	91.2 days	56.2 days
(xii) Interest cover	5 times	6.4 times	6.2 times	1.2 times	0.1 times

Commentary

Notwithstanding the quantity of financial information available to assist in the interpretation of the firm's progress over the five-year period, further in-depth knowledge of the business and of the general economic environment in which it operates is vital in order that the statistical results and ratios can be considered in their proper perspective. Furthermore, the results of the Law Society of Scotland's annual inter-firm comparison should help provide benchmarks against which Frederickson and McCarthy's own performance could be judged. As previously mentioned in the main text, legal firms will get access to the results of this survey only if they themselves contribute to the initial survey carried out each year.

Bearing in mind the above caveat, the information which is available through the question is still sufficient to at least provide a basic starting point to assist in measuring the firm's progress, in diagnosing its strengths and weaknesses and consequently in planning future courses of action.

A full analysis of all of the information given in relation to this task could result in a report several pages long, with ease. However, the key issues may be summarised as follows:

(a) *Profitability*

Profitability has generally improved over the 5-year period although it has tailed off in recent years (see the 'net profit percentage', 'ROCE', 'net profit per employee', 'net profit, before appropriations' (as in **Illustration 13.11**), and the original figures given in **Illustration 13.10**).

Expenses have fluctuated over the years. The firm began the period under review in a relatively poor position, improved over the years before suffering an apparent setback in 1997 (see 'total expenses as a percentage of turnover', look at 'staff costs' between 1997 and 1996 in **Illustrations 13.10/11/9**).

(b) *Financial Standing/Solvency/Liquidity etc*

Generally, the firm appears in a secure financial position (see 'partnership solvency/capital adequacy', 'current ratio', **Illustration 13.12** and the narrative of this question relating to the firm's balance sheets) although some aspects do give cause for concern (see 'Acid test', 'debtor days', and again the source information on the firm's balance sheets).

The firm should review its WIP since it appears very large relative to fees rendered for example, or indeed relative to other balance sheet items. (Also, see the Law Society of Scotland's Guidance Notes on capital adequacy and partnership profitability given in the Appendices. Frederickson and McCarthy's balance sheet would be subject to adjustment in terms of its WIP if the Law Society's provisions in this respect are followed, before the calculation of its key ratios).

The firm should also review its credit control policy since it appears that its debtors are getting almost three months to settle invoices, which is too long a period.

Finally, the various management reports mentioned earlier in Chapter Thirteen could provide information to further explain the reasons behind the firm's present position relative to previous years. For example, see the section in the text which deals with fee analysis by fee earners/work category, analysis of WIP, debtors ageing schedules etc.

Appendix 1

SOLICITORS (SCOTLAND) ACCOUNTS RULES 1997

RULES MADE BY THE COUNCIL OF THE LAW SOCIETY OF SCOTLAND
UNDER SECTIONS 34, 35 AND 36 OF THE SOLICITORS (SCOTLAND) ACT 1980
ON 25th APRIL 1997.

Citation, commencement and repeal

1(1)　These Rules may be cited as the Solicitors (Scotland) Accounts Rules 1997.

(2)　These Rules shall come into operation on the 1st day of January 1998 and from that date the Solicitors (Scotland) Accounts Rules 1996 shall cease to have effect.

Interpretation

2(1)　In these Rules, unless the context otherwise requires:

'the Act' means the Solicitors (Scotland) Act 1980;

'Certificate' and 'accounting period' shall have the meanings respectively assigned to them in the Solicitors (Scotland) Accounts Certificate Rules in force from time to time;

'balance his books' means to prepare and bring to a balance a Trial Balance being a schedule or list of balances both debit and credit extracted from the accounts in both firm and client ledgers and including the cash and bank balances from the cash book;

'bank' means the Bank of England, the National Savings Bank, the Post Office in the exercise of its powers to provide banking services and an authorised institution within the meaning of the Banking Act 1987 and which operates within the bankers automated clearing system provided however that a recognised bank not operating within the bankers automated clearing system may be approved by the Council for the purposes of this sub-section;

'client account' means a current, deposit, or savings account or other form of account or a deposit receipt at a branch of a bank in the United Kingdom in the name of the solicitor in the title of which the word 'client', 'trustee', 'trust', or other fiduciary term appears and includes an account or a deposit receipt with a bank, a deposit, share or other account with a Building Society authorised under the Building Societies Act 1986, a current or general account with a Building Society operating such an account within the bankers automated clearing system or an account showing sums on loan to a local authority being in such cases in name of the solicitor for a client whose name is specified in the title of the account or receipt;

'clients' money' means money (not belonging to him) received by a solicitor whether as a solicitor or as a trustee in the course of his practice;

'the Council' means the Council of the Society;

'Faculty' means a faculty or society of solicitors in Scotland incorporated by Royal Charter or otherwise formed in accordance with law, but does not include the Society;

'the Keeper' means the Keeper of the Registers of Scotland;

'local authority' means a local authority within the meaning of the Local Government etc (Scotland) Act 1994;

'Money Laundering Regulations' means the Money Laundering Regulations 1993 (SI 1993/1933), and

'Regulation' means a regulation of the Money Laundering Regulations,

'relevant financial business' has the meaning given by Regulation 4, and ,

'other business' means any business which is not relevant financial business;

'partner' means a member of a firm of solicitors or a director or member of an incorporated practice;

'print out' means a printed or typewritten copy of any account or other information stored in a computer;

'the Society' means the Law Society of Scotland, established under the Act;

'solicitor' means a solicitor holding a practising certificate under the Act and includes a firm of solicitors and an incorporated practice under Section 34(1)(a) of the Act.

(2)   The Interpretation Act 1978 applies to the interpretation of these Rules as it applies to the interpretation of an Act of Parliament.

Rules not to apply to solicitors in certain employments

3   These Rules shall not apply to a solicitor who is in any of the employments mentioned in sub-section (4)(a), (b) and (c) of Section 35(1) of the Act so far as regards monies received, held or paid by him in the course of that employment.

Clients' money to be paid into Client Account

4(1)   Subject to the provisions of Rule 7 every solicitor shall:-
   (a)   ensure that at all times the sum at the credit of the client account, or where there are more such accounts than one, the total of the sums at the credit of those accounts, shall not be less than the total of the clients' money held by the solicitor; and
   (b)   pay into a client account without delay any sum of money exceeding £50 held for or received from or on behalf of a client.

(2)   Where money is held by the solicitor in a client account in which the name of the client is specified and where no money is due to that client by the solicitor or the amount due is less than the amount in the specified client account, the sum in that account or, as the case may be, the excess, shall not be treated as clients' money for the purposes of paragraph (1)(a) of this Rule.

(3)   Nothing herein contained shall:
   (a)   empower a solicitor, without the express written authority of the client, to deposit any money held by the solicitor for that client with a bank or on

share, deposit or other account with a building society or on loan account with a local authority in name of the solicitor for that client, except on such terms as will enable the amount of the share or deposit or loan or any part thereof to be uplifted or withdrawn on notice not exceeding one calendar month;

(b)   relieve a solicitor of his responsibility to the client to ensure that all sums belonging to that client and held in a client account in terms of these Rules are available when required for that client or for that client's purpose; and

(c)   preclude the overdrawing by a solicitor of a client account in which the name of the client for whom it is held is specified where that client has given written authority to overdraw, and an overdraft on such account shall not be taken into account to ensure compliance with paragraph (1)(a) of this Rule.

Other payments to client account

5   There may be paid into a client account:

(a)   such money belonging to the solicitor as may be necessary for the purpose of opening the account or required to ensure compliance with Rule 4(1)(a); and

(b)   money to replace any sum which may by mistake or accident have been withdrawn from the account.

Drawings from client account

6(1)   So long as money belonging to one client is not withdrawn without his written authority for the purpose of meeting a payment to or on behalf of another client, there may be drawn from a client account:

(a)   money required for payment to or on behalf of a client;

(b)   money required for or to account of payment of a debt due to the solicitor by a client or in or to account of repayment of money expended by the solicitor on behalf of a client;

(c)   money drawn on a client's authority;

(d)   money properly required for or to account of payment of the solicitor's professional account against a client which has been debited to the ledger account of the client in the solicitor's books and where a copy of said account has been rendered;

(e)   money for transfer to a separate client account kept or to be kept for the client only;

(f)   money which may have been paid into the account under paragraph (a) of Rule 5 and which is no longer required to ensure compliance with Rule 4(1)(a); and

(g)   money which may by mistake or accident have been paid into the account.

(2)   For the purposes of paragraph (1)(b) of this Rule and of Rule 7(e) hereof a debt due to the solicitor by the client shall not include dues payable in respect of deeds

which have been sent to the Keeper for recording or registration until receipt by the solicitor of the Keeper's invoice in respect thereof.

(3) Where money drawn from a client account by cheque is payable to a person's account with any bank or building society, the cash book and ledger entries relating thereto and said cheque shall include the name or account number of the person whose account is to be credited with the payment.

Exceptions from Rule 4

7   Notwithstanding any of the provisions of these Rules, a solicitor shall not be obliged to pay into a client account, but shall be required to record in his books, clients' money held or received by him:

 (a) in the form of cash which is without delay paid in cash to the client or a third party on the client's behalf,

 (b) in the form of a cheque or draft or other bill of exchange which is endorsed over to the client or to a third party on the client's behalf and which is not passed by the solicitor through a bank account;

 (c) which he pays without delay into a separate bank, building society or local authority deposit account opened or to be opened in name of the client or of some person named by the client;

 (d) which the client for his own convenience has requested the solicitor in writing to withhold from such account;

 (e) for or to account of payment of a debt due to the solicitor from the client or in repayment in whole or in part of money expended by the solicitor on behalf of the client;

 (f) expressly on account of a professional account incurred by the client, or as an agreed fee or to account of an agreed fee for business done for the client where a copy of said account has been rendered; or

 (g) in the form of a cheque, draft or other bill of exchange payable to a third party on behalf of a client which relates to the consideration in relation to a transaction involving heritable property.

Bridging Loans

8   A solicitor shall not enter into or maintain any contract or arrangement with a bank or other lender in terms of which the solicitor may draw down loan or overdraft facilities in his name for behoof of clients unless:

(1)   the solicitor shall, in every case before drawing down any sums in terms of such contract or arrangement, have intimated in writing to the bank or other lender:

 (a) the name and present address of the client for whom the loan or overdraft facilities are required; and

 (b) the arrangements for repayment of the loan or overdraft facilities; and

(2)   the contract or arrangement does not impose personal liability for repayment of any such loan or overdraft facilities on the solicitor.

Borrowing from clients

9 A solicitor shall not borrow money from his client unless his client is in the business of lending money or his client has been independently advised in regard to the making of the loan.

Prohibition on solicitor acting for lender to the solicitor or connected persons

10(1) A solicitor shall not act for a lender in the constitution, variation, assignation or discharge of a standard security securing a loan which has been advanced or is to be advanced to:

  (a) the solicitor,
  (b) the spouse of the solicitor,
  (c) any partner of the solicitor,
  (d) any incorporated practice of which the solicitor or his spouse is a member,
  (e) the spouse of any such partner,
  (f) any company in which any person specified in sub-paragraphs (a) to (e) inclusive and (g) of this paragraph holds shares, whether directly or indirectly, other than a holding amounting to not more than 5% of the issued shares in a public company quoted on a recognised stock exchange, or
  (g) any partnership of which any of the persons specified in sub-paragraphs (a) to (e) inclusive of this paragraph is a partner, and, for the avoidance of doubt, Rule 5(1)(f) of the Solicitors (Scotland) Practice Rules 1986 shall not apply to any such loan.

(2) For the purposes of this Rule 'loan' shall include an obligation *ad factum praestandum* or any obligation to pay money and 'lender' shall include any person to whom said obligation is owed.

(3) This Rule shall not apply if:
  (a) the lender to any of the persons specified in paragraph (1) is the solicitor, or
  (b) the borrower's obligations under the Standard Security have been fully implemented before a discharge is obtained from the lender.

(4) The Council shall have power to waive the provisions of paragraph 1(f) and (g) of this Rule in any particular circumstances or case.

Powers of Attorney

11(1) This Rule shall, subject to paragraph (2) below, apply to monies received or payments made by a solicitor by virtue of any Power of Attorney in his favour.

(2) In the event of any Power of Attorney granted in favour of a solicitor continuing to have effect by virtue of section 71 of the Law Reform (Miscellaneous Provisions) (Scotland) Act 1990 any money of the granter held or received by the solicitor shall be clients' money.

(3) Every solicitor shall deliver to the Council a list of any Powers of Attorney in the solicitor's favour held or granted during an accounting period, the list to be as set

out in the Certificate set out in the Solicitors (Scotland) Accounts Certificate Rules 1997 or such other terms as the Council may from time to time prescribe.

Accounts required to be kept in books of solicitor

12(1)   A solicitor shall at all times keep properly written up such books and accounts as are necessary:

- (a)   to show all his dealing with:
  - (i)   clients' money held or received or paid or in anyway intromitted with by him;
  - (ii)   any other money dealt with by him through a client account;
  - (iii)   any bank overdrafts or loans procured by him in his own name for behoof of a client or clients; and
  - (iv)   any other money held by the solicitor in a separate account in the title of which the client's name is specified; and
- (b)   (i)   to show separately in respect of each client all money of the categories specified in subparagraph (a) of this paragraph which is received, held or paid by him on account of that client; and
  - (ii)   to distinguish all money of the said categories received, held or paid by him from any other money received, held or paid by him.

(2)   Without prejudice to paragraph (1) above, this Rule shall apply to money received or payments made by a solicitor by virtue of any Power of Attorney in his favour.

(3)   All dealings referred to in paragraph (1) of this Rule shall be recorded:
- (a)   in a clients' cash book, or a clients' column of a cash book, or
- (b)   in a record of sums transferred from the ledger account of one client to that of another;

as may be appropriate, and in addition in a clients' ledger or a clients' column of a ledger.

(4)   Every solicitor shall:
- (a)   at all times keep properly written up such books and accounts as are necessary to show the true financial position of his practice; and
- (b)   balance his books monthly and on the last day of the accounting period.

(5)   The 'books', 'accounts', 'ledger' and 'records' referred to in these Rules shall be deemed to include loose-leaf books and such cards or other permanent records as are necessary for the operation of any system of book-keeping, mechanical or computerised.

(6)   Where a solicitor maintains the accounts required by these Rules on a computerised system which does not rely on a visible ledger card for its operation such system must be such that:
- (a)   an immediate printout can be obtained of any account notwithstanding that immediate visual access is available; and
- (b)   all accounts which for any reason may require to be removed from the working store of the system must before removal be copied on to a storage medium which will enable a visual record of the detailed entries therein to

be produced and be filed in alphabetical or other suitable order, indexed and retained for the period set out in paragraph (7) of this Rule.

(7)   A solicitor shall preserve for at least ten years from the date of the last entry therein all books and accounts kept by him under this Rule or a copy thereof in a form which will enable a visible record of the detailed entries therein to be produced from such a copy.

Client bank statements to be regularly reconciled

13(1)   Every solicitor shall within one month of the coming into force of these Rules or of his commencing practice on his own account (either alone or in partnership or as an incorporated practice), and thereafter at intervals not exceeding one month cause the balance between the client bank lodged and drawn columns of his cash book or the balance on his client bank ledger account as the case may be to be agreed with his client bank statements and shall retain such reconciliation statements showing this agreement for a period of three years from the dates they were respectively carried out.

(2)   On the same date or dates specified in paragraph (1) of this Rule every solicitor shall extract from his clients' ledger a list of balances due by him to clients and prepare a statement comparing the total of the said balances with the reconciled balance in the client bank account and retain such lists of balances and statements for a period of three years from the dates they were respectively carried out.

Client funds invested in specified accounts

14(1)   Every solicitor shall within three months of the coming into force of these Rules or of his commencing practice on his own account (either alone or in partnership or as an incorporated practice), and thereafter at intervals not exceeding three months and coinciding with the date of a reconciliation in terms of Rule 13 hereof, cause the balance between the client deposited and withdrawn columns of his cash book or the balance on his client invested funds ledger account as the case may be to be agreed with his client passbooks, building society printouts, special deposit accounts, local authority deposits, joint deposits or other statements or certificates and shall retain such reconciliation statements showing this agreement for a period of three years from the dates they were respectively carried out.

(2)   On the same date or dates specified in paragraph (1) of this Rule every solicitor shall extract from his client ledger a list of funds invested by him in his name for specified clients and prepare a statement comparing the total of the said balances with the reconciled investment funds and retain such lists of balances and statements for a period of three years from the dates they were respectively carried out.

Interest to be earned for a client

15(1)   Where a solicitor holds money for or on account of a client and, having regard to the amount of such money and the length of time for which it or any part of it is likely to be held, it is reasonable that interest should be earned for the client, the solicitor shall so soon as practicable place money or, as the case may be, such part thereof, in a separate interest bearing client account in the title of which the client's name is specified and shall account to the client for any interest earned thereon, failing which the solicitor shall pay to the client out of his own money a sum equivalent to the interest which would have accrued for the benefit of the client if the sum he ought to have placed in such an interest bearing client account under this Rule had been so placed.

(2)   Without prejudice to the generality of paragraph (1) of this Rule it shall be deemed reasonable that interest should be earned for a client from the date on which a solicitor receives for or on account of the client a sum of money not less than £500 which at the time of its receipt is unlikely within two months thereafter to be either wholly disbursed or reduced by payments to a sum less than £500.

(3)   Without prejudice to any other remedy which may be available, any client who feels aggrieved that interest has not been paid under this Rule shall be entitled to require the solicitor to obtain a certificate from the Society as to whether or not interest ought to have been earned and, if so, the amount of such interest, and upon the issue of such certificate any interest certified to be due shall be payable by the solicitor to the client.

(4)   Nothing in this Rule shall affect any arrangement in writing, whenever made, between a solicitor and his client as to the application of a client's money or interest thereon provided such arrangement was made prior to the said application.

(5)   For the purposes of this Rule only, money held by a solicitor for or on account of a client:
   (a)   for the purpose of paying dues in respect of deeds which have been sent to the Keeper for recording or registration; or
   (b)   for or to account of the solicitor's professional account where said account has been rendered shall not be regarded as clients' money.

Money Laundering

16(1)   Every solicitor shall in respect of all other business carried on by the solicitor comply with the provisions of the Money Laundering Regulations as if such other business constituted relevant financial business, but as if:
   (a)   for the figure '1' where it appears in the second line of Regulation 7(1) there were substituted the figure '2'; and
   (b)   Regulation 12(4)(a) were deleted.

(2)   For the avoidance of doubt, this Rule is without prejudice to the application of the Money Laundering Regulations to relevant financial business.

Investigation of accounts on behalf of Council

17(1)   To enable them to ascertain whether or not these Rules are being complied with, the Council may by written notice require any solicitor to produce at a time to be fixed by the Council and at a place to be fixed by the Council, or in the option of the solicitor at his place of business, his books of account, bank passbooks, loose-leaf bank statements, deposit receipts, documents of joint deposit, building society passbooks, local authority deposits, separate statements of bank overdrafts or loans procured by him in his own name for behoof of a client or clients, statements of account, vouchers and any other necessary documents including magnetic storage disks and microfilm records and any Powers of Attorney in his favour (in this Rule referred to as 'books and other documents') for the inspection of a person appointed by the Council being a professional accountant.

(2)   A solicitor duly required to do so under paragraph (1) of this Rule shall produce such books and other documents at the time and place fixed.

(3)   The person appointed by the Council to make the inspection shall investigate the solicitor's books and other documents with the object of ascertaining whether or not these Rules are being complied with by the solicitor, and thereafter shall report to the Council upon the result of his inspection.

(4)   In any case in which a Faculty request that an inspection should be made under this Rule of the books and other documents of a solicitor, such Faculty shall transmit to the Council a statement containing all relevant information in their possession and a request that such an inspection be made.

(5)   A written notice given by the Council to a solicitor under paragraph (1) and where appropriate paragraph (6) of this Rule shall be signed by the Secretary, a Deputy Secretary or the Chief Accountant of the Society and sent by recorded delivery service to the solicitor at his place of business as defined in the Constitution of the Society or in the case of a solicitor who has ceased to hold a practising certificate at his last known address, and shall be deemed to have been received by the solicitor within forty-eight hours of the time of posting. In the case of a firm or incorporated practice the written notice shall be given to each person who is known to the Council to be a partner of the firm or a director of the incorporated practice and it shall not be necessary to give notice to the firm or incorporated practice also.

(6)   Where following an inspection of the books and other documents of a solicitor in terms of paragraph (1) of this Rule it appears to the Council that the solicitor has not complied with these Rules and the Council instructs a further inspection of the books and other documents of the solicitor, the Council may by written notice require the solicitor to pay to the Council such sum as may be required to meet the fees and costs incurred by the Council in carrying out such further inspection, provided always that such written notice is given to the solicitor not more than one year after the date of the inspection first referred to in this paragraph. The amount of such sum shall be fixed by the Council and intimated to the solicitor following such inspection.

(7)   It shall be the duty of a solicitor upon whom a notice in terms of paragraph (6) of this Rule has been served to make payment forthwith of the amounts so intimated.

(8)   Any sum paid to the Council in terms of paragraph (7) hereof shall accrue to the Guarantee Fund.

Application of Rules in case of firm of solicitors or incorporated practice

18(1)   Each partner of a firm of solicitors or member of an incorporated practice shall be responsible for securing compliance by the firm or incorporated practice with the provisions of these Rules.

(2)   Without prejudice to paragraph (1) of this Rule within one month of the coming into force of these Rules or of its commencing practice on its own account every firm of solicitors or incorporated practice shall designate one or more of the partners of the firm or the members of the incorporated practice as Designated Cashroom Partner or Partners who will be responsible for the supervision of the staff and systems employed by the firm or incorporated practice to carry out the provisions of these Rules and for securing compliance by the firm or incorporated practice with the provisions of these Rules.

(3)   Every firm of solicitors or incorporated practice shall deliver to the Council a Certificate in the form as set out in the Solicitors (Scotland) Accounts Certificate Rules 1997 or in such terms as the Council may prescribe listing the name or names of the Designated Cashroom Partner or Partners and the period or periods in respect of which he was, or they were, designated during the accounting period in respect of which the Certificate is delivered.

Savings of rights of solicitor against client

19   Nothing in these Rules shall deprive a solicitor of or prejudice him with reference to any recourse or right in law, whether by way of lien, set-off, counter-claim, charge or otherwise, against monies standing to the credit of a client account or against monies due to a client by a third party.

Index for the Solicitors (Scotland) Accounts Rules 1997

APPENDIX 2

SOLICITORS (SCOTLAND)
ACCOUNTS CERTIFICATE RULES 1997

RULES MADE BY THE COUNCIL OF THE LAW SOCIETY OF SCOTLAND UNDER SECTION 37(6) OF THE SOLICITORS (SCOTLAND) ACT 1980 ON 25th APRIL 1997.

Citation, commencement and repeal

1(1) These Rules may be cited as the Solicitors (Scotland) Accounts Certificate Rules 1997.

(2) These Rules shall come into operation on the 1st day of January 1998 and the Solicitors (Scotland) Accountant's Certificate Rules 1996 are hereby revoked but such revocation shall not affect any outstanding obligation to deliver an Accountant's Certificate in terms thereof nor the rights of the Society against any solicitor in respect of his failure to do so.

Interpretation

2(1) In these Rules, unless the context otherwise requires:
'The Accounts Rules' shall mean the Solicitors (Scotland) Accounts Rules 1997 and 'solicitor', 'clients' money', 'client account', 'balance his books', 'bank', 'the Society', 'the Council', 'Building Society', 'local authority' and 'Money Laundering Regulations' shall have the meanings respectively assigned to them therein;
'practice year' shall have the meaning assigned to it by the Solicitors (Scotland) Act 1980;
'accounting period' shall mean:
- (a) a period not exceeding six months in duration commencing with the expiry of the immediately preceding accounting period after the commencement of these Rules; or
- (b) where there is no immediately preceding accounting period a period commencing with the date on which the Accounts Rules apply to the solicitor or, having ceased to apply, apply again to that solicitor;

or

- (c) a period not exceeding 12 months which includes the date of commencement of these Rules.

'Certificate' shall mean a certificate in the form set out in the Schedule to these Rules, or in such other form as the Council may from time to time approve.

(2)   The Interpretation Act 1978 applies to the interpretation of these Rules as it applies to the interpretation of an Act of Parliament.

Obligation to deliver a Certificate

3(1)   A solicitor shall deliver to the Council within one calendar month of the completion of each accounting period a Certificate in respect of that period.

(2)   The Council may, in any case on cause satisfactory to them being shown, extend the period of one calendar month within which a Certificate is required following a balancing of books, but such extension shall in no case exceed three months from the date on which the Certificate should have been delivered.

(3)   If appropriate, the solicitor may deliver an interim style of Certificate in respect of the accounting period which includes the date of the introduction of these Rules. The period covered by the interim Certificate shall not exceed twelve months.

Who may sign a Certificate

4   The Certificate under these Rules must be signed by two partners, one of whom must be the current Designated Cashroom Partner, unless the solicitor is a sole practitioner.

Where a solicitor practises in two or more places

5   In the case of a solicitor who has two or more places of business and where separate books and accounts are maintained for each office a separate Certificate shall be submitted in respect of each such place of business. In any such case the client account balance shall be struck on the same date in respect of each place of business.

Notice to a solicitor under these Rules

6   Every notice to be given by the Council under these Rules to a solicitor shall be in writing under the hand of the Secretary or a Deputy Secretary or the Chief Accountant of the Society and sent by the recorded delivery service to the solicitor at his place of business as defined in the Constitution of the Society and shall be deemed to have been received by the solicitor within forty-eight hours of the time of posting. In the case of a firm or incorporated practice the written notice shall be given to each person who is known to the Council to be a partner of the firm or a director of the incorporated practice and it shall not be necessary to give notice to the firm or incorporated practice also.

Reservation of power of Council to require inspection of a solicitor's books

7(1)   The delivery of a Certificate to the Council in terms of these Rules shall not prejudice the power of the Council to require the inspection of a solicitor's books as provided for in Rule 17 of the Accounts Rules.

(2)   In the event of a solicitor failing to produce a Certificate timeously, the Council may instruct an inspection of the solicitor's accounting records and other documents. The inspection shall be carried out by a suitably qualified accountant with the costs being borne by the solicitor and a copy of the report shall be sent to the Society.

SCHEDULE

FORM OF INTERIM CERTIFICATE

(IN RESPECT OF AN ACCOUNTING PERIOD COMMENCING
BEFORE THE COMING INTO OPERATION OF
THE SOLICITORS (SCOTLAND) ACCOUNTS CERTIFICATE RULES 1997)

The Secretary,
The Law Society of Scotland,
26 Drumsheugh Gardens,
EDINBURGH
EH3 7YR

Dear Sir,
I /We confirm that, within the premises at (Note (a)), ...
....
being the address at which I/we carry on practice as solicitor(s) I/we have maintained the necessary books of account, bank passbooks, bank statements, deposit receipts including building society or local authority deposits, statements, deposit receipts and other accounting records required by the Solicitors (Scotland) Accounts Rules 1997 for the accounting period from .... to
....
and I/we certify, subject to the points referred to under item 4 of additional matters noted overleaf.

(Note (b))
1.   That the accounting records are up to date and balanced as at the last day of the accounting period, and
2.   That the accounting records, to the best of my/our knowledge and belief, are in accordance with the terms of the Solicitors (Scotland) Accounts Rules 1997, and
3.   That all outstanding reconciling entries noted as at the balance dates disclosed overleaf under Rules 13 and 14 have been entered in the records or confirmed as correct.
4.   That the following Powers of Attorney were held by the undernoted or granted in favour of the undernoted during the accounting period:

GRANTER   ATTORNEY   DATE GRANTED

and

5.   That during the said accounting period the Designated Cashroom Partner(s) in terms of Rule 18 of the Solicitors (Scotland) Accounts Rules 1997 was/were as follows:

NAME	DATE DESIGNATED	DATE DESIGNATION CEASED

I solemnly and sincerely declare that the information given by me in this Certificate is true to the best of my knowledge and belief.

CURRENT DESIGNATED CASHROOM PARTNER . . . .

PARTNER . . . .

                                         DATE . . . .

ADDITIONAL MATTERS

1.   Client account reconciliations as at . . . .
(Note (c))

(i)   (a) Monies held on general client account   £   £   £   £

      (b) Monies due to clients

      (c) Surplus or deficit   £   £   £   £

(ii) (a) Funds held for named clients   £   £   £   £

      (b) Monies due to named clients   £   £   £   £

2.   Firm's account balances
      Due to the firm   £   £   £   £

      Due by the firm   £   £   £   £

3.   If the assistance of an external accountant was needed to prepare this Certificate please indicate the scope of the assistance here (If none, state NONE):

(Note (d))
4.   Other matters which require to be reported:
      (If no other matters state NONE)

NOTES

(a)   State addresses of all places of business of the solicitor or firm of solicitors in respect of whom the Certificate is granted.
(b)   This balance is to be a balance of the whole books covering client and non-client accounts.
(c)   These dates are those quarterly dates required to be reconciled under the terms of Rule 14.
(d)   It is anticipated that many solicitors will instruct an external accountant to assist them in the checking of the accounting records and/or the preparation of the

Certificate in respect of Investment Business. If the services of an external accountant are required you should indicate the extent of the help offered. The following tasks are examples of the assistance which may be obtained from the accountant:

(a) The preparation of day books, ledgers and other records for clients or firm's accounting records; or

(b) Reconciling the funds position under Rules 13 and 14; or

(c) Testing for compliance with aspects of the Accounts Rules as agreed per a letter of engagement; or

(d) Balancing the client or firms accounting records; or

(e) Conducting a review of compliance with all aspects of the Accounts Rules in support of the solicitors certification of compliance with the Rules.

SCHEDULE

FORM OF CERTIFICATE

(IN RESPECT OF AN ACCOUNTING PERIOD COMMENCING ON OR AFTER THE COMING INTO OPERATION OF THE SOLICITORS (SCOTLAND) ACCOUNTS CERTIFICATE RULES 1997)

The Secretary,
The Law Society of Scotland,
26 Drumsheugh Gardens,
EDINBURGH
EH3 7YR

Dear Sir,

I /We confirm that, within the premises at (Note (a)), ... being the address at which I/we carry on practice as solicitor(s)) I/we have maintained the necessary books of account, bank passbooks, bank statements, deposit receipts including building society or local authority deposits, statements, deposit receipts and other accounting records required by the Solicitors (Scotland) Accounts Rules 1997 for the accounting period from . . . . to . . . . and I/we certify, subject to the points referred to under item 4 of additional matters noted overleaf:

(Note (b))

1. That the accounting records are up to date and balanced as at the last day of the accounting period, and

2. That the accounting records, to the best of my/our knowledge and belief, are in accordance with the terms of the Solicitors (Scotland) Accounts Rules 1997, and

3. That all outstanding reconciling entries noted as at the balance dates disclosed overleaf under Rules 13 and 14 have been entered in the records or confirmed as correct.

4. That the following Powers of Attorney were held by the undernoted or granted in favour of the undernoted during the accounting period:

GRANTER	ATTORNEY	DATE GRANTED

and

5. That during the said accounting period the Designated Cashroom Partner(s) in terms of Rule 18 of the Solicitors (Scotland) Accounts Rules 1997 was/were as follows:

NAME	DATE DESIGNATED	DATE DESIGNATION CEASED

I solemnly and sincerely declare that the information given by me in this Certificate is true to the best of my knowledge and belief.

CURRENT DESIGNATED CASHROOM PARTNER . . . .

PARTNER . . . .

DATE . . . .

ADDITIONAL MATTERS

1. Client account reconciliations as at   . . . .

(Note (c))

(i)   (a) Monies held on general client account   £   £

(b) Monies due to clients

(c) Surplus or deficit   £   £

(ii) (a) Funds held for named clients   £   £

(b) Monies due to named clients   £   £

2.   Firm's account balances
Due to the firm   £   £

Due by the firm   £   £

3.   If the assistance of an external accountant was needed to prepare this Certificate, please indicate the scope of the assistance here (If none, state NONE):
Note (d)

4.   Other matters which require to be reported:
(If no other matters state NONE)

NOTES

(a)   State addresses of all places of business of the solicitor or firm of solicitors in respect of whom the Certificate is granted.
(b)   This balance is to be a balance of the whole books covering client and non-client accounts.
(c)   These dates are those quarterly dates required to be reconciled under the terms of Rule 14.
(d)   It is anticipated that many solicitors will instruct an external accountant to assist them in the checking of the accounting records and/or the preparation of the

Certificate in respect of Investment Business. If the services of an external accountant are required you should indicate the extent of the help offered. The following tasks are examples of the assistance which may be obtained from the accountant:

1) The preparation of day books, ledgers and other records for clients or firm's accounting records; or
2) Reconciling the funds position under Rules 13 and 14; or
3) Testing for compliance with aspects of the Accounts Rules as agreed per a letter of engagement; or
4) Balancing the client or firms accounting records; or
5) Conducting a review of compliance with all aspects of the Accounts Rules in support of the solicitors certification of compliance with the Rules.

SCHEDULE

FORM OF CERTIFICATE

(IN RESPECT OF AN ACCOUNTING PERIOD FOR WHICH NO CLIENT MONIES HAVE BEEN HELD)

Name . . . .

Business Address   Home Address:

. . . .

. . . .

. . . .

Tel No: . . . .   Tel No: . . . .

Fax No: . . . .   Fax No: . . . .

I hereby confirm to the Council of the Law Society of Scotland that:

(Note 1)   (a)   I have contributed to the Guarantee Fund in respect of the practice year.

          (b)   I do/do not submit accounts to the Scottish Legal Aid Board for payment to my own account;

          (c)   I do/ do not accept instructions directly from clients;

(Note 2)   (d)   I have not handled client monies during the accounting period from: . . . . to: . . . . ;

          (e)   I keep up to date records of fees earned and expenses incurred in my practice and have balanced my books as required by Rule 12(4) of the Solicitors (Scotland) Accounts Rules 1997.

          (f)   If circumstances change with the result that I require to hold or intromit with client monies, shall immediately advise the Council.

I solemnly and sincerely declare that the information given by me in this Certificate is true to the best of my knowledge and belief.

Yours faithfully

.... (Sign Full Name)

.... (Print Full Name)

.... (Date)

Note 1. The current practice year for this figure commences on 1 November within the accounting year which includes the six month period shown at item (d);

Note 2. The accounting period must be six months or less and follow immediately on from the previous accounting period without a gap or overlap in the dates concerned.

INDEX FOR THE SOLICITORS (SCOTLAND) ACCOUNTS CERTIFICATE RULES 1997

Appendix 3

THE LAW SOCIETY OF SCOTLAND
GUIDANCE ON CAPITAL ADEQUACY

Introduction—why issue guidance on this subject?

Following a period of consultation and discussion the Guarantee Fund Committee Working Party has recommended the production of Guidance Notes on the subject of Capital Adequacy in legal practices. The Guidance Notes are thought to be a valuable and confidential method of allowing solicitors to measure their own firms financial standing. The problem of not having any standard to apply to the firm's balance sheet and profitability means that each firm is forced to make a personal decision about its level of reserves. This healthy independence has drawbacks in dealing with banks and other financial institutions because there are no opportunities for solicitors to make comparisons with other equivalent businesses.

The Law Society is increasingly aware of market pressures and tighter lending policies combining to give real problems to practices where these questions have never been faced before. The Guidance Notes are intended to help the independent firm to check on its financial health. Help and advice is also available if the standard is not being met by the practice. Telephone 0131 226 7411 and ask to speak to Leslie Cumming or one of his team on the subject of Capital Adequacy.

The Guidance Notes are intended to help solicitors to assess their financial position by fixing realistic values in areas where business optimism can traditionally over-rule prudence. It is also recognised that many solicitors have adopted conservative accounting policies in dealing with debtors and work in progress. If the test check produces a negative or poor Balance Sheet result because of these accounting policies e.g., cash based accounts or nominal work in progress values, it is recommended that a realistic value be included in the adjusted figures in order to produce the most accurate result.

The trend of the business measured consistently and regularly can be a powerful management tool. In addition to testing earlier years accounts, the ratios can be done quarterly or half-yearly to measure the rate of improvement and decline. The more regularly this check is carried out the better judgement can be made on the state of the practice's financial health.

The basic standards

The standard measures are intended to look at balance sheet ratios and profitability. The results of the tests should be considered in three stages, action being taken or advice being sought depending on the results of your firm's own calculations.

1. Is the practice solvent?

If the method of calculating the value of your Balance Sheet as set out in Schedule 1 is applied to your firm's balance sheet, does the result show a negative value? If the answer is yes, get some advice on how to deal with the situation. The position is serious and must not be ignored.

2. Are the capital reserves inadequate?

The standard measures should be applied to the balance sheet figures. If the firm is solvent but the partner's capital does not achieve 20% of the value of total assets then the balance sheet needs some action to be taken in order to strengthen the position. Again, advice should be sought if the remedial action to be taken is not obvious.

3. Profitability

The net profit before tax should be at least 20% of income.

If equity partners charge salaries to the Profit and Loss account these should be added back to the profit.

If the results of the calculations do not achieve the 20% level on both balance sheet and profitability calculations the practice is considered to be in a marginal position. If this is the case, then action must be taken to improve the ratios without delay. Again, advice should be sought if the remedial action is not obvious.

The benchmark tests

The two key tests are defined as follows:

(1) Partnership Solvency Test/Capital Adequacy Test

$$\frac{\text{Total partners capital reserves} \times 100}{\text{Total gross partnership assets}} = X\%$$

where X% is less than 0% the partnership is deemed to be insolvent and advice must be sought at once. Where X% is a positive figure, this measures the extent capital cover in the practice. A target of over 20% is thought to be prudent.

(2) Profitability of the practice

$$\frac{\text{Total annual profits before tax} \times 100}{\text{Total annual income}} = Y\%$$

where Y% is targeted to be more than 20% of income.

The higher the assets and profitability ratio are, the stronger the firm's position is. Results in the 0%–20% range are a cause for concern and indicate a lack of financial stability. Well run partnerships may be targeting annual profit ratios in excess of 30%.

Strong balance sheets will include a 50% partnership funding of working capital and at least a 30% stake in any properties owned by the partnership.

It will be helpful to check the equivalent figures in the previous two years in order to measure whether the position is stable, improving or declining. Any reduction in performance even in a strong set of accounts should be treated as an early warning.

Conclusion

If you are unable to meet the basic minimal standards as set out above you must take advice from another experienced solicitor, accountant or the Law Society. The smaller the ratios, the more urgent is the need for advice. Firms with losses or negative capital reserves must act at once.

Schedule II shows three examples where the original profit and partnership reserves range from adequate to strong. The tests show up inherent weaknesses in the figures. Complacency is dangerous in these circumstances.

SCHEDULE I

Benchmark Tests
Definitions and calculations to be used.

Step 1. Valuing assets

—*Fixed assets.* Using written down values per your balance sheet is generally acceptable and will include properties, office equipment and cars.
—*goodwill.* This asset is ignored for the purposes of the test.
—*work-in-progress.* This must be prudently valued. Any estimate of work-in-progress must be capable of being confirmed by reference to time records or files and should not exceed three months average fee income (excluding any element of profit).
—*debtors.* The value must exclude any bad or doubtful debts. The total for this asset must be linked to the annual fee income. The test value should be the lesser of the actual total or three months fee income.
—*cash.* Actual value on deposits.
—*listed investments.* Cost or market value. If market value is the lesser figure this should be used.

The total assets value which has resulted from these calculations are used for the balance sheet ratio calculation.

Step 2. Calculating liabilities

This will include any bank overdrafts, loans or business mortgages or personal loans by third parties to the partnership or the sole practitioner in his business.

Also to be included are creditors of the business hire purchase liabilities on the firms assets and income tax and VAT liabilities on the profit and income figures included in the accounts.

Step 3. Adjusted Balance sheet Partnership reserves

The partnership capital reserves which form the balancing figure to the revised balance sheet calculations will reflect the balance sheet adjustments for the value of any assets which require to be written down or excluded as set out under Section 1 above. The gross balance sheet value of assets including current assets and the net partnership capital figures devised from the adjusted balance sheet are used in the calculation of the balance sheet ratios required under Test No. 1 and 2. The resulting figure is used for the balance sheet ratio calculation.

Step 4. Calculating the ratio

The revised capital reserves figures (Step 3) should be divided by the adjusted gross assets (Step 1) and expressed as a percentage.

Step 5. Total income and net profit

The figures for total income should be as per the annual accounts and may include fees, commissions, interest earned or other income generated by the practice.

The figure of annual profit after all overheads and operating charges including finance and depreciation charges but before tax and partners drawings is used for this calculation.

Step 6. Profitability in the Practice

The calculation of the annual figure of profitability as a percentage is done by using the values set out in Step 5.

SCHEDULE II

Sample calculations—Example 1

(a)   Balance sheet adjustments

	Actual	Test
Goodwill	£100,000	£NIL
Property at valuation	120,000	120,000
Other fixed assets	60,000	60,000
	280,000	180,000
Current assets		
WIP	140,000	61,000
Debtors	45,000	45,000
Clients account surplus (net)	1,000	1,000
	186,000	107,000
Total assets	£466,000	£287,000
Liabilities		
Trade creditors	£ 15,000	£ 15,000
Bank overdraft	50,000	50,000
Term loan	100,000	100,000
Total liabilities	165,000	165,000
Partner capital	301,000	122,000
	£466,000	£287,000
Comparative ratios—capital/assets	65%	43%

(b)   Profit and loss statement

	Actual	*Actual*
Income—fees		£280,000
—commissions		20,000
		300,000
Expenses		
Salaries	£160,000	
Office expenses	30,000	
Car expenses	15,000	
Professional fees	7,500	
Miscellaneous	12,000	
Interest	6,000	
Depreciation	15,000	245,500
Net profit before tax		£ 54,500
Profit ratio		18%

(c)   Benchmark ratios
Balance sheet

$$\frac{\text{Capital} \times 100}{\text{Total Assets}} = X\%$$

$$\frac{£122,000 \times 100}{287,000} = 42.5\%$$

Profitability

$$\frac{\text{Net Profit} \times 100}{\text{Total Annual Income}} = Y\%$$

$$\frac{£54,500 \times 100}{300,000} = 18.2\%$$

Note: The WIP figure is replaced by three months' costs as a reduced valuation. The strong balance sheet is being threatened by a weak profit position. If this three partner firm can't live on the profits a slow decline in the balance sheet position will result in a problem.

Sample calculations—Example II

(a)   Balance sheet adjustments

	Actual	Test
Goodwill	£100,000	£NIL
Fixed assets	60,000	60,000
	160,000	60,000
Current assets		
WIP	140,000	43,000
Debtors	45,000	45,000
Client account surplus (net)	1,000	1,000
	186,000	89,000
Total Assets	£346,000	£149,000
Liabilities		
Trade creditors	£ 25,000	£ 25,000
Bank overdraft	100,000	100,000
	125,000	125,000
Partners capital	221,000	24,000
	£346,000	£149,000
Comparative ratios—capital/assets	64%	16%

(b)   Profit and loss statement

	Actual	Actual
Income—fees		£280,000
—commissions		20,000
		300,000
Salaries	£160,000	
Office expenses	42,000	
Car expenses	15,000	
Professional fees	7,500	
Miscellaneous	12,000	
Interest	5,000	
Depreciation	15,000	256,500
Net profit		£ 43,500
Profit ratio		14.5%

(c)   Benchmark ratios

Balance sheet

$$\frac{£24,000 \times 100}{149,000} = 16.1\%$$

Profitability

$$\frac{£43,500 \times 100}{300,000} = 14.5\%$$

Note: Balance Sheet. The strong position shown per the original Balance Sheet is undermined by the lack of property assets, the high goodwill and work in progress figures. Revalued WIP is included in the revised Balance Sheet at an actual valuation of files.

Note: Profit and Loss statement. Below average results. The problems have to be addressed before they get worse. Profits must be improved and the balance sheet strengthened. There is very little leeway.

Sample calculations—Example III

(a) Balance Sheet adjustments

	Actual	*Test*
Goodwill	£ 50,000	£NIL
Fixed assets	15,000	15,000
	65,000	15,000
Current assets		
WIP	25,000	13,000
Debtors	15,000	15,000
Client account surplus	1,000	1,000
	41,000	29,000
	£106,000	£44,000
Liabilities		
Trade creditors	10,000	10,000
Overdraft	35,000	35,000
	45,000	45,000
Partners capital	61,000	(1,000)
	£106,000	£44,000
Comparative ratios—capital assets	58%	Negative

Note: WIP is revised to actual values from the original estimate used. The reduction in asset value has produced a negative capital value—insolvency on this benchmark test.

(b) Profit and loss statement

Total Income	£85,000
Total expenses (not set out in detail)	65,000
Net profit	£20,000

(c) Benchmarks ratios

Balance sheet   Insolvent

Profitability $$\frac{£20,000 \times 100}{85,000} = 23.5\%$$

The sole practitioner's profitability is acceptable but modest. Take advice on the apparent insolvency. How can the weak balance sheet be improved. Action to reduce borrowings and improve profit should be taken now.

APPENDIX 4

THE LAW SOCIETY OF SCOTLAND: A SIMPLE GUIDE TO THE SOLICITORS' (SCOTLAND) ACCOUNTS RULES 1997 SOLICITORS' (SCOTLAND) ACCOUNTS CERTIFICATE RULES 1997 AND THE MONEY LAUNDERING REGULATIONS 1993

This booklet is issued as a guide and is not a substitute for the rules and regulations of which all solicitors should have a thorough knowledge.

Some questions and answers

1. What is the main purpose of the Accounts Rules?

To protect clients' money and to ensure that at all times solicitors identify and record client funds so that they may be clearly identified from the solicitor's own monies and to ensure that at all times solicitors have enough money in their client bank accounts to meet the total amount that they are due to clients (irrespective of any money due to them by clients) both as a solicitor and as a trustee in the course of their practice.

2. What is a client account? **(Rule 2(1))**

It is any account with a recognised bank or building society in the name of the solicitor but specifically identified in its title as being for clients or for a named client or trust etc. You can have as many client accounts as you need. The client account may also be a loan (but not a general deposit) to a local authority but in this case it must be in the name of the solicitor for a specific client. In the case of a joint deposit this should be recorded in the books of the first named firm.

3. Can the client account be with any bank or building society? **(Rule 2(1))**

No. It must be with an authorised institution within the meaning of the Banking Act 1987 or the Bank of England, National Savings Bank or the Post Office. It may also be an authorised building society under the Building Societies Act 1986. Any such institution must be able to operate within the bankers automated clearing system. Details of 'recognised' institutions can be obtained from the Society or the Bank of England. If you deposit a client's money with an institution that does not come within the definition of a client account then you must have the client's written consent.

4. Clients' Funds outwith the UK   (Rule 2(1))

Client account funds may only be invested in accounts outwith the UK with the express consent of the clients and suitable risk warnings must be given to the clients in advance of any decision to place funds in accounts which are outwith the scope of the Accounts Rules.

Note that the Channel Islands and the Isle of Man are deemed to be *outwith* the UK.

5. What books must we keep and can they be electronic?   (Rule 12)

You must keep a cash book and a ledger in which there must be an account for every client in respect of whom you have any financial intromissions. The Rules also require a separate record to be kept for inter-client transfers within the client ledgers. You must also keep a record of all other financial dealings of the firm and all accounting information must be up to date. The narrative for the entries needs to be clear and each entry should be self explanatory. If the books are on a computer it must have software to allow the accounting information to be printed out on request. Alternatively, books can be hand written. This must be in indelible ink and not in pencil.

6. We only do legal aid work, do we need to keep clients' accounts?   (Rule 4 and 6)

It is common practice for cheques paid by The Scottish Legal Aid Board to be paid directly into the firm's bank account or another special bank account set up for this purpose. Many firms do not have a client bank account for this. However, it is important to note that when SLAB's cheque or telegraphic transfer is paid into the firm's bank account it is essential that you have already paid out the outlays due to third parties and these funds are simply reimbursements. If some, or all of the outlays have not been settled then that portion of SLAB's remittance in this respect is clients' funds and should be treated as such. Settlement of such outlays on the date of receipt is acceptable. If you are not able to do that then you must have a client bank account or you will be in breach of the Accounts Rules. Similarly contributions received from clients who are in receipt of legal aid or legal advice and assistance *must* be treated as client funds until an account has been rendered in accordance with Rule 6(1)(d).

7. Should we have a surplus or float in our general clients bank account?   (Rule 13)

Yes. Most firms do as a simple precaution to cover minor mistakes which may occur from time to time. The reconciliations have to be listed and the statements kept *for at least three years*.

8. Do we need a Compliance Partner?   (Rules 16 and 18)

Yes. You require a designated cashroom partner who is responsible for compliance with the Accounts Rules.

You also require a money laundering reporting officer to be appointed.

9. What do we do with money coming into the firm? **(Rules 4(2) and 12)**

Immediately clients' money comes in to the office, ensure that appropriate entries are made in the cash book; **do it today and not tomorrow!** Clients' money must be lodged in a properly designated bank account—it must not go through the office bank account.

10. What do we do about money going out?

Firstly ensure that you have funds to make the payment, normally by cheque. If you do not have sufficient client funds from the client account then you must use the firm's funds to meet any shortfall. If clients' funds are in a Solicitors Special Deposit Account or similar they must be uplifted and paid into the bank account on which the cheque is to be written before you issue the cheque or make payment from that account.

11. Why must we record entries for funds not paid through the
Client Bank Account? **(Rule 7)**

The Rules now emphasise the need to record entries which are needed for completeness and to ensure that the client accounting records deal with the whole consideration involved in conveyancing transactions. If part of the price of a property is paid to the solicitor in the form of a cheque made out to a third party, the cheques should be recorded on the face of the ledger card as a contra entry.

12. How do we deal with bridging loans? **(Rule 8)**

You must not enter into a bridging loan agreement on behalf of a client in circumstances which may impose on you personal liability for repayment in the event of default by the client. Bridging loans must always be in writing and you must give the lender full details of the client and what the arrangements are for repayment.

13. Can we lend money to a client?

Yes, but you should consider whether a conflict of interest might arise.

14. Can we borrow money from a client? **(Rule 9)**

No, unless the client has been independently advised about the loan or is in the business of lending money.
(NB Personal and business loans are not covered by the Guarantee Fund.)

15. Do we need to keep a list of Powers of Attorney? **(Rule 11)**

Yes, each year the designated cashroom partner must complete a list of active and dormant powers of attorney in the name of any solicitor.

16. What records do we have to keep to operate a power of attorney? **(Rules 11 and 12(2))**

A clear record of money paid in or out of the client's own bank account should be kept in a client ledger and cash book. Where you have exclusive control of the client's bank account then that bank balance should be treated as client funds which should be included in invested funds held for named clients.

17. *What do we have to do on a daily basis?*   (Rule 12)

For a manual system ensure that the cash book entries are also entered in the clients' or the firm's ledger. The cash book and the ledger should be summed up to date and regularly balanced. They should clearly identify monies which you hold in separate client accounts.

A computer system will do this automatically provided you enter the information accurately and daily

18. *What are other funds?*   (Rules 2(1), 12(1) and 14)

These are funds which you hold in individual accounts in the firm's name or in a solicitor's name in trust for a client. These include funds held under powers of attorney. Keep an extra column or section in your cash book or day book to record these. There must also be an additional column in the client's individual record headed 'other funds' or you could have a separate ledger card dealing with investment funds only. You are required to keep this separate record and to reconcile (physically check the balances in the account against the records) at least four times a year (many firms do this monthly).

19. *What do we have to reconcile?*   (Rule 14)

You check that all interest earned on building society or SSD Accounts has been written up in the passbook or bank statements and that there is an equivalent entry on the face of the client records. You then prepare a list of investment funds and check this against the total of funds held in the Investment account for the various authorised bodies. Any differences between the figures must be identified and adjusted to the correct amount. You must also keep the reconciliation *for at least three years*.

20. *What do we have to do about interest on a client account?*   (Rule 15)

As a general rule when you have received money from a client you should put it into some form of interest bearing account for that client. This, however, depends upon the amount of money being lodged and/ or the time it is likely to be held. You must always act fairly and reasonably. Smaller sums (under £500) which should be paid out within two months do not require to earn interest for the client. However, larger sums, even for short periods, do. Particular attention should be paid to executry funds. Make sure that they too earn interest for the client.

You need not account to clients for interest earned on your general clients account(s), subject to the above rule.

RECENT SCHEMES introduced by banks or building societies offer differential rates for client funds. Arrangements to retain any element of the interest should be agreed with the client.

21. What about the money laundering regulations? **(Rule 16)**

(a) To whom do they apply? Everybody.

(b) To what do the provisions apply? To every one-off transaction which involves the payment by or to the client of an amount of ECU 15,000 (approximately £12,000) or more, and to any one-off transaction for a smaller amount which appears to be *linked with others where the aggregate of the amounts involved is in excess of ECU 15,000.*

— to every case where the firm forms or resolves to form a business relationship for relevant financial business only,
— if you suspect that your client is engaged in money laundering, or that a transaction is being carried out on behalf of someone else who is engaged in money laundering.

'Relevant financial business', 'business relationship' and 'one-off transaction' are defined in the Regulations. The definitions are wide and any transaction which involves the handling of money of ECU 15,000 or more, is likely to be subject to the money laundering provisions.

(c) What does this mean in practice? Some matters are **exempt.** Examples are:
Existing clients do not require identification checks.
Instructions from other solicitors who confirm to you that they have complied (Reg 10).
Cheques drawn on the client's own UK bank account (Reg 8).
Criminal work, wills, licensing and gaming work, insurance claims, certain matrimonial matters etc.

(d) Can you give us one or two practical examples? Matters which are unlikely to be exempt and therefore covered would be:
House purchase (unless all funds from client's own UK bank account).
Investment of client's funds.
Receipt of funds for onwards transmission to the client or a third party.

(e) When did the regulations come into effect? The Money Laundering Regulations 1993 (the 'Regulations') came into force on 1 April 1994.

(f) What are the Regulations supposed to do? Prevent the proceeds of unlawful activities being legitimised by being applied to carry out legitimate transactions.

(g) What do we have to do under the Regulations?

1 Verify the identity of every person with whom you intend to form a business relationship, or carry out a one-off transaction;
2 maintain record keeping procedures; and
3 maintain internal reporting procedures.

(h) What happens if we do not comply? Failure to comply with the Regulations constitutes a criminal offence, punishable by a fine and/or imprisonment for a term of up to two years.

(i) What else do we have to do? Set up and maintain a procedure for establishing the identity of a client where required in terms of the rules and regulations (see (b) above).

(j) Do we have to identify clients?   Yes. If satisfactory evidence of the identity of new clients is not obtained then the business relationship or one-off transaction as the case may be shall not proceed any further.

(k) How do we go about deciding if we need to comply and also in identifying new clients?   Common sense.

However, if in doubt there is a style of Verification of Identity Flowchart annexed at Schedule 1 and an evidence of identity form at Schedule 2.

(l) When is evidence of identity satisfactory?

1   when it is reasonably capable of establishing that the client is the person he claims to be; and
2   when the person who obtains the evidence is satisfied, in accordance with the procedures maintained under the Regulations, that the evidence does establish that the client is the person he claims to be.

For **individual clients** it is suggested you obtain:

the true name and/ or names used
current permanent address, including postcode
'wherever possible' the date and place of birth
a document from a reputable source which has a photograph of the applicant eg, a current valid full passport or national identity card should be requested and the number recorded.

Other suggestions:

check the voters' roll
make a credit reference agency search
see an original recent electricity, gas, telephone, council tax bill or bank statement
check a local telephone directory
visit their home.

For **corporate clients**. No specific steps are needed if clients are:

a listed company or a subsidiary of a listed company
a private company or partnership one or more of whose directors/ partners are already known to the firm.

Steps are needed if clients are:

an unquoted company or a partnership and none of the directors/partners is already known, then the firm should verify the identity of one or more of the principal directors/partners and/or shareholders as applicable as if they were individual clients see above.

It is suggested you also obtain copies of:

Certificate of Incorporation/Certificate of Trade or equivalent
and perhaps for companies their latest report and accounts (audited where applicable).

(m) What records do we have to keep and for how long?   The evidence of identity you obtained needs to be kept for at least five years from completion of the relevant business or transaction concerned.

(n) Do we have to have a Money Laundering Reporting Officer?   Yes.

(o) What do we have to tell him/her?   Any information or other matter which comes to the attention of a person handling relevant financial business which in the opinion of the person handling that business gives rise to a knowledge or suspicion of money laundering.

(p) What does the Money Laundering Reporting Officer have to do?   Consider all such reports and any other relevant information and decide if this gives rise to a knowledge or suspicion of money laundering. If so pass that information to NCIS.

(q) How?   Use the style of form in Schedule 3 In serious cases telephone or fax NCIS to get guidance on how to proceed with a suspicious transaction. Telephone Number: 0207 238 8274. Fax Number: 0207 238 8286

(r) What else should they do?   Keep a record of what they decide to do and why.

22. Inter-client loans—Are they protected by the Guarantee Fund?   **(Rule 6(1))**

Normally not. Make sure the lending client gives written consent to the loan and written confirmation that they understand that they will have no claim on the Guarantee Fund. Consider very carefully the question of conflict of interest in any such transaction.

23. When can we take fees?   **(Rule 6(1)(d))**

After you have rendered a fee note and if you have funds in the client account. Do not draw fees when you do not have a balance to meet them as this is likely to result in a deficit in the client bank account and lead you to being in breach of the Rules. Take care to ensure that interim fees are fair and reasonable and reflect the work which has already been done.

24. Do we have to balance the firm's books?   **(Rule 12(4))**

Yes. You must keep all your accounting records up to date at all times and balance your books monthly. That is all your books, your clients' account, your own funds and your assets and liabilities. The obligation is to have them balanced throughout the practice year and certify that this has been done by submitting an Accounts Certificate every six months. You must also properly maintain your own firm's records so the true financial position of the practice can be ascertained at all times. If in any doubt of this aspect of the Rules contact your own Accountant or the Accountants' Department of the Law Society (see below).

25. What is an accounts certificate?

The annual certificate produced by your accountant under the Accountant's Certificate Rules had to be produced annually and within six months of the end of your year. **This requirement has been completely removed and replaced by a form of accounts certificate completed by two partners one of whom should be the designated cashroom partner (sole practitioners require only one partner). The forms of interim and final certificates are in the Schedule to the Certificate Rules.** You may retain the services of an accountant to check all or part of your records as frequently as you consider to be needed. The certificate is due to be completed every six months and sent to the Law Society within *one month*. The very tight time limit is a key part of the control over client accounts. **Do not leave it until the last minute!**

26. What information is needed for the certificate?

The certificate should be prepared on the solicitor's own letter headings and disclose the following details:

(a)   The start and finish dates of the accounting periods.
(b)   The list of powers of attorney should be included. A separate list can be attached to the certificate if the volume of powers held is large.
(c)   Cashroom partners should be disclosed.

On the reverse of the certificate, information taken from the accounting records each quarter should be included as follows:

(a)   Total sums due to clients in the general client accounts.
(b)   Total monies held in general client bank accounts.
(c)   Surplus or deficit which results.
(d)   Total sums due to named clients.
(e)   Total monies held for named clients.
(f)   The firm's financial position shown as a total. Monies held in the practice balance sheet for the firm should be shown in total. If the firm has term loans, practice loans, overdrafts or other borrowings shown in the balance sheet then these must be disclosed. Hire purchase liabilities which fund partnership assets are included but unexpired leases are not. Personal loans arranged outwith the firm are excluded.

If an accountant is instructed to help with the work of preparing the new certificate, an explanation of the extent of help is needed. This is best done by attaching a copy of the letter of engagement as arranged between accountant and solicitor.

27.Do the Rules and Regulations apply to incorporated practices

Yes.

Note: This brief guide has been prepared by the Guarantee Fund Committee who are solicitors just like yourselves. None of us likes rules but they are there to help us all keep proper records, to protect clients' money, to reduce the risk to the Guarantee Fund and to keep the Guarantee Fund contributions to a minimum.

Please play your part. If you are at any time in doubt about what you are doing, please do not hesitate to contact the Society's Chief Accountant, Leslie Cumming, or one of his staff at:

The Law Society of Scotland   Telephone: 0131 226 7411
The Law Society's Hall   Fax: 0131 225 2934
26 Drumsheugh Gardens   E-mail:
Edinburgh   Document Exchange DX ED 1
EH3 7Y   Edinburgh

who are always willing to help and advise.

SCHEDULE 1
VERIFICATION OF IDENTITY FLOWCHART

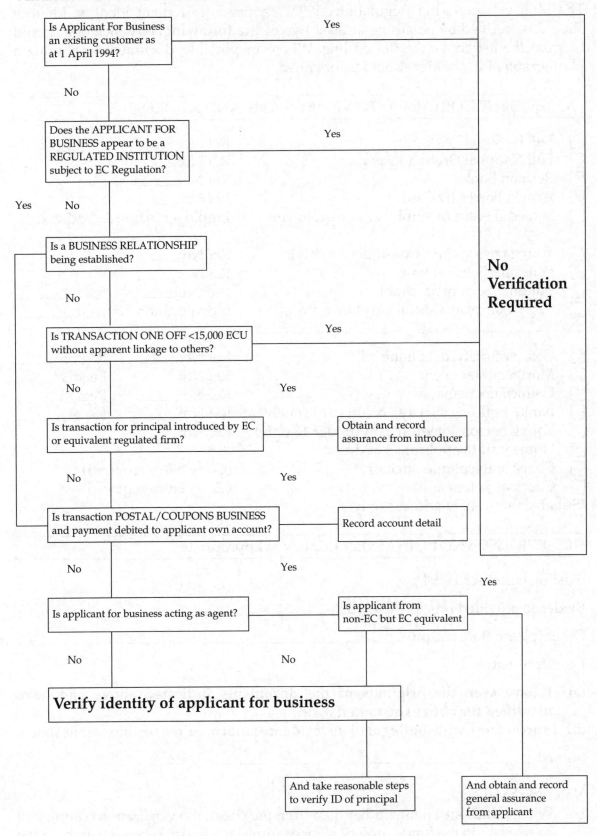

Note: If money laundering is known or suspected then a report must be made to NCIS and verification procedures undertaken if not already done so.

SCHEDULE 2

The Money Laundering Regulations 1993. Verification of client identity. Identity should be verified by obtaining **at least two of the following,** of which one should be from the list above the dotted line. Wherever possible, documents including a photograph of the holder should be obtained.

A.   EVIDENCE OBTAINED TO VERIFY NAME AND ADDRESS

☐ Full National Passport   Ref No:_____
☐ Full National Driving Licence   Ref No:_____
☐ Pension Book   Ref No:_____
☐ Armed Forces ID Card   Ref No:_____
☐ Signed ID card of employer known to you   Employer Name & Address:___

☐ Young persons NI card (under 18 only)   Ref No:_____
☐ Pensioner's travel pass   Ref No:_____
☐ Building Society passbook   Roll No:____   BS:_____
☐ Copy Company Certificate of Incorporation   Incorporation No:_____

....

☐ Gas, electricity, telephone bill   Ref No:_____   Region:_____
☐ Mortgage statement   Ref No:_____   Lender:_____
☐ Council tax demand   Ref No:_____   Region:_____
☐ Bank/ building society/ credit card statement Ref No:_____   Issuer: _____
☐ Young persons medical card (under 18 only) Ref No:_____
☐ Home visit to applicant's address*
☐ Check of telephone directory*   (Copy entry required)
☐ Check of voters' roll*   (Copy entry required)
*Suitable for proof of address only

B.   EVIDENCE NOT OBTAINED Tick box as appropriate

Existing customer 1.4.94

Evidence provided previously on date_____

Other (please state reason) _____

I confirm that:

(a) I have seen the originals of the documents indicated above and have identified the above Customer(s), or

(b) In accordance with the Regulations, evidence is not required for the reasons stated.

Signed_____**Date** _____

Notes to checklist:
1   Where funds are coming other than from the client, the verification criteria will be relevant to the funds provider. For example, if a house is being bought in the name of X for £15,000 but the funds are paid by Y, then a verification form would need to be completed for Y if an individual or other appropriate check made with the issuer of the funds.

2   A 'business relationship' is defined as any arrangement between two or more persons designed to govern the dealings between those persons where the dealings are to be on a 'frequent, habitual or regular' basis and where the monetary value is not known or capable of being known at outset.

3   Under the regulations of a transaction is considered to be a one-off transaction, the funds must be linked to any other transaction made by the same applicant/fund provider to assess whether the total funds over the last 3 months is in excess of £12,000.

4   In terms of the regulations a calendar year means a period of twelve months beginning on 31 December.

SCHEDULE 3

0++N++   **NCIS FINANCIAL DISCLOSURE**
Please be careful to align typing on the same line as the plus sign coding

Test typing on this line ++   ++T++

Disclosure Type ++   ++1++Category++   ++2++

Name of Institution ++   ++3++

Your Reference No. ++   ++4++

Sort Code ++   ++5++

Town or Branch ++   ++6++

Surname ++   ++7++

Forename(s) ++   ++8++

Address ++

++9++ Do not type on this line

Postcode ++   ++A++ Date of Birth   ++B++

Other searchable Factors ++

++C++ Do not type on this line
Information ++

++D++ Do not type on this line.

Key:	Disclosure Type	DTOA 1986/CJ Scot/CJA 1988/POTA 1989
	Category	Type A for New or B for Update
	Surname	Surname of subject of disclosure or business name
	Date of Birth	Enter date as DD /MM/YY
	Other Searchable Factors	Identification Procedure, Associated Names, Tel Nos, Fax/ Mobile Tel Nos, Passport No. Etc.
	Information	Details of Transactions arousing suspicion and other information considered to be relevant to disclosure i.e. Accounts details, Occupation/ Employer. Continue on next page if necessary.

SUGGESTED LIST OF ITEMS THAT SHOULD BE SPECIAL AREAS OF CONCERN TO DESIGNATED CASHROOM PARTNERS

Consider:

1. The methods used to record incoming funds and make sure that all funds are lodged in the bank on the day of receipt.
2. Your arrangements to handle cash handed in by clients.
   eg Do you have special arrangements to cope with larger cash sums brought to you by clients?

Do you see the detailed workings of the client account balances each month?

How much checking do you do each month on:

(a) List of client balances.
(b) Bank reconciliation working papers.
(c) Statements of surplus/deficit?

Do you have an automatic reporting and investigation procedure set up if your accounting system discloses a temporary shortage?

Can you confirm at least quarterly that all client funds including funds invested for named clients are properly accounted for? What checks are done to verify the position?

Are all large fees reviewed to confirm they are fully charged but not excessively or prematurely charged? Do you have any controls over the level of interim fees being charged during an ongoing piece of business?

GUIDANCE ON RETENTION/DESTRUCTION OF FILES AND RECORDS

Specific obligations regarding the retention of financial records are noted in the Solicitors' (Scotland) Accounts Rules. The client ledger records and day book records of journals must be retained for a period of ten years. The Law Society therefore recommended that any documents which may be required to be produced to vouch payments or receipts within the client ledger account should be retained for a period of ten years.

Client files which deal with conveyancing, executry or trust accounting matters would contain within the general correspondence files matters of importance which would require to be kept for the full ten year period. Bank statements, cashed cheques, VAT fee notes or any passbooks or print-outs which relate to funds invested or borrowed on behalf of clients would fall directly into this category.

Those solicitors who use a system of debit/credit posting slips to instruct the cashroom in their work should also ensure that these documents are retained safely for the ten-year period. Previous advice from the Society had suggested that these posting slips might not require to be retained for the full ten year period. Police enquiries into matters of employee or solicitor fraud have now indicated that these documents are of vital significance to their enquiry since the handwriting will give significant evidence as regards the source of instructions in respect of any misleading or false entries. You may wish to take account of this advice.

The only financial records which are not covered by the ten-year rule are the documents which comprise lists of client balances, bank reconciliation workings and statements of surplus/ deficit prepared in respect of the monthly client ledger account reconciliation. These working papers are now required to be kept for a period of three years.

The Society is aware that a convention has grown up amongst solicitors who carry out a significant amount of Criminal Legal Aid whereby files which relate to completed cases are routinely destroyed twelve months after the matter has been concluded. The Society has no concerns regarding this procedure provided there are no client account funds involved in the transaction. In the event that the solicitor is dealing with client funds any relevant vouchers would require to be separated and stored for the full ten-year period prior to the contents of the file being destroyed.

Generally if you are in doubt with regard to the destruction of specific client files or papers then every effort should be made to retain all documents for the minimum ten years.

Appendix 5

THE COMPANIES ACT 1985 REQUIRED ACCOUNTS FORMATS
BALANCE SHEET FORMAT 1

A Called up share capital not paid

B Fixed assets

   I   Intangible assets
      1 Development costs
      2 Concessions, patents, licences, trade marks and similar rights and assets
      3 Goodwill
      4 Payments on account
   II   Tangible assets
      1 Land and buildings
      2 Plant and machinery
      3 Fixtures, fittings, tools and equipment
      4 Payments on account and assets in course of construction
   III Investments
      1 Shares in group undertakings
      2 Loans to group undertakings
      * Interests in associated undertakings
      * Other participating interests
      4 Loans to undertakings in which the company has a participating interest
      5 Other investments other than loans
      6 Other loans
      7 Own shares

C Current assets

   I   Stocks
      1 Raw materials and consumables
      2 Work in progress
      3 Finished goods and foods for sale
      4 Payments on account
   II   Debtors
      1 Trade debtors

---

* These items, which are inserted by Schedule 4A and, although not assigned references, are to be treated as if they had been assigned Arabic numbers, replace the items 'Participating interests' for an individual company.

        2   Amounts owed by group undertakings
        3   Amounts owed by undertakings in which the company has a participating interest
        4   Other debtors
        5   Called up share capital not paid
        6   Prepayments and accrued income

III   Investments
        1   Shares in group undertakings
        2   Own shares
        3   Other investments

IV   Cash at bank and in hand

D Prepayments and accrued income

E Creditors: amounts falling due within one year

        1   Debenture loans
        2   Bank loans and overdrafts
        3   Payments received on account
        4   Trade creditors
        5   Bills of exchange payable
        6   Amounts owed to group undertakings
        7   Amounts owed to undertakings in which the company had a participating interest
        8   Other creditors including taxation and social security
        9   Accruals and deferred income

F Net current assets (liabilities)

G Total assets less current liabilities

H Creditors: amounts falling due after more than one year

        1   Debenture loans
        2   Bank loans and overdrafts
        3   Payments received on account
        4   Trade creditors
        5   Bills of exchange payable
        6   Amounts owed to group undertakings
        7   Amounts owed to undertakings in which the company has a participating interest
        8   Other creditors including taxation and social security
        9   Accruals and deferred income

I   Provisions for liabilities and charges

  1   Pensions and similar obligations
  2   Taxation, including deferred taxation
  3   Other provisions

J   Accruals and deferred income

**   Minority interests

K   Capital and reserves

  I   Called up share capital
  II   Share premium account
  III   Revaluation reserve
  IV   Other reserves
    1   Capital redemption reserve
    2   Reserve for own shares
    3   Reserves provided for by the articles of association
    4   Other reserves
  V   Profit and loss account

**   Minority interests

**   This item, which is inserted in either position by Schedule 4A, although not assigned a reference is to be treated as if it had been assigned a letter.

PROFIT AND LOSS ACCOUNT

FORMAT 1
1   Turnover
2   Cost of sales
3   Gross profit or loss
4   Distribution costs
5   Administrative expenses
6   Other operating income
7   Income from shares in group undertakings
*   Income from interests in associated undertakings
*   Income from other participating interests
9   Income from other fixed asset investments
10   Other interest receivable and similar income
11   Amounts written off investments
12   Interest payable and similar charges
13   Tax on profit or loss on ordinary activities
14   Profit or loss on ordinary activities after taxation
**   Minority interests
15   Extraordinary income
16   Extraordinary charges
17   Extraordinary profit or loss
**   Minority interests
19   Other taxes not shown under the above items
20   Profit or loss for the financial year

FORMAT 2
1   Turnover
2   Change in stocks of finished goods and in work in progress
3   Own work capitalised
4   Other operating income
5   (a)   Raw materials and consumables
    (b)   Other external charges
6   Staff costs:
    (a)   Wages and salaries
    (b)   Social security costs
    (c)   Other pension costs
7   (a)   Depreciation and other amounts written off tangible and intangible fixed assets
    (b)   Exceptional amounts written off current assets
8   Other operating charges
9   Income from shares in group undertakings
*   Income from interests in associated undertakings
*   Income from other participating interests
11   Income from other fixed asset investment
12   Other interest receivable and similar income
13   Amounts written off investments
14   Interest payable and similar charges
15   Tax on profit or loss on ordinary activities
16   Profit or loss on ordinary activities after taxation
**   Minority interests
17   Extraordinary income
18   Extraordinary charges
19   Extraordinary profit or loss
20   Tax on extraordinary profit or loss
**   Minority interests
21   Other taxes not shown under the above items
22   Profit or loss for the financial year

In each format, Schedule 4A:
*   replaces the item 'Income from participating interests' with these items and
**   adds this item in either position
which, although not assigned references are to be treated as if they had been assigned an Arabic number.

Index